WORKFLOW THAT WORKS

Instructional Design Tools

Kelly Goto

Emily Cotler

Taken From:

Web ReDesign 2.0: Workflow That Works
by Kelly Goto and Emily Cotler

Web ReDesign 2.0: Workflow That Works
by Kelly Goto and Emily Cotler

Published by Peachpit Press
A division of Pearson Education
Berkeley, California 94710

This special edition is published in cooperation with Pearson Custom Publishing.

Printed in the United States of America

13 14 15 0BRV 14 13 12 11

ISBN 0-536-20707-0

2006200045

EM

Please visit our web site at *www.pearsoncustom.com*

PEARSON CUSTOM PUBLISHING
75 Arlington Street, Suite 300, Boston, MA 02116
A Pearson Education Company

ACKNOWLEDGMENTS

Many thanks to Dr. James Kirkwood, Doug Wintin of the Ft. Wayne, Indiana campus, ITT Technical Institute and to Instructional Designer Gail Trout for their editorial review and selection of this textbook.

Table of Contents

Foreword by Jeffrey Zeldman xiii

Introduction 1

Case Study: Baby Center 8

1 Keys to a Successful Redesign 9

Why This Book Right Now? 10

Presenting a Workflow That Works 11

Expert Topic: Leigh Duncan on Identifying Redesign Issues and Strategy 13

Case Study: Port of Seattle 16

2 Core Process Overview 17

Phase 1: Define the Project 21

Discovery 21

Clarification: Determining Overall Goals 22

Planning 23

Phase 2: Develop Site Structure 25

Content-View 25

Site-View 26

Page-View 26

User-View 27

Phase 3: Design Visual Interface 28

Creating 28

Confirming and Testing Flow and Functionality 29

Handing Off 29

Phase 4: Build and Integrate 30

Planning 30

Building and Integration 31

Testing 32

Phase 5: Launch and Beyond 33

Delivery 33

Launch 34

Maintenance 35

Chapter Summary 36

Case Study: Janus 38

3 Phase 1: Define the Project 39

Gathering Information 42

The Client Survey 42

Customizing the Client Survey 42

Analyzing the Client Survey 46

The Maintenance Survey 47

Understanding Your Audience 49

Outlining Technical Requirements 51

Expert Topic: Kate Gomoll on User Profiling 52

Understanding Audience Capabilities 53

Analyzing Audience Capabilities 55

Determining Technical Needs 56

Expert Topic: Nathan Shedroff on the Emotional Future of Branding 58
Analyzing Your Industry 59
Understanding Discovery 60
Determining Overall Goals 62
Preparing a Communication Brief 62
Creating a Project Plan 65
Details and Assumptions 66
Setting the Budget 67
Understanding Scope Creep 68
Estimating: What and How to Charge 69
Tracking Time 71
Client-Initiated Changes 74
Creating Schedules 75
Overview Schedule 76
Detailed Schedule with Deliverables 76
Assigning Your Project Team 78
Setting Up Staging Areas 80
Planning for User Testing 81
Developing a User Testing Plan 81
What Are Online Surveys? 81
What Is Focus Group Testing? 82
What Is Usability Testing? 82
Kicking Off the Project 83
Phase 1 Summary 84

Case Study: BearingPoint 86

4 Phase 2: Develop Site Structure 87

Addressing Content 90
Auditing Existing Content 91
Expert Topic: Christina Wodtke on IA Toolkits 92
Outlining Content 94
Creating a Content Delivery Plan 95
Sitemapping 98
Addressing Existing Site Organization 100
Determining Site Structure 101
Setting Naming Conventions 103
Organizational Naming 105
HTML Naming 105
Wireframing 106
Addressing Navigation 111
Naming and Labeling 111
Defining Key User Paths 112
Developing The HTML Protosite 113
Creating User Scenarios 115
Phase 2 Summary 116

Case Study: About.com 118

5 Phase 3: Design Visual Interface 119

Starting the Creative Process 121
Defining Smart Design 121
Reviewing Site Goals 122
Developing Concepts 123
Designing for Your Audience 124
Expert Topic: Eric Meyer on CSS 126
Presenting Designs and Gathering Feedback 127
Confirming Flow and Functionality 132
Testing Functionality 132

Expert Topic: Lynda Weinman on Designers as Problem Solvers 133
Creating Graphic Templates 134
Creating a Design Style Guide 137
Phase 3 Summary 140

Case Study: gotomedia, inc. **142**

6 Phase 4: Build and Integrate **143**
Assessing Project Status 145
Establishing Guidelines 146
Scope Expectations Meet Scope Reality 147
Expert Topic: Chad Kassirer on Knowing Your Client Before You Code 148
Readdressing Audience Capabilities 152
Checking Content Status 152
Checking Design Status 154
Confirming the Backend Integration Plan 155
Setting File Structure 155
File Structure and Scalability 156
Slicing and Optimization 157
Creating HTML Templates and Pages 159
Implementing Light Scripting 162
Creating and Populating Pages 163
Expert Topic: Jeffrey Zeldman on Web Standards 164
Invisible Content 166
Integrating Backend Development 166
Understanding Quality Assurance Testing 167
Conducting QA testing 168
Light/Informal QA 171
Semiformal QA 172
Formal QA 173
Identifying, Prioritizing and Fixing Bugs 174
Conducting a Final Check 175
Phase 4 Summary 176

Case Study: Melanie Craft **178**

7 Phase 5: Launch and Beyond **179**
Handing Off 181
Completing the Production Style Guide 181
Creating the Handoff Packet 185
Tracking Documentation 186
Conducting a Postlaunch Meeting 186
Scheduling Maintenance Training 187
Expert Topic: Stephan Spencer on Information as Power 188
Going Live 190
Prepping an Announcement Plan 192
Optimizing for Search Engines 192
Expert Topic: Barbara Coll on Designing for Optimal Placement in Search Engine Results 194
Launching the Site 198
Maintaining the Site 198
Assessing Maintenance Team Capability 200
Internal vs. External Maintenance Teams 201
Developing a Maintenance Plan 202
Confirming Site Security 204
Planning Iterative Initiatives 206

Measuring Success 206
Phase 5 Summary 208
Core Process Summary 208

Case Study: Coldwell Banker Walter Williams 210

8 Testing for Usability 211

Understanding Usability 212
Getting Started 214
Usability and Redesign 215
When to Test 215

Expert Topic: Jakob Nielsen on the Value of Small-Study Usability Testing 216
Costs of Testing 218

Conducting Usability Tests: A Four-Step Process 219
Step 1: Plan and Prep 219
Step 2: Find Participants 222
Step 3: Conduct the Session 226
Step 4: Analyze Data and Make Recommendations 229

Chapter Summary 231

Case Study: WebEx 232

9 Working with Complex Functionality 233

Gathering & Documenting Requirements 240
Determining When Requirements Are Necessary 241
Understanding Requirements 241
Gathering Requirements 242
Documenting Requirements 242

Prioritizing, Rating, and Analyzing 244
Prioritizing Business Needs 244
Rating Requirements 244
Analyzing Requirements 245

Drafting a Functional Specification 246
What to Include in the Functional Specification 247
How Detailed Should the Specification Be? 250

Getting Sign-Off 251

Expert Topic: Sean Dolan on Fostering Productive Collaboration Between Designers and Engineers 252

Implementing the Functional Specification 254
Integrating Your Efforts 254
Preparing to Launch 255

Chapter Summary 256

Case Study: Banana Republic 258

10 Analyzing Your Competition 259

Formal Industry Analysis vs. Informal Features Analysis 261
Becoming an Expert in the Client's Industry 262

Conducting an Analysis 263
Step 1: Defining the Process 264
Step 2: Creating a Features List 268
Step 3: Conducting Analysis and Testing 270
Step 4: Creating a Final Report 272

Chapter Summary 276

Index 277

ABOUT THE AUTHORS

Kelly Goto is the principal of gotomedia, inc. (www.gotomedia.com), a San Francisco–based strategic consultancy specializing in user experience and interaction design. A self-proclaimed "design ethnographer," Kelly continues to seek new methods of applying research-oriented design to interfaces, products, and mobile devices for clients such as Adobe, Apple, Macromedia, Veritas, and BearingPoint. Kelly is a sought-after lecturer and instructor, specializing in topics of usability, user experience, and branding. When not tethered to her laptop, Kelly can be found trekking the Third World — where she does not check her email.

Emily Cotler is the founder and creative directrix of Waxcreative Design, Inc. (www.waxcreative.com), an Oakland-based studio focused on site development and strategic maintenance for authors, photographers, performers, and other creative professionals as well as small enterprises. Prior to co-authoring *Web ReDesign*, Emily was a regular contributor to industry periodicals, including *Publish Magazine*. With clients in five countries, Emily is a sought-after leader in her niche market and regularly speaks on successful branding and building of fan-based web presences. Her preferred method of escape from cyberspace includes a snowboard and a Colorado mountain.

Emily and Kelly, hard at work on the first edition of this book, May 2001, Oakland, California.

Photo courtesy of deborah sherman photography (www.deborahsherman.com).

ABOUT THE TECH EDITORS

Sean Dolan is Senior Producer/Project Manager for gotomedia, inc., in San Francisco, where he has guided the development of projects for clients such as the FDIC and WebEx. Prior to gotomedia, Sean was Director of Program Management for Idea Integration/San Francisco and Executive Producer at Food.com. He was also Senior Managing Partner at AOL/Digital City in Boston.

Chad Kassirer is the founder of What?Design (www.whatdesign.com), an award-winning, full-service website design, development, maintenance, and internet consulting firm located in Oakland, California. In addition to managing, designing, and coding websites for clients such as Macromedia, Adobe, Disney, Oracle, and SFMOMA, Chad also finds time to teach HTML and JavaScript workshops at the University of Hawaii's Outreach College and serves as a judge for local and international web competitions. Prior to What?Design, Chad was the director of production for web development shops Idea Integration/San Francisco and Red Eye Digital Media.

ACKNOWLEDGMENTS

We did not create this book (first or second edition) by ourselves. Writing it in a Kelly-and-Emily-vacuum would have taken twice as long (at least) and resulted in a far less information-rich volume. We are indebted to many talented individuals, and many thanks are to be had...

Thanks to our families and our friends who continued to love and humor us despite our constant unavailability and ubiquitous insertion of the words "The Book" into just about every conversation and excuse for asocial behavior.

Thanks to the editorial team at New Riders — Steve Weiss, David Dwyer, Linda Bump, Jennifer Eberhardt, Chris Nelson, Audrey Doyle, Ellen Butchart, Wil Cruz, Jake McFarland, and everyone else — your enthusiasm, attention to detail, and unfailing understanding were instrumental in shaping and producing this book. And a big thanks to the new team at Peachpit — Nancy Davis, Marjorie Baer, Doug Adrianson, and the rest — for taking over the project midstream and running with it.

Thanks to Steve Cotler, walking thesaurus, grammar god, voice police, and critical reviewer throughout the entire process — your unparalleled editorial assistance, generous-beyond-description availability, and blatant honesty made this book better (say very little more!).

Thanks to Chad Kassirer and Sean Dolan, wide-ranging experts in production and processes — your off-hours spent reviewing the material and contributing expertise are very appreciated.

Thanks to our book designers — layout designer Renée Frisbie and cover designers Darren "Dag" Marzorati and Serena Howeth — you outdid yourselves... again. Thanks also to Kim Scott (layout production) for your amazing speed and attention to detail, and to Deb Sherman (photographer extraordinaire) for getting the perfect shot.

Thanks to the gotomedia team: Serena Howeth, Lisa Crosina, Rachel Kalman, Subha Subramanian, Craig Drake, Jeffrey Chiang, Irene Sandler, Regina Sherman, and the rest of the "creative collection" — for ongoing support, encouragement, and contributions to the book. Also much appreciation to the original team at Red Eye Digital Media/Idea Integration — especially Eric Tam, whose original support and loyalty made this book possible.

Thanks to the support team at, and associated with, Waxcreative Design — Abi Bowling, Renée White, Beth Barany, Judith Lumbreras, Candace Apple, Brian Cogley, Deb Sherman, Elizabeth Yarnell, Julie Rozelle, Caitlin Lang, Julie Pottinger (special extra thank you for the contract and royalty statement deciphering assistance), and of course, Emily's mom, Jane, who uncomplainingly did much typing.

Thanks to Jim Heid, Steve Broback, and Tobi Malina for creating the original venue for the evolution of this material. And to Kandice Boyle and Lisa Li for being constant sounding boards and endless sources of encouragement.

Thanks to the companies and colleagues that contributed material to this book: Netconcepts; nGen Works; Phinney/Bischoff Design; Werkhaus Design; Idea Integration/San Francisco; Idea Integration/Houston; gotomedia, inc.; and Waxcreative Design, Inc.

Thanks — huge thanks — to all of this book's expert contributors: Jeffrey Zeldman for his insightful foreword to the second edition *and* his expertise, Barbara Coll, Sean Dolan, Leigh Duncan, Kate Gomoll, Chad Kassirer, Eric Meyer, Dr. Jakob Nielsen, Nathan Shedroff, Stephan Spencer, Christina Wodtke, and Lynda Weinman. Thanks also to the participating experts from the first edition: Jim Heid, Leslie Phinney, Ani Phyo, David Siegel, and Eric Ward, and to Jeffrey Veen for his foreword to the first edition.

And Emily thanks Kelly and Kelly thanks Emily — mostly just for not killing each other inside the tunnel and for coming back into the sunlight as good friends.

DEDICATIONS

For the teachers who have inspired me — Henrietta Davis, Polly Bragg, and Bill Brown. And to my mom and dad — for a lifetime of learning, encouragement, and support.

And to Serena Howeth, creative extraordinaire, who has been a source of inspiration and strength through the years, both professionally and personally, and who has collaborated with me on many creations: this book, gotomedia, umpteen projects. Thanks for all you do.

— Kelly Goto

For my parents, Steve and Jane, who instilled in me the belief that I could accomplish almost anything in life so long as I worked hard and had a little luck…

And for two incredible, accomplished, and kind women who continue to be role models and collaborators in many areas of my life, professional and creative: my sisters, Julie Pottinger and Abi Bowling. Lucky me, they're also two of my very best friends. Thanks for everything.

— Emily Cotler

FOREWORD

In a 10-year career, I've designed about a dozen websites. I've redesigned 10 times that many.

Redesign is not only the meat and potatoes of our business, it's also the salad and beverage. But just when and how should you redesign and for what reasons? What questions should you ask before putting pen to paper or stylus to tablet? And how can you manage the process to keep it creatively and financially rewarding?

People often redesign for the wrong reasons. They do it because they've just learned a new technological skill (I'm guilty) or because someone in the organization is tired of the existing look and feel, even though people who use the site may like it just the way it is.

Some launch into redesigns without considering how their users feel or what they need. Still others who've done their brand and user analysis homework up front find themselves losing control of the process further along. What starts as an exciting project can quickly turn into a black hole, sucking up time and money without generating benefits for anyone.

This wonderful book, written in down-to-earth language by professionals for professionals, will help you ask the questions that will start your redesign on a sound footing. It shows how to construct scenarios that lead to people-friendly sites… and how to manage even the most difficult clients every step of the way. The first edition of this book saved my company thousands of dollars by pointing out potential pitfalls so that my clients and I did not have to act them out in the real world.

Read this book, learn its lessons, and three good things will happen:

1. Your client or boss will be happy.

2. The people who use your site will be happy.

3. And most importantly (let's be honest), you will be happy. You'll have done your best work for an appreciative audience — and you'll get to go home before sunrise.

Today is the first day of the rest of your web redesigns. Enjoy.

Jeffrey Zeldman
Autumn 2004

> The workflow of a project is exactly that: a planned flow for the work involved.

Introduction

Introduction

We did not suddenly think, "Web redesign, now there's a topic for a book." The concepts behind this book have evolved over many years. They were a direct result of the process methodology that was born out of Kelly's appearances at the Thunder Lizard conferences (www.thunderlizard.com) beginning as far back as 1997. Kelly was then, and continues to be, on the Thunder Lizard roster at several conferences each year, where she lectures extensively on the topic of web design workflow in its many stages.

As the market shifted from reengineering to redesigning, it became apparent that points specifically directed at redesigning websites needed to be addressed. And with every successive conference came The Question: "When are you going to write a book?" Kelly's PDF documents that accompany her lectures have always been widely and freely distributed, but clearly it wasn't enough, and by 1999 The Question was ever present. Then The Idea was born: *Web ReDesign*. But then The Idea sat. It was too big for one person.

The Kelly-and-Emily team came together over bagels and coffee. Emily, having attended one of Kelly's Thunder Lizard workflow sessions, interviewed her for an article for *Publish Magazine*, an industry periodical for which she had been writing for years. When Kelly read Emily's article, she realized that here was the co-conspirator who could help turn The Idea into The Book.

This book — a true collaborative endeavor — puts the topics of web management and workflow, information design, and usability all together under the umbrella of the timely topic of redesign. A guide for web development methodology, with heavy emphasis on the additional and specialized needs of redesign projects, this book is a roadmap that shows you how to proceed with minimal guesswork and budget-draining fuss.

Our focus is workflow; our process — we call it the "Core Process" — is workflow that works. It is based on our experience and expertise, and it has been tested and used in the real world, on real projects, and has been shared, modified, updated, streamlined, and simplified into what you see here today. This book provides a complete, top-down view of a web redesign plan, presented in an accessible, usable format. This is about process; there is very little preaching here.

We do not put this methodology forth as something set in stone. You are not a dummy (and this is not a dummy book); you'll know when to follow and when to modify.

A TOOL KIT IN A BOOK

We've included tools in this book — tools you can use today, as in right now, as in on your current project. We offer checklists, surveys, worksheets, and forms to help you keep your project on track from initial planning through launch and beyond. Many of these tools are downloadable from this book's accompanying website (www.web-redesign.com). These tools, like the Core Process itself, have been tested, used, and refined. Plus, we have added new and updated ones for the second edition. We received a lot of feedback on the tools after the first edition was published, and we hope that this interaction will continue.

HOW THIS BOOK IS ORGANIZED

The best way to use this book would be to read it from beginning to end before starting your next project. But who has the time?

With that in mind, this book is organized to be picked up and restarted and put down and skimmed over and browsed through and read in detail. We've included lots of tips and pulled additional pertinent information into sidebars. We've repeated ourselves in places. We do this because we know you are probably reading in spurts and not necessarily in a linear fashion. We don't want you to miss out on anything.

The Core Process comprises five phases, presented in Chapters 3 through 7. In addition, we supplement the Core Process with a selection of expanded steps (in Chapters 8 through 10) that, depending on your time, budget, and needs, will help further round out your redesign process.

Most readers will probably want to use this book by familiarizing themselves with the overview (Chapter 2), reading the chapters, and reviewing the tools available. Then, while actually running your project, use the overview for reference and the chapters for detail. And, of course, utilize the many tools we provide during the course of your own production, including the checklists at the end of each chapter, to help keep you on track.

WHO IS THIS BOOK FOR?

This book is designed to streamline the process for everybody involved, not just the project manager and key decision-makers. Our goal is to put everybody — client and team alike — in the same frame of reference and have them all use the same terminology and understand the steps necessary for any web project. When we say any project, we really mean any — redesign or initial design, $10,000 budget or $500,000 budget. Truly, even if your project is under or over this range, the Core Process will still be helpful.

When we say "core," we mean exactly that: the basic and necessary functioning parts. We like to think of "core" as a tool kit that you wouldn't venture into a project without. No matter the type of site being redesigned or the scope of the project itself, the Core Process remains essentially the same, with variation dependent upon circumstances and expertise. Approaching any project in an organized and comprehensive manner will save time, budget, and headaches along the way.

Who Are You?

Whether you are a designer, an in-house webmaster, or a company owner trying to move your web presence to the next level, this book is for you. If you have ever felt frustrated because a web project was run inefficiently ("My client delivered site content five weeks late, yet the site launch date remained immovable"), this book is for you. If you are embarking on your first web project (from "This is the opportunity I have been waiting for" to "What am I going to do?"), whether taking over your company's website or being asked to build a department to do so, this book is for you.

This book is for every person — designer and nondesigner — who has ever lived through a workflow nightmare and wants to avoid it in the future. ("We went straight to visual design, figuring we could deal with navigation and content at that stage. The result? Total disorganization and much backtracking.") From the seasoned pro to the newbie, this book will help. If you already have significant experience, you will probably find yourself customizing the Core Process to fit your existing processes. If you are a newbie, this is the place to start — the whole process is right here.

Bonus

This book also works for straightforward website development in addition to redesign. The techniques and tools modify easily and provide a solid workflow for either. If you're designing a site for the first time, simply ignore the redesign parts and focus on the Core Process.

What Kind of Company Are You?

Are you a small to midsize web development firm or a huge company with an existing intranet department? Perhaps you are a small corporation with a web department in-house or a midsize company with an outside design firm contracted. Maybe you are a sprawling university system in which every department is using a different branding...

The Core Process outlined in this book applies to all of the above and then some. It truly is a one-process-fits-all workflow.

WHO IS THE CLIENT?

For the purposes of this book, "the client" is a somewhat schizophrenic, catch-all term. The client is one entity to the design house and a different entity — but not-so-entirely different — to the internal department.

If you are a design firm or web development company, the client is external — the company that contracted you. This is pretty straightforward client management.

For those of you in in-house departments, the client is internal — specifically, the person (or group) who is responsible for the content, the concept, and perhaps most importantly, granting approval. This is not necessarily the head of the internal web department; it might be a group including someone in marketing, someone in product development, a couple of VPs, and perhaps the CEO. Less straightforward client management.

Throughout this book, we frequently reference "the client." Wherever we do so, we mean either the external or internal client — whomever is in the position to give project, budget, and design approvals. Even if you are your own client, know and accept that whether excellent to work with or patience trying, the client always requires managing. There are spots in this book where we specifically reference a situation for an in-house team with an internal client, or for a web development/design firm with an outside, contracted client. Only you can know how to interpret "the client" as it relates to you.

WHAT THIS BOOK IS NOT

No book can be everything to everybody. We focus on workflow and, at that, on a Core Process. With the goal of creating a basic (albeit comprehensive) book, we necessarily had to make the conscious decision to omit several facets of web development that were not strictly project management and workflow oriented.

This Book Is Not a Technical Manual

This book is not a step-by-step workflow for back-end implementation. If your site requires a backend database, e-commerce capability, dynamic content, and so on, you need an additional, parallel plan. The workflow for the redesign is this Core Process, this book. But backend development needs its own, totally separate workflow, a whole book unto itself.

Levels of Formality

The management of internal projects — specifically the presentation of deliverables — tends to be less formal than when a firm contracts an outside client. This informality has its pros and cons, though none so pronounced as in the cycles of approval of deliverables. PRO: It's often as easy as walking down the hall to get sign-off, plus the level of formal presentation can be greatly diminished. CON: There is a great propensity for items to slip through the cracks in internal setups. When you don't have to formally invoice a client, the tendency to be lax on administrative details becomes more prevalent.

However, while we don't outline the backend workflow in detail, we do indicate points in the Core Process where the front-end and backend workflows meet, where the project managers for the two processes must confer. For more on this and additional processes for working with complex functionality, please refer to Chapter 9, new to this second edition.

To this end, this expanded second edition provides not only an overview of the technical considerations that need to be clear and understood so that you can evaluate the project's scope, but also a step-by-step model to help manage a project that has both a front-end and a backend. This book provides you with surveys, suggestions, and tips, all geared toward helping you identify your overall technical needs. Our goal is to help you determine what these needs are and how realistic they might be so that you can budget and plan for them.

We can tell you for certain — and we repeat it in several places because it is so very, very important — that whatever your technical requirements, whether significant backend or not, you will want to talk with your technical team — HTML production and engineering alike — throughout the project. And yes, that means from the get-go, all the way through the lifecycle of the redesign project.

Know Your Ends

Sites are developed in layers. All sites have a design/presentation layer — essentially everything the site user actually sees. This is the graphic user interface (GUI). Some sites have an application layer, where much of the functionality that the user interacts with resides (for example, for registration, login, shopping cart transactions, personalization, etc.). The design/presentation layer and the application layer form the front-end of web development, as we know it, on the web today.

The application layer, being in the middle of the front-end and backend, sometimes crosses over between simple scripting (e.g., JavaScript, DHTML, CGI) and complex programming (for example, for shopping carts or secure transaction integration). It is the conduit and link between the front-end and backend of web development.

For sites with complex content-retrieval systems, database architecture, and massive engineering needs, a separate workflow is in order. This is the "backend" of web development.

For the purposes of this book, however, "front-end" is the design/presentation layer only. "Backend" refers to everything behind the front-end, application layer included. Please note: Not all sites have or need backend development, but 100 percent of websites have a front-end.

We have no explanation as to why front-end is hyphenated and backend is not.

This Book Is Not a How-To Design Manual

We address the workflow of a redesign project, not the specifics of design itself. We go into a cursory overview step by step of how the creative track is managed. For design graphics, we recommend Lynda Weinman's *Designing Web Graphics.4* (New Riders, 2002). For site design and production, try Jeffrey Veen's *The Art & Science of Web Design* (New Riders, 2001); Jeffrey Zeldman's two books, *Designing with Web Standards* (New Riders, 2003) and *Taking Your Talent to the Web* (New Riders, 2001); or David Siegel's industry classic (still a great resource after all these years) *Creating Killer Web Sites* (Hayden Books, 1997). For more recommendations and links, consult www.web-redesign.com.

This Book Is Not a How-To Manual for Usability Testing

Again, this book is about workflow. Usability testing is definitely something we talk about — frequently. We believe very, very strongly in its value. We go into detail on the subject in Chapter 8, but primarily from a project management and workflow approach. For an immediately accessible (and entertaining) handbook on usability, we recommend Steve Krug's *Don't Make Me Think* (New Riders, 2000). For an in-depth background and philosophical approach, we suggest Jakob Neilson's *Designing Web Usability* (New Riders, 1999). Both these books remain on target despite being several years old. For actual how-to, try Jeffrey Rubin's timeless *Handbook of Usability Testing* (John Wiley & Sons, 1994). For more recommendations and links, consult www.web-redesign.com.

WWW.WEB-REDESIGN.COM

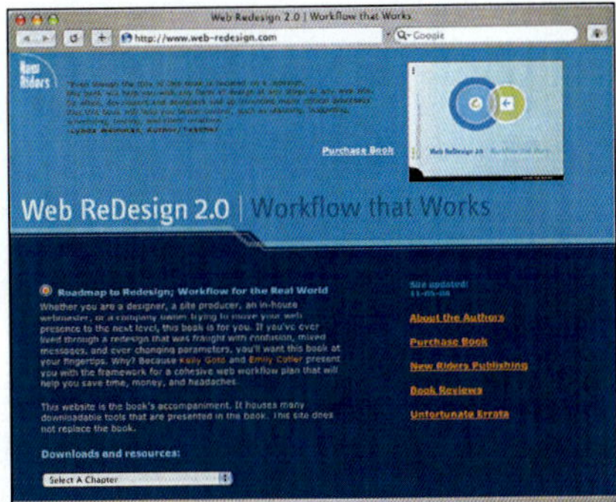

Unlike a companion CD, a website is a resource that can be updated, accessed, and actually used. The idea of creating a companion book site is not new. This one, however, comes with downloadable tools, references, and resource links. Throughout this book, we identify tools as being "downloadable from www.web-redesign.com." We are inviting you to take these tools and use them. Please be aware that our publisher gets cranky if the copyright is removed, so credit to the book is appreciated.

The website is not a replacement for the book. Even calling the website a supplement is a stretch. It is a resource. In addition to providing all the tools featured in the book, www.web-redesign.com will include links to related sources, updated information about us (where we are and what we are doing), and of course, a section that deals with errata and the publishing time lag.

We welcome feedback and look forward to hearing from you.

Kelly Goto (kelly@gotomedia.com)
Emily Cotler (emily@waxcreative.com)
Autumn 2004

Baby Center

Company: Baby Center
URL: www.babycenter.com
Design Team: In-house
Design Director (Original Design): Jonathan Tuttle
Project Manager (Original Design): Jon Stross

Design Director (Redesign 2000): Allyson Appen
Associate Art Director (Redesign 2000): Shannon Milar
Project Manager (Redesign 2000): Alissa Cohen Reiter
Design Director (Redesign 2004): Allyson Appen
Art Director (Redesign 2004): Mary Kate Meyerhoffer
Project Manager (Redesign 2004): Kate Handel

BabyCenter.com focuses on providing pregnancy, infancy, and toddler information as well as offering maternity and baby products. The company's founding mission was to build the most complete resource on the internet for new and expectant parents.

<PREVIOUS>

BABYCENTER.COM [OLD] went through several iterations as it evolved from a small startup to a full commerce and community site. Each redesign was based on evaluations of customer needs.

<INTERIM>

BABYCENTER.COM [REDESIGNED 2000] drives membership with prominent messaging and links. The redesigned site improves usability through a simplified design that retains several successful elements from the old site, including effective use of personalization.

<CURRENT>

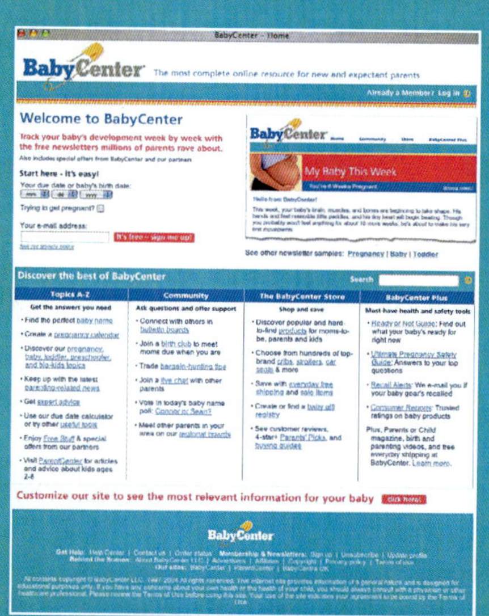

BABYCENTER.COM [REDESIGNED 2004] replaced the old tab structure with directory-style content in easy-to-access columns. Better customization and personalization gives the audience even easier access to information particularly relevant to their needs.

Results: In-house expertise allows for quick response to users' needs and ongoing improvements, including increased personalization and content offerings.

> Web design, whether starting from scratch or redesigning, is all about planning and organization. Think long-term but focus on short-term — and never lose sight of your customer.

Keys to a Successful Redesign 01

Keys to a Successful Redesign

WHY THIS BOOK RIGHT NOW?

There is no question that a web presence is a critical component to a company's services and offerings (externally and internally). Business and the web are inextricably entwined. Sites of all sizes need to grow in iterative stages as part of ongoing business strategy. Staying on the leading edge is key, and that means reevaluating, redesigning, and revamping what worked — or at least what seemed to work — yesterday.

Companies everywhere feel the urgency to hit shorter deadlines with smaller budgets. Higher expectations with an eye toward measurable results are a given. In this way, some things haven't changed since the first edition of this book was published in 2001. The pressure is still astounding, and it doesn't stop with the launch. Companies like yours (and clients like ours) that met the original challenge of getting online continue to face the need to scale, grow, and increase internet initiatives in order to stay current with competition and technology.

Why this book right now? Because it was needed in 2001 and is still needed now. Why a second edition? Because while the process and tools we originally introduced still apply, many technical points need updating (for example, browser versions, treatment of CSS, etc.). Because budgets have been significantly streamlined. Timeframes are shorter. Resources have been reduced. Sites that were originally given 18 to 24 months to redesign and relaunch are now granted mere 3- to 6-month turnarounds, with a need to justify costs and benefits at each step. Because almost three years after the first edition, we continue to receive emails with validating regularity from all over the world, reporting widespread, successful integration of the

Core Process, asking us questions, and requesting additions ("If you ever write another book..."). We listened.

There are many good reasons to redesign. You inherited an old, mostly ineffective, brochure-ish site... Your company has gone through a reorganization and/or has taken a new direction... You want to update the look and feel... You need e-commerce capabilities... You need a content management system... Your navigation is a mess... Your branding has fallen apart... You never really had branding in the first place... You want your site to load faster... You want your site to look the same on different browsers and/or platforms...

If any of the preceding applies to you (and these are just some of many examples), you are probably questioning what your next move should be. You may be somewhat unsure about how to go about doing this. What is the process?

There must be a process.

Web design, whether you are starting from scratch or redesigning, is all about planning. Taking the time to visualize and follow a solid workflow is the most important key to any multi-phase project, not just a web-related one.

The one thing everyone can count on is that the web will continue to evolve. It will become smarter, more competitive, and more service-oriented. Your site visitors will get savvier. The web will keep changing all the rules. You can count on that.

PRESENTING A WORKFLOW THAT WORKS

Many factors can derail or delay a project: technical roadblocks, disorganized clients, poorly defined goals and schedules, sloppy budgeting. We have all experienced them, whether as a designer or a manager or both. "Designers are utterly starved for guidance on workflow," says web conference chair and *LA Chronicle* technology columnist Jim Heid. "Kelly is mobbed after her strategy and workflow sessions at our web design conferences. You can just tell that every designer in the room has lived through some kind of workflow nightmare, but Kelly shows how careful planning and organization can keep things on track."

Take Kelly's methodology, mix in a healthy dose of collaboration from Emily, and you have this book, now in its second edition complete with the following:

- **A focus on iterative design cycles with an eye on measurable results**
- **A brand new chapter covering technical requirements for gathering, documentation, and implementation**

Redesign Cycles

Many corporations ask, "How often should we redesign?" Our experience recommends average time necessary to complete a full-scale redesign and rebranding/repositioning effort to be 12 to 24 months. We call this the 1.x to 2.x effort. The old site becomes the 1.x site. The newly redesigned look, feel, and branded site is the 2.x site. Between full-scale efforts, iterative site improvements or initiatives should be made quarterly — each with measurable goals tied to ROI. These initiatives are site "refreshes" numbered 2.1, 2.2, 2.3, etc. A year or two later, you are ready for the 3.x release. Much like software.

Iteration Is Key

Today's web workflow is not just about redesign, but redeploying a site in stages with each iteration aiming to achieve measurable objectives. One key to a successful redesign is taking an iterative approach with each initiative defined, planned, and executed on time and on target. By breaking large projects up in to smaller, more regularly paced and manageable releases, iterations can more closely be tied to specific business goals. It is important to note that not all iterative site improvements will be visible to the end-user. Cost-effectiveness drives these improvements. Examples include implementing CMS, converting to CSS, and bringing the site development in-house.

- **A streamlined workflow to condense the information design and Protosite development phase**
- **A focus on separating content from presentation**
- **Updated examples, images, data, tools, and pertinent sidebars and tips**

This streamlined workflow plan for redesign includes tools we have used, revamped, reused, etc., for designing and redesigning websites. These tools are instantly applicable and are already tested and proven successful. Yes, instantly — you can use these tools today. We have some serious answers here, and we're sharing.

This book is a readable, understandable, industry-needed workflow plan. Use this book as a toolkit. Adapt it into a methodology that works for you. Call it a plan, call it a roadmap, call it a guide — we like to call it *Workflow That Works*, because that's what it is.

Why this book right now? Because the need for a cohesive web workflow plan — particularly one that addresses a strategic approach toward redesign — is more timely than ever — especially for in-house departments madly trying to keep up with initiative after initiative or for small to midsize firms without a solid methodology in place. Corporate heads and company owners need to understand how their websites fit into an overall strategy of business goals with profits tied directly into a successful user experience. A website is an extension of a company's services and offerings for consumers, for business to business, and for internal communication, and it is time to approach new site designs and redesigns with long-term goals in place and a clear understanding of how a company's brand value is keenly connected to an individual's experience with the company — *online and off.*

Web redesign doesn't need to be that hard. All it takes is planning and organization.

LEIGH DUNCAN ON IDENTIFYING REDESIGN ISSUES AND STRATEGY

"Gut-level" instinct isn't enough to support the case for internet redesign. When companies cannot clearly articulate why they are redesigning, their efforts often result in rework, expense, and partial or total failure. The instinct to redesign, while often on target, must be supported by fact, analysis, and comprehensive strategy to lead to success.

Simply defined, strategy is the development of a clear action plan to "bridge the gap" between current state and future vision. Web redesign strategy, therefore, involves creating an organized plan to improve an existing site to better serve customers and drive desired business outcomes. Ultimately, good redesign strategy examines the underpinning technology, business model, institutional process, content structure, and brand positioning of a web initiative. Good web redesign also fully examines the unique role the web can play in synchronizing the online and offline customer experience to better inform, educate, engage, persuade, and sell to customers.

It's easy to become overwhelmed during a redesign. Rapid business changes and technology growth make juggling multi-departmental concerns a constant management challenge. However, it is paramount to approach the project from one central position: the customer's perspective. Good redesign strategy starts here.

Developing a customer-centric perspective is the most important aspect to a successful redesign strategy. This perspective requires all redesign participants to step back from detailed business considerations and approach customer needs in a uniform fashion. A helpful way to do this is to simplify the site's audience segmentation into the site's Primary, Secondary Audience, and Tertiary Audiences.

Many companies find this exercise to be a challenge because it forces clear prioritization, articulation of behavior, and discussion of customer need. Once basic audience segments are defined, it becomes much easier to map out a site based on weighted audience need and detailed business considerations, such as the following:

- **Business plan review**
- **Current state assessment**
- **Future state vision**
- **Audience validation and testing**
- **Content and services planning**
- **Communication brief/design strategy**
- **Technical implementation approach**
- **Marketing and business planning**

These exercises, though not an exhaustive list, outline some next steps that prepare the way for a successful redesign and illustrate how a customer-centric focus sets the stage for the practical evaluation of business, technical, and design concerns. Once the stage is set for website redesign, any project manager is better empowered to move forward with confidence.

Leigh Duncan is a 14-year industry veteran with a depth of knowledge in online and offline business strategy, marketing, CRM, customer experience design, and enterprise content management. She currently consults for BearingPoint where she has provided counsel to world-class clients including 1-800-FLOWERS, Procter & Gamble, Chevron, America Online and Bristol-Myers Squibb.

KEY EXPERT TIPS TO A SUCCESSFUL REDESIGN

Processes evolve. Methodology expands or becomes more streamlined, depending on the case or cause. From the start of the internet to its evolution through the dot-gone era into the new "prove it" economy, we have seen the approach to web design and web services streamlined down to the essentials. There are keys to a successful redesign — items that should remain high in priority while considering approach, development, and launch of a new or redesigned site. Consider the following:

TIP 1>

FOCUS ON YOUR AUDIENCE

A successful user experience continues to be the main reason people return to a company or website. One bad experience and your customer is lost. (Harsh, but true. Ask your customers!) Your company's brand value is established by the experience, positive or negative. By focusing on your audience, you are building your credibility and value proposition through successful interaction.

TIP 2>

SET MEASURABLE GOALS

Sites often launch or relaunch with loose or no measurable goals in place. Aim to have specific, targeted goals in place for each launch or relaunch, including iterative refreshes. And instead of a full site redesign, focus on specific areas of your site and iterate toward your long-term goals. Clear benchmarks are necessary to determine design success. Invest in tracking and survey software for qualitative details.

TIP 6>

CLEARLY DEFINE YOUR TECHNICAL GOALS

For sites with complex functionality, integrating a separate and parallel workflow is necessary. Have a clear understanding of what you are doing and assign the right team to the effort. For an overview, refer to Chapter 9. For details, buy another book.

TIP 7>

KEEP SITE MAINTENANCE IN MIND

Many sites are developed by people who don't work with the site after launch and often have little sense of to how the content will change on a regular basis, or who will change it. Have the right design/coding resources ready for regular updating. Arm maintenance with the appropriate skills. Ensure fluidity of growth.

TIP 3>

REDESIGN TOWARD WEB STANDARDS

Efforts to establish browser standards and incorporate style sheets are finally being followed. Smart design in this new generation of websites means streamlining code and separating content from presentation to achieve greater flexibility and updating ease.

TIP 4>

CUSTOMIZE YOUR OWN PROCESS

Every project and situation requires its own level of customization. Use this book as a springboard: Take the tips, tools, and methodologies in this book and develop your company or team's own process for designing and developing web initiatives.

TIP 5>

ESTABLISH A METHOD OF CONTENT CREATION AND DELIVERY

Content will always be late! Factor it in — determine a structured method of content creation and delivery. By operating in a proactive, organized manner, you can help your copywriter (or yourself) set reasonable goals and keep to the proposed schedule.

TIP 8>

BELIEVE IN USABILITY TESTING

One-on-one testing with actual site visitors is still the best way to gather relevant data and real-world input. Conducting usability tests informally throughout a redesign and on an ongoing basis ensures proper feedback and allows you to adjust accordingly for a more successful user experience.

TIP 9>

DON'T HIDE FROM EXTERNAL SEARCH ENGINES

Accessibility means many things. Make sure your site is friendly for individuals as well as for search engines. Using frames, a Flash intro, and graphic text are some of the best ways to hide from search bots.

TIP 10>

THINK LONG TERM BUT FOCUS ON SHORT TERM

It is easy to lose sight of the big picture when you're hit with emergencies and urgent requests. Making a company and team commitment to stay on target (18- to 24-month goals) will enable the kind of focus necessary to strategize successfully.

Port of Seattle

Company: Port of Seattle
URL: www.portseattle.org
Design Team: Phinney | Bischoff Design House
Creative Director: Leslie Phinney
Technical Director/Information Architect: Mark Burgess
Brand Strategist: Dave Miller

The Port of Seattle website is an information center for entities working with or affected by the port's business and community activities. These include Seattle-Tacoma Airport, cargo and cruise ships, regional transportation initiatives, and real estate and economic development. The redesigned site is functional, accessible, and visually appealing.

<PREVIOUS>

PORT OF SEATTLE [OLD] used a site structure based on the port's internal structure versus what readers wanted to learn. Persona development and user testing helped to determine who was using the site and what kind of information they were looking for.

<CURRENT>

PORT OF SEATTLE HOME PAGE [REDESIGNED] was built using XHTML for structural markup and CSS for presentation, including layout. Redesign goals included current and relevant content; clear, efficient, and intuitive navigation; and a compelling, unique visual design. Information architecture called for an "entry" page, giving access to a series of equally weighted home pages.

PORT OF SEATTLE COMMUNITY PAGE [REDESIGNED] highlights port activities within the community and promotes greater understanding of the port's role locally and regionally. This is one of six home pages designed to give equal weight to the various divisions of content, as accessed via the entry page.

Results: The port's website combines form, fit, and function into a satisfying user experience for each of the different types of readers it serves by applying the experience design process.

The Core Process: A comprehensive, modifiable plan. A starting point for all kinds of teams and all kinds of budgets.

Core Process Overview 02

Seeing is comprehending. Presenting a visual of the Core Process: all five phases, each consisting of three interwoven and/or parallel tracks, including points where front-end and backend workflows intersect. This comprehensive flowchart illustrates how the Core Process — from start to finish — is really a roadmap of the workflow of redesigning a website. (Ignore the redesign aspects and it works for initial web development as well.) Use this chart both as a starting point and as a reference.

In addition to this visual representation, we offer a detailed list of action items in this chapter. The flowchart and the action item lists correspond but are not identical. Yet each approach is helpful.

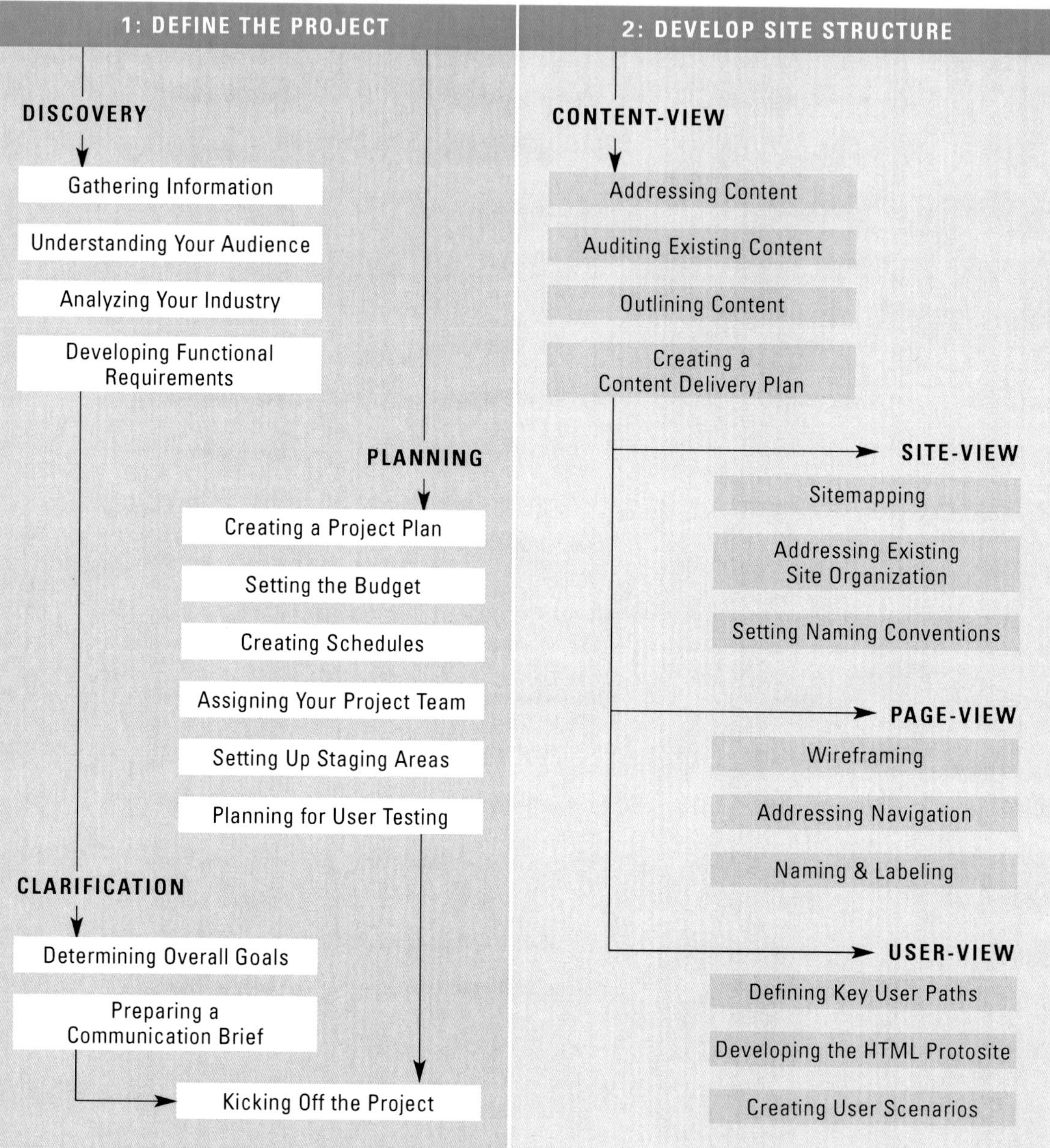

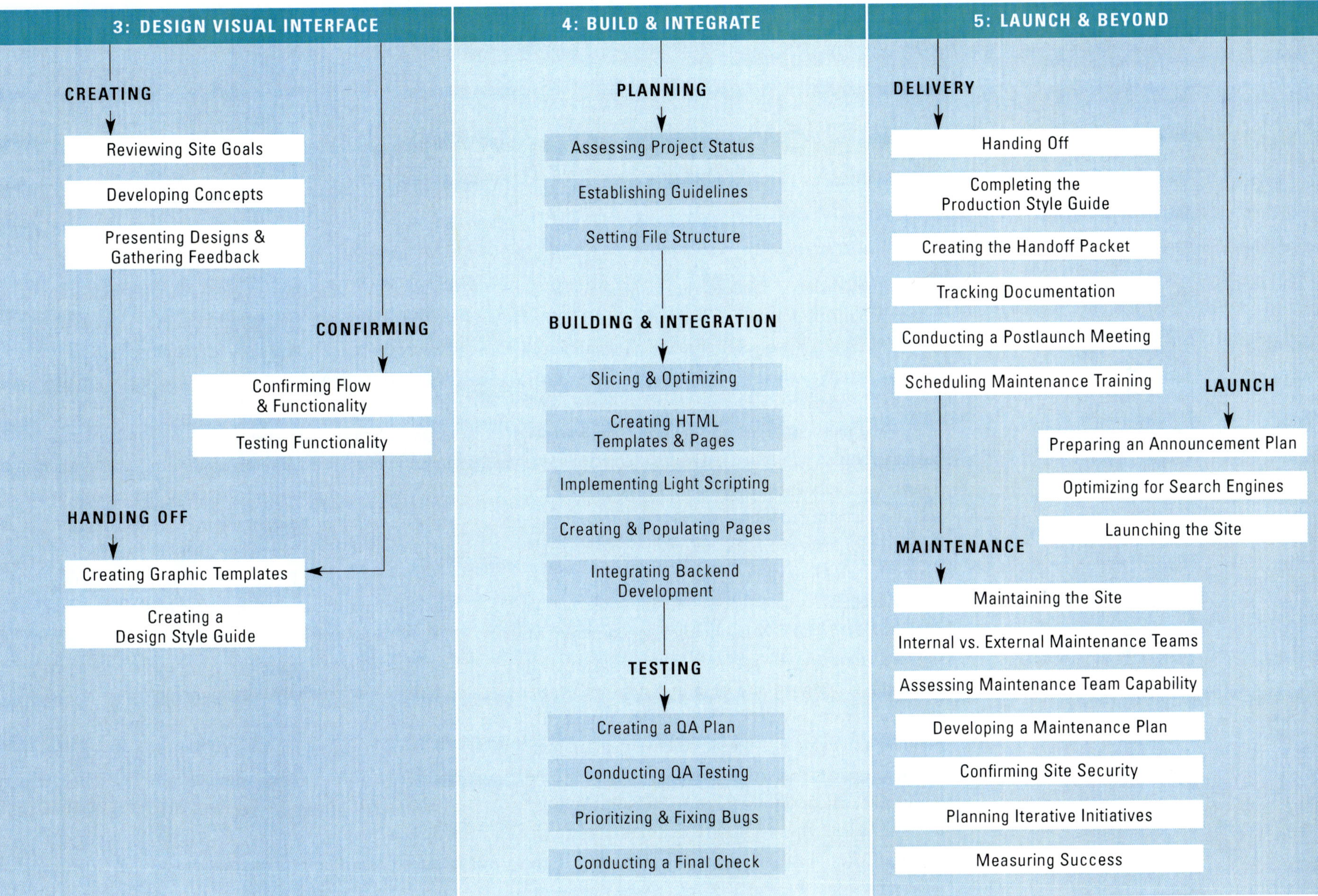
3: DESIGN VISUAL INTERFACE
CREATING
Reviewing Site Goals
Developing Concepts
Presenting Designs & Gathering Feedback
CONFIRMING
Confirming Flow & Functionality
Testing Functionality
HANDING OFF
Creating Graphic Templates
Creating a Design Style Guide
4: BUILD & INTEGRATE
PLANNING
Assessing Project Status
Establishing Guidelines
Setting File Structure
BUILDING & INTEGRATION
Slicing & Optimizing
Creating HTML Templates & Pages
Implementing Light Scripting
Creating & Populating Pages
Integrating Backend Development
TESTING
Creating a QA Plan
Conducting QA Testing
Prioritizing & Fixing Bugs
Conducting a Final Check
5: LAUNCH & BEYOND
DELIVERY
Handing Off
Completing the Production Style Guide
Creating the Handoff Packet
Tracking Documentation
Conducting a Postlaunch Meeting
Scheduling Maintenance Training
LAUNCH
Preparing an Announcement Plan
Optimizing for Search Engines
Launching the Site
MAINTENANCE
Maintaining the Site
Internal vs. External Maintenance Teams
Assessing Maintenance Team Capability
Developing a Maintenance Plan
Confirming Site Security
Planning Iterative Initiatives
Measuring Success

Core Process Overview

A comprehensive workflow that can be incorporated, modified, and adapted by all web development teams... A set of best practices you can apply to all projects...This is our process — the Core Process. It consists of five sequential phases (with additional methodologies for backend technologies suggested on an as-needed basis). In this chapter, we present an overview with a focused emphasis on the specific needs of redesign.

The Core Process can be followed by all types of teams, for all kinds of companies, and with all sizes of budgets. Every site faces common construction choices: Flash or HTML, complex functionality or nothing more involved than simple JavaScript rollovers, redesigned site or brand new web presence. All web projects need to be thoroughly planned and defined. All need to have their content organized and structure blueprinted. All need to be designed aesthetically. All need to be built. All need to be launched. All sites. Every last one.

The Core Process takes you through these necessary steps. We describe what you should do (necessary), what you can do (extra), and what you should watch out for. We also highly recommend two additional processes — testing for usability (see Chapter 8) and analyzing your competition (see Chapter 10). We've also added a new chapter in this second edition that covers working with complex functionality (see Chapter 9.) If time and budget allow, your adaptation of the Core Process should incorporate these processes as well.

What follows in this chapter is the CliffsNotes version of the Core Process — an overview. But just like your English teacher in high school used to say, "Do not rely on the overview alone!" There is no detail here, no description of why and how. We provide that information in the chapters to come. We include tools there, and charts, and helpful lists. While subsequent chapters are comprehensive, this chapter is a concise overview. Refer to it and use it to familiarize yourself with the Core Process. Each project is unique, of course, and every team and budget has different demands pressed upon it, so variation will obviously be at your discretion.

PHASE 1: DEFINE THE PROJECT

The first phase of the Core Process covers gathering and analyzing the necessary information, identifying the scope and direction of the project, and then preparing for kickoff. You will start by asking a lot of questions (relax, we'll give you the questions), and you will amass a lot of data — data that you will use to shape and communicate the expectations of the project. No matter the size or scope of the project, the need to plan is ever-present.

In Phase 1: Define, you set the stage for your redesign. Many of the items that get addressed here affect every phase, and a few, like knowing your audience, figure into every step. When defining project scope, you must have an understanding of everything from budget to maintenance.

This is the most important phase of the Core Process. The work you do here will define the entire project — every move you make and every deliverable you create.

DISCOVERY — CLARIFICATION — PLANNING

Discovery

Spend as much time as possible understanding the company, the outgoing site, and the redesign project. Gather information and ask questions. Learn about the audience. Analyze the current site and compare it to the competition, both on- and offline. Become an "expert user" in the client's business. Develop an understanding of the strategy behind the site and what the value is for the target audience.

DISCOVERY

- > Gathering Information
- > Understanding Your Audience
- > Identifying Your Audience's Technical Capabilities
- > Developing Functional Requirements
- > Analyzing Your Industry

> Distributing/Collecting/Analyzing Surveys

Gather information. The Client Survey and the Maintenance Survey should be handed to the client at the project's outset. These concise and comprehensive questionnaires prompt the client into articulating expectations. The data collected will aid in gaining insight into the site's audience and goals. Both surveys appear in full in this book and are downloadable from www.web-redesign.com.

> Collecting Existing Materials from the Client

Request materials: brochures, annual reports, collateral, sample products, etc. Go on a tour of the facility, store, and/or existing site. Understand the client's current marketing materials and general marketing plan.

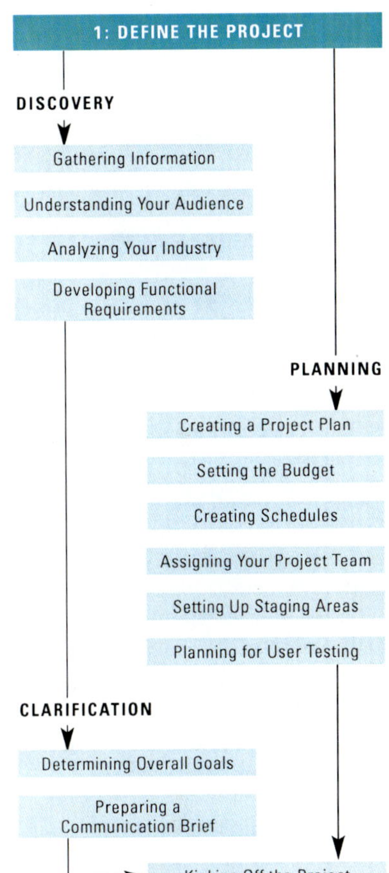

Prepare for Scope Creep

Understand the concept of "Scope Creep" and how it will affect your project. The slow, inevitable swelling of a project's scope from something defined to something significantly bigger, Scope Creep happens with almost every project. Little things add up. Beware of seemingly casual client requests for small changes. Scope Creep is subtle; you usually don't recognize that it is happening. At your kick-off meeting, define Scope Creep to both your client and your team and explain how keeping careful tabs on the schedule, deliverables, and process will help keep the project on target. See Phase 1: Define for more on Scope Creep.

> Understanding Your Audience

Use the data gathered from the Client Survey to get a strong sense of who your site visitors are, why they will come to the site, and what tasks they will be performing. Define both target and secondary audiences. Create a visitor profile. Keep in mind that you may need to profile more than one target group.

> Identifying Your Audience's Technical Capabilities

Once you know your audience, you need to know what kind of site they can access. From platform to connectivity speed, types of programming languages to plug-ins, determine your audience's abilities. An extensive survey, the Client Spec Sheet, should be given to the client shortly after project kick-off. The Client Spec Sheet is a production item. Part of it appears in Phase 4: Build, and it is downloadable in full from www.web-redesign.com.

> Identifying Backend Programming Needs

This is an only-if-it-applies step. A straightforward tool, the Expanded Tech Check, asks the client a few questions. If any are answered "yes," your project needs backend programming, and an additional workflow will have to be employed. See Chapter 9: Working with Complex Functionality for more detail. The Expanded Tech Check can be downloaded from www.web-redesign.com.

> Analyzing Your Industry

Analyze the client's industry to see what the competition is doing on- and offline. The goal is to become an "expert customer" in the client's field. Visit multiple sites, perform tasks, call customer service, and see what is successful and what is frustrating. For a detailed description of an extended process, see Chapter 10.

Clarification: Determining Overall Goals

Now that you have the data you need, determine the site's goals (such as increasing traffic, decreasing calls to customer service, streamlining sales, improving navigation, achieving a different look, etc.). This will help you identify the main goals of the redesign and communicate them to all involved. It will also help answer the seemingly obvious yet often-glossed-over question, "Why are we redesigning?"

CLARIFICATION

- > Determining Overall Goals
- > Preparing a Communication Brief

> Preparing a Communication Brief

The Communication Brief is a summary of overall visual and conceptual goals. This document restates the target audience, user experience goals, and communication strategy. It also lists the proposed style and tone of the redesigned site. The client signs off on the Communication Brief, and it is used extensively by the team. Use the provided worksheet as a guideline when writing the Communication Brief. The worksheet is downloadable from www.web-redesign.com.

Planning

There's no shortage of administrative tasks here: budget, schedule, team assignment, and more, each focusing on another defining aspect of the project. Now that the goals of the site have been defined, you can actually plot the course of action for the development of the redesign. The documents you generate in this stage become components of your Project Plan.

PLANNING

- > Creating a Project Plan
- > Setting the Budget
- > Track Time
- > Creating Schedules
- > Assigning Your Project Team
- > Setting Up Staging Areas
- > Planning for User Testing
- > Kicking Off the Project

> Creating a Project Plan

Documentation requirements vary from project to project. A Project Plan contains the budget, schedule, Communication Brief, technical documentation, and any other information that sets the scope for the project. The presentation varies, as does the page count; these most often depend on the formality of the project. A list of suggested Project Plan components appears in Phase 1: Define.

> Setting the Budget

Budget defines the size, boundaries, and feasibility of a project. Although the budget always depends on what the client has to spend, actual costs get based on hours. Take a realistic view of the resources, time allocation, and deliverables and consider that the budget that the client has and the specific budget for the scoped project may differ and a scope change may be in order. Use the budget tracker tool to aid in the estimating and tracking process. View this tool in Phase 1: Define or download it at www.web-redesign.com.

> Track Time

Have a reliable method in place to track time — and then really do it. Track actual against projected hours. When you actually track hours, you are able to see when a project is going over budget. There are many methods of tracking time. Find one that works for you. We suggest a couple in Phase 1: Define.

Track Your Hours

In general, organizations that track their hours — and know where their budget stands and how it is being utilized — are usually profitable. Those that don't track their hours either are usually unprofitable or hope to get lucky. Establish a method for tracking hours... and then actually, truly, diligently track them. Time tracking is critical for both design firms and in-house departments; it helps track profitability and keeps team members accountable for their projected hours (and your projected budget). For more on tracking time, see Phase 1: Define.

Get Signed Approvals

Nothing makes a client more accountable than a signature. Here's a good rule to live by: If it discusses scope, budget, or schedule, get it signed. Establish one contact from the client side who has final sign-off. Email approvals are a good start, but follow up with a hard copy to protect yourself — get a signature via fax whenever possible. For every project, create a project folder (or a binder) to house all signed documentation: contracts, briefs, the initial proposal and subsequent revisions, the approved sitemap, visual design directions, etc. Clients sometimes suffer from short-term memory loss. Gently remind them of things they have approved and dates they have agreed to throughout the process.

> Creating Schedules

People respond to deadlines. Establish them in two ways: first in an overview schedule and then in a detailed, date-by-date schedule. Both the overview (a broad-scope look at the project) and the detailed schedule (complete with deliverables, approval reviews, and due dates) communicate a sense of urgency.

> Assigning Your Project Team

Select your team. When identifying individual roles, understand that people often wear multiple hats, so clarify responsibilities for each team member. Maintain clear communication with all team members throughout the process.

> Setting Up Staging Areas

A staging area acts as a hub of communication. Whether you call it a "client site" or a "project site," create a project-specific URL for posting current material for review. This client staging area should be kept current, be easy to maintain, and contain very simple navigation. Don't confuse the client staging area with your own internal web space. Create a different area for the team to work and share information that is not for client viewing.

> Planning for User Testing

Decide what form of user testing your project will employ, if any. There are many valid forms of feedback (focus groups, online surveys, etc.), but usability testing differs in that it shows what your audience *actually* does, not what they *think* they might do. If you're going to test, decide the scope of testing and get it in the schedule as soon as possible. In Phase 1: Define, we present the different forms of user testing. For more on usability testing, see Chapter 8.

> Kicking Off the Project

Bring the client together with the team and review the discovery materials, align expectations, and establish project scope. Set a clear means of communication and a standing weekly meeting or conference call for the duration of the project. Either face to face or via conferencing, these should be your primary goals for a kickoff meeting that starts the project right.

PHASE 2: DEVELOP SITE STRUCTURE

With Phase 2: Structure, the actual hands-on work begins with content and information strategy — determining how to organize information so that site visitors can find it quickly and easily. Whether working on a brand new site or a redesign, whether the budget is $5,000 or $250,000, the need for a logical structure is a constant across all websites. Yes, the client is anxious to see the look and feel of the redesign, but devising a solid, well-thought-out plan will lay the foundation for everything to come — including the visual design.

CONTENT-VIEW SITE-VIEW PAGE-VIEW USER-VIEW

Content-View

Without good, relevant content, your site won't be compelling. Content and structure are intertwined — you cannot create one without defining the other. Division and categorization of pages is necessarily determined by content, and the way in which you organize a site's content defines the backbone for the structuring process.

CONTENT-VIEW

- > Addressing and Organizing Content
- > Auditing Existing Content
- > Outlining Content
- > Creating a Content Delivery Plan

> Addressing and Organizing Content

Content should be addressed as early as possible. Start organizing the content conceptually and examining it from an audience perspective. What content would site visitors logically expect to see together? Contract or assign a dedicated person to the role of content management, preferably on the client side.

> Auditing Existing Content

Be careful not to fall into the trap of using old content just because it is available and easier. A content audit is a thorough review of all existing material: copy, images, diagrams, media, etc. It is an excellent opportunity (don't overlook it!) to determine what content should get carried over and incorporated into the redesign and what should be tossed.

> Outlining Content

Use the simple, familiar, Roman-numeral-outline format to further organize your content. Determine content sections, including new material. You can expect the client to provide the outline, though you may have to guide and urge. You don't have to have all the content written/revamped/received, but you do need to know what is coming.

> Creating a Content Delivery Plan

A Content Delivery Plan clarifies what content is due when — existing, revamped, and new content alike. Responsibility for copy, images, and other

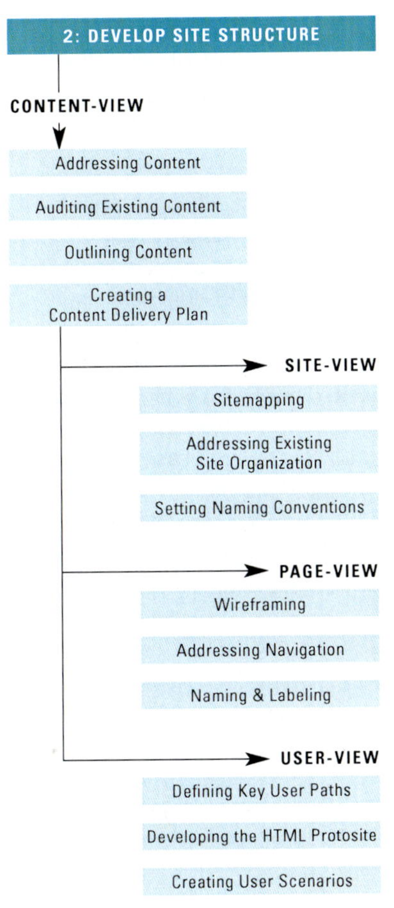

Combat Content Delay

Late content is consistently one of the biggest reasons for project delay. Why? The task itself and the resources needed to complete said task are severely underestimated. Accept it. Plan for it. Charge for it. One way to combat content tardiness is to HIRE A CONTENT MANAGER, a person to manage and oversee the entire content-delivery process. A second way is to CREATE A CONTENT DELIVERY PLAN. This is a schedule that outlines realistic dates for delivery according to readiness. See Phase 2: Structure for more on content.

necessary elements is assigned. Due dates are established. Here's a content truth: Content will inevitably be late, but this plan will help.

Site-View

Being able to see the whole site at once is an important perspective while structuring. In much the same way that a house needs to be architecturally blueprinted, a site also needs to have its structure drawn. This information will translate into a sitemap, which will serve as the backbone for the entire site.

SITE-VIEW

- > Sitemapping
- > Addressing Existing Site Organization
- > Setting Naming Conventions

> Sitemapping

The sitemap shows proposed links and main navigation. It works with the content outline (but not in place of it). If the sitemap changes, it should be updated, reapproved, and redistributed. The sitemap we discuss in this book outlines content, organization, and some functionality, but it does not replace a technical or functional schematic.

> Addressing Existing Site Organization

As you develop the future site's sitemap, take a look at the current site's organization from a visitor's perspective. How can it be changed to be more intuitive? Examine a site map of the current site and then of the planned redesign. Compare the two. Make sure you are truly fixing flow issues in your redesign.

> Setting Naming Conventions

All files, whether assets or pages, must have some sort of methodology to their naming. There is no correct or industry-standard method to name them, so just pick a method and establish it with your team — then be consistent. Apply naming conventions to your sitemap and Content Delivery Plan for ultimate organization.

Page-View

Structuring a site from a Page-View is a lot like storyboarding. With content addressed and the sitemap created, you can look carefully at the site on a page-by-page basis. By examining what goes on what page and how the pages work with one another, you can confidently take the organized content and present it in a way that is meaningful and logical to your audience.

PAGE-VIEW

- > Wireframing
- > Addressing Navigation
- > Naming and Labeling

> Wireframing

A wireframe is a purely informational, architectural schematic that shows major content placement, primary and secondary navigation, and perhaps light functionality. By putting all the page elements down on paper, you can see what you are designing before you start the visual/graphic design phase of the project. Plus, looking at wireframes in relation to each other (interactive wireframes) gives you an idea of page flow.

> Addressing Navigation

Navigation connects the site visitor with the content. Buttons, links, and graphics can be used to maintain a sense of place, offering visitors familiarity: Where are they in the site? Where do they need to go? How do they get back to where they were? Redesign project leaders should be aware of the tendency to rely on the old site's navigation.

> Naming and Labeling

The naming of buttons and labels, including the tone of the wording, should be consistent throughout the site. Determine at this stage what type of cues (icons and/or text) will be necessary to support the naming, labeling, and navigation. Consistency here is key.

User-View

Unlike Page-View, which looks at one page at a time, User-View looks at how each page relates to the others. The goal is getting from point A to point B in the most efficient and easy-to-follow manner possible. Testing paths by following navigational cues and direction will expose awkward spots before they get built in.

USER-VIEW

- > Defining Key User Paths
- > Developing the HTML Protosite

> Defining Key User Paths

If your site does not require the user to actually perform any tasks (for example, fill out a form, log in, make a purchase), you can skip this step. But if the user's experience includes tasks, identify the task's path and build wireframes for each page in the path. With these interactive wireframes, you can check page flow and judge the validity of the path. For an example of a real user path in both wireframes and screenshots, see Phase 2: Structure.

> Developing the HTML Protosite

While working in User-View, have your production team start with an HTML click-thru. This "Protosite" enables you to examine content, navigation, and page flow. Establish whether your informational model makes sense. In other words, can someone actually go through your site as planned?

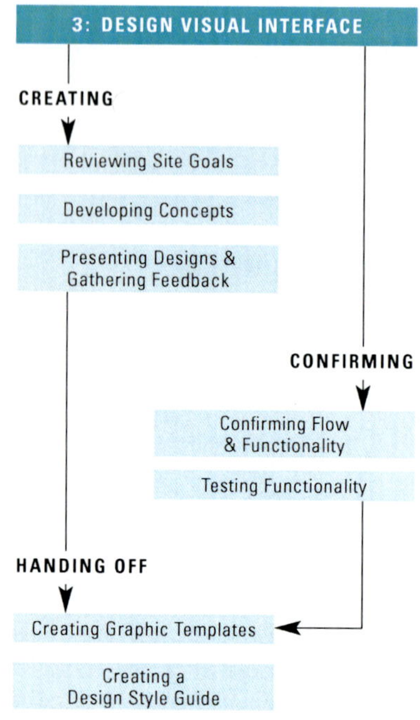

PHASE 3: DESIGN VISUAL INTERFACE

The visual design, the look and feel, the graphic interface — it's the first experience the audience has with the site. Even before users know if the site is easy to use, they see what it looks like. Designing the visual face of any site is exciting, and in this phase designers finally get to be creative. At this stage, all design elements are created based on the established information design and the tone and goals set forth in the Communication Brief. The design is then approved, refined, and tested.

CREATING **CONFIRMING** **HANDING OFF**

Creating

Finding the balance between creative expression and technical constraints is challenging. Visual design is not just about creating a pretty interface; it is about matching the site visitors' needs with solutions on multiple levels. Even if the design is compelling, if it is difficult to use, it is unsuccessful.

CREATING

- > Reviewing Site Goals
- > Developing Concepts
- > Presenting Designs and Gathering Feedback

> Reviewing Site Goals

Visual design should not be done in a vacuum. Review site goals and technical specs. Reread the Communication Brief; refamiliarize yourself with the audience. Aim to design for your audience, not for any designer's ego.

> Developing Concepts

Conceptual brainstorming involves coming up with visual solutions that function and that meet overall site objectives. Visual designers start experimenting with colors and layouts, thumbnails and sketches. The production team is also involved; all concepts should be passed by development to confirm feasibility before being presented to the client.

> Presenting Designs and Gathering Feedback

Present the client with a few rounds of designs, each refining the previous. Set clear expectations; control the client and avoid "endless tweaking syndrome." If the client pulls toward a direction not originally stated in the Communication Brief, be prepared for additional billing. Refine the agreed-upon design until it is approved. Get client approval in writing.

Confirming and Testing Flow and Functionality

During the visual design phase, take time to confirm the content, page flow, navigation, and proposed functionality developed in Phase 2: Structure. Without doing this, moving on to HTML production is a risk. Involve the production designers at all points — from initial sketches through presentations — to ensure that the designs are producible. For special needs, such as pop-up screens, DHTML pull-down menus, and other elements involving light scripting, conduct advance testing against multiple browsers and platforms before the designs are formalized. This minimizes the risk of major issues appearing during production.

CONFIRMING

> Confirming Flow and Functionality

> Testing Functionality

Handing Off

Once the look and feel is refine, approved, and tested, it needs to be applied across multiple pages, and then each of those pages must be prepped for optimization and HTML production.

HANDING OFF

> Producing Graphic Templates

> Creating a Design Style Guide

> Producing Graphic Templates

The transition from final, approved design to production takes form in a handoff of graphic templates. These files call out all functionality (including on/off/over states) and contain placeholders or dummy text for content — all the information that production needs to translate the visual design into HTML.

> Creating a Design Style Guide

For the purposes of ongoing production, design, and maintenance, a Style Guide is an excellent reference document. The Design Style Guide lists established standards for fonts, colors, headers, and many other treatments to help maintain the integrity of the design. A chart of recommended Design Style Guide components appears in Phase 3: Design, along with a visual example.

Incorporate Smart Design

Smart Design serves the audience's environment and capabilities. Smart Design is functional and fast loading. It is focused on the audience's experience rather than on the ambitions of the designer, the desire to use Flash, the positioning of the company's advertisers, or even the personal quirks of the CEO of the client's company itself. If it detracts from your audience, it is not Smart Design — even if it is cool. How do you practice Smart Design? Simple. Think like your audience. Browse, click, and download like your site visitors. Incorporate your information design rather than fight it.
For more on Smart Design, see Phase 3: Design.

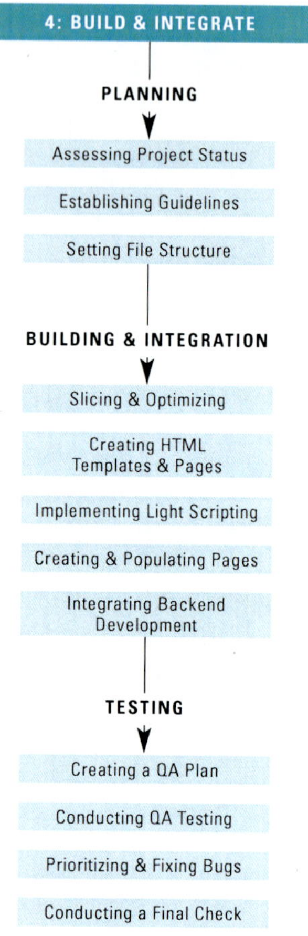

PHASE 4: BUILD AND INTEGRATE

Phase 4 is where you put together all the pieces and make them work. Everything comes together at this point. Production merges content, design, and HTML/CSS and/or Flash production into the completed site. Phase 4: Build sees the backend technical implementation (if applicable). This is also the time when you should conduct quality assurance (QA) testing on your site. Test the site against your requirements. Test for code fluidity. Run QA. Identify the bugs, prioritize the fixes, and then fix them. Get audience feedback and iron out the kinks. Launch is imminent.

PLANNING | **BUILDING** | **TESTING**

Planning

Before starting actual production, take time to re-address both the original expectations and the scope of the project. Review the audience's technical specifications, confirm that graphic templates are ready to be handed over, check content status, and prepare for the work of the building stage.

PLANNING

- > Assessing Project Status
- > Establishing Guidelines
- > Setting File Structure

> Assessing Project Status

Projects often change midstream. Assess your project with regard to time, budget, expectations, and scope. How many hours did you budget for, and how many hours have you used so far? Compare your original projections to the current reality. Now, before building actually begins, is the time to add resources or to ask for additional budget if there have been miscalculations and/or unforeseen technology glitches.

> Establishing Guidelines

Specific questions regarding browser, platform, technology, and file structure need to be answered early in the Core Process, long before production begins and ideally right after the project kicks off. Accessibility needs should each be determined at this point. The Client Spec Sheet is a survey for the client's key technical person to answer. The answers provide the production team with all necessary parameters for establishing guidelines. The Client Spec Sheet is long and detailed. It appears in part in Phase 4 and can be downloaded in full at www.web-redesign.com.

> Setting File Structure

Start clean. Chances are the old site's folder structure is a mess. When determining what naming convention and organization will work best for the project, keep future maintenance and scalability in mind. Even for dynamic sites, there are still static pages to consider. Know in advance of starting production how the files will be named, saved, and archived.

Building and Integration

HTML production is ready to begin in earnest. If all questions are answered and all details already addressed, this can be a very streamlined process. If not, it can be costly. The goal is to touch each HTML page or template only once. Maintaining clear standards for HTML production is extremely important, especially when working with a team of HTML production designers. Strive for consistency. Test and troubleshoot along the way.

BUILDING AND INTEGRATION

- > Slicing and Optimization
- > Creating HTML Templates and Pages
- > Implementing Light Scripting
- > Creating and Populating Pages
- > Integrating Backend Development

> Slicing and Optimization

Translating graphic templates into HTML pages is a challenge and a skill. Here is where the production designers actually cut up, or slice, the graphic templates into individual GIFs and JPGs that will turn into the flat graphics, animations, and rollovers that will compose the HTML templates and pages. Strive to keep page sizes down. Use flat colors with images and background colors for table cells and DIVs whenever possible.

> Creating HTML Templates and Pages

All sites, whether static or dynamic, start with an HTML template. This master page, or set of masters, will be used to create the rest of the site. If the site will be built in static HTML pages, this is the start of actual HTML site production. If layout and positioning will be CSS-driven, that code is developed and tested here. Anything that appears site-wide, such as pull-down navigation menus in DHTML, is included, as well as any footer text (including privacy policy and copyright information) and other global elements. After this master template is created, all sub-templates are built. From there, HTML pages can be produced.

> Implementing Light Scripting

"Light" means do-it-yourself scripting in JavaScript. Features such as rollovers, forms, pull-down menus, pop-up windows, frames, etc. need to be implemented as the HTML templates are created (or in an individual page if the feature is for that page only) and tested.

> Creating and Populating Pages

If content isn't in, you can't populate your templates or pages. This is a spot in the Core Process where the flow often clogs. Content is due, but chances are it

Incorporate Usability Testing

Of all forms of audience feedback, the information collected from usability testing is some of the most valuable because it measures not how you *think* your audience will behave, but rather how an individual site visitor *actually* navigates, finds information, and interacts with your website. Results are immediate and indisputable. By conducting informal testing throughout the development process, you can test assumptions and make decisions, thus refining your site's information design, navigation, naming and labeling, and visual design along the way. Incorporate usability testing into your process. For more on usability testing, see Chapter 8.

Include Invisible Content

While building the individual pages and populating them, add the invisible content to the pages (for globals, add the information when building the HTML templates). Invisible content includes ALT attributes, META, and TITLE tags and is often left (if not forgotten) until production is well under way. Some invisible content is a deliverable from the client, but mostly production designers decide. As a result, naming conventions are necessary.

will be late, and this creates a domino effect that often adds days and dollars to the production schedule. Avoid this. Stay on top of content delivery and set clear and realistic deadlines that can (and should) be adhered to.

> Integrating Backend Development

If your project involves backend engineering, see Chapter 9: Working with Complex Functionality. This new-in-the-second-edition chapter outlines the steps necessary to develop technical specifications and to define your engineering needs. This one of the key crossover points at which engineering begins to integrate with production: here, toward the end of the building stage of Phase 4: Build.

Testing

You've built your site; now make sure it works. Quality assurance testing is simply the exhaustive checking of your site for bugs and against the original specifications outlined in Phase 1: Define. You tested at various stages up to this point. Now that the site is built, it is time to test it as a whole. Whether your testing is formal or informal, using a test plan or just "winging it," there are tools, resources, and expert-level firms that can make QA a breeze.

TESTING

> Creating a QA Plan
> Conducting QA Testing
> Prioritizing and Fixing Bugs
> Conducting a Final Check

> Creating a QA Plan

From informal to semiformal to full testing, there should be a plan in place. A QA test plan specifies the methodology used to test against browsers, platforms, and technical specifications. Resources, schedule, equipment, and assumptions are listed, along with a plan for bug tracking and fixes prior to release. In Phase 4: Build, you can find a tidy list of items to include for a core QA plan.

> Conducting QA Testing

QA testing should be conducted in multiple stages. Internal testing (sometimes called alpha testing) comes first and then beta testing, hopefully on the actual server (before launch if you have access, or after going live if not a soft launch). Testing levels depend on budget, time, resources, and expertise. The main aim of QA is to identify bugs. If you have a separate, formal QA team, it will only track the bugs. The production team needs to fix them.

> Prioritizing and Fixing Bugs

Establishing a method of tracking, prioritizing, and fixing bugs will make the process run much smoother. Determine priorities and monitor and recheck fixes prior to launch. A list of items to note when bug reporting is available in Phase 4: Build, as are suggestions for downloadable, helpful tools available online for in-house QA teams.

> Conducting a Final Check

You're ready to go "live." All testing and fixes have been completed on the staging server (or hidden URL). Before moving the site to the live server, however, a last check should be conducted on design, content, production, and functionality. Also make sure the client has signed off on the site. The final check, in detail, is listed at the end of Phase 4: Build.

PHASE 5: LAUNCH AND BEYOND

Getting to this phase means you are ready to go live with your redesign. Congratulations! Launching your site is a major milestone, but you're not done yet. This phase covers what you need to think about before, during, and after your site goes live. It is about gathering loose ends and wrapping the project up before the site moves into the next phase of production: ongoing maintenance.

Phase 5 is where the distinction sharpens between in-house teams and external web development firms. Although we don't go into this distinction here in the overview, in Phase 5: Launch, we are careful to note where the responsibilities of the different teams usually begin and end.

DELIVERY LAUNCH MAINTENANCE

Delivery

Most projects have one team designing and building and another team managing the ongoing maintenance. The transition between a site-in-development and a site-in-maintenance is usually determined by launch. During this transition, one team hands off all design and production files to the other team for ongoing design, production, and updating.

DELIVERY

- > Handing Off
- > Completing the Production Style Guide
- > Creating the Handoff Packet
- > Tracking Documentation
- > Conducting a Post-Launch Meeting
- > Scheduling Maintenance Training

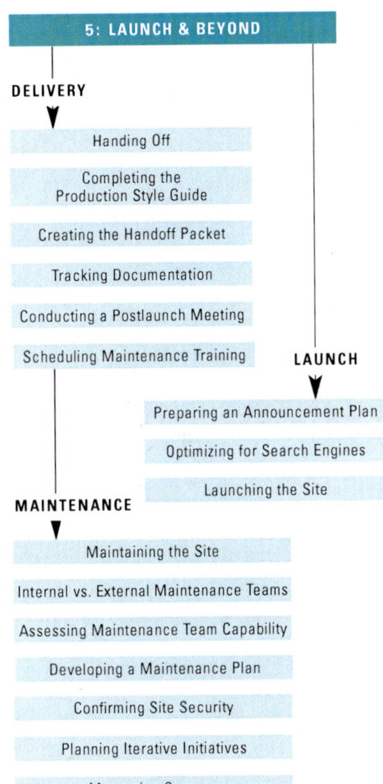

> Completing the Production Style Guide

After launch, production-specific guidelines are added to the Style Guide started in Phase 3: Design. (If the internal team is producing pages with the design team is delivering only templates, the style guide may be necessary before launch.) The Production Style Guide should include code information for HTML tags, attributes, and definitions of graphic elements — all information necessary for one production designer to hand off to another. A chart of recommended Production Style Guide components appears in Phase 5: Launch, along with a visual example.

> Creating the Handoff Packet

All relevant design and production materials should be organized and put into a packet for distribution to the client and the maintenance team. See Phase 5: Launch for a list of suggested handoff materials.

> Tracking Documentation

All documents (electronic and hard copy) having to do with project scope changes, budget issues, and client approvals should be saved. Hard copies of the initial contract, proposal, Project Plan, and any other relevant documentation should be filed and archived. Cull and organize. A suggested archival list can be found in Phase 5: Launch.

> Conducting a Postlaunch Meeting

Every project is a learning experience. The postlaunch meeting (sometimes called the postmortem meeting) is a chance for all key players to get together and constructively rehash the project. Seeing what worked and what could be improved on the next time around — this is the goal.

> Scheduling Maintenance Training

Some training for the maintenance team is almost always needed. This is usually accompanied by specific guidelines outlined in the Style Guides. For larger sites and in-house teams, this maintenance may include additional phases of ongoing application development, content management systems, and relaunches.

Launch

With QA testing completed and production frozen, you are ready to announce the live site. Most likely, there are still some bugs to be fixed, but the site has been given the "go" for public viewing. While the actual launch is really nothing more than a blip in the project timeline, a few factors requiring much more time and resources should accompany the upload.

LAUNCH

- > Preparing an Announcement Plan
- > Optimizing for Search Engines
- > Launching the Site

> Preparing an Announcement Plan

An announcement strategy has been planned long in advance of the launch date — usually by an in-house or outside marketing team. Hopefully, that plan includes notifying your existing audience in advance of the site's redesign to encourage buy-in and feedback. As outside factors may be involved, make sure there is clear communication as to the site's readiness and launch status before any major advertising is started.

> Optimizing for Search Engines

Even if your site is already listed in search engines, plan to resubmit after the redesign launch. Make sure to refer to regularly updated sites such as www.searchenginewatch.com for the most current information.

> Launching the Site

Pull the switch. You're live. Congratulations! Plan to upload the site during nonpeak hours to allow for troubleshooting of last-minute snafus. If appropriate, have a temporary home page in place during the transfer between old and new sites. Larger sites may relaunch in phases if upload and testing will take several hours or days. Have a rollback ready in case of major problems.

Maintenance

Make sure a team is in place for content creation, HTML production, and any necessary visual design changes. How often will the site update? Daily? Monthly? How will you be archiving material? Who will be maintaining the site? How savvy is that person? You filled out the Maintenance Survey at the beginning of the project in order to plan, now it is time to assess, reassess, and transition into a whole new workflow: maintenance.

MAINTENANCE
> Maintaining the Site
> Assessing Maintenance Team Capability
> Developing a Maintenance Plan
> Confirming Site Security
> Planning Iterative Initiatives
> Measuring Success

> Assessing Maintenance Team Capability

The individual(s) responsible for updating must have a high enough level of skill to handle the maintenance of the redesigned site. The web development team should assess the abilities of the maintenance team against the complexity of the redesigned site. Advise the client if the team is understaffed, underskilled, or over-resourced.

Conduct a Competitive Analysis

Analyzing both your industry and your competition can help you better understand how your site rates. Review the main features and usability of a cross-section of competitive sites. An informal analysis conducted from the audience's point of view allows for a greater understanding of features, services, and ease of use. Further formal research and analysis can allow for an in-depth look into the client and the industry, coming with a higher budget and utilizing greater expertise. A competitive analysis should be part of the Discovery process, no matter the level of your approach. Incorporate regular competitive analyses as you plan significant future changes to the site. For more on conducting a competitive analysis, see Chapter 10.

> Developing a Maintenance Plan

Determine the frequency and details of maintenance updates. Create a spreadsheet or official plan outlining the sections and content that will be updated on a daily/weekly/monthly/quarterly basis. Set deadlines that include a regular check of the site against the standards set in the Style Guide.

> Confirming Site Security

Site security is a very specialized field, and we don't go into it in depth, but in Phase 5: Launch, we do present a list of things to consider as you plan for your redesign's security. Hackers are relentless; it helps to safeguard.

> Planning Iterative Initiatives

With site improvements and refreshes ideally occurring regularly, revisiting planned initiatives should happen right after launch. What happens next? Don't delay; begin planning quarterly releases. Out-of-scope items raised during the development process should be scheduled.

> Measuring the Success of the Site

Now that you have launched, it is time to track and measure results. Does your new site actually improve on your original redesign goals? Have sales increased? Have calls to customer service decreased? Having both qualitative and quantitative feedback on usage and customer satisfaction helps you analyze your redesign's success.

CHAPTER SUMMARY

This overview offers a singular panorama of the entire workflow — you can actually see the entire Core Process from start to finish. It is often helpful, especially when in Phase 1: Define, to see everything still to come. When you are building your budget, you can look through the pages of this chapter and budget by task, ticking off each one in each phase as you allocate hours. When you are scheduling, you can see all the steps laid out in list format and gain a better timeline view. For project management, being able to see the next several steps at any point in the process can be valuable as far as staying on top of your team.

Finally, this chapter is sort of a summary, but instead of following the main subject, we present it here at the beginning. This way, you can familiarize yourself with the Core Process and then read about it in detail. We believe it is more helpful this way.

Janus

Company: Janus Capital Group
URL: www.janus.com
Design Team: Janus in-house and selected vendors
Maintenance Team: Janus in-house

Janus Capital Group, a key player in the mutual fund business for 30 years, primarily targets the individual investor and investment advisors with diversified asset-management opportunities. Based in Denver, the majority of its business is conducted online or over the phone.

<PREVIOUS>

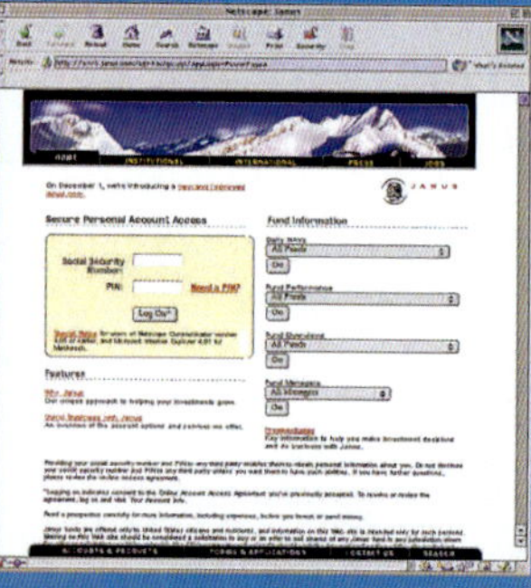

JANUS.COM [OLD] shows a very task-oriented process. 24-hour self-service through the web was the goal, even with the old site.

<INTERIM>

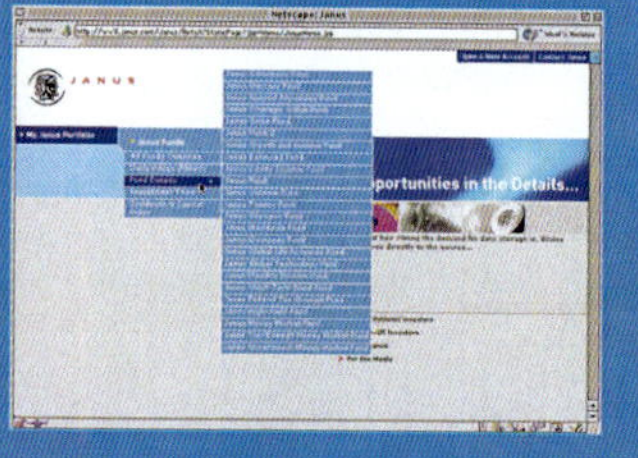

JANUS.COM [REDESIGNED 2000] used a layered navigation system which rendered the landing page nearly useless and it was difficult to glean relevant information quickly and intuitively.

<CURRENT>

JANUS.COM [REDESIGNED 2004] employed social research findings to understand how investors behave. Intuitive navigation offers separate paths for three types of investors. The visual iconography was changed to position Janus' brand more effectively.

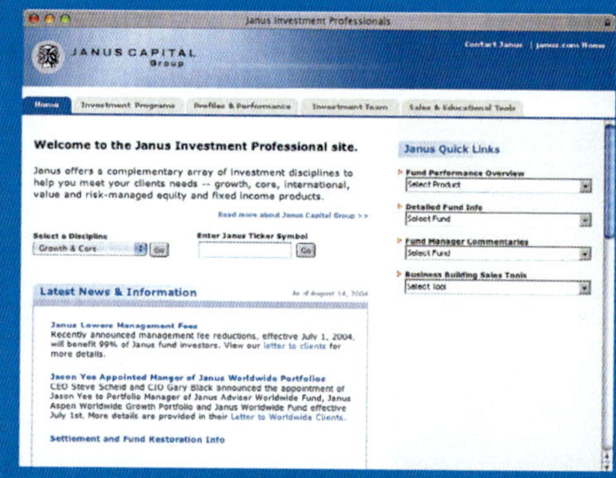

JANUS.COM INVESTMENT PROFESSIONALS [REDESIGNED 2004] uses quicklinks and scannable, relevant content to create a landing page for the investment professional. Information is easy to review and access in this newly structured and content rich site.

Results: Greater productivity and lower costs. In January 2001, 62 percent of investors contacted Janus through Janus.com as compared to 32 percent in January 1999. More intuitive design in 2004 has attracted more traffic from retirement plans and investment professionals.

> Set parameters and expectations — develop methods for clear communication throughout the project's lifecycle.

Phase 1: Define the Project 03

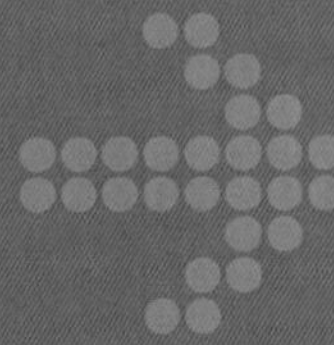

Phase 1: Define the Project

Starting a web redesign project can be daunting. So much to do... where to begin? Although you — and the client — may have a general understanding of what will be involved in getting the project done, the details and process of starting a redesign project can be elusive. The first part of this first phase is all about gathering information.

This chapter will help you set the stage, plan, and prep. Here we focus on developing methods of communicating expectations and making sure there are no mistaken assumptions. We include a lot of handy tools designed to help you help your client provide the necessary information you need to define goals, objectives, budgets, timelines, and of course, the audience. (Don't miss this one; defining your audience and their goals is one of the most important and overlooked preparatory points in any development project, web or otherwise.)

Please note that this chapter outlines the workflow steps necessary for defining a project. We do not go into getting a project. We present workflow, not business development. But because it is often necessary to define quite a bit of the project in order to get it, there is a great deal of information here that is potentially helpful.

WHAT THIS CHAPTER COVERS

DISCOVERY	CLARIFICATION	PLANNING
> Gathering Information	> Determining Overall Goals	> Creating a Project Plan
> Understanding Your Audience	> Preparing a Communication Brief	> Setting the Budget
> Analyzing Your Industry		> Creating Schedules
> Understanding Discovery		> Assigning Your Project Team
		> Setting Up Staging Areas
		> Planning for User Testing
		> Kicking Off the Project

Discovery is an industry-wide term that can mean several things. It can have a budget (often significantly into five figures) and a plan all its own. We have simplified the Discovery process so that it is accessible across a range of projects and pricing.

Also, a project may not be a complete redesign. You might be overhauling a site's architecture without changing the look and feel. Or you might be addressing a specific path through your site in order to increase sales leads. Whatever the project or initiative, take the time to define and clarify goals before starting. Overkill is not required, but some advance planning is necessary in order to operate efficiently instead of haphazardly.

We have divided this first phase of the Core Process into three tracks: Discovery, Clarification, and Planning. Through a series of surveys, discussion, and research, Discovery leads to understanding three critical things: the client's online goals, the audience and its needs and online capabilities, and the industry and the competition as it relates to the web. Discovery is all about gathering information and asking a lot of questions. The answers will serve as a reference for nearly every step that follows.

Clarification and Planning each consist of taking the information gathered and putting it together into documentation — the former into a Communication Brief and the latter into a Project Plan. This documentation is designed to communicate several topics clearly and concisely to both client and team:

- **What are the client's wishes and goals? What is the proposed plan to carry these out?**
- **How much is the entire project going to cost, how is that cost broken down, and how many hours are allocated to each individual task?**
- **Who are the team members, and what are their responsibilities?**
- **What are the client's responsibilities?**
- **What are the specific project deliverables (both client and team), when are they due, and what are the budgetary and scheduling impacts of missing deadlines?**
- **How will the site be tested against audience needs?**
- **What are the immediate measurable goals of the site redesign? What are the long-range goals for the site?**
- **What, if any, are the technical requirements for complex functionality? (For these and other backend references, please see Chapter 9: Working with Complex Functionality.)**

At the end of this defining phase, the preparatory materials are distributed at the kick-off meeting, attended by all team and key client members. The goal is to communicate clearly, to keep the members of the team aligned with the same goals and terminology during the life of the project, and to make sure no one is ever left guessing as to what comes next or when what comes next is due.

Internal Discovery

If you are working internally you are probably incorporating the Discovery process into your daily workflow. This includes looking at competitive sites, interviewing or meeting with your customers and any other method of gaining insight into your industry and audience. If this is the case, the Discovery process can be shortened and details incorporated into the Project Plan and Communication Brief.

DISCOVERY >

> Gathering Information

> Understanding Your Audience

> Analyzing Your Industry

GATHERING INFORMATION

Discovery is a thinking process. Its purpose is to allow team members to put themselves in the minds of the site's users and to understand as much as possible about the target audience(s), the company, the outgoing site, and the redesign project as a whole. To start, you need information. There are a lot of questions to ask; the surveys will get you going.

For more technical projects, especially those that require complex functionality (and therefore a back-end), anticipate Discovery and Planning taking anywhere from a week with one tech-savvy person to several weeks or months with a team of engineers. For more information, see Chapter 9.

On the whole, Discovery can take one week or many weeks, depending upon budget and approach. The Discovery team can be one person or a posse of researchers. Regardless, Discovery starts with the Client Survey.

The Client Survey

Clients usually have clear business objectives, but are notorious for not having clear site objectives. And why expect them to? They are neither designers nor web experts. By asking clients the right questions, you guide them into aligning their business objectives with the constantly changing, evolving, and demanding web.

The Client Survey (available for download from www.web-redesign.com) should be a straightforward distribute/collect/analyze process. Distribution of the survey is the very first thing to do with a redesign project — with any web development project. Encourage feedback within a short timeframe.

Recommend to the primary client contact that the Client Survey be distributed to all decision-makers. Many organizations have several key players, and feedback from varying sources usually gives a broader feel for any project. It is the client's responsibility to manage this distribution and then to process all answers into one response for the development team to use. If you head an internal team, it is probably your responsibility to manage the Client Survey's distribution, collection, and consolidation.

Customizing the Client Survey

The Client Survey should be customized to be client- or industry-specific. If you are in-house and you know the company and industry well, certain basic questions can be eliminated and more in-depth questions added. In fact, if you are the project manager on an internal team, you may be filling out the survey yourself.

All projects differ in size, scope, and focus. The Client Survey asks for in-depth, but basic, information necessary for general site redesign. Using the Client Survey as a base, determine whether any additional information is required. Don't overwhelm the client with dozens of extra questions, however. If the client's eyes glaze over, it's likely you won't get even the basic information you need.

The Client Survey as a Screening Tool

We've all had nightmare clients. Unreasonably demanding, capricious, unrealistic, cheap.... Use the Client Survey as an interviewing or screening tool for prospective clients as soon as a project presents itself. Completing and returning the survey makes clients accountable. The ones who take the time to answer your questions in a thoughtful, well-organized manner are likely to put proper thought into the creation of a site and have the makings of a good client. Clients who exhibit a number of red-flag-client characteristics (see chart below) are sometimes better left alone. If you have the luxury of choice, screen and choose projects and clients wisely.

GOOD CLIENT

A good client has some of the following attributes:

- Is goal-oriented: focused on the big picture and how the site fits into the business as a whole
- Answers the Client Survey in a clear and detailed manner
- Supplies a Request for Proposal (RFP) or a clear outline of goals and scope
- Understands the web environment and the development process
- Gives final sign-off and approval in a timely manner
- Is in agreement on deliverables, schedule, and budget
- Is responsive to email and phone calls
- Has a team-oriented approach
- Gets you content on time and establishes a point-of-contact for content and/or a copywriter
- Is part of the solution instead of the problem

RED FLAG CLIENT

This is not necessarily a nightmare client, but here are some things to watch out for:

- Has a "get-it-up-quick" attitude with unrealistic schedule requests
- Wants to shortcut the process and feels it is a waste of time to address audience needs or overall strategy.
- Doesn't know what the content should be but wants it to "look cool"
- Asks to create a demo site, says "the real one will come later"
- Cannot give final approval or is not putting you in touch with the decision-makers
- Doesn't have time to fill out the survey
- Small budget, swift deadline
- Unresponsive, cannot make decisions, does not email or call back in a timely manner
- Indecisive, changes mind frequently, unable to articulate feedback
- Wants to handle the creative and/or production aspects to "save money"

Unifying Goals

Do key players in the client's company have differing opinions and goals for the redesign? This is usually a red flag indicating that the client is experiencing an internal tug-of-war or is suffering from a significant level of disorganization. Depending upon the source of the dispute, it is possible that data collected from a round of usability tests on the outgoing site and/or on some competitor sites might help client personnel agree on common goals. Real users will clearly demonstrate what is working and what isn't. Understand, however, that user-based feedback, while incredibly insightful, is not a substitute for having clear business objectives. For more on usability testing, see Chapter 8: Testing for Usability. For more on competitive analyses, see Chapter 10: Analyzing Your Competition.

Client input is the foundation on which successful websites are built. This survey will help you articulate and identify the overall goals of your site redesign, including specific questions regarding message, audience, content, look and feel, and functionality. Each key decision-maker should fill out his or her own survey, answer each of the questions in a thorough but brief and clear manner, and add any additional notes or comments at the end of the survey. When finished, all compiled information should be emailed back to the project manager on the web development team.

This survey presented here is available for download on our book website www.web-redesign.com. We recommend expanding and customizing the survey to create your own version if you are working with specific project types, including branding and identity, back- to front-end integration, etc., or if you simply feel you need more information. If you are working in a niche market, you will undoubtedly have the opportunity to get significantly more specific in your questions.

This survey is available for download at www.web-redesign.com >>>

THE CLIENT SURVEY

General Information

1. What is the name of your company and your current (or intended) URL?
2. Who are the primary contacts from your organization, and who has final approval on the project? Please list names, titles, email addresses, and phone numbers.
3. What is your intended launch date for the new site? Are there any outside considerations that might affect the schedule (for example, PR launch, tradeshow, annual report)?
4. Do you have a specific budget range already established for this project? Can this project be divided into phases to accommodate budget and timing constraints?

Current Site

1. Do you feel your current site promotes a favorable user experience? Why or why not?
2. What specific areas of your current site do you feel are successful? Why are they successful?
3. What shortcomings exist with the current site, and what three things would you change on the site today if you could?
4. Have you conducted usability tests or gathered visitor feedback for your current site? If so, how long ago? Please include any reports or findings.
5. How important is it to maintain your current look and feel, logo, and branding?

Reasons for Redesign

1. What are the main reasons you are redesigning your site (new business model, outdated site, expanded services, different audience)?
2. What are your primary online business objectives with the site redesign? What are your secondary objectives? (Examples include increased sales, marketing/branding awareness, and fewer customer service calls.) Please discuss both long- and short-term goals.
3. What is the main business problem you hope to solve with the site redesign? How will you measure the success of the solution?
4. What existing strategy (both on- and offline) is in place to meet the new business objectives?

Audience/Desired Action

1. Describe a typical site visitor. How often are they online, and what do they generally use the web for? Give basic demographics: age, occupation, income level, purchasing habits. (Use as much detail as possible in profiling your target user. Profile more than one type if appropriate.)
2. What is the primary "action" the site visitor should take when coming to your site (make a purchase, become a member, search for information)?
3. What are the key reasons why the target audience chooses your company's products and/or services (cost, service, value)?

4. How many people (as far as you can tell) access your site on a daily, weekly, or monthly basis? How do you measure usage? Do you forecast usage to increase after the site launch and by how much?

Perception

1. Use a few adjectives to describe how your site visitor should perceive the new site. (Examples include prestigious, friendly, corporate, fun, forward thinking, innovative, and cutting edge.) Is this different than the current image perception?

2. How is your company currently perceived offline? Do you want to carry the same kind of message through your website?

3. How does your company differentiate itself from competitors? Do you think your current audience differentiates you from your competition? Please list competitor URLs.

4. List the URLs of any sites you find compelling. What specifically do you like about these sites?

Content

1. Will this site use existing content from the current site? If so, what is the source, who is responsible for approval, and has the content been audited? If not, will you be creating content in-house or using an outside provider?

2. What is the basic structure of the content, and how is it organized? Is it a complete overhaul of the current site or an expansion?

3. Describe visual elements or content that should be utilized from your current site or marketing materials (logo, color scheme, navigation, naming conventions, etc.)

4. How will the content of this site (along with functionality and navigation) expand or differ from your current site? Do you have an existing sitemap for the outgoing site structure? Do you already have a sitemap or outline for the proposed redesign?

Technology

1. What is your target platform and browser? Whom can we talk to in your organization to help respond to technical issues?

2. Are there specific technologies (Flash, JavaScript, DHTML, etc.) that you would like to use in the site? If so, how will they enhance the user experience? Please describe in detail.

3. Will you have database functionality (dynamic content generation, personalization/login)? Do you already have a database in place? Please describe it in detail, including specific information regarding existing programs and software.

4. Will you have a need for secured transactions (e-commerce)? Do you already offer transactions online? Please describe in detail.

5. Will you require other specific programming needs (such as personalization or search capability)? Please describe in detail.

Marketing/Updating

1. How do most people find out about your current website? What kind of triggers prompt a visit (referral links, incentives, search engine terms)? What methods of distributing the URL already exist within the company on and offline?

2. Briefly, what are your short-term marketing plans (specifically, for the site redesign and the 6 to 12 months following launch)?

3. Do you have an existing or planned marketing strategy in mind to promote this site redesign? If so, please describe.

4. Do you intend to keep the site updated? If so, how often? Who is responsible for updating and providing content?

Additional Notes/Comments

Please take as much space as you need.

____

____

____

____

____

____

____

Redesign vs. Refresh

Sometimes a site does not have to go through a complete top-to-bottom change. When analyzing scope, keep in mind that sometimes you may only need to focus on one area of your site at a time.

Analyzing the Client Survey

Once analyzed, the client-answered survey serves many purposes. You will refer to it regularly, especially to define site goals and to build schedules, the budget, and the all-important Communication Brief. It is, quite simply, the project's springboard.

When you are finished analyzing the Client Survey, you should have clarity on several points, concepts, and ideas:

- **Site goals.** What are the overall goals of the site redesign? What is the primary business problem that will be solved (for example, increase traffic, increase sales)? What other goals will be achieved (decrease calls to customer service, create a more user-centric site)?
- **Audience.** What are your audience profiles and demographics? A sample demographic includes occupation, age, gender, online frequency, connection speed, and online habits (the sites users visit and why, how often they purchase online, how web savvy they are). It also includes their type of computer, their browser, and where they live. An audience profile takes that demographic and puts a real name and person to it.
- **Redesign issues.** What are the redesign issues and goals? Have a clear understanding of old site vs. new site in terms of usability, tone, perception, and message. Some examples of uses for this list: to help create the Communication Brief, to review at the kick-off meeting, and as a check-off list during subsequent phases of development.
- **Tone.** What is the client's desired tone and audience perception? Sophisticated? Sleek? Fun? Credible? Dependable? Inexpensive? Have a clear interpretation of this; you need it to write the Communication Brief.
- **Scope.** What are the project boundaries from all angles including budget, schedule, creative vision, technical needs (including the extent of engineering needs), and overall size (as clearly defined as possible with existing knowledge)? You cannot create a budget without a defined scope.
- **Maintenance.** What is the client's vision for future site updates? Formulate a basic idea of how often and to what degree the site will be updated. The Maintenance Survey will provide additional data.
- **Contacts.** Who is involved on the project? Start a contact list for both the client and development teams. This should contain all contact names, email addresses, telephone and fax numbers, and snail mail address (for deliveries and billing). Plan to keep this list updated and available on the password-protected client staging site (discussed later in this chapter).

EXAMPLES OF ADDITIONAL CLIENT SURVEY QUESTIONS	
If promoting the site is a specific redesign issue/goal, try some of these additional questions:	If the redesign project will include a brand and identity overhaul, ask the client about the company's desired brand identity and how it differs from the current perception. Here are some sample questions:
1. What methods of promoting your URL do you currently utilize outside your own organization both online and off? Do you currently have a way of monitoring and/or measuring traffic to your site? Is your site reliant on search results or keywords? 2. How will your encourage site visitors to return to your site? What factors will motivate positive word-of-mouth solicitation? 3. What are your short-, medium-, and long-term goals to increase traffic and awareness of your site?	1. How would you describe your company's brand identity? What is the promise you make to your customers? How will this website help to fulfill this promise? 2. What specifically do you want to communicate with your logo and brand? What kind of emotional response should the customer feel when they come to the website? 3. Are you open to modifying or altering your current logo? How has the logo been modified over time? 4. Who is responsible for maintaining consistency of the brand company-wide? Is this person also responsible for the website? Who has final approval over the logo and brand? 5. If a new logo is required, please attach any examples (or URLs) of logos you feel effectively communicate that company's brand personality.

The Maintenance Survey

It may seem premature to address site maintenance this early in the redesign process, but it is far more streamlined in terms of effort and budget if the following is known early: the level of growth anticipated in the first 12 months following launch, and the post-launch plan, including who will be responsible for the updating (coding, project management, content management, and copywriting), and what skill level will be required for the actual coding. Please note that the Maintenance Survey (available for download from www.web-redesign.com) does not need to be filled out and analyzed prior to the project's kick-off, but it is an issue to consider before the site structure is set.

The client should answer the questions as thoroughly as possible, and the project manager should then use the results from this survey as a guide. By addressing these questions at the beginning of the project, you are able to plan in advance for maintenance needs once your redesign is live.

This survey is designed to help you determine how your site maintenance will be addressed after launch. Answer the following questions briefly and clearly and to the best of your knowledge. When you are finished, email all compiled information back to the project manager on the web development team.

This survey is available for download at www.web-redesign.com >>>

THE MAINTENANCE SURVEY

General Information

1. What areas of the redesigned site will be updated (for example, news, photos, horoscopes, products, reviews) and how often (for example, daily, weekly, monthly, quarterly, annually)?

2. Describe the maintenance team and individual responsibilities and time allocation, if known. (Full time? Part time? Split jobs?)

3. How will the site be updated? Will you be inputting content manually into HTML or XML files? Will you be using a content management system (CMS) to dynamically update and deploy content (useful, for example, in the management of e-commerce inventory or text-publishing databases)? If using a content management system, please describe in detail.

4. Who is responsible for maintaining the site from a technical standpoint, and what is this person's technical expertise level? What experience and capabilities does he or she have? Will the person require training?

5. Who is responsible for making graphic changes on the site? What is his or her design expertise level?

Content Creation

1. Who is responsible for creating the content for the site? Is this person able to dedicate part- or full-time resources to content creation?

2. Who is responsible for approving look-and-feel changes (as the site expands) to ensure that the quality of the site is maintained?

3. How often will new sections or areas be added to the site? Will they be based on the existing site's template or be independent sections?

Production Expertise

1. What technological expertise is necessary to update the site (basic HTML knowledge, light scripting knowledge)?

2. Is there an automated process of changing content on the home page (an automatic refresh of images or text each time a person comes to the site, a randomly generated quote, or a date change)?

Promotion

1. How will the user know the site has been updated? Will there be email announcements or specials tied into the site updates?

2. Who is responsible for continued search engine and keyword updates and submissions? How often will keywords and META tags be revised?

UNDERSTANDING YOUR AUDIENCE

The web is all about the audience. What needs, capabilities, wants, and fickle characteristics of your audience will you need to know? All of them (or at the very least, as many as possible). But because speculation is not credible here, do some sleuthing.

Use the initial data gathered from the Client Survey to get a strong sense of who your site visitors are, why they are coming to the site, and what tasks they will be performing. A typical audience demographic description is a very general listing of stats and data pertaining to everything from where and how they connect to the internet to age and income. You may need to profile more than one target group (with multiple audiences, create separate audience demographics). And keep in mind that your client may not have a clear or complete vision of audience; you may have extra work in store.

Use this demographic information to create a general profile for each visitor type, which will be used in the Communication Brief. This should be a concise paragraph about each visitor type, describing who they are and what they do as a real person, written without using overarching descriptions or nonspecific stats. Here is an example of a general profile:

> **"Typical site visitor is a university student between the ages of 18 and 22, who accesses the web on a daily basis. S/he is extremely web savvy and completes online purchases for books, CDs, DVDs, and gifts regularly — 2 or 3 times per month. S/he has high-speed internet access both at the dorm and at the library, most often using the library computers for research and the dorm computer for personal correspondence. Typical tasks on the site include searching for authors, titles, and products to purchase. S/he has a username and password and is able to complete purchases quickly and easily."**

If you have the resources, we highly recommend building a few detailed individual profiles **[3.1]**. To achieve this, you may need to interview both the client and a few actual users to gain a real-world view of the target audience. The results will be worth the effort.

Request Existing Material

The client may have existing research about the target audience and market. Ask questions. Gather as much information as possible. Keep in mind, however, that the client's business model may have changed in a year's time, so the provided information may no longer be relevant... or complete.

Paige McCormick

Paige McCormick

Paige McCormick is an elementary art teacher, artist, and girls' Little League Track coach in Portland, Oregon. She is 35 years old and lives in Northwest Portland near Forest Park with her dog Ruth Ann (Ruthie).

Paige owns her house and spends a great deal of time fixing it and gardening. She has a very busy and active lifestyle. When not working, Paige spends her time outdoors running, mountain biking, and playing with Ruthie.

Paige is an enthusiastic dog owner and goes out of her way to provide for her dog. She has given up on stuffed animal toys — they're so cute, but Ruthie guts them immediately and eats the fiberfill. Paige casually studies dog behavior and training techniques. She enjoys living near Forest Park because it provides an excellent place for Ruthie to chase squirrels.

Paige uses a Mac G4 PowerBook and considers herself very computer savvy. She connects to the internet at home via 56K modem (but is thinking about upgrading to DSL service soon). At work and at cafés she connects via high-speed wireless. She does a significant amount of her shopping online, which she finds saves her a great deal of time, although sometimes the shipping is a deterrent. She appreciates the automatic monthly deliveries of dog food.

She loves smaller pet shops that specialize in items that appeal to her aesthetics and dislikes large warehouse-style pet stores such as PetCo.com, although she admits they provide necessities at a reasonable price.

< 3.1

This sample audience profile gives a detailed description of a typical site visitor. Also called a "persona," this document can be as brief or as detailed as your information, creativity, and time allow. Most sites draw several distinctly definable audience types. You may need to create more than one profile.

Outlining Technical Requirements

What technological "latests and greatests" will your redesign project require? This is, without question, one of most significant factors in defining the project. A redesign project that is front-end only — even if extensive in scope — is a very different project from one that also includes dynamic content and security capabilities. It is not unusual for clients to want all kinds of bells and whistles without understanding the associated costs, or if a better, more appropriate solution could be found (content should determine the technology, not the other way around). Analyzing both basic and backend technology needs will gather the data necessary to show where client expectations do not match reality **[3.2]**.

Because the client may have (and often does have) unrealistic expectations, it is the project manager's responsibility to make sure the client understands not only the fundamentals of redesigning the website, but also how each choice and decision that is made impacts both the scope, timeframe and therefore the budget of the project.

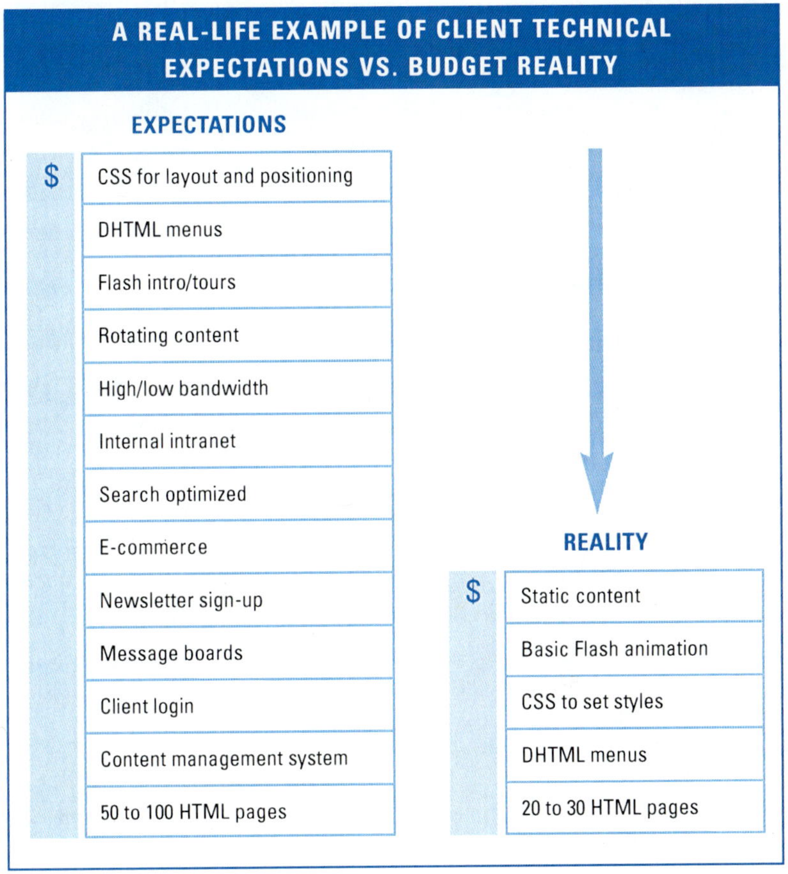

A REAL-LIFE EXAMPLE OF CLIENT TECHNICAL EXPECTATIONS VS. BUDGET REALITY

EXPECTATIONS ($)	REALITY ($)
CSS for layout and positioning	Static content
DHTML menus	Basic Flash animation
Flash intro/tours	CSS to set styles
Rotating content	DHTML menus
High/low bandwidth	20 to 30 HTML pages
Internal intranet	
Search optimized	
E-commerce	
Newsletter sign-up	
Message boards	
Client login	
Content management system	
50 to 100 HTML pages	

3.2 >

Clients often have only a vague idea of what features actually cost. Once true costs and timing are communicated, clients frequently adjust their technical expectations.

KATE GOMOLL ON USER PROFILING

Designers and developers need to keep real people in their minds as they design. Reality TV has been so successful because real people are endlessly fascinated by the unexpected things that other real people actually do and say. As you define your audience, if you can write a story about an actual person — complete with pictures, hobbies, quirks, product preferences, pet peeves, and details about that person's daily life — the designers and developers will actually read it and, more importantly, absorb it.

Typically, companies run focus groups or conduct market surveys to learn about the potential users of their products. The results from this research are traditionally presented in summary reports that describe user goals, needs, and desires in terms of percentages and trends. While this information is useful for overall product planning and marketing, it often isn't specific enough for product designers and web developers.

The summary reports that most research departments create are an abstract representation of people. They are usually a discussion of trends and market breakdowns, lacking any details about individual customers. But designers and developers need details when they create a product. Details about users' motivations, frustrations, and desires help the development team make important and strategic decisions. There will always be disagreement over how a new or redesigned product should look and work. But when you have profiles of real users at your fingertips, the arguments shift from "I would never do that" or "My Mom would hate that" to arguments about actual users like Paige **[3.1]**. Suddenly, team members are asking whether Paige would require instant-on functionality — meaning that the functionality automatically loads and doesn't need to be called upon by a visitor — or whether Paige would be turned off by an advertising banner. The designers use the data in the profiles to help make sensible design tradeoffs.

I'm not saying that you shouldn't conduct research using a decent sample size or that you should stop doing focus groups and conducting surveys. But often, schedules don't allow even the most minimal research. Still, if time is spent figuring out what types of users fall into the target market group and then visiting at least one person from each of the market segments, very useful profiles can result. Sometimes teams will launch a grassroots profiling effort — even when it's not in the budget — simply because designers need them! Designers simply can't do their jobs without knowing specific information about the potential users.

What kinds of information should you include in your profiles?

- **Basic demographics**
- **Day-in-the-life stories**
- **Photographs of people, their environments, their tools**
- **Likes and dislikes**
- **Observational data**
- **Product usage patterns**
- **Frustrations with your product or similar products**
- **Product-related desires**

Because these profiles are only useful if people want to read them, take the time to write a compelling narrative; make each person you profile memorable. Use the details you collect from users to develop each person as a character. If you have the time and budget, create profiles for many potential users. Then roll them up to create just a few composite characters to represent the user segments. These profiles, also called personas, will become shorthand descriptions for the user segments that your product serves. The key to successful user profiling is to work from actual user data, not hypothetical, made-up stories. You'll find that the truth really is stranger — and more revealing — than fiction.

Kate Gomoll is president of Gomoll Research & Design Inc. (www.gomolldesign.com), *a consulting company that specializes in user experience design. The company's recent clients include DirecTV, Charles Schwab, WebTV, Hewlett-Packard, Internet Appliance Network, and Compaq. Kate has published chapters on user observation in* The Art of Human Computer Interface Design *(Addison-Wesley, 1990) and* The Macintosh Human Interface Guidelines *(Addison-Wesley, 1992). A nationally recognized expert in the field of software interface design and usability, Kate teaches customer research methods at conferences and workshops worldwide. She also taught user-centered design workshops through UCLA Extension for many years. Prior to starting her consulting business, Kate was an interface designer in the Advanced Technology Group at Apple Computer.*

Understanding Audience Capabilities

It comes down to this question: Who is the client willing to leave behind? Some sites such as Amazon.com or eBay depend on appealing to all audiences. If your targeted audience is everybody-with-a-computer-and-then-some, users with older — and sometimes newer — technologies must be accommodated, and bandwidth requirements must be kept low. Many web users have small monitors, use older browsers, and still connect with modems — these users may be as valuable to the client as those with a T3 connection and the absolute latest browsers. High-bandwidth requirements would frustrate and alienate someone on a slow modem and would probably cause that user to abort the page load. Result: lost business.

High or low bandwidth? Most clients will know which group they want to target. It is your job as project manager to determine what that audience can accept technically and then scope the project accordingly.

When catering to high-bandwidth users, the client wants to show all the latest and greatest with little concern for who gets left behind. Clients want an audience that supports all their high-end technologies (the newest Flash plug-ins, extensive use of style sheets, the very latest browsers, etc.). These sites tend to be experimental and artistically cutting edge **[3.3]**.

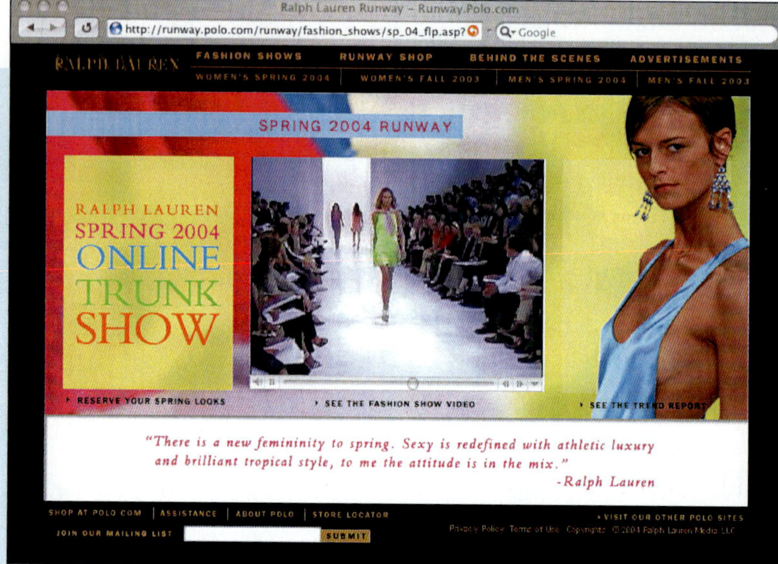

< **3.3**

High bandwidth: www.runway.polo.com loads in seconds with a high-speed connection, but it takes over a minute for users with a modem. It requires multiple plug-ins (which may deter some visitors) and the streaming media will crash some older browsers, even if the connection speed is adequate.

Sites that need to be accessible to anyone (including the wireless market), anywhere (even where DSL is unavailable), must appeal to a low-bandwidth-capable audience. These sites need to load quickly even on slower modems. (We are no longer targeting 28.8 modem speeds but must consider 56K if considering a broad, at-home market.) Examples include www.amazon.com **[3.4]**.

Most companies want to shoot for a widely targeted audience, one that includes users on both modem and higher-speed connections. These companies don't want to lose the users needing low-bandwidth access, but they want to accommodate some higher technology and appeal to users who can and do appreciate what high bandwidth can allow. The site for the Issey Miyake fashion collection **[3.5]** accomplishes this by loading a home page that offers broadband and modem options. Some sites, like www.macromedia.com, even take the choice away from the audience and incorporates programming to detect which browser is being used and automatically directs users to the site they can access.

Analyzing Audience Capabilities

Once you know who your audience is, start determining their technical capabilities. What percentage of your audience is still at an 800×600 screen resolution? What percentage has the latest RealPlayer plug-in installed? At what browser level is most of your audience? What bandwidth can these people comfortably handle? (Does the client even care? Maybe not, if the purpose of the site is merely to display.)

Your goal is to identify your target audience's technical capabilities so you can set standards for the team to work within. These standards must be in alignment with the expectations of the client. Keep in mind that your key client contact may not be the best person to answer these questions. Interviewing the client's technical team, if there is one, will probably yield better results. Depending on your expertise, you may want your tech lead to talk to your client's tech lead.

3.4 >

Low bandwidth: www.amazon.com downloads in a snap, even on 56K modems, and designs its functionality to be stable. It is even accessible to audiences still on 4.x browsers.

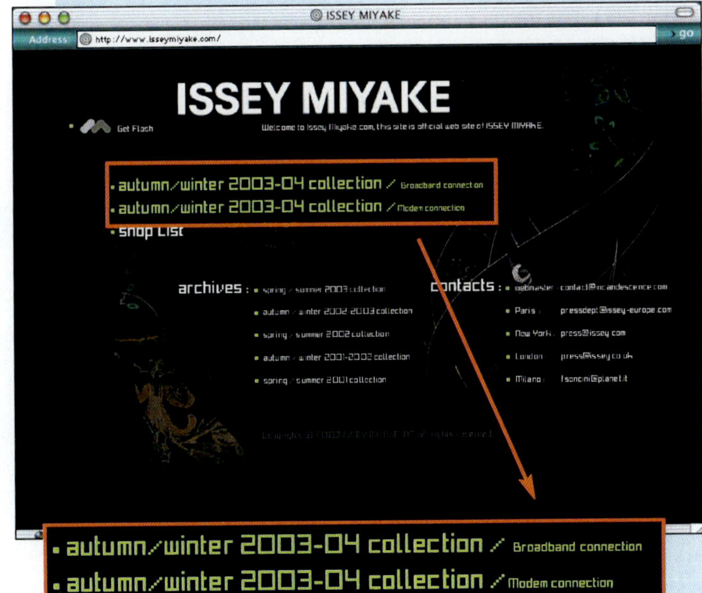

3.5 >

Aiming to satisfy both high and low is usually achieved by making concessions to each. www.isseymiyake.com (circa December 2003) loads a home page that shows none of its actual product and offers the option not between Flash and HTML but broadband vs. modem. The broadband option crashes some not-quite-up-to-the-minute browsers, but the online experience of this option is (at press time) cutting edge.

Site Specific Statistics

Many organizations continuously audit the internet audience at large, tracking overall audience statistical data. However, much more specific stats are also available to show the percentage of browser types and screen resolutions accessing *your* site. Though much of this information might be available for free through your ISP or server software, a paid account with www.hitbox.com, www.webtrends.com, or www.hitslink.com **[3.6]** may be able to offer better information.

Bring in Your Technical Expert Early

Whether a straightforward front-end redesign or a technical behemoth, now is the time to bring the design and the technical expertise together. Getting key tech personnel in synch with the front-end team early, especially as the project is being defined, will help identify — even eliminate — potential issues along the way.

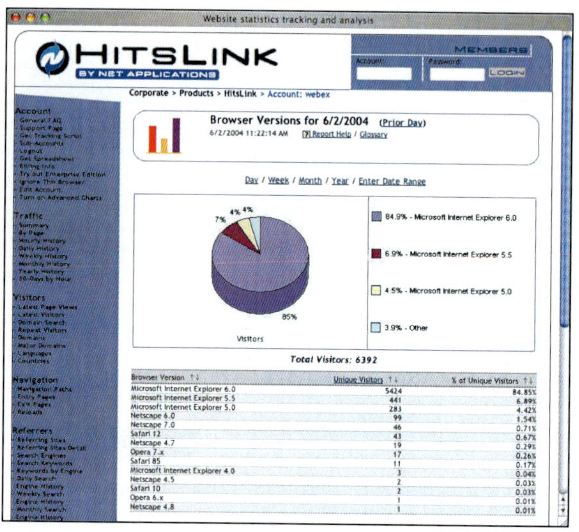

< 3.6 >

Data from a Hitslink account tied to a specific domain shows customized and meaningful information.

Determining Technical Needs

Use the Expanded Tech-Check worksheet (available for download from www.web-redesign.com) to determine what, if any, backend programming needs you have. When you have completed this simple worksheet, you will know whether you need to implement a separate workflow for backend development. Either way, front-end only or front-end and backend together, the completed Expanded Tech-Check worksheet is a good thing to have on hand as reference for your team.

Tech Spec

Creating a written specifications document that details and itemizes how a conceived site will function is a must-do for most large websites. (A less comprehensive version is a should-do for smaller sites.) If the website can be programmed entirely on the front end, you can ensure that everyone is using the same terminology and has an identical understanding of the site's technical parameters by preparing a Tech Spec. However, if complex functionality will be required and backend engineering is necessary, a considerably more detailed document called a Functional Spec will need to be created. In either case, you will want input and sign-off from all project decision-makers, both team and client. For further information on the Functional Spec (it documents all the technology involved in all planned database-dependent functionality or other complex interactivity), or on working with complex functionality, see Chapter 9.

THE EXPANDED TECH-CHECK

These questions will help determine larger-scale technology issues that may include high-level programming and backend development needs. This is used initially as a checkpoint at a very basic level to identify client expectations. When you are finished, email all compiled information back to the project manager on the web development team.

1. Please identify whether you currently use any of the following features on your site. Describe in as much detail as possible. (Check all that apply and describe briefly below.)

   ☐ Search engine
   ☐ Personalization (login/cookie set)
   ☐ Security features
   ☐ Survey/voting tools
   ☐ Email newsletter distribution
   ☐ Shopping cart
   ☐ Discussion board/bulletin board
   ☐ News/press release area
   ☐ Other ______________________

   ____
   ____

2. List any other features that you hope to add to your site, now or in the future.

   ____
   ____
   ____

3. Are there or will there be any e-commerce transactions on the site (secure transactions, interface with inventory database, and fulfillment)?

   ☐ Yes (Please describe in detail below.)
   ☐ No

   ____
   ____

4. Is there or will there be login, registration, and/or personalization incorporated?

   ☐ Yes (Please describe in detail below.)
   ☐ No

   ____
   ____

5. Do you currently or will you in the future use a content management system (useful, for example, in the management of e-commerce inventory or text-publishing databases) to dynamically update and deploy content?

   ☐ Yes (Please describe in detail below.)
   ☐ No

   ____
   ____
   ____
   ____

6. Does the site need to integrate with any preexisting database system? If so, what kind of database is currently being used (FileMaker, Access, Oracle, SQL)?

   ____
   ____
   ____

7. Will you be using any scripts or code that have already been established? Are they server-side or client-side (if known)?

   ☐ Yes (Please describe in detail below.)
   ☐ No

   ____
   ____

8. Please list names and contact information for the current tech lead and any third-party vendors/providers that we may need to talk with to gather additional details.

   ____
   ____
   ____

If you answered "yes" to any of the preceding Expanded Tech-Check questions, you will need to begin a separate workflow track of development, engineering, and execution. Please refer to Chapter 9 for more information.

NATHAN SHEDROFF ON THE EMOTIONAL FUTURE OF BRANDING

"Brand" and "branding" are now common words in the lexicon of both designers and businesspeople. Since the late 1990s, these have been discussed at all levels in companies and other organizations — especially online. While there is still disagreement over definitions, the discussion alone points to an acceptance of importance. In fact, online media is what forced a new understanding of brand and thrust it into a new position in both design and business. Interactive media, in general, and online media, specifically, remind us that brands are interactive and are not the static material that our complacency had defined them as (print, outdoor, packaging, etc.). Now that we've begun to rediscover that brands are interactive, what's next?

We still need to foster a more coherent definition about what is and isn't a brand and where brand boundaries lie, but beyond that the conversation quickly dies. There is little discussion about where the state of branding is going — or should go — and little about its growing or waning influence in business and culture, online or off.

Added to this is a pronounced rise in anti-brand and anti-corporate rhetoric and demonstration. Often this is the result of frustration with corporate and consumer culture more than it is a true reflection of the power or satisfaction of branding among the public. All people appear to use brands, but which ones they support or demonstrate against depends more on which brands reflect values they share or don't than whether the mechanism of representing values itself is the problem.

Perhaps the most value that online media can bring to the brand equation is connectivity. For sure, online media have unique and particular traits, but one of their greatest strengths is their ubiquity and ability to serve as a nexus for the brand experiences in all other media. For example, websites and email are one of the best ways for companies to serve at their customers' convenience. No customer service or "relationship management" system would be complete without online tools and solutions, precisely because interactive media are, inherently, two-way. Companies are learning that their experiences (and brands) are only built successfully over time by engaging people in an ongoing conversation or relationship.

The more companies can engage their customers (and vendors, suppliers, etc.) on a personal and appropriate level, the more they do so on an emotional level. This is where brands gain their strength. Our interaction with websites providing services, features, and functionality carries with it emotional weight and value. Sometimes these experiences are poor, other times exactly what the company hoped to achieve... and sometimes online experiences exceed expectations. Successful companies build their brands by focusing on a positive user experience — combining the best of user interaction and customer service to provide value throughout the relationship. It isn't surprising at all, in fact, that brands that once had popularity decades ago (ESPRIT, Looney Tunes, Atari, and Puma, for example) have rebuilt their mindshare and returned with new popularity, in part based on rebuilding a positive user experience online. Likewise, the best websites have a look, feel, and tools that are consistent with that company's product and service experiences in other media. One of the best examples of this is the Apple website. The tight integration between the website, Apple's retail stores, phone-based customer support, and the products themselves provides a consistent — and consistently comfortable, focused, and wonderful — experience that builds a corresponding relationship.

The history of branding has always been in this emotional space between product/service and audience/customer. And branding will need to address this space even more in the future. Online and off, brands are undoubtedly emotional at some level, but brand professionals will probably need to be as dispassionate as possible in making decisions regarding brands in order not to break this illusion of shared "ownership" that their trusting audience feels.

The future of branding for site redesigns will be defined by tools to measure and better understand emotions and will be tied to ever more meticulous measures of emotional feedback, instead of merely profits and losses or statistics based on sales.

Nathan Shedroff (www.nathan.com) *is a pioneer in Experience Design, an educator, an entrepreneur, and the author of* Experience Design 1 (www.experiencedesignbooks.com). *In addition to speaking and teaching internationally, he is the chair of the AIGA Center for Brand Experience. He is currently developing design books and tools to help designers develop more successful experiences.*

ANALYZING YOUR INDUSTRY

Some projects have the luxury of a contracted or in-house marketing team. These researchers run exhaustive market and audience research and in-depth competitive analyses. An analysis this extensive, however, is not usually an option for most projects in which budget and time are real considerations. No matter the budget level, however, spend time looking at the competition and the industry. Look at the current, outgoing site's features and learn about the online features that competitors use. What is working? What isn't? All this will greatly help you learn about your audience. With this information, you will be better armed to re-create and redesign a successful website.

You can do a cursory analysis, but we highly recommend expanding Discovery by conducting a competitive analysis. See Chapter 10 for a detailed discussion of methodology for this process.

Technical Summary

By the end of the Discovery phase, the technical legwork should be complete, and the technical liaison should be able to gauge both the scope and the complexity of the backend development needs. The Discovery process for technical development can be a project in itself, with a large document referred to as a Technical Specification. For more information, see Chapter 9.

UNDERSTANDING DISCOVERY

Discovery is an information-gathering process meant to dig deep into the details of what is important to a client's business, target audience, and industry. Scope and depth of research and inquiry will differ from project to project, but the results are the same: valuable data. The more information you gather, interpret, and comprehend, the more prepared you will be to execute a site on budget and on target.

Keep in mind that parts of the Discovery process (such as audience profiling and competitive analysis), specifically those that may require additional budget allocation, may not be completed before moving into other aspects of defining the project. However, the goal should be to get as much exploration completed before moving to the next phase of the project. Clear information about the goals and obstacles of the project will allow you to execute your solutions effectively.

DISCOVERY CHECK-OFF LIST

To help ensure that you have all the information you need to move forward, use this check-off list to make sure you touch on all aspects of the company, industry, and audience.

1. Company/Client

- ☐ Distribute the Client Survey to all key decision-makers and align expectations for primary goals, target audience(s), desired tone, etc.
- ☐ Gather existing company information, marketing materials, studies, existing research, and printed materials and reports.
- ☐ Follow up with email or phone interviews and determine reasons for the change (current issues, possible solutions, and specific goals for redesign).

2. Industry

- ☐ Research the client's industry on- and offline. Use traditional research methods (the library, online searches, the phone book) as well as paid research methods (Jupiter Research, Gartner, etc.) if the budget allows.
- ☐ Research industry-specific publications, newsgroups, subscribed materials, organizations, white-papers, etc.

3. Strategy/Marketing/Branding

- ☐ Gather information on current and planned marketing and advertising efforts (on- and offline advertising, placement, strategy).
- ☐ Understand marketing strategy and measurable goals, both short and long term. (An immediate goal might be to sign up new customers.)
- ☐ Understand branding strategy, desired perception, message/tone, and approach (current thinking and desired thinking).

4. Current Site

- ☐ Conduct usability testing and analysis of the current site. Determine what is working and what is not working with the site (navigation, content, functionality).
- ☐ Gather existing quantitative data. Using logs and marketing data, what types of purchasing habits and traffic patterns exist?
- ☐ Gather qualitative data. Using customer feedback and customer service data, what do customers like and dislike about the current site? What areas are successful and why?
- ☐ Gather technical/functionality specifications. Have a general understanding of how the current site functions and the specific technologies involved.
- ☐ Conduct a content audit. What is relevant and not relevant on the site? How effective is the current content to meeting the overall site goals?

5. Competition

- ☐ Identify primary and secondary competition, both on- and offline (from client and team research).
- ☐ Conduct a formal or informal competitive features analysis (see Chapter 9).
- ☐ Identify main features and differentiators for each site and/or company.

6. Audience

- ☐ Define the primary target audience(s) (use the client and Client Survey).
- ☐ Gather demographic information about the target audience(s) (occupation, gender, income, online and offline habits, connection speeds, browser and platform specifications).
- ☐ Create audience profiles and user tasks (showing lifestyle, work and home environment, income range, occupation, internet usage, and typical tasks performed on the client site).
- ☐ Create user scenarios (specific situations for the target user to complete or engage in an online task or transaction).

7. Products/Services

- ☐ Identify and familiarize yourself with what products or services the company offers.
- ☐ Understand buying habits — factors that enable the potential customer to become a paying or registered customer.
- ☐ Determine effectiveness of customer service. Is it helpful or not?

8. Technical Needs

- ☐ Define the extent of the functionality required for the site. Can it be done with forms, light scripting, and/or passwords, or will a backend layer need to be incorporated? If so, what is the extent of those technical requirements? (For more on backend integration, see Chapter 9.)

9. Other

- ☐ Use any additional areas specific to your client or industry that may give additional insight and information to your research.

CLARIFICATION

> Determining Overall Goals

> Preparing a Communication Brief

DETERMINING OVERALL GOALS

"What is the goal of this redesign?" "Why are we redesigning?" "What will the redesigned site accomplish that the present site doesn't?" You need answers to these questions. Don't get sidetracked, though. You are not yet looking for the answer to "How are we going to redesign the site?" For now, you are seeking to identify specific goals. Review the Client Survey. What did the client list as goals? Were the goals specific or general? In conversation with the client, were any other goals mentioned? Pull these together into a concise list of overall goals.

Here are some possible client goals:

- To increase traffic
- To increase sales
- To highlight a new product
- To make a dynamic, content-driven site
- To decrease calls to customer service
- To create intuitive navigation
- To streamline browsing and purchasing
- To create a scalable structure for growth

What are goals, however, without a way to measure whether they have been reached? How will the client determine whether the site has met the stated goals upon launch? Are there methods in place for assessing return on investment (ROI)? Take your list of goals and sort them into primary, secondary, and tertiary priorities. Identify measurable ways in which you can determine whether these goals have been met postlaunch (for example, a statistical increase in purchase process completion). To determine the site's success, suggest that the client identify both measurable goals and milestones and do so both quantitatively and qualitatively. Redesigned sites should be able to compare statistics to the old site. Make a note of these measurable goals and revisit them in Phase 5: Launch when maintenance is readdressed.

PREPARING A COMMUNICATION BRIEF

An effective way to make sure you understand what someone has said to you is to repeat it back to the person clearly and concisely. In addition to being the basis for understanding the overall tone, goals, and direction of a project, the Communication Brief (also called the Creative Brief) restates the client's wishes by organizing the answers from the Client Survey. List the overall site goals in the Communication Brief. This will serve to align both the team and the client under the same terminology. With everyone talking the same language and working toward the same goals, the project has an excellent chance of staying on target.

Take thoughtful time when preparing the Communication Brief (**[3.7]** is a generic sample) because you and your team will be referring to it throughout the project, but don't sweat over it for weeks. It is a short and simple statement of site objectives, from overall goals to targeted audience to end-user perception. It should identify — among other things — style, audience, and message. In addition, the Communication Brief sets the project's tone (how people should perceive the site and the company).

The Communication Brief should articulate visual and conceptual goals for the new site, both independent of and in comparison to the existing site. This document should be nonvisual — no sketches or layouts — and it should be short (only one to two pages) to ensure that it actually gets read. It can be as informal as an email or formal enough to be included in a bound report. No matter the form or format, it needs to be client approved. Get it signed.

Pull information you need from the answered Client Survey and from your various meetings thus far with the client. Use the Communication Brief Worksheet to get started. Further questioning may be necessary.

3.7 >

This sample communication brief has been abbreviated in its printed form here. Both Audience B and Audience C received as much of a description as Audience A. Your communication briefs should do the same for all your target audiences.

Company XYZ
Communication Brief v_02

Project Overview
Company XYZ is undergoing a complete overhaul. The company is moving in a new direction — with the goal of creating an organization that conveys usability, interaction design, and user experience expertise. The redesigned website will reflect the combination of compelling theme and approach combined with effective, straightforward navigational approach to create an experience that is intuitive and smart.

The single purpose of the new site is to highlight Company XYZ's brand, expertise, and services. The site should be a showcase of our abilities while offering easy access to case studies and our 1-2-3 approach to create customizable, integrated solutions for web development teams. We are the "external/internal" team — focusing on measurable results for iterative web initiatives. The secondary purpose of the site is to create a reputable resource for web design and development teams to access information on process, information design, visual design, and usability. The site will be a showcase for CSS-based design. Company XYZ will also be promoting speaking events, lectures, teaching, and published works, as well as updates for press releases and latest news.

The long-term goal of the company is to become a recognized, credible global presence on- and offline and to continue to build the Company XYZ brand as a leader in user experience, interaction design and research.

Target Audience
Audience A is a marketing director or VP of a Fortune 1000 company. She has been given the approval to move forward with a site redesign and possible rebranding of the company. As a highly paid executive, her recommendations are seldom ignored. She accesses the internet on a high-speed connection on a daily basis and works on a PC. She has seen read articles written by various Company XYZers about iterative site design, branding, and workflow practices, and goes to the site to determine if Company XYZ is a good fit for the site redesign. She contacts the company and requests to start with a general site analysis and consulting to determine how she should approach the redesign. Primary tasks include reviewing the case studies and client list, the process and approach, and background information to ensure a credible fit.

Audience B is an in-house webmaster with a technology-based web team in place. His company wishes to ...

Audience C is an independent web designer and owner of a small web design studio who has heard of gotomedia through various lectures and publications. She wants to ...

Perception/Tone/Guidelines
The target audience feels Company XYZ is a credible resource. They know Company XYZ via word of mouth, past client/vendor relationships, and through various conferences and speaking engagements.

Perception: Intuitive, intelligent, compelling, streamlined, focused, user centered, flexible, responsive, successful, industry leader, integrated, collaborative, strategists, real-world, effective, educators, straightforward, honest, trustworthy, smart.

Communication Strategy
The overall message we would like to convey is credibility and intelligence. We will convey this message by simplifying the experience and create a compelling intuitive experience. Messaging and action items will be clear throughout the site, and the visual design and concept will make people remember the Company XYZ brand.

Single-Minded Message: Smart

Signature Date

THE COMMUNICATION BRIEF WORKSHEET

Answering the questions on this worksheet will effectively build the skeleton for your Communication Brief. The information gathered in the Discovery process (Client Survey, research, interviews) will provide you with the answers.

Project Summary: State general project information, goals, and relevant background information for the site redesign. This paragraph should be a statement overview of the project as a whole.

1. What is the basic overview of the project? Briefly include background information if relevant.
2. What is the single purpose of the new site?
3. What are the secondary goals of the new site?
4. What are the long-term goals?

Audience Profile: Profile the target audience. Provide enough detail to enhance everyone's understanding of who the audience is. Include some audience demographic information. Use these questions as a guide. Add some of your own.

1. Who is your target audience? Choose a typical visitor and profile in detail. Include occupation, age range, gender, online frequency, online activities, and any other relevant information. Profile more than one if applicable.
2. What is a typical task the visitor might perform on the new site? (For example, register, log on, search for information, buy a specific product, send their email address, call for more information.)
3. What do these people care about? Why are they interested in the product the site will be offering? What trigger would prompt them to visit the site, and why would they be enticed to return?

Perception/Tone/Guidelines: How should your target audience respond to your new online presence?

1. What does the target audience think and feel about the company and the current website?
2. What do we want them to think and feel?
3. How will this new website help achieve this goal?
4. What adjectives can be used to describe the way the website and the company should be perceived by the target audience?
5. What are some specific visual goals the site should convey?

Communication Strategy: How will we meet our measurable goals?

1. What is the overall message you are trying to convey to your target audience? (For example, cost-effective, secure, reliable, efficient.)
2. How will you convey the overall message? (For example, effective messaging through copy, directed path towards goal, specific offer on home page.)
3. Identify stages of development (if appropriate) used to execute goals.
4. How will you measure the success of the redesigned site?

Competitive Positioning: How you are different from your competition and the factors that will make you a success.

1. How is your company or your web presence different from your competition?
2. What specifically sets your company apart from your competition?
3. What areas of the current site are successful and why?

Targeted Message: State a to-the-point word or concise phrase that will appropriately describe the site once it is launched.

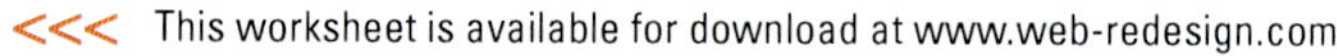

CREATING A PROJECT PLAN

With all Discovery data collected and site goals defined, you can move confidently into the creation of a Project Plan. There are separate and distinct aspects of the project to plan, but when you have finished, you will have assembled several deliverable documents that help define the project and plot the course of action for the development of the site design. Compiled, these documents form your Project Plan. Larger companies put far more effort and resources into these documents (which can swell in size to 100 or more pages), but we live in the real world. What we present here are the key items that make up the Core Process — the minimum amount of planning and organization necessary for a project's success.

Sometimes referred to as a Scope Document or a Project Charter, the Project Plan should contain at least the following (each of which is described in detail elsewhere in this chapter and is listed here in suggested order):

- **Project overview**
- **Schedule (including deliverables and methodology)**
- **Budget breakdown, with allocated hours**
- **Communication Brief**

Additionally, the following are suggested, though not mandatory.

- **Target audience information**
- **Audience profiles**
- **Audience technical capabilities**
- **User testing plan**
- **Details and assumptions**
- **A line for the client's signature**

PLANNING

- Creating a Project Plan
- Setting the Budget
- Creating Schedules
- Assigning Your Project Team
- Setting Up Staging Areas
- Planning for User Testing
- Kicking Off the Project

Proposal or Project Plan?

We're not offering marketing, sales, or business-development advice here. The Core Process assumes you have the project already. We hardly touch proposals (maybe next book). With that disclaimed...

What is the difference between a proposal and a Project Plan? Both are used to define the project, outline overall goals, and announce the plan of action. Both contain a budget and a schedule with deliverables clearly defined. But as far as the Core Process is concerned, the main difference is this: The proposal is a skeletal overview, or starting point, and is dealt with before you have a signed contract. The Project Plan goes much deeper into details and execution strategy. It comes after the signed contract.

Details and Assumptions

- This project includes concept development, design and layout, production, and programming for the <client/project> website.
- The structure and hierarchy of the site will be based on client-provided information, with feedback and direction from <web development firm> when creating site architecture.
- The client will provide all text content in electronic format on disk as well as a proofed hard copy. Video and audio material will be provided in digital format, ready for online use. Production and schedule are based on receiving all content by a targeted date specified elsewhere in writing. Late delivery will directly impact budget and schedule.
- Production of the site includes creation and optimization of all files/images (except for those audio/video as noted above) and HTML coding for up to <___> pages. This site contains light scripting that only includes JavaScript rollovers. If more functionality is added, an additional charge form will be issued to accommodate the expanded scope. The site will be created to exist on a UNIX or NT server and will be compliant with Netscape 7.x+ and I.E. 6.x+ for PC and Safari for Macs.
- This project is scheduled and estimated for a 10-week turnaround, starting <date>. Because development team resources are available in a predetermined window only, the project is not scheduled past <date>. Factors that increase or decrease the production schedule (for example, late content or additional features added) may incur additional charges as applicable.
- The estimated budget is based on existing information. Once criteria and direction of the site are finalized, additional costs may apply for custom application development and other programming needs.

< **3.8**

Use this sample Details and Assumptions list as a guide. As these are only examples, you should modify them as your project requires. Be as descriptive as possible. Note that although the Details and Assumptions list can be included in a contract (and therefore be part of a legally binding agreement), on its own it does not substitute for a legal contract. It is for clarification and reference only.

The Project Plan protects both the team and the client. It spells everything out and forms a referential starting point for the project. By agreeing to the contents of the Project Plan, the client acknowledges that they understand what the team is preparing to undertake on their behalf.

The Project Plan is a deliverable. It can be submitted to the client, along with a legally binding contract and initial invoice. Once the project officially starts, any changes to this document will result in an additional charge (AC), so take care when listing needs and details. With a client signature on the Project Plan or proposal (whichever you create), you can move forward.

Details and Assumptions

At the end of the plan, near where a signature is required (and the client is sure to be paying attention), include a list of Details and Assumptions **[3.8]**. The Details and Assumptions list is concise and confirms specific items that often are inadvertently subject to independent thinking (which is a diplomatic way of saying "Items the client assumes can be randomly

Make sure the client approves and signs off on the Project Plan. Nothing creates accountability more than a signature.

changed at their whim, such as the schedule"). Its main purpose is to protect the team, primarily against situations concerning scope changes. It achieves this by clearly identifying the boundaries of the project in an easy-to-understand list format. Perhaps these three items appear in your Details and Assumptions list:

- **This site will contain 20 to 25 pages.**
- **This project is scheduled to be completed in 10 weeks.**
- **All stock photography/illustration fees are the responsibility of the client and are not included in the budget. Obtaining any/all usage rights for stock work is the responsibility of the client.**

This document covers you against unanticipated changes in scope and provides the team with a point of reference for increasing the budget. The more detail you provide, the more protected you are. (This is especially important for web development firms.) Please note — this documentation does not replace a legal contract, which is generally drawn up by the hiring firm if you are an outside vendor. For more information on legal contracts, please refer to *Web and Software Development: A Legal Guide* by Stephen Fishman.

SETTING THE BUDGET

Estimating the cost of web development projects can be especially challenging due to the myriad variables involved and the alarming propensity for "Scope Creep." It takes practice and experience to predict how long each phase and task will take. Underestimate and you end up not even covering your overhead. Yes, it is possible to invoice $50,000 and still lose money. Know this much to be true: Everything will take longer than you think, especially project management. Build cushions. Cover yourself.

The project's budget will define the actual scope of the project; the words "depending on budget" will dictate how much time and resources you can allocate to any individual task. Of all administrative tasks, this one naturally comes first because it defines the size, boundaries, and feasibility of a project. And keep in mind that a $25,000 budget handled wisely can yield a far more effective redesign than an $80,000 budget mishandled.

For the Dedicated

The Project Management Institute (PMI) is a professional organization dedicated to providing resources, education, and certification for the project management industry. The group's book, the *PMBOK Guide*, is a respected standard for project management principles and should be utilized by serious players. Professional project managers will also find the website (www.pmi.org) very helpful.

Web ReDesign is a guide for website redevelopment and design and should not be mistaken as a comprehensive project management guide (although we offer great insight to the realities of the web design world.)

Marking Up

Multiply your total by a percentage to allow for contingencies and overhead costs. A 10% to 20% markup is a standard protective measure. A 50% to 100% markup is often applied to cover overhead such as rent, phones, administrative tasks, and sometimes the ugly necessity of legal fees.

Understanding Scope Creep

Scope Creep is the slow, inevitable migration of a website redesign from a straightforward, comprehensible project to an out-of-control nightmare. Seemingly insignificant modifications and unplanned extra time spent handholding and babysitting your client lead to budgetary increases and time delays. Little things add up.

Scope Creep is subtle; you seldom realize it is happening. At your kick-off meeting, define Scope Creep to both client and team and explain how the various schedules and delivery plans all work together to keep the project on target.

Help avoid Scope Creep by having a very clear list of deliverables. Establish and state unequivocally in the Details and Assumptions list of the proposal or the Project Plan that client-initiated changes mean budget increases. It will help to refer to these written statements if the client suffers from selective memory loss.

Keep meticulous track of hours and all client-initiated changes. As soon as you see that you are going over budget, ask yourself and your team why. Does the client send seemingly casual emails, asking for little changes and minor additions? Does the client send 10 emails a day instead of streamlining into one concise communication? Worse, is the client emailing suggestions, instructions, and/or requests to the production designer or visual designer, bypassing the project manager altogether? Are you

BUDGET REALITIES		
Budget Reality #1: We Charge What We Can	**Budget Reality #2: It Comes Down to Hours**	**Budget Reality #3: Base Estimates on Facts**
Most companies charge what they can. While individual projects are dependent on the team's experience, client expectations, and current market conditions, all the following should also be considered: availability and resources, overhead and outside costs, technology and backend programming, timing and expectations, and documentation.	Estimating can be based on task or by team. Whatever your methodology and regardless of budget presentation (whether fixed cost, projected range, or based entirely on time and materials used), when all formula is stripped away, it comes down to one thing: hours. As a result, tracking time is crucial for staying within budget.	When finalizing scope and budget, you already have a general idea of what has been preliminarily agreed upon with the client. To close the deal, however, the temptation is strong to shave off hours and tasks to save costs. Yet despite how much you may want to woo the client, certain tasks take a certain amount of time no matter what, and time always equals money.

receiving content, feedback, and sign-offs when these items are due and needed, or are you having to chase after them? All of this contributes to Scope Creep. A certain amount is expected, but it is the project manager's job to educate the client and clearly define what is within budget and what is out of scope. You can produce an amazingly successful redesign, but if you go way over budget and do not account for it, you're not going to feel great about losing money on the project, no matter how many accolades it garners.

Avoid Scope Creep. Make it your mantra.

Estimating: What and How to Charge

Estimating projects is a developed skill. We can offer some suggestions that will help improve your forecasts, but it will mostly depend on your ability to properly estimate scope (how big is the project really?) and client management (how much time will it take to educate and control the client?). Start with the basics; determine your timeframe and resources and then do the math. How many hours will you allocate to each task? Who will make up your team? What deliverables will be due? Forecast realistic hours necessary to complete the goals. Be baldly

Documentation

Here's a good rule of thumb: If the client signs it, save it. Email approvals are a good start, but follow up with a hard copy to protect yourself — get a signature via fax whenever possible. For every project, create a project folder (or a binder) to house all signed documentation: contracts, briefs, the initial proposal and subsequent revisions, approved sitemap, visual design directions, etc.

You don't have to three-hole punch and save every email, but you should print all emails relating to budget, scope, sign-off, and especially requests for changes and have them at your fingertips. Save everything electronically as well. Avoid messy files and lost documents; start organized and stay that way.

All the forms, briefs, and schedules are key to both keeping the project streamlined and maintaining your credibility. Most documents can be as abbreviated as an email or as formal as a written, multipage report complete with 8×10 color glossy pictures with circles and arrows and a paragraph on the back of each one.

The importance of each piece of documentation lies in clarity of communication, not necessarily in the extravagance of delivery. However, sometimes more documentation is prudent, especially if you have a capricious client or an inconsistent team.

Fixed Bid Concerns

Many clients request a fixed bid. If you do submit a fixed price, it is the responsibility of the project manager and the team to keep the project scope under control. This means being firm about client-requested "small" changes and keeping track of time to ensure that the project stays within the budgeted hours or — on a more depressing note — at least being aware that you are working in the red or at a reduced rate.

When to Invoice?

Invoicing expectations should be established prior to the start of work. A normal payment schedule is 30% upon approval of the proposal or Project Plan, 30% upon approval of the visual look and feel, and the remainder upon delivery of the final site. Be clear that any additional charges will be clearly identified and approved at any point in the development process where they apply and that those charges will be added to the final invoice.

PHASES OF DEVELOPMENT	low range 150 hr total	medium range 300 hr total	high range 800 hr total
Phase 1: Define the Project Conduct the Discovery process. Define overall goals. Write the Communication Brief. Create a budget and schedules. List deliverables. Put together a team. Develop audience profiles. Determine a user testing plan. Outline technical requirements. Build staging areas. Kick off the project.	project manager 50 hrs	project manager 100 hrs; usability test 20 hrs	project manager 200 hrs; info design 100 hrs; strat/brand/analysis 60 hrs; usability test 60 hrs
Phase 2: Develop Site Structure Develop site structure, navigation, and page flow. Begin information design and wireframing. Begin content acquisition.	info design 10 hrs; usability test 5 hrs	info design 30 hrs	
Phase 3: Design Visual Interface Develop visual design, combining conceptual direction, tone and functionality, and look and feel. Identify branding, copy flow, and incorporation of content. Create an HTML Protosite and test for usability.	design 40 hrs; art & HTML prod 40 hrs	design 60 hrs; art & HTML prod 60 hrs	design 180 hrs; art & HTML prod 100 hrs
Phase 4: Build and Integrate Graphic optimization, HTML production, and light scripting completed. Test for usability. Run QA testing and debug the site. Freeze content.	QA 5 hrs	QA 20 hrs; progr/javascr 10 hrs	progr/javascr 40 hrs; QA 60 hrs
Phase 5: Launch and Beyond Debugged site is ready for launch. Address maintenance and marketing. Have a celebration. Have a post-mortem meeting.			

< 3.9 >

A typical breakdown of hours for three sizes of projects. This is only an example; each project will differ based on size, scope, expectations, and deliverables. Please note that this chart takes neither integration nor implementation of a backend layer into consideration. Those estimations will vary greatly with scope and level of expertise.

honest: Can the project even be done before the launch date? Work backwards from launch. You may find that you need to increase resources and negotiate with the client for additional funds.

The chart provided [3.9] illustrates a typical allocation of hours for three different sizes of projects, each running on the five-phased Core Process. (Note that backend is not included.) Take notice of how much of the total resources project management takes. With this conceptual, phase view of your project understood, you can then break it into weeks on a spreadsheet [3.10] that can be used during the project to track against budget projections. To further calculate your costs, two useful methods are estimating by team or by task [3.11].

Tracking Time

If you take away only one thing from this book, let it be this: TRACK YOUR HOURS. (We hope you get more out of the book than that, though.) In general, organizations that track their hours, and therefore always know where their budget stands and how it is being utilized, are profitable. Those that don't track their hours either aren't profitable or are lucky. It's as simple as that.

3.10 >

This budgeting time tracker is a straightforward spreadsheet that takes each role and sets up an hourly charge, estimated hours, and a weekly tally. This example shows a typical eight-week breakdown with a small team in place. (A blank form is available for download at www.web-redesign.com.)

team member/role	rate	wk 1	wk 2	wk 3	wk 4	wk 5	wk 6	wk 7	wk 8	wk 9	wk 10	wk 11	wk 12	total hrs	total $
project management	$50.00	40	40	40	40	40	40	40	40					320	$16,000.00
art direction	$50.00	12	12	40	40	40	20	20	20					204	$10,200.00
information design	$50.00	12	40	40	20									112	$5,600.00
														0	$0.00
art production	$35.00	2		20	20	40	40	40	40					202	$7,070.00
														0	$0.00
														0	$0.00
														0	$0.00
														0	$0.00
														0	$0.00
														0	$0.00
														0	$0.00
														0	$0.00
														0	$0.00
														0	$0.00
[hours]		66	92	140	120	120	100	100	100	0	0	0	0	[total]	$38,870.00

< 3.11 >

Often, with an experienced and set team in place, it is most effective to estimate by team member (for example, "Kate usually needs about 40 hours for information design on a site of this size and complexity"). This method might apply better to a web development firm.

Sometimes it is easier to break a project down by task rather than by the time needed for each role ("This project will probably take between 30 and 40 hours for information design"). Whether estimating by team or by task, use whichever method helps the client understand the total cost.understand the total cost.

Blank estimating forms are available for download at www.web-redesign.com >>>

ESTIMATING METHODS

Estimate by Team

Who is on your team, and how much time will they be spending on the project? Take each role (remember, some team members wear multiple hats), determine an hourly rate, and multiply by the hours or days that each role requires.

Add a safe markup to allow for contingencies and overhead. The percentage of this markup depends on overhead costs, risk of project, studio policy, and/or what the market will bear. Fifty percent is common. In the end, provide your client a range of pricing based on your totals.

Team Member	$ Rate	Est. Hours	Days	Subtotal	X % overhead	TOTAL
Project Manager	$50	200	25 days	**$10,000**		
Art Director	$50	20	2.5 days	**$1,000**		
Designer	$40	40	5 days	**$1,600**		
Usability Specialist	$50	30	5 days	**$1,500**		
Production Designer	$40	40	5 days	**$1,600**		
Programmer	$60	10	1.25 days	**$ 600**		
Copywriter	$35	40	5 days	**$1,400**		
QA Lead	$25	12	1.5 days	**$ 300**		
				$18,000	50%	**$27,000.00**

Estimate by Task

Break the project into appropriate tasks and give time estimates to each task in terms of days and weeks. Apply rates depending on the type of task: creative, production, programming, admin/management.

Add a 50% markup to allow for contingencies and overhead. In the end, provide your client a range of pricing based on your totals.

Task	Est. Hours	$ Per Hr	Days	Subtotal	X % overhead	TOTAL
Project definition	40	$50	5 days	**$2,000**		
Information design	40	$50	5 days	**$2,000**		
Visual design	60	$50	7.5 days	**$3,000**		
Flash animation	20	$50	2.5 days	**$1,000**		
Production	80	$40	10 days	**$3,200**		
Programming	10	$60	1.25 days	**$ 600**		
Usability testing	30	$50	5 days	**$1,500**		
Competitive analysis	20	$50	2.5 days	**$ 1,000**		
Copywriting	60	$50	7.5 days	**$ 3,000**		
QA/testing	15	$40	1.5 days	**$ 600**		
				$17,900	50%	**$26,850.00**

Rates shown here are generic and are representative neither of varying levels of expertise nor of all markets.

Establish the method by which you and your team are going to track time... and then actually, truly, diligently track it, even in small increments (not accounting for answering email is notorious for driving Scope Creep). It is the only way to know whether you are making $10/hr or $100/hr. Time tracking is critical for both design firms and in-house departments, though it is more important for many design firms because they bill hourly.

Make sure your team submits accurate hours on a regular basis, at least weekly (this keeps them accountable) and keep a running check of total team hours used against your budget and allocation of hours **[3.12]**, **[3.13]**. Staying on top of project time spent is crucial to maintaining budget and scope requirements. Any time used that was not budgeted for either is eaten by the web development company or, if authorized, scoped, and tracked properly, is billed to the client as an additional charge. The time to tell your client that you are going over budget — especially if it is due to Scope Creep — is as early as possible.

Use whatever tracking system works. And be diligent. Your project depends on it.

3/24/00	Time Budgeted	Time Used	Time left	Comments
Design	248	207.5	**43.5**	
Production	325	18.5	**306.5**	
Admin	128	36.5	**91.5**	

3.12 > *Each week, generate a short report for hours budgeted, hours used, and hours left. Track hours weekly to maintain scope and time estimates. Be accountable. This report means nothing if people are not forthcoming with how over, on, or under budget they really are.*

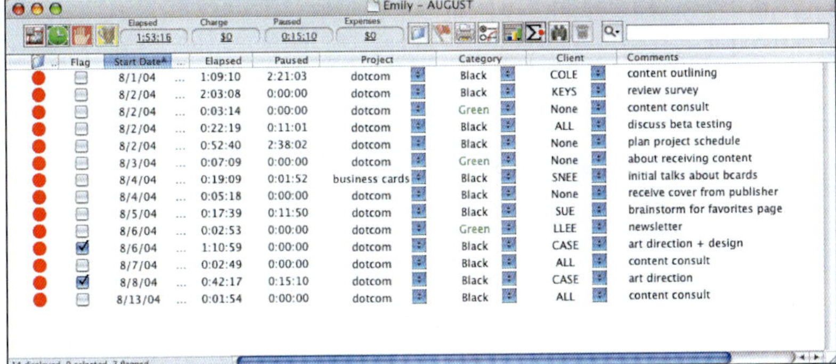

3.13 > *Timeslice (www.timeslice.us) allows for time tracking at a click and makes sorting easy. Available for both PC and Mac, is cross-platform, reasonably priced and does not require a subscription.*

Additional Charge (AC) Form
(Change Order or Track Changes Document)

Project Title:
Project ID:
Date:

Client Name:
Client Email:
Client Phone:

[company] contact:

This item is a:
1. Client-requested change
2. Additional item request
3. Outside original budget/scope
4. Other ____________________

Description of change or addition:

Description of Services	Estimated Hours	Cost
		$
		$
		$
	Total	$

I am in agreement with the additional charge, description, timeline, and details outlined above. Please sign the document below and fax back to [xxx-xxx-xxxx].

Client Signature ____________________ Date ____________

Client Name (printed) ____________________

< **3.14**

Use this sample Additional Charge (AC) Form as a basis for your own.

Client-Initiated Changes

Scope Creep is subtle. Blatant requests for project changes are not. If the client asks for an additional feature or section that is not within the original definition of the project, smile and respond confidently, "No problem, I'll get back to you with a separate schedule and budget by the end of the day." You'll be surprised at how effective this approach is at controlling Scope Creep. Clients will react by retracting the request or agreeing to the scope change.

An Additional Charge (AC) Form is a handy way to document increases in scope **[3.14]**. Even if you decide to not charge for a change, you can still issue an AC, mark the change as "gratis," and have a record of the change. ACs work as amendments to the approved budget.

Requests that are out of scope for the current phase of the project don't have to die on the table. If it can't be added in now (2.0), consider inclusion in subsequent phases (2.1, 2.2, etc.) as a planned item.

<<< The form seen here is available for download at www.web-redesign.com

CREATING SCHEDULES

Projects need a schedule, and people respond to deadlines. Whether in a check-off list, calendar view, text in an email, or a weekly breakdown, there are many different ways to communicate timeline and sequence. In addition, a project schedule should emphasize immediacy of needs. Distribution of a schedule is the proverbial lighting of a fire under everybody's seat. It is a wake-up call with an obvious message: "We are starting now. Here is what is due and when." Strive for clear communication. Fully explain how missed deadlines have a domino effect. Many clients do not understand that when they are late with feedback, it retards the flow of the schedule and therefore the final delivery date. Some client education may be necessary and, if done in a goal-oriented manner, will probably be appreciated.

We recommend approaching the scheduling task in two ways. First, create an overview schedule that shows methodology chronologically. Then build a detailed date-by-date format that itemizes deliverables and approval reviews according to due dates. One follows and evolves out of the other; each communicates the message from a different perspective. Get both schedules approved by the client. Leave nothing up to interpretation.

No one should ever have to dig for a deadline. This information should always be available, front and center, and perhaps even emailed or posted to the online staging area as a weekly reminder. Schedules should communicate a sense of urgency and should keep both your team and your client on track.

Project Management Applications

For serious project management, Microsoft Project is an industry standard. When tracking multiple timelines and deliverables, MS Project can be a blessing. The application's greatest strength is its ability to recalculate an entire schedule based upon a single change. If client feedback is two days late, the program will automatically construct a new schedule for all remaining tasks. But be warned: except for the individual who created the plan, most people can't decipher it. A Gant chart is a Gant chart no matter how prettily displayed, and however much the reaction might be, "Wow, what a great Gant chart!" most people won't make the connection with the schedule. When creating a detailed schedule in MS Project, be prepared to create a modified version in Word or Excel for distribution. And remember: designers and engineers like to know the deadlines, not just the duration.

Show Methodology

When you build the overview schedule, include methodology steps (i.e., these five phases) alongside due dates. Doing so provides an excellent visual overview of the process as a whole as it relates to the project's timeline.

Use Different Styles

The visual methods shown in this section are merely suggestions. People respond to different types of stimuli, and therefore different formats may benefit your projects. Some prefer a listing of key dates, and some prefer an overview schedule showing each day in calendar style. Use whatever style is necessary to communicate to your client and to your team.

Date	Deliverables/Notes	Deliverables
Weeks 1 to 2 07/30 to 08/10	**Define:** Overall budget and schedule approved. Technical needs addressed and clarified. Scope of project and deliverables defined. Project plan created and approved. User testing and maintenance needs addressed and clarified. Creative brief composed (based on client survey) outlining vision and perception. Conduct competitive analysis; begin initial audience profiling. Client signs off on all materials.	CLIENT SURVEY(S): DISTRIBUTE TO CLIENT PROJECT PLAN **30% payment due to begin work* CREATIVE BRIEF COMPETITIVE ANALYSIS
Weeks 3 to 4 08/13 to 08/24	**Structure:** Site structure defined; navigation and page flow developed. Sitemap completed and approved by client. User profiles created and user tasks defined. Create content-delivery plan. Content acquisition and editing/writing started. Wireframing of primary and secondary pages begins. Establish navigation, page flow, content organization, and layout and user paths. Conduct paper prototype testing.	SITEMAP USER PROFILES CONTENT DELIVERY PLAN WIREFRAMES USER PATHS
Weeks 5 to 6 08/27 to 09/07	**Design | Protosite:** Present first round of page design/layout. Design of "look and feel" approved; begin art production. User interface (UI) design begins. Necessary materials are digitized for online use. HTML protosite (nondesign oriented) developed following approved page flow and UI design. Content is collected, modified, and finalized. Production of design template begins.	ROUND 1 CREATIVE: PRESENTED ONLINE FOR REVIEW PROTOSITE: INFORMAL USABILITY TESTING **30% payment upon approval of creative*
Weeks 7 to 9 09/10 to 09/28	**Production:** Production begins using protosite as outline and structure. HTML production and programming begins, incorporating content and design. Continue production, testing, and build out of site. Confirm all specified browser and platform compatibility. Begin internal QA. Beta version of site is "live" for client sign-off and internal testing and QA begins. Site moved to end server for testing/QA/cross-platform testing.	BETA SITE: PRESENTED ONLINE: MTG 09/24
Week 10 10/01 to 10/05	**Launch:** Public launch. Announcement. Postlaunch: hand off assets and templates, set up maintenance training, and conduct postmortem meeting.	FINAL SITE: PRESENTED ONLINE: MTG 10/02 **Final balance due*

< 3.15

A sample 10-week overview schedule shows methodology and a summary of tasks and deliverables. (This example is in a simple table format created in Microsoft Word. Use whatever format best communicates to your client and your team.)

Overview Schedule

The overview schedule is just that, an overview. Easily referenced and descriptive, it's an excellent forum to present a big picture view — the whole project, complete with methodology and breakdown of major milestones and deliverables. This schedule, which can be quickly built, is appropriate both for the proposal stage and kick-off meeting and throughout the project as a point of reference.

Begin by separating the project into weeks or months as well as into phases and steps. We suggest using the core phases put forth in this book. See **[3.15]** for a generic example.

Detailed Schedule with Deliverables

Action items — deliverables being submitted or milestones that need to be met — push both team members and the client forward. A detailed schedule with deliverables becomes a concise, day-by-day list of action items. It communicates pacing to everyone involved, and pacing is critical to keeping the project on track.

The detailed schedule with deliverables grows out of the overview schedule. Keep your overview for reference (and, of course, update it if suddenly the scope balloons from 8 weeks to 13), but itemize and delineate on the detailed schedule **[3.16]**. Keep schedules current as the project moves forward and changes, and make sure schedules are easily accessible in your staging area. Communication is the key to avoiding schedule lags.

Date	Deliverables/Detailed Summary	Notes
Week 1	**Define | Discovery**	
Mon 07/30	CLIENT SURVEY(S): ANSWERS DUE BACK FROM CLIENT	**Client Survey submitted to client 07/14*
Thurs 08/02	PROJECT PLAN: OVERVIEW BUDGET/SCHEDULE/ DELIVERABLES DEFINED AND SUBMITTED TO CLIENT FOR REVIEW	**30% payment due to begin work*
Fri 08/03	**Creative brief: Submit to client for approval.** USER TESTING PLAN: SUBMIT TO CLIENT FOR APPROVAL. FEEDBACK DUE EOD; SIGNOFF DUE ASAP. COMPETITIVE ANALYSIS: FINALIZE COMPETITIVE SET, DETERMINE APPROACH, USABILITY PLAN, AND TEAM	**Begin informal usability testing on site; begin informal competitive analysis*
Week 2	**Define | Discovery** (continued)	
Tues 08/07	KICK-OFF MEETING: ALL TEAM MEMBERS PRESENT, REVIEW PROJECT PLAN, CREATIVE BRIEF, USER TESTING PLAN, AND OVERALL SCHEDULE	**Weekly status meeting: need client to review all materials*
Fri 08/10	COMPETITIVE ANALYSIS: INFORMAL REPORT DUE INTERNALLY (REPORT USED TO INFORM DESIGN TEAM, NOT A FORMAL DELIVERABLE)	
Week 3	**Structure | Content**	
Tues 08/14	SITEMAP: SITE STRUCTURE AND ORGANIZATION PRESENTED CONTENT DELIVERY PLAN: ALL CONTENT/ASSETS LISTED	**Weekly status meeting (present sitemap and content)*
Thurs 08/16	SITEMAP: CLIENT APPROVAL/MODIFICATIONS DUE EOD	
Fri 08/17	USER PROFILES: TARGET AUDIENCE DEFINED	
Week 4	**Structure | Content** (continued)	
Tues 08/21	WIREFRAMES (ROUND 1)	**Weekly status meeting (present wireframes)*
Thurs 08/23	USER PATHS	
Fri 08/24	WIREFRAMES (ROUND 2)	
Week 5	**Design | Protosite**	
Tues 08/28	ROUND 1 CREATIVE: PRESENTED ONLINE FOR REVIEW	**Weekly status meeting (present creative)*
Wed 08/29	ROUND 1 CREATIVE: CLIENT FEEDBACK DUE EOD	
Thurs 08/30		
Fri 08/31	ROUND 2 CREATIVE: PRESENTED EOD (CLIENT TO REVIEW ON MONDAY, CAN WORK OVER WEEKEND IF NECESSARY)	**Weekend work if necessary*
Week 6	**Design | Protosite** (continued)	
Tues 09/04		**Weekly status meeting*
Thurs 09/06	DESIGN TEMPLATES: HOME PAGE TO PRODUCTION FOR BUILD-OUT AND TESTING/OPTIMIZATION	
Fri 08/07	PROTOSITE: INFORMAL USABILITY TESTING	
Week 7 09/10 to 09/14	**Production**	**30% payment upon approval of creative*
Week 8 09/17 to 09/21	Continue production, testing, and build-out of site. Confirm all specified browser and platform compatibility. Begin internal QA.	
Week 9 09/24 to 09/28	**QA** Beta version of site is "live" for client sign-off and internal testing and QA begins. Site moved to end server for testing/Quality Assurance/Cross-platform testing.	BETA SITE: PRESENTED ONLINE: MTG 09/24
Week 10 10/01 to 10/05	**Launch | Public Launch** Announcement Post-launch: Hand off assets and templates, set up maintenance training, and conduct post mortem meeting.	FINAL SITE: PRESENTED ONLINE: MTG 10/02 **Final balance due*

3.16 >

A detailed 10-week schedule with deliverables breaks the project down into weeks and days. (Set up in table format using Microsoft Word, specific deadlines and deliverables are clearly identified.)

For smaller projects, the schedule overview and the detailed schedule with deliverables can be combined, or the overview can be used alongside a detailed task list.

ASSIGNING YOUR PROJECT TEAM

You've heard the adage: You're only as good as your weakest link. With web development teams, this holds true. To minimize potential breakdowns in your well-crafted and streamlined plan, look for people with proven track records, even if it takes additional funds to hire more experienced people. If you have newbies involved, balance them with expertise. Then, by clearly establishing individual roles and responsibilities — for both client and team — you can safeguard against tasks falling through the cracks.

On the client side, establish one contact who has final sign-off on behalf of all client decision-makers. Avoid redesigning for an unorganized committee and encourage a single point of feedback. With regard to the project team, remember that a single person can fill more than one role — thus the term "wearing multiple hats" — and hire or delegate as necessary to avoid overloading a single resource with more than he can handle.

This chart shows a description of the roles of a project, not necessarily all the people who must be involved.

PROJECT ROLES		
Project Manager	**Programmer/Backend Engineer**	**Art Director/Visual Designer**
Also called site producer or account manager, the project manager organizes a web project from start to finish and is the primary contact for the client as well as the central point of communication for the team. Project managers are responsible for determining and defining the site's actual needs and for educating the client as to how much technology and development time is required to meet the stated goals within the specified budget and/or timeframe. The project manager keeps the project on track, troubleshoots, and communicates with all team members and the client in every phase of the Core Process. Project management is the glue that holds it all together.	Depending on the technical needs of the project, varying levels of technical expertise are necessary to make a site work. From basic JavaScript to more complex programming — Perl, PHP, Java, etc. — a careful analysis of the project from the onset is important in determining your backend needs. The backend engineer runs a parallel workflow behind the front-end site development. This individual can also act as point person or liaison between backend and front-end, especially critical during production. Please remember that backend workflow runs on a separate, parallel workflow. See Chapter 9 for more information.	The art director/visual designer creates stunning, effective graphics while working within the limitations of the capabilities of the target audience. A fluency in industry-standard programs (Fireworks, Flash, Dreamweaver, Photoshop, GoLive) should be a given. As with any other team position, the art director/visual designer should know how to follow a schedule, must check in regularly with the project manager, and should be adept in the art of client communication. If there are several visual designers, the art director is responsible for leading the others in shaping the creative vision. (For more information on visual design, see Phase 3: Design.)

PROJECT ROLES

Production Lead/Production Designer

The production lead heads a team of HTML production designers to facilitate HTML production and testing, while keeping an eye on scope and schedule at all times. It is ideal for the production designer to have a background in visual design and have working knowledge of CSS (Cascading Style Sheets) web standards.

On smaller projects, the production lead often is also the HTML production designer. The individual fulfilling this role should be fluent in HTML and art optimization standards, including use of CSS, tables, frames, and cross-platform and browser issues. The production designer can also be expected to have a fluid understanding of PHP, Perl, ASP, JSP and Java., etc. Responsibilities include building the HTML Protosite and implementing final HTML layouts, as well as combining design specifics and art integration into the site. (For more information on production, see Phase 4: Build.)

Copywriter/Content Manager

One of the most important (and often overlooked) roles in effective web development is that of copywriter. The copywriter should have experience with web-specific needs, including style and tone.

In some situations, the copywriter is also the content manager — in charge of tracking all assets (i.e., photos, media, copy) and ensuring that they are delivered to production in accord with the content delivery plan. For content-heavy sites, it is not uncommon for there to be several copywriters and a full-time content manager. Regardless, those involved in creating the content should work closely with the information designer.

We suggest that the copywriter(s) and the content manager be hired by, and work directly for, the client, with their output being defined as a deliverable. (For more information on content, see Phase 2: Structure.)

Information Designer

With an eye for design, structure, and usability, the information designer translates content and business goals into functional schematics. This person develops the site map and structures the way content navigation is laid out on a page — all of this in a non-design-oriented manner. The information designer defines site navigation, functionality, and user interaction. And when working with web-based applications, this person will be responsible for developing Use Cases (user task flows in scenario format). See Chapter 9 for more on Use Cases.

Information design is sometimes a shared role with either visual design or production. (For more information on information design, see Phase 2: Structure.)

QA Lead

Sometimes known as the Exterminator, the quality assurance (QA) lead checks for bugs starting right after production or engineering starts, and, in some cases, testing after launch. Responsibilities include building a Test Plan and checking browser compliance, HTML, and content placement. The QA lead also works hand-in-hand with engineers while testing individual applications or functional components. The QA lead also develops and tests use case and test plans. (For more information on QA testing, see Phase 4: Build.)

Usability Lead

The usability lead gathers firsthand information about how site visitors actually use a site and analyzes what works and what doesn't. The usability lead works with the information designer on navigation and user paths and then tests the redesigned site for usability issues at the HTML Protosite phase, alongside QA, and at launch. This person generally has a background in cognitive psychology or human factors engineering. (For more information on usability testing, see Chapter 8.)

Additional Expertise

Other experts are often brought in for specific projects. As an example, a search engine expert can be hired as a consultant during Phase 2: Structure, and Phase 4: Build, in order to impart the most up-to-date knowledge of search engine tips and tricks for higher rankings and search optimization. When accessibility is critical (for government and educational sites) it may be necessary to bring in someone with a working knowledge of W3C (World Wide Web Consortium) standards.

< **3.17**

The Catchword staging area shows one way to set up a client staging site. Four primary sections divide the posted deliverables into contacts, design, production, and documentation.

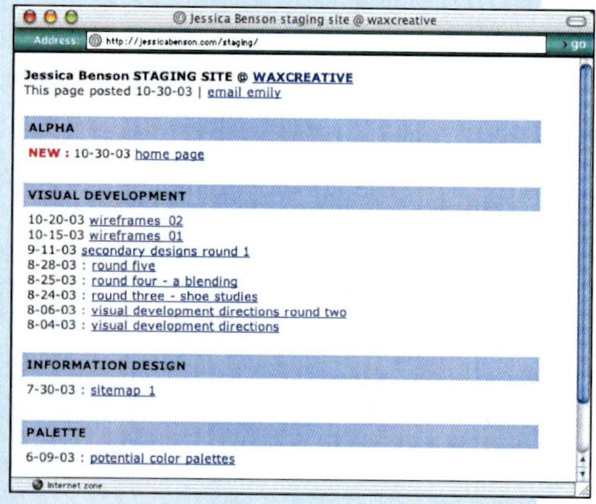

< **3.18**

The jessicabenson.com staging site is even simpler. It is a much smaller project with a much smaller team, so a single page of links suffices.

SETTING UP STAGING AREAS

The staging area acts as a hub of communication. Divide it into two sections: a client staging site and a team development area. For the client, or internal decision-makers, set up a central HTML staging area to post all deliverables and project documentation **[3.17]** and **[3.18]**. Although email is very effective for transmission of information, for work in progress, and as a point of administrative reference (email links, schedules, etc.), create and use these staging areas.

Reserve a spot on your own server for the team development area. Password protect it. The team development area serves as a place to stage and view work-in-progress. It is not for client viewing. It becomes very handy for projects with team members working remotely and needing FTP access and is ideal for developing an HTML alpha site.

For the client, or internal decision-makers, set up a central HTML staging area to post all deliverables and project documentation. Whether you call it a "client site" or a "project site," this staging area should be kept simple, easy to maintain, and current. Consistency and organization will reflect your professionalism.

Once you set up the staging area, make sure the client bookmarks it and is reminded via email when the site is updated. With each reminder include the URL, username, and password so neither the client nor the team has to look it up each time.

PLANNING FOR USER TESTING

A usable site promotes a positive user experience, which in turn creates loyalty and trust. This translates into brand equity for the company. With so much at stake, it is not surprising that one of the leading reasons for redesigning a site is the need to make it more usable. Sites must cater to the end user. If your customers can't use your site, they won't come back. Bottom line: If your site isn't usable, your redesign will fail.

In this book, we mention usability testing frequently, always touting it as a truly effective method by which to test your site. But there are also other valid methods of gathering feedback and information (see the chart on the following page). Throughout the development process, learning about your audience — and making sure that your navigation, information design, and visual designs are working as you intended — can only raise the chances of the site being a success.

Developing a User Testing Plan

Decide here, while still building your Project Plan, how and where within the workflow you want to test your redesign project against your audience. You may want to conduct usability testing upfront on the existing site to see what specifically is in need of fixing. Perhaps you want to use an online survey to gather audience information to aid in the Discovery process. Maybe you want to conduct focus group testing as early as Phase 2 to gather outside opinions. The following overview descriptions of different testing will help you decide on methodology. Once reviewed, decide where you want to integrate it into your workflow and then communicate that on your schedules.

What Are Online Surveys?

Email and online surveys are a valuable way to gather feedback from large groups to reach statistically significant conclusions. This type of information gathering is best for general questions with yes/no answers and should not be used to amass feedback on specifics. Online surveying is one method for finding out about your audience's online habits, tastes, and needs as well as, perhaps most importantly, what about the current site does the respondent feel needs redesigning.

Surveys can be frustrating in that the response rate is generally low. On a mass emailing to a targeted group of site visitors, you may only get a 10% to 15% return. However, if you send out 500 surveys, even 50 responses are a lot with which to work.

Gathering Information

There are many ways of gathering stats and data; however, deciphering the information can be as overwhelming as reading Tolstoy. SurveyMonkey.com (www.surveymonkey.com) and Zoomerang (www.zoomerang.com) have low-cost options for customer feedback and online surveys that allow quick insight into audience behavior. This task should not replace actual usability testing (see Chapter 8); but rather serve as an addition to the development cycle and information gathering process.

The Truth About Focus Groups

Although focus groups are great for gathering opinions, the feedback you get from a focus group does not specifically address what is working and what is not working with your site. Plus, if your focus group has a particularly strong personality in it, that single individual can overshadow and tilt the group as a whole. For these two reasons, focus group testing should not be used in place of usability testing.

What Is Focus Group Testing?

Focus group testing is used to gather opinions from and get into discussions with a representative cross-section of your audience. An advantage of focus groups is that you can test early in the process. Visual look and feel, content organization and presentation, and navigation — all these (and more) can be tested in focus group settings. Focus group testing seeks general and objective opinions. You may ask: "What do you think about this content organization?" or "What about this navigation? Is it logical?" or "What do you think about this advertising placement?" You may present several initial design directions and inquire which is preferred and why. Opinions from an independent but representative group give great insight as to whether you are on target with your assumptions. But remember, they are still only opinions.

What Is Usability Testing?

Usability is literally the "ease of use" or the understanding it takes to make something work. Website usability is the understanding of how an individual site visitor navigates, finds information, and interacts with a website. Unlike online surveys or focus groups, usability testing is a one-on-one process in a watch-and-learn approach — one person (the tester) observing another person (the end user) as he or she actually uses the site and completes tasks. Usability is goal oriented; the site visitor should have a series of specific tasks to perform when using the site but not step-by-step instructions. Leading your audience will skew your results.

Usability testing shows what site visitors actually do, not what they think they might do. This is invaluable. If testing is done during the actual development process, results can be incorporated, direction shifted, and major problems avoided. We go into far more detail on usability testing in Chapter 8.

METHODS OF GATHERING USER FEEDBACK AND INFORMATION

Online/Email Surveys	Focus Groups	Usability Testing
50 to 1,000 participants, representative of target audience. No direct interaction. Statistically significant feedback. **What they are generally thinking.**	8 to 20 participants. Valuable initial feedback and opinions. Facilitator-to-group interaction. **What they think they might do.**	4 to 8 participants. Task/action oriented. Actual results based on observation, one-on-one interaction. **What site visitors actually do.**

KICKING OFF THE PROJECT

Have a kick-off meeting. Consider it the opening ceremonies of your redesign project. Now bring everyone face to face into one stadium (a conference room will do) to announce the guidelines and goals to everybody involved. A kick-off meeting is a wonderful opportunity to open up the project to include everybody — both client and team key decision-makers — and officially start.

Be ready for this meeting; bring the Project Plan (which includes at least the following: project overview, schedule, deliverables and details and assumptions) and prepare a meeting agenda. Include these points in your kick-off meeting agenda and modify it to fit your project:

- **Introduction of the Project Plan.** Introduce the project, client, and team; show Discovery items; go over Details and Assumptions; make sure everybody understands the project scope; distribute contact lists to both sides; go over roles and responsibilities of both the client and team; establish means of communication.
- **Overall site goals.** Distribute the Communication Brief and go over it in detail.
- **Schedule and timing.** Discuss the project calendar; make clear the relational importance of feedback and content delivery to the final launch date; establish and adjust the project calendar according to individual schedule conflicts; discuss known risks and Scope Creep issues.
- **Content.** Who will provide content? How will the content schedule be worked out?
- **Next steps.** Briefly describe what happens next and who will be in contact with whom, specifically for the immediate next steps: organizing the content and structuring the site.
- **Regular meetings.** With all decision-makers in one place, pull out your calendars and establish a standing day and time that is amenable for the entire team. This scheduled meeting can be changed as necessary from week to week, but it helps to check in on a regular basis — at least weekly.

The kick-off meeting is where expectations are aligned and scope is established. Fill everybody in on the boundaries of scope. State that the next steps for the client include determining content, while the team will begin to structure the site.

PHASE 1 SUMMARY

The kick-off meeting signifies the end of the first phase of our Core Process. Your project has been organized, approved, scheduled, budgeted, staffed, and kicked-off. Defining the scope of a redesign project, as we have shown in this chapter, involves a great deal of legwork and a huge amount of planning. After reading through this, the longest chapter in this book, you may be questioning the effort. Why spend the time? Why poll the client so extensively? Why not simply take the information the client provides to the team and work with that?

Data. The more data you have at the outset, the better you will set the stage for your redesign project. The Client Survey alone contains more than 30 questions. The Expanded Tech Check worksheet, the Maintenance Survey, and all the tools presented in this chapter are designed to help you gather the information you need for your redesign project.

A project that is clearly defined establishes several points of reference, including the tone and the overall goals for the redesign. By making these known to all team members as well as to the client, you have ensured that everyone is working with the same assumptions and terminology; everyone sees the same finish line. Also high in importance, you have defined your target audience(s) and their needs. You know all about their online habits and their technical capabilities. At each step in every phase that follows — Structure, Design, Build, Launch — the entire team must work at redesigning for the end user. But if you don't understand your audience... Enough said. Only after defining the project can you begin hands-on site development.

Structuring the site, the second phase of the Core Process, begins right on the heels of the kick-off meeting. Armed with defined goals and specified direction, you will begin to design the site's information and address site content.

PHASE 1 CHECK-OFF LIST

Discovery

- ☐ Distribute/collect/analyze the Client Survey
- ☐ Distribute/collect/address the Maintenance Survey
- ☐ Collect existing marketing and research materials from the client
- ☐ Identify audience demographics
- ☐ Create audience profile(s)
- ☐ Identify the audience's technical capabilities
- ☐ Identify backend programming needs (if any exist, employ additional workflow)
- ☐ Analyze your industry (see also Chapter 10)

Clarification

- ☐ Determine overall goals
- ☐ Prepare a Communication Brief

Planning

- ☐ Set your budget
- ☐ Establish a means of time tracking
- ☐ Create schedules
- ☐ Assign your project team
- ☐ Set up a client staging site
- ☐ Set up an internal team development area
- ☐ Plan for user testing (see also Chapter 8)
- ☐ Assemble your Project Plan
- ☐ Have a kick-off meeting
- ☐ Get client signatures on all documents

BearingPoint

Company: BearingPoint (formerly KPMG Consulting)
URL: www.bearingpoint.com
Design Team: BearingPoint in-house
Director, Interactive Marketing: Todd Dorff
Art Director: Nick Iacona

Content Manager: Sandra Dowker
Content Specialists: Mike Sen, Amy Currens
Technology Lead: Brady Hivner
Developers: Jitka Byrd, Ajay Ajmera
Design Support: Arnold Interactive

In 2002, KPMG Consulting, a global consulting and systems-integration firm with a 100-year history, changed its name to BearingPoint and then implemented a complete rebranding… in 90 days.

<PREVIOUS>

KPMG CONSULTING [OLD] was a successful representation of the old company brand and services.

<DURING>

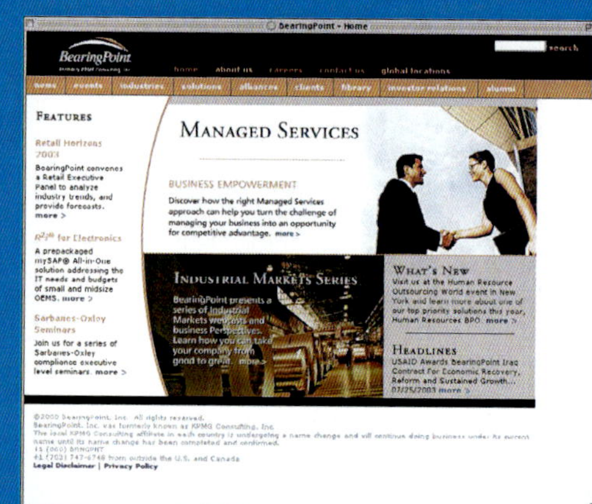

BEARINGPOINT [INTERIM] was relaunched in 90 days with a new look and feel. The extremely accelerated design cycle meant that the name, positioning strategy, logo, visual system, and messaging were all evolving throughout the project, with severe ripple effects.

<CURRENT>

BEARINGPOINT [REDESIGNED] was relaunched with unique messaging and rebranding aimed simultaneously at both internal and external audiences under a single set of guidelines and art direction (2004).

Results: In the 18 months following the launch of the new brand and new site, traffic steadily increased to show a 110% increase in visits and a 180% increase in registered visitors.

> Structure and content go hand in hand. Intuitive navigation and a positive user experience is information properly designed and presented.

Phase 2: Develop Site Structure 04

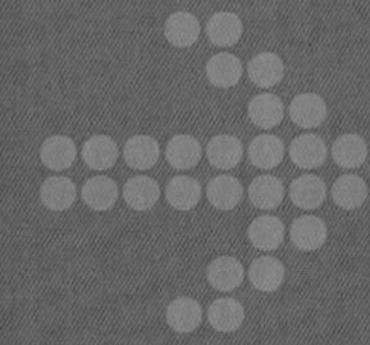

Phase 2: Develop Site Structure

Some people race in and out of a website, looking for a quick assessment of a company. Other people take the time to browse, not unlike strolling through a store. Others come in with a specific goal — to find information or to purchase an item.

Using the web is all about seeking and finding information quickly and easily. The goal? To connect your visitors to relevant content. Whatever the task, your audience needs to be clearly directed to their desired goal. Effective design is seamless, and that extends to the presentation of the information as well as the visual look and feel. Good information design provides "street signs" that keep users from getting lost or discouraged. Peter Morville, author of the famous "Polar Bear" book on information architecture (www.semanticstudios.com) succinctly sums up good information design as "creating consistent and functional systems for navigation, graphics, page layout, and title languages so that the user knows where to go, what to do, and it encourages them to return."

Structuring any site — whether from scratch or as part of a redesign — involves viewing the content of your site from three perspectives: Site-View, Page-View, and User-View. Content seems self-explanatory, but understanding how it is organized and how it flows together is sometimes elusive. Why three views? Each achieves a different goal. The Site-View

WHAT THIS CHAPTER COVERS

CONTENT-VIEW	SITE-VIEW	PAGE-VIEW	USER-VIEW
> Addressing Content	> Sitemapping	> Wireframing	> Defining Key User Paths
> Auditing Existing Content	> Addressing Existing Site Organization	> Addressing Navigation	> Developing the HTML Protosite
> Outlining Content	> Determining Site Structure	> Naming and Labeling	> Creating User Scenarios
> Creating a Content Delivery Plan	> Setting Naming Conventions		

(sitemapping) sets the overall structure and creates a "blueprint" of the site. The Page-View (wireframing) presents and organizes copy, navigation, and visuals in a way that is logical and meaningful to the end user. The User-View is the relationship of one page to the next, including actions and task flows intended for visitors to follow. User-View outlines paths and decision points from start to finish. (Please note that any complex and/or complicated functionality requiring additional technical specification is addressed in Chapter 9: Working with Complex Functionality.)

Structuring the site on paper before starting visual design is a critical step toward effective presentation of content to your intended audience. Understand that information design is often the most difficult and mismanaged — even outright neglected — component of a web design or redesign. Clients sometimes question the time allocation for information design. Some clients just want to keep their site navigation and organization "as is" and defer to the old site as the structure for the redesign. Other clients present pages of copy and consider the information design unnecessary. We strongly suggest not skimping on information design no matter how badly the client wants to jump straight to visual design. Redesigning is a process, and removing a step compromises the outcome.

Try this metaphor: Redesigning a website is like remodeling a kitchen — you must figure out what features and capabilities you need and how you will use them before you design your layout, place appliances and plugs, and select tiles, curtains, curtains and countertop colors. If you don't plan this information before building, the final product will look thrown together and patchworked. Worse, it may not function properly. Whether in a kitchen or on a website, if you have a good experience, can complete tasks, and can find what you are looking for quickly and easily, chances are you'll enjoy yourself and come back (or at least not be forced to tear out your brand-new tiling and cabinets). Advance planning from a user's vantage is key. Only by envisioning using the redesigned kitchen (or the redesigned website) can you competently design its framework.

Use this point of view: Think like your site's visitors. Be one of those visitors. What are they coming to the site to do? What are their needs, and how can the site's navigation and structure be planned to help meet those needs? Just as important, what do you want your audience to do, and how can you plan the content to entice them in that direction? In Phase 1 of the Core Process, the site audience was defined. Now, as the structuring begins, revisit that target audience. Look closely at the overall demographics and at individual user profiles. How you decide to communicate with your audience obviously depends on who they are and how they see and use the internet. Only by knowing this can you employ a user-centric approach and think like a user — a goal that's important in every phase of this book.

Information Design as a Role

In Phase 1: Define, we listed several roles involved in this Core Process, and one of the roles was information designer. Not all projects will have the luxury of a dedicated information designer. That's okay. We are referring to roles, not necessarily people. The project manager may double up as information designer, or the role may be split between the project manager and the art director. You might have a small army of information designers hammering out the structure of a huge site, with one leading and the others handling individual structural tasks. Any way it works on your project, someone is responsible for the information design. It is that person to whom we refer.

A good resource and forum for Information Design is www.boxesandarrows.com.

CONTENT-VIEW

- > Addressing Content
- > Auditing Existing Content
- > Outlining Content
- > Creating a Content Delivery Plan

In this phase, you will organize your redesigned site, merging the planned content with the information design to create a solid structure. This completed, your visual designers will have a clear blueprint with which to create a look and feel, and your production designers will understand how the site is organized and how it functions.

A note on terms: Information design, site architecture, and information architecture are often used interchangeably in the web development field. Here's our nutshell position on their subtle differences. Information design focuses primarily on organizing information from a Page-View or content layout perspective. Site architecture focuses more on the way the site is physically structured on a server (i.e., where the files are kept, on what server, etc.). The distinction becomes clearer when incorporating backend engineering. But whether you are an information designer or an information/site architect, your role is the same — to organize information and navigation in a way that is meaningful to the user. For clarity's sake, we lump all three terms under the umbrella of information design (process) and information designer (person). Our apologies if this attempt at simplification offends any information architects or site architects.

Christina Wodke has a collection of helpful definitions on her personal site Elegant Hack (www.eleganthack.com). Her expert topic follows.

ADDRESSING CONTENT

Content is critical to any site. Without good, relevant content, your fancy technology and whipsmart graphics are simply empty placeholders. But even having good content is not enough. You need to have good, *organized* content.

Content development is a major task — a humdinger in some cases — often worthy of its own workflow and its own manager. Any site with content-rich channels that requires a constant influx of information cannot function without dedicated copywriters and content managers. For sites that are less content heavy, it is possible that all the content can be both written and managed by the same person. But in between these two extremes, we recommend appointing someone to act as a liaison between the client and the development team to facilitate the development, gathering, and organization of content.

Furthermore, we strongly suggest that clients contract a dedicated copywriter or content manager and that this individual work client-side. If in-house, assign an individual to the task. (If the redesigned site is slated to be content heavy, chances are the client already has a dedicated copywriting staff.) But for many sites, the client is simply not prepared for the enormity of gathering and preparing content and may have heaped the responsibility on some hapless individual who already has a full plate. As a web development project manager, you will find professional life much more livable when there is someone on the other side who is responsible for the content.

AUDITING EXISTING CONTENT

A content audit is, by definition, an evaluation of every piece of content (text, imagery, or media) in the outgoing site that is relevant to the redesign. Looking at each piece of content in the existing site may seem daunting, but it can be as refreshing as moving into a new home, sorting through all your boxes, and keeping what you deem valuable while tossing out what no longer has relevance in your life.

To avoid reusing existing content without close evaluation, encourage your client to audit the content on the current site. The client may balk, however. A content audit can be viewed as such a huge undertaking that the client may suggest simply using the existing content so that the project can move forward. The plan may be to fold in new content as necessary and withdraw old content down the road. This is counter-constructive. Clients opting out of auditing should be educated about the risks of appropriating existing unreviewed content. Doing so compromises new organizational decisions and often results in delays and backtracking in subsequent phases. The common reasoning is: "We're in a hurry. We'll go through the content after the redesign launches." But we all know that will never happen. New priorities will always take precedence.

Ideally, your client already reviewed existing content before the project started and has communicated plans for redeveloping content and/or incorporating old material. But if the client has yet to address existing content, it doesn't mean they are a bad client, just a client with something immediate to do. It may be up to you, the project manager, to urge the client into action. Here are a few things you can say to the client to help explain why this step is so important:

- **The existing content may be part of the problem. A content audit not only removes unnecessary content, it helps minimize less important content and maximize the content and messaging that fulfills branding and business goals. Think of this as a content tune-up. Your site will run better.**
- **As the content is audited, it will begin to naturally organize itself. When finished, there will be groupings on a spreadsheet or several piles of printouts, each representing like areas of content. This is a great preliminary step toward chunking.**
- **A content audit is a perfect opportunity to organize the content for physical delivery. If a piece of content is being kept for the redesigned site and needs no reworking, drop the web-ready digital file into a folder slated for delivery. (Auditing content while gathering content for delivery? Killing a few tasks in a single swipe never got anybody fired.)**

Ultimately, the content audit is the client's responsibility. You may have to help with this, but only the client can truly analyze their own current content and determine what needs to be rewritten or created from scratch. If you are an in-house department, however, this is probably your job. Remember to budget both time and money for it.

Preparing for Growth

Without driving yourself into an anxious frenzy, consider and speculate where and how the redesigned site might grow in relation to the structure that is coming together. What areas of content might be added, and will those areas comfortably fit within one of the main chunks you have organized? With technology and business changing monthly/weekly/daily, you will never be able to plan exactly what you will be doing in two or three years' time. No one expects you to divine the future, but as you categorize and group your content and begin to hone in on what will be your navigation, leave room for logical changes. If you can anticipate areas of added content down the road, decide now where they will go.

CHRISTINA WODTKE ON IA TOOLKITS

The web, once a homogenous home for brochureware and hobby pages, now houses as many different kinds of sites as there are human interests. Although there are still simple sites made up of a handful of pages, more and more sites are becoming dauntingly complex. For example, there are applications like Oddpost.com that mimic mail program functionality online, monster megapage sites like Smithsonian.org, and hybrids of the two like Amazon.com, which mixes the complexity of thousands of pages with intricate interactions such as wish-list management.

Imagine trying to design these using a single methodology, perhaps the classic of "audit and organize." It sounds like it might work for any site: Collect all the current content, card-sort the items into similar piles, and then create your sitemap from that. But what about Oddpost, where content is user created and thus unknown? Or Amazon.com — a content audit won't tell you how to help a user track a misplaced order. To solve a range of difficult problems, today's information architects need to arm themselves with a toolkit of techniques.

You begin building your IA toolkit with a set of basic techniques, just as you build your first household toolbox of simple tools: a hammer, screwdriver, and wrench. The jigsaw comes later (if at all). Your starter IA toolkit needs to hold techniques from the areas of content organization, interaction design, interface design, and user research.

For content architecture, your basic kit should include how to do a content inventory; how to create and/or harvest metadata; how to collect content that has yet to be created (a nifty trick but doable); how to create enumerative, hierarchal, and faceted classification systems; and when to use each type.

For interaction design, you should put task analysis, competitive analysis, and persona/scenario creation in your toolbox. Task analysis is the fine art of taking apart a task (checkout) and breaking it down into its subprocesses (enter billing address, enter shipping address). Personas and scenarios make sure your task analysis is humane.

For interface design, you'll need to find a partner in graphic design or make sure you have a grounding in graphic design basics, especially layout, typography, and color theory.

And for user research, you'll again want a professional partner, but you should know a bit about ethnography, participatory design, questionnaires, and usability testing. You don't need to know how to do it so much as how these techniques affect the decisions you are making and how they reduce the risk of building a poor user experience.

The experienced information architect has a good grounding in all these techniques so that she can then create an architecture design strategy from them.

For example, if the IA were asked to design architecture for a photo site, she might begin with competitive analysis of other photo sites and visit people's homes to understand their digital photo use (ethnography). She might then create scenarios describing the most important tasks — uploading photos, creating photo albums, sharing photos perhaps. Perhaps she might even discover that most folks organize photos in the same way and might make a preset taxonomy such as "family," "pets," and "vacation."

A different site — perhaps a movie review site — would require a different set of tools. She might inventory the content and then design a faceted classification system that would allow users to find reviews based on the movie's title, stars, director, or rating. The movie review site might have almost no interaction beyond rating and not need ethnography or scenarios.

Each site has its own user base, its own set of functionality, and its own content. Taken individually, each aspect of the problem has a best approach for a solution. Taken in aggregate, you have a unique site with unique design needs, and redesigning it requires a unique architecture strategy. An IA toolkit gives you the flexibility needed to approach — and solve — a variety of problems.

Christina Wodtke has been an information architect since the dawn of the dotcom era. She founded Boxes and Arrows, *an online magazine of IA; authored the book* Information Architecture: Blueprints for the Web; *co-founded the Asilomar Institute of Information Architecture; and has spoken on the topic of IA at conferences from Seybold to Web World. Formally a partner at the renowned user experience agency Carbon IQ, she has worked with clients such as Shockwave.com, Coca-Cola, and Houghton Mifflin, as well as non-profits. To learn more, visit her personal site at* www.eleganthack.com.

Section: 0.0 Home Page			
HTML Page: index.html			
Item	**Description (text, imagery, and so on)**	**Importance (1 low, 5 high)**	**Action (x = delete, k=keep)**
Intro text	2 to 3 lines of text with a jumplink	1	x
Company overview	2 paragraphs describing company services	3	Rewrite, add to content list
Logo	Company logo	5	k
Animated marketing message	Gif animation 12K	2	Will have something similar, add to content list
Ad banners	1 main banner, 2 smaller banners	4	Will move to new site, keep main banner at top and move smaller banners to bottom (under fold)

Audit Methodology

A highly effective way to approach a content audit is to take the site section by section and determine which areas of the site will be KEPT, MODIFIED, or DISCARDED. Then you move into the page-by-page review. Here are two effective techniques: 1) Print out every page (or at least all key pages) of each main section of the current site and circle the pieces of information and graphics that will be kept, highlight what needs to be rewritten, and cross out that which is being retired, or 2) Create a grid in Excel or Word and, using it as a check-off list, hit each and every page and section with scrutiny. Depending on the size of your site, copying content that will be kept and pasting it into a document for use on the redesigned site might be helpful, regardless of which audit methodology you follow. Be sure to assign next steps to the content manager and determine a plan for the review and modification of content. Either way, call for a pizza... you're going to be at it a while.

OUTLINING CONTENT

Luckily, the content doesn't have to be completely written at this point (soon though), but it does need to get outlined before actual structuring can begin in earnest. It is entirely possible that the client has already put together information, probably in the form of a bulleted list of content. If so, fabulous. Review it, refine it, and suggest ways it can be fleshed out. If the client hasn't started outlining, however, offer a few words of guidance as to how to proceed (for example "Create a content plan," "Hire a dedicated copywriter") and then give the client a deadline. You can't move much further forward without a content outline.

If the client has no outline to deliver, if the outline is of very little use, or if you are part of an internal team, plan on building one yourself. Using a bird's-eye view of your redesign, begin your outline using the familiar and simple Roman numeral outline format from your high school years, dividing your content into logical groupings and subgroupings. Depending on the expertise and workflow preferences of the information designer and content manager, the content outlining step might be the perfect time to dig deeper into the content itself, planning the nature of the features and the naming and labeling that the user sees. It is wildly helpful at this point to identify which items are pages, what is just going

Chunking and Organizing

And now we present the incredibly technical term "chunking," as in "chunk your topics together." Apples with apples, oranges with oranges... and tangerines go with the oranges, too. It's close; it follows (unless your site is all about citrus, not fruit in general, in which case a tangerine is not an orange). As you structure your site, begin by organizing your information into broad chunks first and then more detailed chunks, eventually creating a hierarchy of chunked-together content. You'll develop more and more detail with each successive view of the site.

In determining the content, you start to get a real feel for how to organize. Look at addressing your content as one big sorting exercise, as if you dumped your entire sock drawer on the floor in front of you. At first the mound of socks feels overwhelming, but that passes quickly, and you can conceptualize broadly and logically about plans to organize. Then audit the socks by getting rid of the ones that are no longer viable, such as those with holes and those lonely without matches, as well as the socks you no longer wear.

With these basic sorting tasks complete, you are ready to sort and outline by more specific categories (or chunks): color, size, style, pattern, etc. By harking back to *Sesame Street*'s "one of these things is not like the others," you can easily separate items. Be logical, but also be wary of too many choices. A plethora of options can confound users. Divide your information into granular subgroupings whenever possible.

to consist of links, what section headings are going to be on the page, and other such details. Knowing this ahead of sitemapping and wireframing will enhance efficiency. However, some information designers like to wait until later in the structuring phase to determine the nature of the content. Regardless, make sure it has been developed and approved before visual development.

> Content management is tricky. For details on defining the role, then doing the job — see www.gotomedia.com/gotoreport/sept2004/news_0921_contentmanager1.html

CREATING A CONTENT DELIVERY PLAN

Is your content ready to go? Probably not. Late content is the number one reason for project delays. (Technical difficulties come in a close second, but sometimes even DHTML pull-down menus will work cross-browser after the third or fourth revision.) About 99% of the time, the content is late. Accept it. Plan for it. Charge for it.

When Is Copy Web Ready?

Getting a stack of brochures and a printed annual report does not a usable deliverable make. There are two ways to consider copy web ready. First is the physical delivery. Copy that comes from the client to the web development team should be delivered digitally in text format and be clearly named. (Create and use naming conventions.) "Digitally" means in a text file so that formatting is not messed up when dealing with special characters such as curly quotes and such. Sometimes copy can come in the body of an email, but some email programs destroy formatting, so this is not advised. All copy should be final. Simply saying, "All copy should be final," will not guarantee that it is. You may need to educate your client as to what final copy means. Final means "final," as in "no longer subject to change without an accompanying change in schedule and/or budget."

The second criterion for judging whether copy is web ready is tone. Web content is usually more casual and friendly than corporate brochures or ad materials. Caution your clients against simply taking brochure copy or old site copy without careful examination. Copy should be short, require as little scrolling as possible, and contain links that will lead the client to other parts of the site. However, some clients go overboard when writing web-ready content and include far too many links. Be judicious. Links should be pertinent. Otherwise, link-happy users will quickly leave the page... and they might not find their way back.

Due Dates

Establish realistic milestones for content to be delivered instead of one major deadline. By breaking the content delivery into manageable chunks, you are actually likely to receive it. Make sure you specify a drop-dead due date for all the final content to be delivered (urgency helps). Aim for this to happen before starting actual production (Phase 4: Build). State clearly, however, that sooner is better in regards to the design process — both information design and visual. Working with placeholder content can be deceptive; actual content may require last-minute designer trickery to expand or shoehorn the content into the space designed for it. Or worse, the content may be so different than anticipated that navigational structure surgery becomes necessary.

There exists no wand-waving solution to the problem of late content, but we suggest a couple things to help keep the process moving forward:

- **Hire a content manager.** Encourage the client to contract a copywriter or appoint a dedicated staff member to manage, gather, write, and submit content.
- **Create a Content Delivery Plan.** Create a comprehensive and doable delivery schedule for the client.

Tam Associates Content Delivery Plan

Ref	Name	HTML Page	Status	Assigned	Draft Due	Final	Notes/Status
	Main Pages						
0.0	Tam Associates	index.html	In progress	Tam - DC	Mon 8/2	Wed 8/4	Need final logo art
1.0	Company Profile	profile.html	In progress	Tam - DC	Wed 8/4	Fri 8/12	
2.0	Projects	projects.html	In progress	Tam - DC			
3.0	Resumes	resumes.html	Review/Approve	Tam - MH			
4.0	Jobs Available	jobs.html	Review/Approve	Tam - MH			
5.0	Contact Us	contact.html	DONE	Tam - MH			
6.0	FTP Client List	ftp.html	No copy	–	–	–	Need to set up password access
7.0	FTP Admin Area	ftp_admin.html	No copy	–	–	–	
	Company Projects						
2.1	Educational	proj_educational.html	Need new copy	Tam - DC	Fri 8/16	Fri 8/20	Need individual photos/bldg.
2.1.1	Educational Template						Need individual photos/bldg.
2.2	Hospital	proj_hospital.html	Need new copy	Tam - DC			Need photos for montage
2.2.1	Hospital Template						Need individual photos
2.3	General	proj_general.html	Need new copy	Tam - MH	Mon 8/16	Fri 8/20	
2.3.1	Correctional	proj_correctional.html	Need new copy				
2.3.2	Commercial	proj_commercial.html	Need new copy				

< **4.1**

A sample Content Delivery Plan. Using Excel or another sortable application, clearly identify each separate piece of content. Specify clear dates for all deliverables. If you are lucky enough to have a very detailed content outline (usually done in Word), you can simply color code the outline, calling out a due date, or an individual responsible, etc.

The Content Delivery Plan, a document built by the project manager or the content manager, is exactly what it sounds like: a plan for the gathering, writing, and delivery of content **[4.1]**. It provides a realistic breakdown of content into deliverable pieces rather than simply imposing a target date such as "All content is due by the 30th of this month." Because having everything due at once is usually impossible, a deadline like that is often ignored.

Clients frequently have an unrealistic view of what they "already have ready to go" and what they need to create. Clarifying when content is due in rough and final form will help, but clarification alone will not solve content-delivery issues. A Content Delivery Plan outlines each page or section in a phased delivery process — existing, revamped, and new content alike. Help the client by breaking the content into digestible chunks, delineating what is ready, what is almost ready, and what needs to be created from scratch. If the redesign is slated to launch in stages, identify what can wait. Be detailed.

The Content Delivery Plan should be created after the content outline so that the client can start gathering content as soon as possible. Invariably, some items on the content outline may shift around during the sitemapping and wireframing phases. The content outline itself should have clear page identification that can translate easily into a Content Delivery Plan. This plan should include primary content (copy for main pages, graphics, media), secondary content (error messaging, forms, and search

The Information Design Intensive

The information design phase, as with any complex task, can be forced into a streamlined process by condensing the timeframe to complete. A good solution to kick start structuring is an Information Design Intensive: a working "summit" with an expressed goal of establishing a working model of the project's information design and structure. By condensing the design and review cycle into a structured series of focused working sessions, the team can — without distractions — gather input directly from the (external or internal) client and determine the site structure, page organization, naming, labeling, and content needs. Through intensive sketching and brainstorming as a group, what might otherwise take weeks (or months!) can be accomplished collaboratively and efficiently inside of a week.

Key decision makers, including content/copy providers, technical team members, and visual and information designers should attend. The team should be small enough to facilitate effective working conditions. Higher-level decision makers do not need to be (and probably shouldn't be) present during the sessions, except for the first three-hour session where high-level goals are discussed and initial brainstorming starts. Engineers and/or technical staff should be available to work out major path flows and answer technical questions, but their input can be gathered after the sessions. Assign a moderator to keep the pace moving and the discussion focused. This person should ideally have some experience with information design processes and content development and should be organized enough to run the sessions, take notes, and document any dry-erase-board sketches with digital photos.

The suggested format requires two days — incorporating two to four three-hour working sessions — to work as a team. Ideal timing calls for a Tuesday and a Friday. Mondays are notoriously bad for hitting the ground running, and in the days between the sessions, the information designer should incorporate the concepts and sketches into wireframes or other documentation to lock down decisions and keep moving forward. These two days can be spread out over two weeks, the first session focused on an overview of the pages, sketches of how the layouts are envisioned by the client, and high-level pages.

Each session must have specific goals; preparation is mandatory. It is a good idea to have the existing site content audit already complete, and having key decision makers available during this process is also important. And stay on target! You are not trying to determine a new business model or argue the current one. You are trying to set the structure and page organization for the new, redesigned site and in order to accomplish this the team must focus!

Scope Creep Alert

Sometimes when clients realize that they cannot get their act together and provide certain content on time, they decide to simply delete those sections, thinking they will, in fact, save money. This is rarely the case, especially if those sections are part of the main navigational scheme. Clients need to understand that each change in scope and structure — both additions *and* deletions — affects the development process and, therefore, the budget. And it isn't just the bottom line that is at stake. A navigational structure can become ugly, less effective, or both if blocks of content are removed or added. Fixing would require further visual design, information design, and/or usability testing.

SITE-VIEW

> Sitemapping
> Addressing Existing Site Organization
> Determining Site Structure
> Setting Naming Conventions

keywords, if applicable), and production-specific content (META tags, ALT tags, TITLE tags, etc.). List as much detail as is necessary to make clear what is due when and who is responsible. Be accountable.

Start by dividing the content into main sections. Begin with the areas that are most "web ready" in the client's mind (that is, text or other elements that are already written and in text format) and therefore easiest for the client to achieve. Make sure the client understands that on-time delivery of content is crucial to maintain the launch schedule. Be firm.

Work with the client and content manager to create a plan that is acceptable to all. Each week, the content plan should be updated, reviewed, and redistributed by the content manager (if the client contracted one). Responsibility for copy, images, assets, and other necessary elements is assigned. With a Content Delivery Plan, you have a shot at getting nearly all of the content in when you need it, if not when you expect it. Build a cushion into your production schedule for late content. Be thrilled if it is on time.

> Content needs differ depending on scope of project. If your team is producing the HTML pages of the site, you need all content for all pages. If you are doing graphic or HTML templates and prepping for a large-scale site implementation, you just need to know the shape/size/nature of the content, and can use placeholder text until the site is ready for the actual text.

SITEMAPPING

We've been surprised to discover how infrequently sitemaps are actually part of web development workflow. At conference after conference, year after year, the audience is asked, "How many of you create sitemaps for your projects?" Out of 800 people, a whopping 20 or 30 raise their hands. "How many of you are using a sitemapping program?" About half of those hands go down. "How many of you are using a program you like?" All hands go down.

This is unfortunate because a sitemap is important. It is the backbone on which the project stands (**[4.2]**, **[4.3]**, and **[4.4]**). A sitemap shows a visual representation of the site's structure, organization, flow, and grouping of content and information. It communicates, it defines, and it structures. It is a representation of the entire project, from a broad vantage point to many of the most minute of details. It is a chance to view the site structure and organization as a whole. And while a content outline can be (should be) very detailed, it does not provide a sense of flow from a user standpoint.

Who will create the sitemap? Because not all projects have the luxury of a dedicated information designer, this task usually falls to the project manager, though sometimes even the client takes it on. It's a big job. For smaller sites, with 20 to 30 pages and static HTML pages, sitemapping is relatively easy to tackle. But for larger sites, with hundreds of pages and a lot of functionality, it becomes daunting.

Once built, the sitemap should clearly show all HTML pages within each section of the site; every page gets a box, and most major links are represented. Please note, however, that the sitemap to which we are referring is not a technical schematic, nor is it a fully functional view of the site. If it were, this task would be far more involved, and we would all get paid what engineers get paid. The sitemapping step, however, is one where the front-end and backend teams must work together. See Chapter 9 for more details.

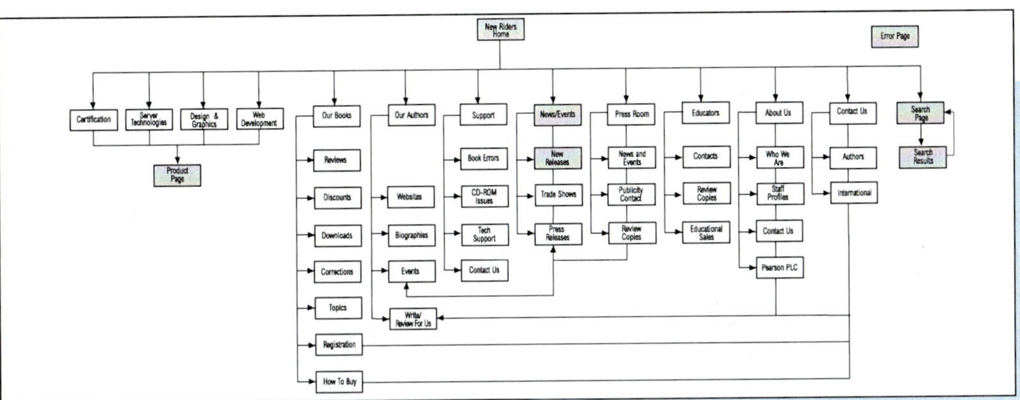

< **4.2** >

A sample sitemap using a top-down schematic.

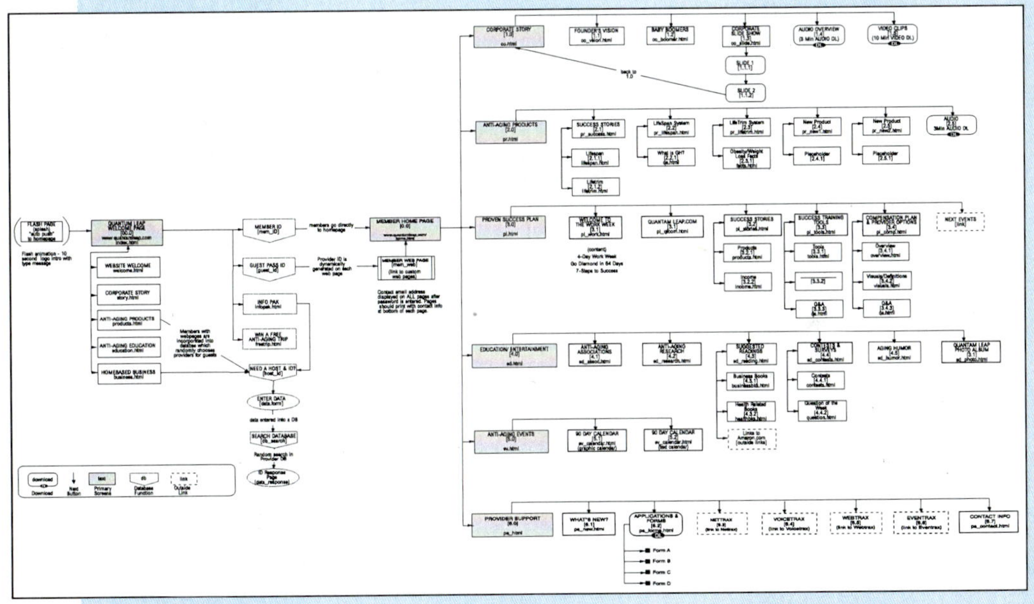

< **4.3** >

A sample sitemap using a left-to-right schematic with category divisions. There is also a key used to identify types of screens and content.

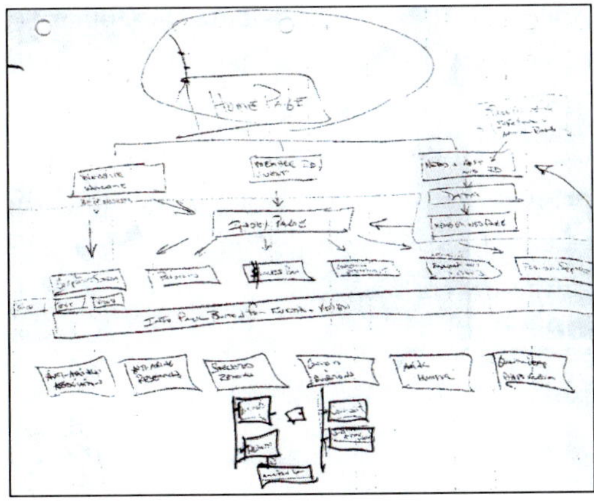

< **4.4** >

The client-provided sketch on which the sitemap shown in ***[4.3]*** *was based. This came over the fax with very little explanation or clarity.*

The sitemap is a deliverable. Get it approved and signed, and if it changes, get every update signed and approved as well. It is imperative that the sitemap be kept available and up-to-date as the site structure changes, no matter how laborious the task. (Hint: Build time into the information design budget for updates.) Keeping the sitemap as updated as possible is important to its validity as a point of reference, even after launch. At each major step during each phase of the Core Process, review the sitemap to ensure that it is still accurate. HTML production designers and content developers use the sitemap to check off their progress during production. This should be reason enough.

ADDRESSING EXISTING SITE ORGANIZATION

Hopefully, you conducted some kind of usability testing on the old site. Assessing what is working, what is not, and how the existing organization relates to the redesign goals is a good move at this point — before you start seriously organizing for the redesigned site. Don't get too caught up in it, though. The existing site organization is likely to show significant patchworking due to growth and migration of the site over time. Your current task is to use existing data to determine the best way to organize and structure your redesign, not to dive into the history of the site and understand why it is failing.

Don't rely solely on the client to provide this information, an objective analysis is imperative. Oftentimes, clients will have only a hazy notion of the overall structure of their existing site — clear on the high levels and areas they use often or deem important, less clear on those seldom updated and neither seen as problematic nor in need of attention. This is particularly true for the areas they do not use regularly, or are either static or "not my department." This content is the first to get overlooked or minimized during restructuring. Unfortunately, such oversights allow for potential surprises later on.

Use logic. You need to anticipate the audience's intuition and employ it strategically. If the current site's organization of information isn't logically working, make a note of it and figure out how to fix it. Remember that there will be no user manual on how to navigate your website... and no one would read it if there were.

DETERMINING SITE STRUCTURE

Generally, you will design and structure your site in a hierarchical style **[4.5]**. If dynamic content is a factor, add sections or "content buckets" and indicate these on the sitemap as well **[4.6]**. Put the home page at the top, the main pages next, and then the secondary pages. Very elementary.

For more high-level presentation, sometimes a visual model can be created **[4.7]** to show how the site is organized from a conceptual standpoint. Being visually appealing never hurt any project, and often client comfort zones require it.

Most often you will want to keep your content in outlined, flowchart format while the site is still undergoing critical changes in content, organization, naming, and labeling. Be aware, however, that although it effectively communicates to the team, it may cause some clients to zone out, especially if the site is huge. At times, you may want to break a sitemap up into individual sections and work with each section like its own mini-site.

Be aware that there are different layout approaches to sitemapping, and no single approach is best. You may find that flowing from the top of the document down rather than from left to right makes more sense to you.

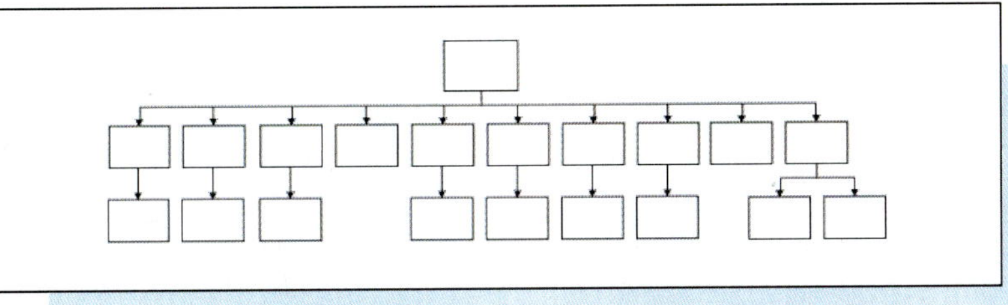

4.5 >

A simple, hierarchical sitemap style.

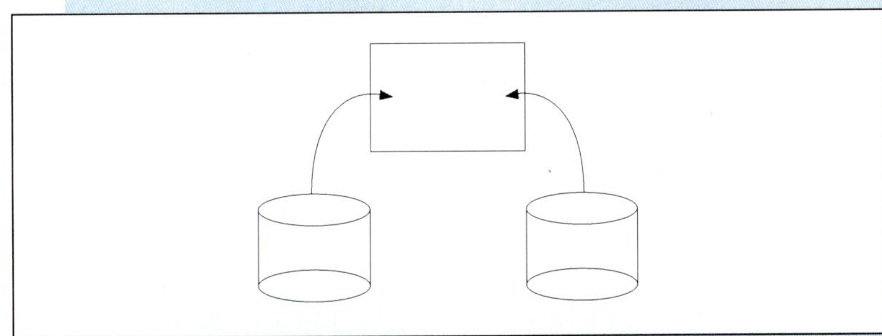

4.6 >

This sitemap style shows how database-stored content (represented by the cylinders) flows into a content bucket (represented by the rectangle) after being called up by the user. Content buckets are built into the HTML pages.

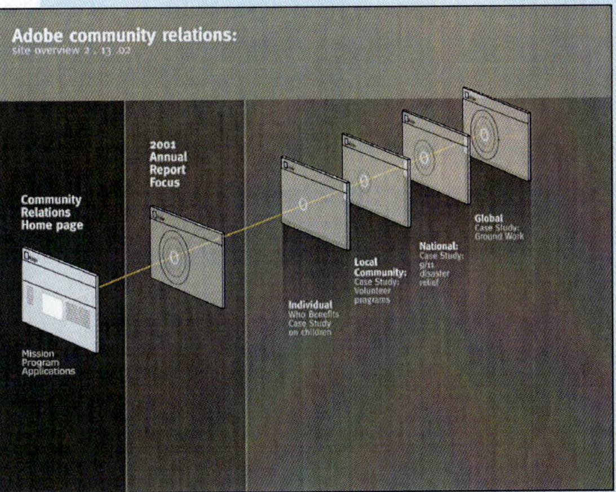

4.7 >

This conceptual sitemap shows how the microsite for Adobe's Community Relations works with the corporate site as well as the levels of content within the microsite itself. It is another approach to visualizing how the content and structure fit into the big picture.

Keep It Simple

A sitemap should show as much detail about the relationship between pages as possible. Keep it readable; include only what is necessary. For instance, jumplinks (links within body copy to other parts of the site or another site altogether) are not often shown on a sitemap. The level of detail you show depends on site complexity. Some sitemaps fit neatly on an 8.5"×11" piece of paper, and some wrap around the walls of a conference room. It is excessive to build out every page on a 2,000-page site if you can otherwise account for what needs to be represented. A good rule of thumb is this: If all pages in a section have similar content, require no unique interface or navigation, and have no functionality beyond content, then go for simplicity and represent them as a single icon representing stacked pages on a sitemap **[4.8]**. Like pages like these will require only one wireframe (later in this chapter) and one graphic template (next two chapters) for the lot of them.

< **4.8** >

Stacked sections represent similar pages.

That Pesky Backend Again

Sitemapping is one spot where both front-end and backend workflows touch. For communicating basic functionality and to identify those parts of the backend with which the visitor interacts (for example, points of login, e-commerce transactions, search, registration, etc.), simple shapes can be used to show where the visitor will interact with the complex functionality. Whatever shapes are used should be agreed on by both the information designer and the engineer. Keep in mind that this is for purposes of flow and should not be considered a Functional Specification. (For more on the Functional Spec, see Chapter 9.)

As an example, "Login Here" should be shown at the point where the visitor logs in, but that is all. You don't need to go into the details of backend verification associated with that login **[4.9]**. Depth of detail from a nontechnical but functional standpoint (i.e., login failure scenarios such as what happens if you forget your password, etc.) depends on the experience of the information designer and the interaction with the engineering team.

Bring in your engineering team to review the sitemap. Their seal of approval means you've accurately represented the path from a user perspective. Then have the information designer, project manager, production lead, and engineer sit down and create a Functional Spec to augment and complement the site map.

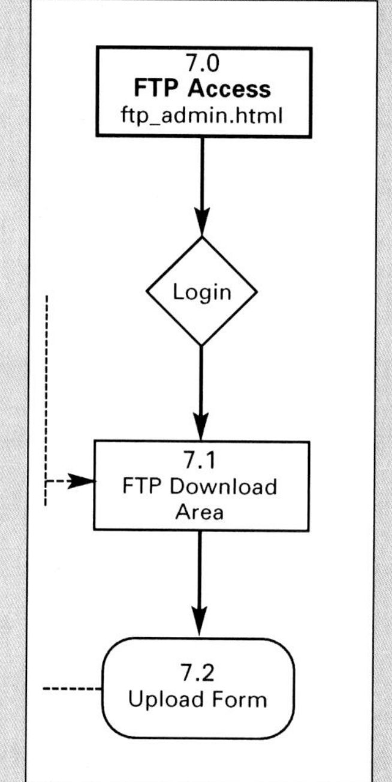

< **4.9**

A portion of a sitemap showing a page where the user would see a point of backend interaction, in this case, login.

As you build the sitemap, keep in mind that it will evolve. The schematic you come up with first most likely will not be the exact structure of the redesign that eventually gets launched, but it will hopefully be representative. To begin, we recommend building your sitemap based directly on the content outline. This will get a working schematic onto paper. With the information now visually represented, start considering organizational options. Should any of your main pages be combined? Should any secondary pages move up to the main level? Would the pages make more sense to the user if grouped differently? Keep thinking like your audience.

SETTING NAMING CONVENTIONS

Establishing a standard for naming files during the structuring phase helps organize the main sections of the site, and this in turn enables easy referencing for all team members and the client throughout the Core Process. Setting naming conventions should be straightforward. There is no need for a verdict by committee on this. There is no "correct way" to do this; each team and individual designer will have his or her own preference. The information designer should get input, confer with production to see what type of naming is preferred, and then make a decision and impose it.

From content/asset organization to HTML production, these conventions will be the key used for reference by anybody associated with the building and maintenance of your site. If you don't set conventions, naming will be determined by developers as they create each file or folder without necessarily seeing the big picture or paying attention to already established naming patterns. This, in itself, can cause additional work and problems (checking links, finding files, updating files, etc.) Plus, it won't be consistent, smooth, or logical.

Most likely, the current site is employing an existing naming convention that may or may not be consistent across the site. Confer with the client as to whether they want to hold over an existing naming convention or if they are open to creating a new system of naming.

There are two types of naming conventions that should be addressed: organizational/numeric naming and HTML naming. Sitemaps should contain them both, but if they only contain one, be sure to include a key that makes it easy to discern the other naming convention.

Why Sitemap?

Many teams balk at the notion of creating a large, potentially unwieldy sitemap and often ask, "Why bother?" The answer is this: Developing a sitemap allows the creator(s) to develop a conceptual model, providing a mental picture of the site as a whole. It is always helpful for any team to be able to wrap their heads around the structure and organization of the site.

However, it is true that some larger sites may need to stay in an outlined format for ease of modification and efficiency. Also, if your site has fewer than a dozen pages, a sitemap may be superfluous (provided your content outline is very detailed). Of course, we recommend following the steps for structuring and developing a sitemap. However, you can modify this step and employ the tools that you will actually use to keep the site diagram updated throughout the Core Process.

HTML Naming Tips

First, note that the web is no longer confined to the eight-dot-three rule. If you have no idea what the eight-dot-three rule is/was, don't worry about it. Next, determine if either .html or .htm works on your server. Pick one or the other and be consistent. Finally, be logical. Most likely, you will not be the only person working on the site. Make the conventions clear and simple. In more complex sites, especially those with dynamic content, naming is even more important. If the content is date specific, name it so. Product specific? Name it so. The key here is to use logic and create clarity. Finding a file shouldn't require bloodhounds.

Sitemap Software

Surprisingly (and annoyingly) there are very few software options — and even fewer good software options — for sitemap creation. Creating or re-creating a sitemap from the ground up is a time-consuming and incredibly detail-oriented task. For charts, graphs, and diagramming, we recommend using OmniGraffle Pro [4.10]. Two versions (standard and professional) are available for purchase at www.omnigroup.com for around $100. Bonus: It is Mac-based (only) *and* is compatible with Visio. Several positive aspects of this program are the toolkit (available in easy-to-manage palettes) and multiple page capability (to keep a stack of wireframes together), as well as helpful automatic guides (appearing in blue in the screenshot) for easy lining up and positioning of boxes and/or objects.

Additional sitemapping tools included in Dreamweaver and Visio now assist in capturing large site structures, using spiders that crawl through a site and capture pages, creating a rudimentary structural representation of your site. It's a helpful start, but nothing mentioned here doth an automatic sitemap create. Advancements notwithstanding, sitemapping is still a painstaking and largely manual process.

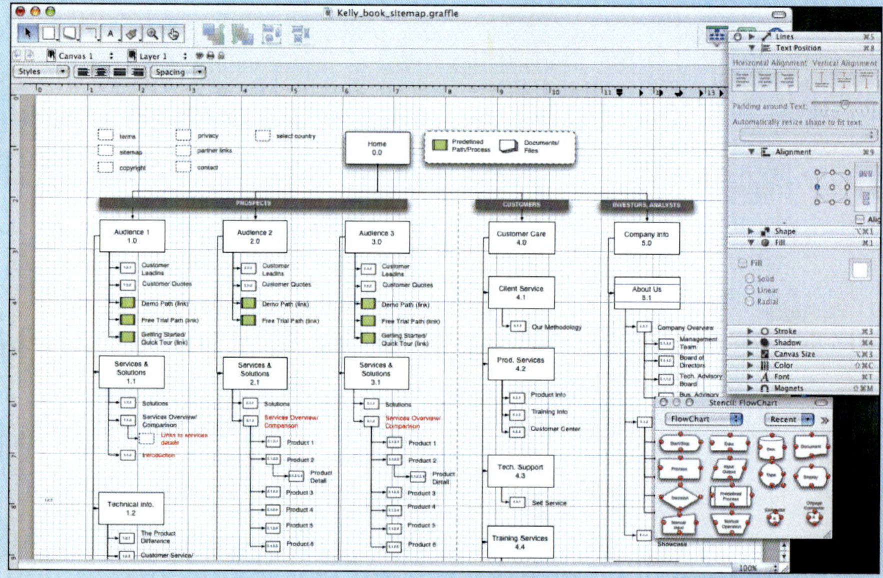

< 4.10 >

Here is an example of a sitemap in progress using OmniGraffle Pro. Using a sitemapping tool doesn't solve all of your problems, but it will make your sitemap easier to create and update.

Organizational Naming

Organizational naming is simply applying a numeric or alphanumeric standard to pages and sections of the sitemap. Begin with the home page as 0.0. The primary sections beneath the home page are labeled 1.0, 2.0, 3.0, etc. Subsections under primary pages are 1.1, 1.2, 1.3, etc. See chart below.

A numeric organizational hierarchy can be applied to content (text files and images) as a streamlined way to easily identify where a piece of content may appear. The downside of numeric naming is that you normally need to have a copy of the sitemap handy for reference, as this naming style is not inherently intuitive, and pages and numbering may change throughout the development cycle.

HTML Naming

There are as many preferences for HTML naming as there are HTML production designers. Some people abbreviate and condense, some use upper- and lowercase to help organize and define, and others ignore all standards and abbreviate some and write out others. We asked three production designers from three different teams to establish naming conventions for a fictitious site by creating a company bio page. They quickly got back to us, each with a different convention:

aboutthecompany.html
about_company.html
co_info.html

All are acceptable; just be consistent across the site. And if you are developing many sites (even more so if you are maintaining them, too), if your naming conventions are consistent, your overall workflow will be much smoother.

Avoid random file naming syndrome. Decide the standard and establish it. If HTML standards for static pages are set up in advance, the chances are better of maintaining an organized site. For redesigns, the existing site has established naming conventions and terminology that should be reviewed, addressed, and either kept or scrapped.

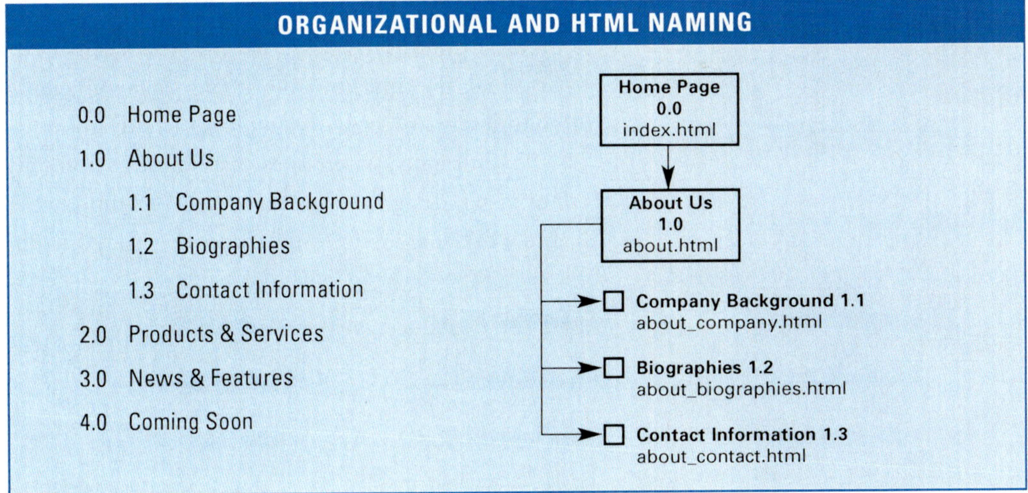

PAGE-VIEW

> Wireframing
> Addressing Navigation
> Naming and Labeling

WIREFRAMING

Simply put, wireframes are storyboards for the site. Also referred to as content layouts or page schematics, these are non–design-oriented sketches (don't worry about colors or button shapes; this is all about information) of unique pages showing rough navigation, copy layout, graphic allocation, key headers, and any other elements that need to appear on a page. Wireframes show a certain hierarchy of information but do not dictate exactly how something should be represented.

Wireframes speak. They aid in communication and are the basis for visual design and HTML production. We strongly recommend that they should be completed for all unique main, secondary, and templatized pages (containing similar content, placement, and layout) and for any pages with unique functionality. Although wireframing can seem tedious at times (especially after revision number two or three), the time you take at this stage will enable your design and production phases to run smoothly.

Traditionally, wireframes carry information only, not visual design. A wireframe can be simple ([4.11] and [4.12]), showing only the content layout and navigational organization of a few key pages within a site. Complex wireframes show copy, light functionality, links, navigation, and graphic content in a more detailed format [4.13]. They can also address production specifications and basic functionality (DHTML, JavaScript, etc.). Additionally, they should call out any kind of dynamically generated content, often challenging to represent on a wireframe due to the nature of database-driven content's dependence on the site visitor's requests. (We recommend blocking out space for a content bucket, a designated area into which said dynamically generated content flows.) For these involved situations, we recommend creating even more detailed wireframes that clearly identify anything more complex than "simple" static content.

Wireframes should include a representation of all major page elements — all content, navigation, media, functional elements, and messaging — that are slated to appear on the page. Of course, having a rough idea of content (that is, knowing text length, imagery, and placement) by this point is a big plus. It is the job of the information designer to break it down into detail.

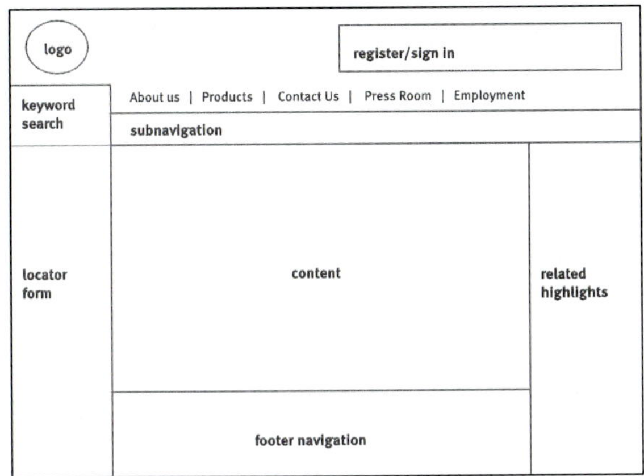

< **4.11**

This simple wireframe shows general content and navigation in a representative format. Loosely indicated areas give an idea of the type and placement of content.

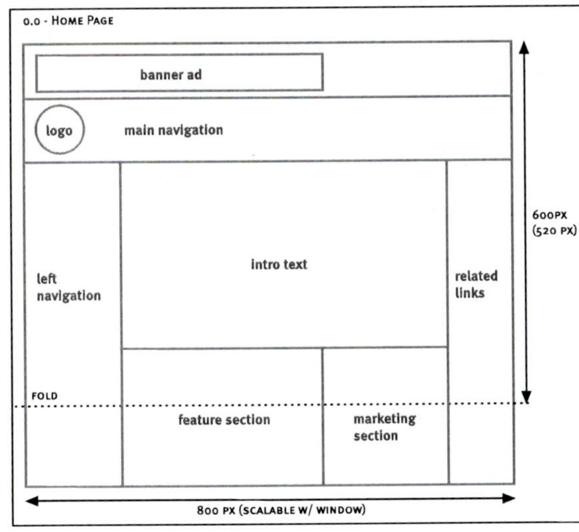

< **4.12**

This simple wireframe is actually a template containing specific callouts for targeted screen dimensions, along with indicators for logo, content, navigation, and some basic functionality above and below the fold.

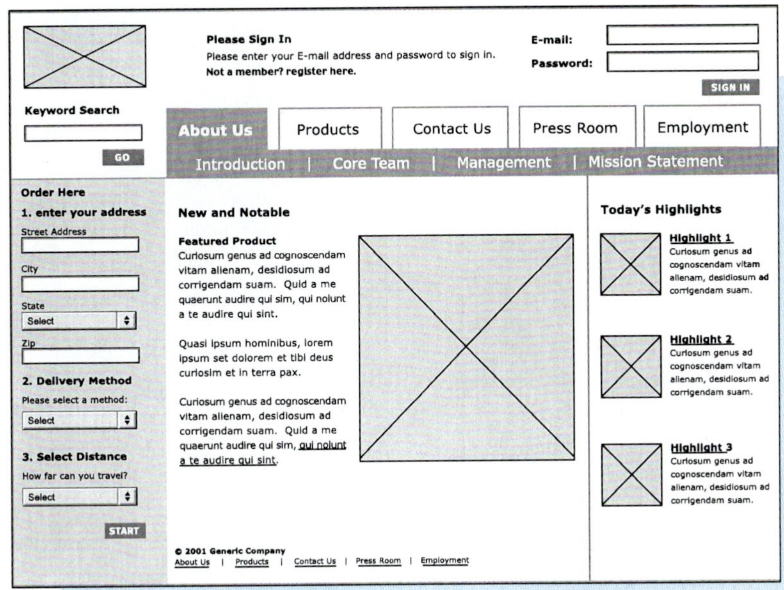

< **4.13** >

Information is presented in a very specific manner. Naming, labeling, placeholder content, and copy are included. This is generally used when content and navigation are well established.

A Refreshing Change

Sometimes, a fast-turn homepage "refresh" is a cost- and time-effective way to reach quick measurable goals. As part of a strategic redesign, WebEx.com opted for a refresh of the branding, organization and messaging on its home page to tide the company over until the entire site was redesigned. As part of this initiative, several steps were taken to analyze the current homepage, maintain the links and global navigation but reorganize the content, and add a familiar face (Lily Tomlin, who was being broadcast as part of a national advertising campaign WebEx wanted the site to tie into) **[4.14–4.18]**. In a short development cycle, the site was given a facelift to simplify the navigation, content and update the brand resulting in a temporary yet effective solution which lasted for the several months it took to complete the entire redesign. Following the launch, an immediate measurable result was a 27 percent increase in traffic toward the primary action. The rise in search engine rankings didn't hurt either.

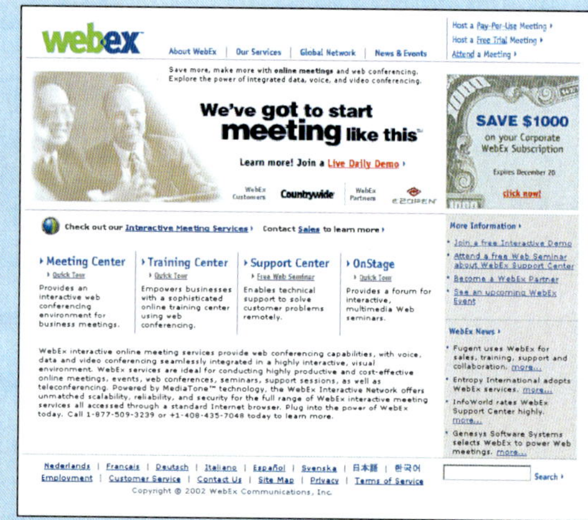

< **4.14** >

WebEx's original homepage — non-branded and cluttered. It was very difficult to understand exactly what WebEx did and how to navigate through all of the information presented.

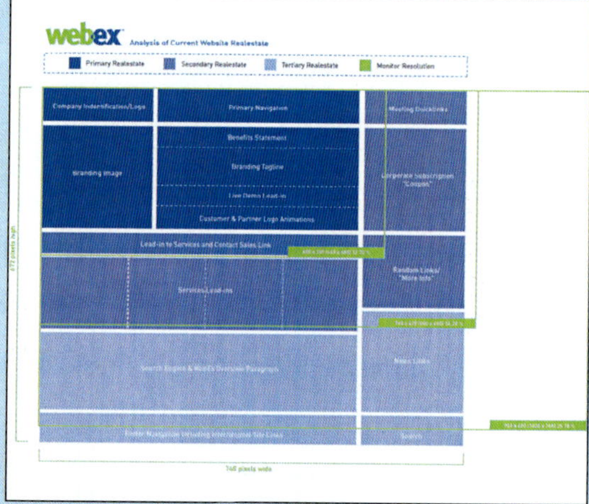

< **4.15** >

Real Estate Analysis — An overview of the existing site's layout and information was broken down into screensizes (shown in green) with the primary, secondary and tertiary levels of information are shown in tones of blue from dark (primary) to light (tertiary.) This helped to determine how the current site was organized.

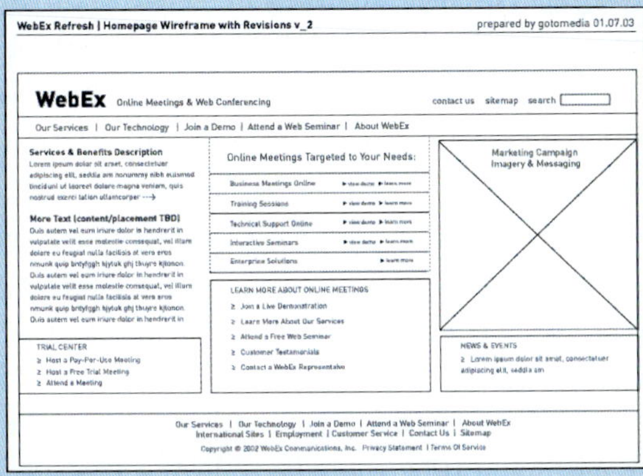

< 4.16 >

Detailed Wireframe — The content and navigation is reorganized into a comprehensive, action-oriented manner directing a new visitor into a specific path, and adding the required branding and search engine optimization information.

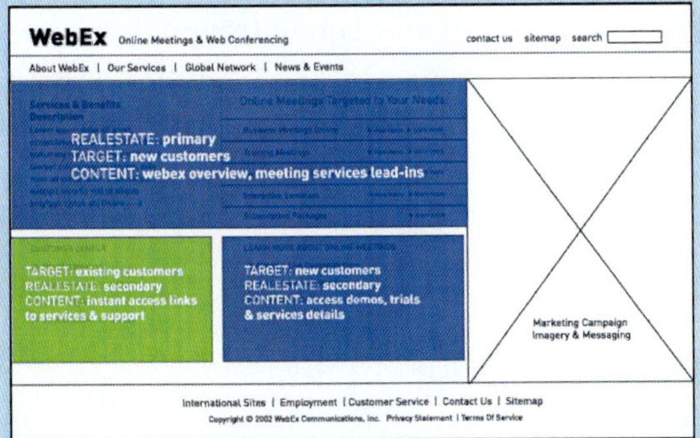

< 4.17 >

Confirming Real Estate — A colorized "overlay" is applied to the final wireframe to help explain items and reasoning to the client (and often to the rest of the team).

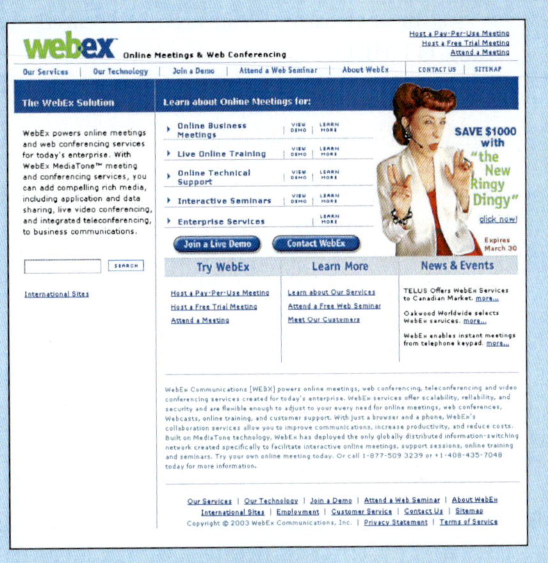

< 4.18 >

The Final Home-Page Refresh — This page served as home until the full redesign launched 18 months later with a new content management system in place (among other redesigned features and aspects). Note the addition of a search-friendly "tagline" which is actually a descriptive piece of HTML text located strategically at the top of the page.

Maintain a Sense of Place

Avoid user vertigo. While navigating from screen to screen, users should feel comfortable wherever they are. Can they get back to the home page? To where they started their task? Does the Back button actually return the user to the previous screen? (This is sometimes a problem when using cookies for session management or using framesets that load multiple pages at one time.) Become the user and navigate. Do you feel lost in the redesigned site? If so, adjust.

Use the following checklist when wireframing:

- ☐ **Images/figures/illustrations** (items in .gif or .jpg or .swf format that are not created using HTML)
- ☐ **Content** (general content direction or actual text if it is available)
- ☐ **Header or global navigation** (nav bar or global elements that appear on each page)
- ☐ **Functionality** (a description of the basic functionality of the page)
- ☐ **Primary links** (proposed navigation)
- ☐ **Secondary links**
- ☐ **Media** (if applicable)
- ☐ **Target window size** (actually draw a box and indicate pixel measurements)
- ☐ **Header and footer documentation** (project name, page name, version number, date, author, copyright)

Start at the beginning: the home page. Beyond that, decide how many more wireframed pages your budget and resources will allow. A wireframe set can consist of 5, 50, or 200 pages, depending on the budget and aptitude of the wireframe creator and/or the requirements of the project. We recommend wireframing at least your home page and all main pages. If you have any significant secondary pages — especially if those pages have a schema that repeats on many pages — we recommend wireframing those as well.

Add detail to every page, calling out specific functional needs (for example, pull-down menus and rollover navigation) and specifying links, graphics, and other information. If you have final copy, by all means use it, but copy on wireframes is usually placeholder text, represented by gray boxes, simple lines, or greeking (fake text, which ironically is almost always the Latin *Lorem Ipsum*). Whatever you use, it should be a good indication of suggested text length per page.

ADDRESSING NAVIGATION

There are many different approaches to navigation, all aimed at directing your audience to and through a desired action. Directed, searchable, tabbed, and linear are four navigational models, and any good information design book will go into deep detail on each (Christina Wodtke's *Information Architecture: Blueprints for the Web* and Louis Rosenfeld's *Information Architecture for the World Wide Web* are excellent resources), though it should be noted that most sites are a combination of two or more models.

NAMING AND LABELING

A solid naming system not only clearly defines the contents of the site, it also sets a tone about the company. Tone is important. The manner in which you name or label your buttons, icons, and navigational elements says a lot about your company and your approach. Naming should be consistent throughout the site. We're talking words or labels here — nongraphic road signs — that help to lead the way. Refer to the site goals. Is the client going for a friendly, accessible approach, or is the goal to be as professional and credible as possible **[4.19]**?

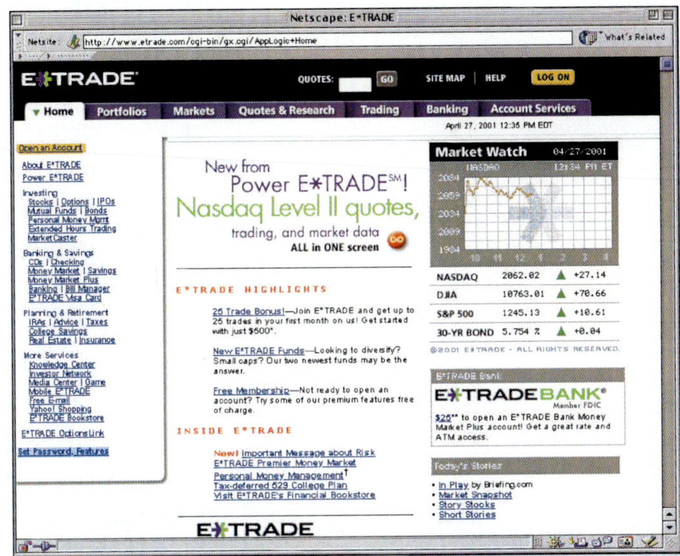

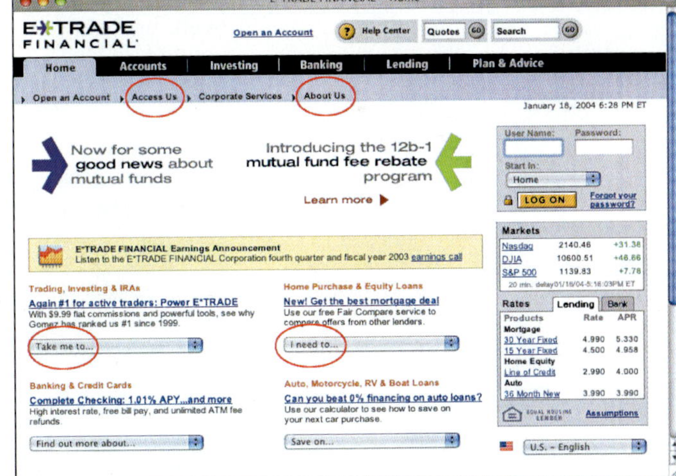

4.19 >

Consider www.etrade.com *then and now. In 2001, E*TRADE went for a very businesslike "login" and offered "Customer Services." There is nothing user-centric in this version, with the generic and impersonal long list of navigational links on the left side of the screen." In 2004, E*TRADE's menus actually prompt site visitors: "Take me to..." and "I need to..." All in a friendly and user-centered manner. [All references marked with red circles by the authors, not E*TRADE.]*

USER-VIEW
> Defining Key User Paths
> Developing the HTML Protosite
> Creating User Scenarios

DEFINING KEY USER PATHS

If your site does not require the user to actually do anything task oriented (for example, fill out a form, log in, or purchase), you do not need to define user paths. Defining key user paths is definitely part of the Core Process but only for sites that need them: sites with tasks, sites where one page must relate to the next in sequence.

What kinds of tasks? Because the goal is to simulate specific paths that a typical user would take when performing a task, defining user paths expands on the user profiles to create user scenarios — specific situations on the site in which real users might find themselves. These situations almost always involve tasks that require a specific path that involves several screens and steps to get through: registering, ordering, searching, etc. These tasks were probably defined in the previous phase of the Core Process and, as they likely involve backend technology, were hopefully detailed in a Functional Spec (see Chapter 9).

Wireframing out a path offers another opportunity to view the site from a user perspective. Also, if usability testing is scheduled, wireframing allows investigation of usability at this early stage.

Here are some sample tasks:

- **Order flowers for Mother's Day delivery.**
- **Fill out and submit an online loan application.**
- **Search for and order a spare battery for your cellular phone.**
- **Purchase a dog bed for your pet.**

Determine the user's primary paths or the actions a user will take through your site. (These are generally the primary actions that were specified by the client in the completed client survey.) Map out the screens

Take the Path of Least Resistance

If you want your audience to perform a task — registering, for instance, or making a purchase — you don't want to force them through a dozen or more screens. Too many forms and fields to fill out, even if important to your marketing department (such as age, income, and marital status), will annoy your users and could lead to them abandoning the task. In defining user pathways, interactive wireframing is a perfect technique for analysis and solution. Is there any way to combine steps so that registering takes only three or four screens? This would be more visitor friendly, and thus the chances for the user completing the task would be higher. Better to work through getting it right on paper or in a simple HTML click-thru rather than having to recode.

necessary to get from point A to point B. These paths (usually linear) follow a visitor through numerous required steps (usually involving filling out information) toward her final goal. This can be as simple as "contact us" or as complex as "prequalify online for a car loan." These paths should be wireframed for two reasons. The first reason is to think about screens you may not have addressed while wireframing. The second, and more important, reason is to think about how one screen relates to the next instead of taking one page at a time.

There are basically two types of user paths: functional and nonfunctional. Nonfunctional paths outline typical tasks that are not dependent on technical requirements (for example, contact the company, look up store locations, read the bio of the company president, etc.). These are simply page-by-page flows to complete a path of information.

Functional paths involve specifications predetermined by the engineering team (for shopping carts, data retrieval, login with password, complex search engines, etc.). These are generally handed over to the front-end team with the raw functionality already set in stone. However, these sections of predetermined functionality are not yet finalized in terms of naming, labeling, button vs. text link, forms to be filled out, or decisions on graphics vs. HTML for the pages. These are things that can be determined in this phase, during the wireframing and user path stages.

If time and resources dictate that defining user paths is in danger of being eliminated from the workflow, consider that even minimal attention at this stage is helpful to both design and engineering, and can aid a client who may not have a good understanding of flow. At the very least, take your wireframes and "click" from one page to the next by flipping to the appropriate wireframe. Also, for any site, complex or simple, keep in mind that even if it takes several levels to get to a specific page that is the endpoint in a user path, you wouldn't necessarily build all the pages in each of those levels, just the pages in the defined path. And you do not have to follow every single path, just the primary ones. We are not advocating extra work here, just what is necessary. Life is too short, and budgets are too tight.

DEVELOPING THE HTML PROTOSITE

Extending the wireframe process into building a Protosite can help to confirm the flow of the pages, the navigation, and the content. This is a nice-to-have, not a must-have. Budget and time allowing, it is an excellent tool to test the information design. The Protosite usually does not include functionality, although sometimes light scripting is involved. Usually the Protosite is just a simple wireframe (purely informational, no visual design, though a few colors are fine to separate navigation) made clickable through HTML **[4.20]**.

Test Content

Populate your click-thru Protosite with text-based content to check the length, tone, and flow. Seeing the content in HTML in context, even if it is not in its final layout position, can assist with internal proofing and evaluation. Once you see copy in place, you can more easily find holes in the content, discern whether a page is too text heavy, or decide that the content just doesn't make sense in the spot for which it was specified.

How Necessary is a Protosite?

The Protosite step can be skipped if you are very confident in your content, navigation, and visual design. If your resources are tight, testing functionality can indeed be folded into production, and confirming your information design can indeed be adequately done with wireframes. But "adequate" isn't great, and if you struggled over your navigation and organization, or if you require other-than-basic coding, you may want the peace of mind that comes from a Protosite at this juncture.

For sites with complex functionality, developers will sometimes create an HTML Protosite of a functional section of the site in order to test the navigation, usability, page-flow, or actual functionality. The creation of a Protosite is not a necessary part of the redesign workflow; however, when time and budget allow, is a useful and often indispensable part of the validation process.

The Protosite, also called an HTML click-thru, is a skeletal representation of the site, or a portion of the site, that allows you to go through the content, navigation, and light functionality (or a mock-up of desired functionality) to establish whether or not your informational model makes sense.

One of the key strengths of the Protosite is exposing content and information-flow design issues as well as navigational issues. When using placeholder content, it can be difficult to put things in their proper perspective. For instance, perhaps you have a main page called "Office Locations" with four secondary pages, one for each of the four offices. Only by plugging in content do you realize that there is nothing (in terms of content) on the actual "Office Location" page — all the content is on the specific location pages instead. This is a great thing for the client (and the team) to discover before production actually begins.

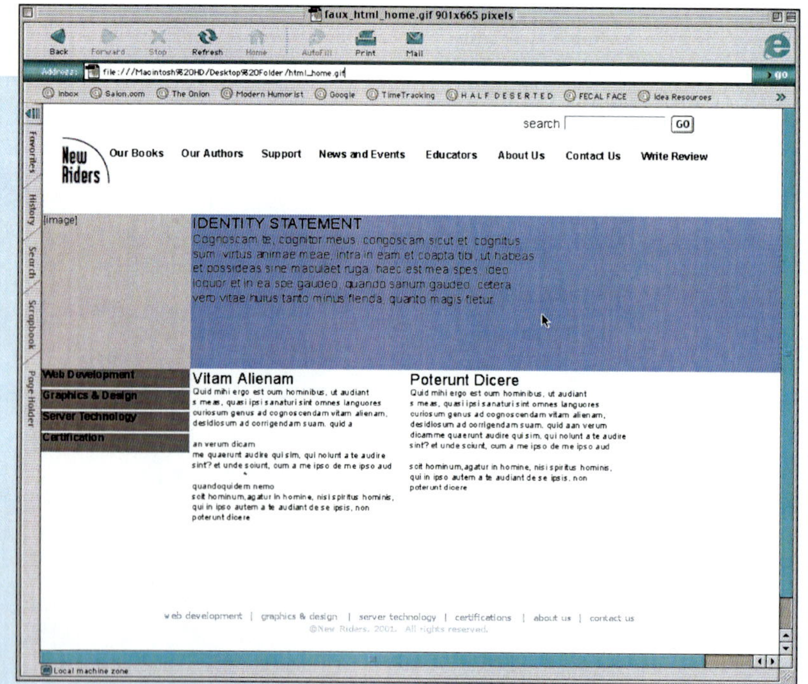

< **4.20**

A sample page for New Riders' Protosite. This click-thru contains navigation, headers, and placeholder content (only some actual content had been received), all in basic HTML — no graphics.

CREATING USER SCENARIOS

Scenarios are situations. User profiling (from the previous phase) is taking a demographic and personalizing it, giving a typical user a name, making the user "real." A user scenario, an expansion of user profiling, puts that "real" person in a real situation on the site **[4.21]**. Anticipate the motivations and the site-specific situations of the target user (or users — you may have more than one target group). What are the actual on- and offline circumstances specific to your users and their tasks? Become your user. Who are you, and why are you at this site?

Creating the various scenarios within the site should take you through several possible tasks, each leading the user down a different path. Examine these sample paths. If they are too complicated, will the user abandon the task? Sample situations need not be complex to be valid; they just need to be real. Real people trying to do real things.

Whatever the situation, it is important to think about the user, the task, and the situation to truly gauge a good path for the user to follow. Without a well-thought-out path, your user will be wandering aimlessly. Chances are, users will not find what they are looking for, and they will leave — and your client will have lost business.

4.21 >

This sample user scenario describes in detail a typical user task for a specific scenario. Refer to Phase 1: Define [3.1] for Paige McCormick's user profile.

Paige McCormick

Paige McCormick: User Scenario for www.petco.com

Paige spoils her dog senseless. Being a devoted dog owner, she is well versed in online pet stores. Her current favorite is www.petco.com, from which she has all her dog food as well as a lovely selection of rawhide chews delivered monthly.

Since Paige's dog, Ruthie, has pretty much managed to gnaw and neurotically dig her current cushion into small, barely identifiable bits of canvas and fluff, today Paige has decided to buy Ruthie a fresh, new bed.

She starts by going to www.petco.com. Here she selects the dog area under the header Go Shopping by clicking the happy, panting dog icon. Once in the Dog Shopping area, she uses the expanding tree menu system to navigate her way into the Cuddler Beds category. After examining a selection of five or six beds, she clicks the Product Options button for the Bed Buddies Lounger in blue.

Here she notes that the cover is stain resistant and machine washable and that it has a comfy faux sheepskin lining. Paige thinks that Ruthie will like that (and is amused by the "Bed Buddies" nomenclature) and clicks the Add to Cart button.

She is prompted to log in or register as a new customer. A regular site user, she logs in with her email address and password. She then reviews her billing and shipping information followed by her saved credit card information. Satisfied that all is in order, she clicks the Place Order Online button and completes her order.

PHASE 2 CHECK-OFF LIST

Content-View

- ☐ Address/organize content
- ☐ Audit existing content
- ☐ Outline content
- ☐ Create a Content Delivery Plan

Site-View

- ☐ Create a sitemap
- ☐ Address existing site organization
- ☐ Determine site structure
- ☐ Set naming conventions

Page-View

- ☐ Create wireframes
- ☐ Establish navigation
- ☐ Establish naming and labeling

Page-View

- ☐ Define key user paths
- ☐ Create an HTML Protosite
- ☐ Create user scenarios

PHASE 2 SUMMARY

Structuring a site for redesign is the spot in the Core Process for issues to be raised (such as concerns over old vs. new content) and for problems to be solved (such as solutions as to how to split the information into sections). Phase 2: Structure answers specific questions: How is the overall structure organized? (Answered with the sitemap.) What exactly goes on each page? (Answered with wireframes.) How do the pages work with one another? (Answered with interactive wireframes.) Planning the design of the site's information is a critical step for any web project. And yet it is a common mistaken assumption that redesign projects can simply appropriate the information, design, and/or content from the existing site and essentially skip this step. Hopefully, this chapter dispelled that notion.

Taking the time to structure the site — specifically to build the sitemap and the wireframes — is one of the most time-consuming and least-expected challenges of a redesign project. It is time well spent, however, because with the site structure and content established, the team is on solid ground to move forward into visual design development. Web design workflow often starts with the designing of the visual graphic user interface before the information design is set — errant sequencing that almost always results in an inefficient use of design resources. Why? Changes at a graphic level generally take more time than do similar changes at a wireframe level. Planning and strategy are always worthwhile.

And that is what structuring a site is truly all about: content and information strategy — where and how to put what information so that users can and will access it. Without this strategy, visual design becomes a gamble.

It is still not standard to have a dedicated information designer on a development team, though more and more teams are recognizing the value. Often this role falls to the project manager or art director. Regardless of who performs the role, however, going through the detail-oriented planning tasks of content organization, sitemapping, and building wireframes always serves as a roadmap to follow for the visual design and production ahead.

About.com

Company: About.com
URL: www.about.com
Design Team: Catalyst Design Group, NYC
Senior Manager, Production: Eric Saam

Senior Producer: Lars Weinrich
Product Manager: Tara Long
Designer: Sayuri Luong
Vice President, Product: Jared Skolnick

About.com is a destination site that connects audiences to relevant content, links, and information. Many topic pages are accessed through search results, so the home page is often unused. This usage analysis led to a complete redesign and rebranding to create a better user experience by making every page a "front door."

<PREVIOUS>

ABOUT.COM HOME PAGE [OLD] looks like a link-oriented portal page. The audience can view the topics they are looking for via alphabetical links and search results, but the site is often mistaken for a directory or portal site instead of a content site.

<CURRENT>

ABOUT.COM HOME PAGE [REDESIGNED] is organized in a new and easy-to-use manner targeting content to specific user groups, and it employs a user login that is presented with options tailored to specific needs.

ABOUT.COM TOPIC PAGE [REDESIGNED] follows the improved architecture to create a landing page for each specific topic. This example of a House & Home page also provides sub-navigation and corresponding links for individuals who find this page through search engines.

Results: The brand is redefined through improved architecture. The number of possible clicks from each page was reduced during this effort by targeting different supporting content to different user types.

> Today's web designer must combine form and functionality to create an intuitive user experience.

Phase 3: Design Visual Interface 05

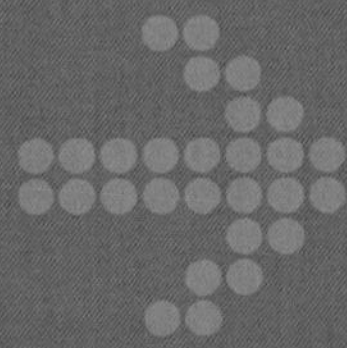

Phase 3: Design Visual Interface

Designing for the web means creating something that looks two-dimensional, like a printed piece, but upon deeper involvement reveals interactivity and layering of information. This makes web design a lot like product design, a discipline in which you design something that you interact with (for example, a better snowboard binding, a more usable corkscrew, or a revolutionary self-sifting litter box). Your website is a product; it gets used.

Today's web design is driven by what is usable and functional; it's not focused on flashy pages and brochureware. With new design advancements, coupled with the standardization of browsers, the time has arrived for visual designers to think like coders and for coders to finally spread their creative wings. Although technical parameters will significantly change in the future (at what rate is anybody's guess), reality now includes some fairly specific demands. Accessible, usable web pages with validated code and an understanding of layouts using CSS for detailed formatting and positioning are only some of the considerations that must be taken into account during visual design.

WHAT THIS CHAPTER COVERS

CREATING	CONFIRMING	HANDING OFF
> Starting the Creative Process	> Confirming Flow and Functionality	> Producing Graphic Templates
> Defining Smart Design	> Testing Functionality	> Creating a Design Style Guide
> Reviewing Site Goals		
> Developing Concepts		
> Designing for Your Audience		
> Presenting Designs and Gathering Feedback		

STARTING THE CREATIVE PROCESS

Here is what the client has been patiently (or not-so-patiently) waiting for: a glimpse at the new branding and layout of the redesigned site. But before that happens, the design team needs to do some serious solution-oriented brainstorming on both creative and technical levels (and sometimes the greatest creative solution is a technical innovation). Creativity doesn't just get churned out, it needs to be kneaded and coaxed and slept on. Don't expect to redesign your visual interface in one take and don't let your client think that this is possible.

DEFINING SMART DESIGN

Visual web design must be more than just a pretty interface; it must also follow overall site objectives while being functional. Here is where information design and advance planning take shape, find a face, and begin to communicate. The Design phase is often called "the fun part." Here is where designers work their magic. Here is also where falling off track can hemorrhage your budget. Hold that tendency at bay. Practice Smart Design.

It is important when designing any site — new or redesigned — to understand the concept of Smart Design. Smart Design serves the audience's environment and capabilities. Smart Design combines style and function and keeps web standards including CSS in mind. Smart Design is focused on the audience's experience rather than the ambitions of the designer, the desire to use Flash (when maybe it isn't warranted), the positioning of the company's advertiser, or even the personal quirks of the CEO of the client's company. If it detracts from the usability of a site, it is not Smart Design — even if it is cool.

How do you practice Smart Design? Simple. Think like your audience. Browse, click, and download like an actual site visitor. Incorporate your information design rather than fight it. And check in with production frequently — think of your HTML production designer as your babysitter: "Can I do this?" "Is this permissible?" "Will I get in trouble if I do it this way?" Even if your designs are beautiful, hip, and perfectly aligned with the needs of the audience, if they are not producible, maintainable, and easily downloaded, they are not smart. Through testing and discussion, production can guide as to what is feasible. Early check-in with production helps start the process of research and investigation into problem solving that is inevitable during the implementation.

Keep Your Designers Happy

Yes, it costs money to upgrade hardware and software, but consider that creativity does not flow from the disgruntled, the overworked, or the under-resourced. Keep your team motivated. Make sure you have a fast system and the latest versions of software. Pay for licenses so that designers don't have to log off the network to launch an application (besides, you'll be legal this way). Provide good workstations. Purchase design magazine subscriptions and send your team to conferences for inspiration from time to time. Be ergonomically proactive instead of reactive. If you care, invest. It will return to you threefold.

< CREATING

- > Starting the Creative Process
- > Defining Smart Design
- > Reviewing Site Goals
- > Developing Concepts
- > Designing for Your Audience
- > Presenting Designs and Gathering Feedback

< **5.1**

An early-stage proposed palette for New Riders Publishing's redesigned site. As the design team progressed, the palette was fine-tuned. Several palettes were presented. In this case, a modified version of these colors was chosen.

REVIEWING SITE GOALS

As the visual designers get ready to begin the Design phase, pull out the Communication Brief and use it as a springboard for the creative process. What was established for the tone? Corporate and solid and clean? Cutting edge and funky? Elegant and smooth? Something else entirely? The Communication Brief also lists the client's redesign objectives, including visual goals such as a more professional look and feel, easy updating through style sheets, search engine optimization, etc. During creative brainstorming, the design team should see and identify the visual problems of the existing site, review the redesign goals, view competitive sites, and discuss the proposed solutions.

The creative process does not develop in a vacuum. While brainstorming on colors and fonts and layout, the visual designers should also muse about technical and structural solutions (for example, use of CSS, JavaScript, DHTML, etc.) Before doing this, review the target audience's technical capabilities. Design with technology in mind, however the design should not necessarily dictate the technology used. And remember, don't use technical solutions just because they are current. You must make sure they facilitate the redesign goals and are appropriate for the audience.

DEVELOPING CONCEPTS

The development of the look and feel can start by gathering colors and putting rough ideas on paper or screen — without concern for the content and labels that the information design will provide **[5.1]**. While waiting for the information design, the visual design team can refer to the Communication Brief for guidance. Only after the sitemap and wireframes are approved, however, can design truly begin. Refer to the Communication Brief for tone and feel, to the sitemap for structure, and to the wireframes for navigational and content elements. Pull together everything to date and begin to "paint" around it.

There are two camps as to how to start designing. Traditionalists like to put pencil or pen to paper; others render straight into the computer and create a series of drafts (**[5.2]** and **[5.3]**). Either way, it is the beginning of concept development, and regardless of technique, at this point in the Core Process visual designers get to start experimenting with colors and layouts. They get to produce design after design. Visual designers should brainstorm until there are two or three solid design directions to flesh out further.

As project manager, make sure the visual designers don't spend hours refining and tweaking the directions for client review until the information design is set.

5.2 >

Initial sketches or thumbnails on paper allow for easy brainstorming on several solutions. By starting on paper, the designers are able to quickly outline grid patterns and layout directions.

5.3 >

Initial design directions started in FreeHand, Illustrator, or Photoshop.

Mac vs. PC

Ninety percent of all websites are designed on Macs, but 97 percent of all sites are viewed on PCs. A PC workstation for your designers will allow them to look at the site they are redesigning in the same way much of the targeted audience will look at it. Get a PC, set the monitor resolution to that of your project's target audience (yes, that will make the designers groan), and then make sure your designers actually review work-in-progress on it.

Gamma Gamma

Colors look slightly different on Macs vs. PCs. Some say brighter on Macs; others claim truer and bluer on PCs. The argument will never die. Just know that they are slightly different, even if you set your Mac gamma to match a PC. Upload your proposed palette onto your server and view it on both platforms before showing it to the client. You may change your mind.

During this initial brainstorming, don't forget that download time, functionality, and browser variables must be addressed. Make sure you run your designs by your production lead and engineer (if applicable). Those who will do the actual building should assist in determining the feasibility of translating the designs into workable web pages for the target audience. The design directions may be really cool but might not come close to working efficiently (or at all) in a live environment. And if you need to ensure that your site follows government accessibility regulations, that's an entire set of parameters against which to measure any potential visual designs.

Involve production early in the design process and confirm that your design can actually be produced. It is embarrassing and it undermines your credibility to present a design that the client loves but that must be retracted as unfeasible.

DESIGNING FOR YOUR AUDIENCE

When the design team is finished brainstorming, the art director or designer should pursue at least three conceptual directions and concentrate on fleshing out the information from the approved wireframes, including navigation, global elements, content, etc. Make sure to determine when and where to place visual/graphic cues (for example, buttons and icons) to help guide the user through the site. Production will need to know. Start with the home page and flesh out at least one subpage during the initial design phase.

As the visual design and testing develop, the team should take the time to truly visualize the site from the audience's viewpoint. What are the goals of the site, and how do you want your target audience to feel when they visit? For instance, if the target audience is largely using T3 lines at the office, go ahead with your Flash and streaming media. Is your audience largely at home, still on modems and/or older browser versions? Reduce graphics and media and employ streamlined code and HTML text. Make sure the visual designers redesign *for* the target audience, not *at* them.

Keeping designers focused on the target audience and on the redesign goals is a challenge. Problems arise when designers get excited and want to design the coolest thing possible. This is perfectly fine as long as this excitement does not overshadow the importance of the audience, the production feasibility, or the client's wishes. Of course, it is entirely possible that the goals of the project *are* to make it as hip and as design-centric as possible. Maybe the goal is to be totally cutting edge. Maybe the audience for your site consists entirely of power users on T1 lines. If so, let your designers go absolutely wild. But anything less than the super-high concept and... well, we've already said it.

Flash Considerations

Flash is everywhere, and it seems that every client thinks they need to have it. The keyword here is "thinks." Don't use Flash just because you can — we call that "Gratuitous Flash," and it's rampant. Flash is fabulous, but have a reason for it — a reason that serves the user. And if you are going to use it, make sure your audience can access it.

With a 96+% penetration rate for the Flash plug-in (though not necessarily the latest version), most browsers are indeed ready to view Flash animations on the web. But even though the Flash technology has enabled the creation of slick animation, sound, and graphics at a relatively low file size, many Flash sites are still too heavy to fully enjoy without a high-bandwidth connection. Design for your audience. What is their connectivity? They could be in for a long (in web-time) loading period, and most users don't like to wait. If you are building a Flash site, consider giving your audience options [5.4].

Connectivity isn't the only concern. Other Flash issues include incompatibilities with text-to-speech translators (for visually impaired or non-graphics-enabled browsers) and the fact that pages are harder to bookmark. Consider also maintenance. The web designer may be a Flash master, but what about the maintenance team? It is considerably harder to update Flash than straight HTML. Plus, Flash tends to thwart search engines. Currently, Flash content cannot be indexed. (For more information on search engines, see Phase 5: Launch.)

Solutions?

1. Provide an HTML alternative site for lower bandwidth and text readers. Many sites use a Flash "sniffer" to determine if the Flash plug-in is in place rather than the splash screens of yesteryear.

2. Provide ALT text alternatives for smaller animation pieces and graphic text.

Macromedia has addressed many of these issues (search for flash+accessibility at www.macromedia.com); however, it is still important to know what you are working with when creating content for a mass audience on the web.

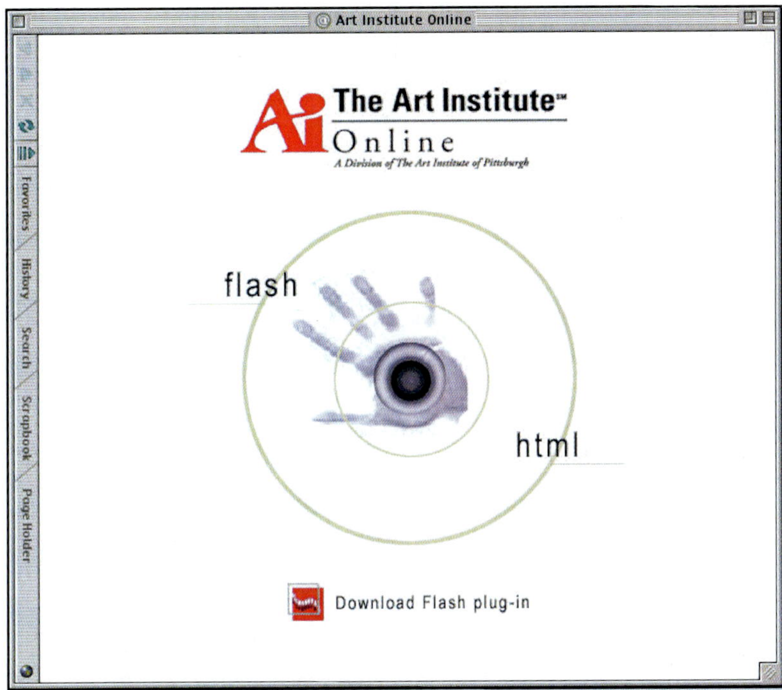

< 5.4 >

For accessibility purposes, create a low-bandwidth version of your website. Give users the option whether to go to the Flash site, or to stick with the HTML version.

ERIC MEYER ON CSS

It doesn't matter what size your business is, even if the business is just you. CSS can deliver major benefits and can potentially save you some money.

The benefit that gets the most attention is the reduction of page weight because, for really high-traffic sites, that translates into bandwidth savings. ESPN.com, for example, at one time stood to save two terabytes of outgoing bandwidth *every day* by converting to a CSS-driven layout. Even smaller sites reap the same benefit as ESPN, Wired, or any other site that moves from table-and-spacer design to standards-oriented design: faster page loads. A large number of redesigns have shown that, typically, a conversion to standards-oriented design cuts markup weight by about 50% and often reduces the number of images needed for the design. That means users wait half as long to get the pages (or, to put it another way, pages come up twice as fast). On the web, speed matters. Standards-oriented design can deliver that speed and without the need to buy a faster (read: more expensive) server.

It's also the case that a standards-based site, if it uses good HTML structure, is more accessible by its very nature. While using standards-oriented design doesn't automatically grant accessibility guideline compliance, it will get you a heck of lot closer. If your site is accessible, guess what will like your site much better? Google. Search engines in general are just like blind users: All they can perceive is the text of your page. Many search engines also give higher rankings to pages that use good HTML structure. So making the move to standards-oriented design can increase your site's accessibility and search engine optimization.

The other benefit of CSS-driven design comes before the design ever goes public. Creating a wireframe layout using HTML and CSS can make the design adjustment phase a lot more efficient. With that wireframe in hand, you can sit in meetings and react in real time to suggestions for change. If the CTO doesn't like that shade of blue you're using, change it and hit reload. The new shade will be right there for him to see. Want to move the navigation to the right and the top news stories to the left? Editing two or three rules in your style sheet is all it takes. Hit reload and see them switch. If that doesn't work as well, switch them back. The process takes almost literally 15 seconds.

Once you've settled on a design arrangement and color scheme, you can take that design and work to make it cross-browser compatible. Maybe you'll end up with a simple table to lay out the page and CSS to style the cell contents, or maybe you'll be able to stick with a tableless layout. Either way, you'll get to that point a lot faster if you do your prototyping with CSS.

Eric A. Meyer is an internationally recognized expert in HTML, CSS, and standards-oriented web design who has been working on the web since 1993. After two years on the standards evangelism team at Netscape Communications, he founded Complex Spiral Consulting (http://www.complexspiral.com)*, where his mission is to help save clients money and improve site experience, performance, and accessibility through the use of open standards. Eric is an author and speaker, and manages a highly active CSS mailing list.*

PRESENTING DESIGNS AND GATHERING FEEDBACK

Before presenting first-round visual directions to the client, the designs should have already gone through several steps internally. Keep two important things in mind: First, presenting too many choices too early in the process slows things down; you're promoting client indecision. Three design directions are good. Second, do not present any design you hate just because you need another design. Chances are, you will end up producing that direction.

Post the designs to the client staging area and invite review ([5.5] through [5.8]). With some clients, you will get your feedback swiftly; with others, it will trickle in. Request written, consolidated feedback. Project management should endeavor to

The Truth About Screen Sizes

Viewable screen sizes vary — they are all totally dependent on the audience's own environment. When the first edition of this book came out in 2001, the most popular setting was 800×600. Several years later that size accounts for only 40 or so percent with 1024×760 gaining momentum. This setting, where most redesigns are now probably aiming, is really only 955×600 viewable. It's true. Where do the extra pixels go? The browser takes them.

Designers like to work at 1024×768 because, almost exclusively, they all use high-resolution screens. But not everyone has a 21-inch monitor. And also, with PC tablets and hand-held devices, screen sizes are getting smaller again. Designers must look at their work-in-progress on a variety of settings. On an average-size monitor or with smaller resolution settings (always determined by the user), you may discover that both the right and bottom get cut off. To combat this problem, consider designing the browser window to be "stretchable," "dynamically resizable," "scalable," "liquid" — all terms to describe pages that expand to the width of the browser. We like the term "liquid" because the page and the text flow with the browser, no matter the size.

Tools exist that will help check a site's individual audience statistics. With only a nominal subscription cost, www.hitbox.com will provide the information necessary to determine your audience's primary and secondary browser size so that your team can design appropriately. WebTrends (www.webtrends.com) also is an industry standard — and both are viable for small to enterprise-sized organizations. There are also a number of free analytic tools, as well as software that comes with your hosting server — make sure you don't already have a statistics tool in place that you are not already utilizing!

Templates to the Rescue? Or Not?

There are many sites offering templatized website designs for the budget conscious. Suprisingly, for less than $100 you can download a nicely designed template (www.templatemonster.com, for example) that contains royalty-free images, Flash movies, buttons, and layered Photoshop and Fireworks files ready to go. Yahoo!, .Mac and AOL also offer simple templates for consumer and small business use. While we are not advocating the use of templatized sites, if you need to get a website up and running quickly, and have some basic HTML text pages (resume, family photos, a vacation rental, etc.) why spend time and money on the look and feel when there are cost-effective options available?

Buyer beware: Confirm the legitimacy of the template vendor. There are sets out there that are knock-offs of copyrighted material. A bit of homework will avoid a significant headache.

Challenge

New Riders' old home page [5.5] was cluttered with content that took up valuable space that could better have been used to convey the New Riders personality and brand. This site needed a new structure and organization to highlight the company's products (books) in a more dynamic fashion. Key words: elegant, informational, professional, high end.

<BEFORE>

< 5.5 The old site was cluttered and static.

APPROACH 1>

< 5.6 > *This initial design direction is modern and friendly in a modular grid system. This approach allows for several features to appear at the top of the home page.*

Approach

Focus the home page on communicating the New Riders personality and vision through the use of strong imagery and a clear welcome or mission statement. Limit content to "teasers" or lead-ins to different areas of the site. This approach also serves the first goal of clarifying navigation, as excessive content does not detract from the user paths.

APPROACH 2>

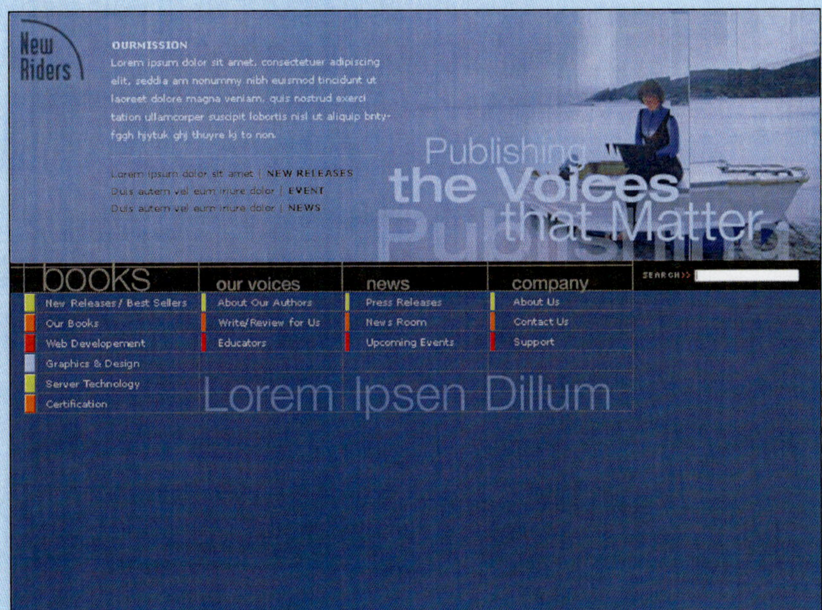

< 5.7 > *This initial design direction shows a subdued/elegant look and feel. This approach highlights the mood and feeling of the company, with a simple linking system to the main areas of content.*

APPROACH 3>

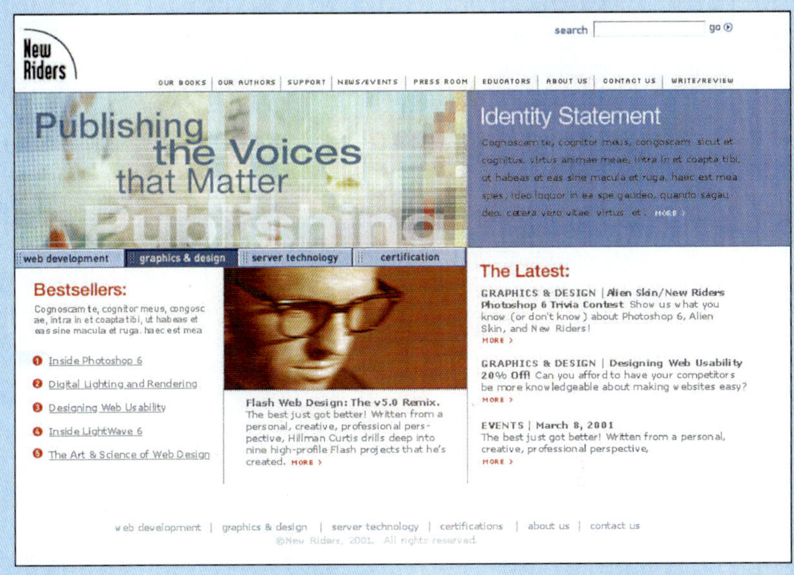

< 5.8 > *This initial design direction shows a corporate/current look as well as a strong company branding and identity treatment. It also allows for book features to appear prominently on the home page.*

Audience Feedback

Take advantage of any and all user-testing opportunities. Right around the presentation of the second round of visual comps, somewhere between initial client feedback and final tweaking, lies a perfect point at which to gather objective audience feedback. Although it isn't appropriate at this point in the Core Process to run usability testing, getting feedback from your target audience will offer you some valuable answers. This can be one-on-one informal interviews, or in a focus group setting. Please note however — we do not suggest you use focus groups in lieu of one-on-one usability testing. Focus groups are good for general opinions and feedback but are not conclusive. What is the purpose of your site and what does your company have to offer (this should be obvious)? What is the first thing a visitor would do when coming to the site? Is the site organized in a comprehensive manner? Is the interface appealing? Should you move forward and execute your designs or backtrack and redo?

educate the client as to what constitutes helpful feedback. Clients can keep you in a frustrating circle of endless tweaking if you let them. Two or three rounds of design are appropriate. Anything after that may need to be renegotiated and additional budget added — dependent, of course, on factors such as level of talent versus expectations, rounds of changes, indecision, etc.

At the end of this first stage of Phase 3, you will have an appropriately smart visual design that fits your client and its audience. The pace just picks up from here. With the design direction finalized (and approved by the client — don't forget to get it signed), you can confidently take the next step toward HTML production.

Client Control

Sometimes clients suffer short-term memory loss. Perhaps the Communication Brief described the corporate brand as "classic, elegant," and that's exactly what you're presenting, but the client says it's not cutting edge. What? "Cutting edge" wasn't in your Communication Brief. What happened? The client wasn't able to articulate their wants until they saw actual designs. Suddenly, none of your brainstorming applies to this new direction, the tone is now wrong, and your schedule feels much tighter.

Sometimes clients love the first thing you present; sometimes they are unpleasable. Regardless, they will often have a hard time articulating their feedback. This is simply part of the creative process — budget for it. But there is also the possibility that your designers may be slow to hit upon a winning design — a few additional rounds of design may be required to fulfill the vision stated in the Communication Brief. You cannot blame (and therefore charge) the client for a slow design process.

You can, however, hold the client responsible for changes in direction, the addition of more pages, or changes in navigation. Gently remind the client about the Communication Brief. Often clients "forget" what they've said about tone and perception, and you budgeted based on knowing certain givens before commencing visual design. It is absolutely acceptable (and common) for clients to change their minds after seeing visual directions, but if you need to significantly backtrack, the scope of the project has changed.

VISUAL DESIGN CHECKLIST: RE-REVIEW (BEFORE SHOWING CLIENT)

Before you present your designs to your client, make sure you have checked the following:

1. **Branding:** Does the proposed design follow the established brand identity, guidelines, and messaging? Is the company logo clearly displayed with a descriptive tagline?

   ☐ Yes ☐ No

2. **Communication Brief Guidelines:** Does the proposed design follow the Communication Brief's stated tone, voice, and direction?

   ☐ Yes ☐ No

3. **Accessibility:** Does the proposed design follow standards for accessibility (mandatory in some cases — you know who you are)? This includes HTML text, quick-loading graphics, and use of CSS where appropriate for positioning and navigation.

   ☐ Yes ☐ No

4. **Screen Display:** Does the proposed design display the most prominent information "above the fold" in an 800×600 (760×420?) window area? Is the design "liquid" so that it will stretch to accommodate multiple screen sizes? Will you be able to easily adjust the layout if you need to switch to 955×600 before you are ready to redesign again?

   ☐ Yes ☐ No

5. **Sliceability:** Have you confirmed that your proposed design is sliceable and can be re-created using HTML and CSS? Have you checked with the production designers to make sure the design can be easily rendered in HTML?

   ☐ Yes ☐ No

6. **Color:** Have you checked the proposed design on both a Mac and PC to ensure that the colors are displaying as designed? Colors often look much darker on a PC than on a Mac.

   ☐ Yes ☐ No

7. **Imagery:** Is the imagery selected royalty free? Most designs require royalty-free imagery from stock photography websites. Check sooner than later to ensure that the visual imagery is affordable.

   ☐ Yes ☐ No

8. **Navigation:** Is the layout dependent on pull-down or rollover menus? Do the second- and third-level pages have a comprehensive navigational system in place?

   ☐ Yes ☐ No

9. **Font Size:** Have you made certain that the design to be submitted is not dependent on a specific HTML font size? (Remember, you have relatively no control over HTML font sizes unless you are using CSS, and even then your control is not total.)

   ☐ Yes ☐ No

If you answered No to any of these questions, you should take a step backward, rethink, and modify the design(s) before submitting them to the client.

Site Visitors Don't Read, They Skim

Information-heavy sites must pass the squint test. As a designer, push your chair back, squint (or take off your glasses), and skim. There, now you are "inspecting" the site just like a majority of users. Can you identify where to click? Quickly and easily? No? Make it more obvious. (Note: More obvious does not necessarily mean bigger and bolder and clunkier.)

Take the squint test one step further. Grab someone totally uninvolved with your site (like your UPS delivery person, someone from personnel, or your mate who's come to meet you for lunch), sit the person in front of your layout, and give him or her all of 10 seconds to find what you want him or her to find. Can the person do so? No? Make it more obvious.

CONFIRMING

> Confirming Flow and Functionality

> Testing Functionality

CONFIRMING FLOW AND FUNCTIONALITY

There is no need to wait until the design is finalized, optimized, and coded in order to test light functionality, content, or navigation. Modify whatever isn't quite working while the visual design is still coming together; you won't necessarily have time to adjust the look and feel during production. We recommend two avenues of testing. Set the production designers to work on testing DHTML, pull-down menus, pop-up screens, multiframe sets, basically anything that needs to be worked out cross-platform and with various browsers. We also recommend building a Protosite (see Phase 2: Structure).

TESTING FUNCTIONALITY

Testing functionality of individual features prior to actual HTML production is a smart move. An innovative idea for a pull-down menu using DHTML might seem like an excellent solution during brainstorming, but if in reality it is neither cross-browser compliant nor Mac viewable, you are losing a significant percentage of your audience, and the solution is not acceptable.

In addition, by testing assumptions now, you are able to determine whether there are changes to project scope with which to contend. Having to build two versions of the site — one for Internet Explorer and one for Safari, or one for high-bandwidth-capable audiences and one for low bandwidth — would be a significant change.

Any of the following scenarios should be tested cross-browser and -platform:

- Complex frame sets (not recommended unless absolutely necessary)
- Functional rollover menus using JavaScript, CSS, or DHTML
- Pop-up windows, especially if size- or placement-specific
- Cascading style sheets (CSS) or any browser-specific treatment
- Forms or surveys requiring data to be stored or sent to a specific email address
- Pull-down menus (especially ones that load pages automatically)
- Basic shopping cart features
- Anything needing light scripting or Server-Side Includes (SSI)
- Testing "Includes" via XML

Testing your functional assumptions during the design phase allows you to fix problems before the design is finalized, a point at which they can still be dealt with in a streamlined manner. Testing also helps prepare the production staff for the task ahead. Working out technical issues in advance saves a lot of time in the end.

LYNDA WEINMAN ON DESIGNERS AS PROBLEM SOLVERS

A designer is a problem solver. By nature, developing a website is a series of problems in need of solutions. Usability, navigability, download speed, etc., are components of the problem. If a designer doesn't pay attention to what problems to solve, he or she will have failed. How good the site looks after those issues are resolved is the measure of how creatively the problems were handled. Visual design should support the functionality and goals of the site and not detract from or overwhelm those issues.

Designer ego can get in the way of problem solving. Just because you're trying to show off your animation skills or you like a certain font or color isn't a reason to put these things into a site design. Design should be deliberate to meet the goals of the site, not to meet your personal design goals. It's great when the two can meet, but the goals of the site need to come first.

When redesigning a site, a design team needs to be armed with critical information. Data should be collected by testers to find out where current end users would like to see improvement, as well as what is currently working very well for them. The design team should keep these points in the forefront of the creative process. Of course, any redesign begins with clearly defined goals. From these, a hierarchy of importance should be established that is carried through with the design.

To that end, team members have to feel what it's like to be in the end users' shoes. Try this exercise to help them do so: Have all the members of your team list the top five things they would look for on a similar kind of site. Instruct them to find five competitive sites, rate them, and write about their strengths/weaknesses. Have them come up with reasons behind the strengths and solutions for the weakness.

When the project is a redesign, there is an insistent lure to employ the latest and greatest technology because it is often perceived as a catchall "fix" for ailing sites. Beware of using technology for the sole purpose of using technology. There should always be a purpose behind every decision. For example, the goal should not be to use Flash, but what can Flash provide that can't be achieved any other way and/or that is necessary to the success of the site?

For any designer, maintaining a solution-oriented, problem-solving approach to the actual design and comping process is possible as long as you make sure that you know the goals of the site, that these goals are measurable (for example, are click-thrus or actual sales more important), and that you approach reaching the goals from the end user's perspective (that is, you want to sell something, but they want to buy something). Keep your eye on the target — make sure your goals are clear and stick to them.

Lynda Weinman is co-founder of lynda.com, a company that specializes in educating creative professionals in digital tools and design for print, web, multimedia, and video. Most recently, lynda.com launched an Online Learning Library (available as a monthly or annual subscription) that contains thousands of instructional movies on dozens of subjects and technologies. She is the co-founder of Flashforward, a conference focused on Macromedia Flash designers and developers that draws attendance from thousands of web developers from all over the world. Visit www.lynda.com *to learn more.*

HANDING OFF
> Creating Graphic Templates
> Creating a Design Style Guide

CREATING GRAPHIC TEMPLATES

Here is where the established look and feel needs to be translated and applied across multiple pages. Download size and feasibility of optimization already should have been addressed as the design was being created. But now that a direction has been decided upon, applying and establishing standards across your site is a must as graphic templates get built for the various types of pages. With several people working on this step, the potential for deviation is significant.

First let's establish the difference between a look and feel and a graphic template. In the first step of this phase, you presented your client with design directions. You established a look and feel. This is different than a final design. The look and feel is just an approved direction; it still has to be refined (there will almost certainly be details to work out) and then reapproved. The application used to create this design could be pretty much any digital design concept tool: Photoshop, Fireworks, FreeHand, Illustrator, QuarkXPress... whatever you are most comfortable with.

A graphic template takes the final, approved look and feel and preps it for optimization and HTML production. It is called a template because it will be used for both the HTML page it is directly designed to be and any similar pages. It is a master graphic file that will soon get handed over to production for slicing and optimization during the next phase of the Core Process. Creating a graphic template is refining a look and feel to achieve a layered file ready for production. The application options for this are more limited. Photoshop and Fireworks are the industry-standard applications for web optimization.

When creating the graphic templates and unique pages in Photoshop or Fireworks, start by establishing the global elements such as headers, footers, colors, and graphic treatments in one layered master file and use this finalized file to create the rest of the templates and unique pages only *after* it has been approved. Graphics for rollovers and pull-down menus (archaic as it may seem with CSS supplying HTML-based solutions for both) should be created and called out in a separate layer in the file. Stick with the elements you will need to create in order for the coders to understand how the page is built. The designer may not need to add every pixeled detail — some of the global elements can be created easily using style sheets during Phase 4: Build. As a general rule, design templates include the following types of pages:

- **Homepage ("graphic template" usually created as an exemplar during look and feel)**
- **Second Level ("graphic template" usually created as an exemplar during look and feel)**
- **Third Level — there is usually a third level, and if there isn't, there soon will be once the site gets to any decent size**
- **Content Page — a normal page — the vast majority of pages on a site.**

- **Content Page with Subnavigation — a normal page with some sort of navigational system to tie together a subset of pages within a site**
- **Search / Search Results (either within a normal search or may be something like a product listing or inventory list, whatever).**

This is just the basics, but when we scope a site, we normally assume that these graphic templates will need to be designed since they are sufficiently unique and/or important to just leave to the production designers to figure out using the Style Guide. If you are talking about an e-commerce site, you can usually assume some templates specific to the purchase path. With a membership-based site, the same thing related to registration / login / account maintenance. You get the picture....

Keep in mind that you will probably have several graphic templates to create, each with one or more similar pages created from this master. Small redesign projects may be able to get away with only a few graphic templates, but large sites can easily have a dozen or more. (www.fdic.gov had nearly three dozen templates!) It is likely that you will have a graphic template for your home page, another for your main pages, a third for your secondary pages, etc. Don't forget about error pages, pop-up windows, or redirects following form submissions or transaction completions. Your visual designers may not need

What Graphic Templates Should Include and Clearly Indicate...

- Text in rendered and unrendered states. (These can be separate files.)
- All individual layers intact (not flattened) for revisions.
- All individual layers clearly labeled. ("Layer 7" helps nobody; "Main Nav" communicates layer content.)
- Each state — on/off/rollover — on separate, clearly identified layers. Indicate rollover treatment on a separate layer if CSS rollovers are used.
- Flash/animation placeholders (use a single-frame, still image with "FPO" placed across).
- Placeholders at points where special technologies and complex functionalities integrate.
- An accompanying GIF or flattened Photoshop or Fireworks file that shows how the page should look once rebuilt in HTML. This reference document is a critical part of any template. In either Fireworks or Photoshop, this can be a single layer on the top of the layers file.

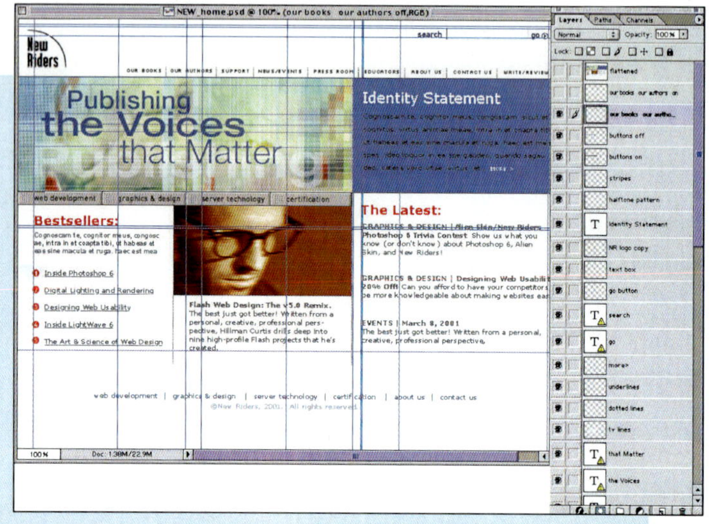

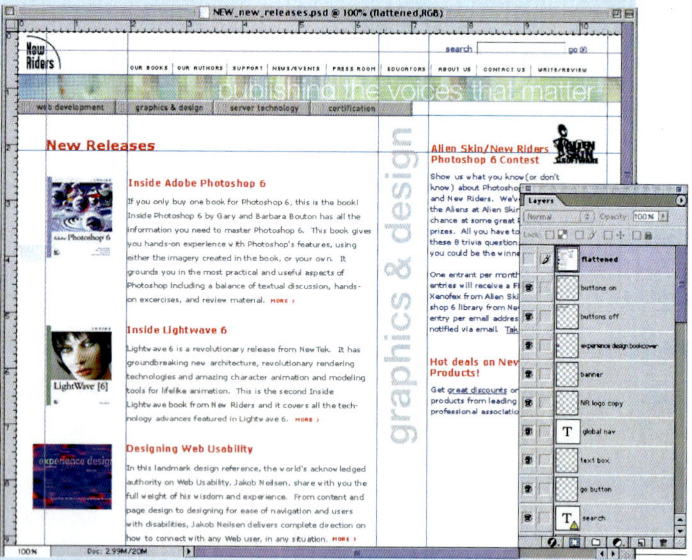

< **5.9**

The home page (top) and a secondary page (bottom) in progress. Each is its own layered file, complete with naming and text carefully called out. The clearly labeled layers indicate rollover states and functionality. Make sure to include a reference layer that contains the entire file flattened. Production designers will need it.

to design them all if they are based on similar styles and attributes. Take care to note standards in the Style Guide (discussed later in this chapter) so that the production designers can improvise if necessary.

Files should go to production as clearly labeled layered Photoshop or Fireworks files that call out all functionality (including on/off/over states) and that contain placeholders or dummy text for content **[5.9]**. Make sure your graphic templates include all the information that production will need to successfully turn the file into an HTML page.

Fonts can be a big issue when creating graphic templates for handoff. Visual designers usually work on Macs, but production workstations tend to be on PCs. Plus, production designers rarely have the same font libraries that visual designers use. As a result, production designers may not be able to work with unrendered, editable text. Consider purchasing the fonts included in the final design for the production team, or at least make sure the production designers have access to a Mac. Regardless, make certain that the visual designers retain a copy of the file in its pristine, unrendered, unflattened (layers intact) state in the likely event that changes have to be made (and there will almost certainly be additions and changes during maintenance as the site grows). Incomplete graphic templates, whether due to font issues or lack of called-out information, will slow down production. Carefully checking over these files before handing them off to production is advised.

CREATING A DESIGN STYLE GUIDE

Every page on your redesigned site is different, and yet each contains global elements. Maintaining consistency should be a priority. Clearly establish rollovers for all states, linking colors, fonts, headers, and HTML size text. Your production designers shouldn't have to ask too many questions.

A Style Guide is a key element for postlaunch maintenance, but it is also extremely helpful for reference as the pages are being built out in production. Created in two parts by both the design team and the production team (one part per team), a Style Guide can be in-depth or very simple — it depends on how much standardization and direction you want to give for the lifecycle of your redesign and, of course, on budget and resources. The more detailed the Style Guide is, the better insured the site is against the almost certain eventuality of design breakdown during maintenance (for more on maintenance see Phase 5: Launch). Clients often take over the maintenance of their own sites, and usually they are not designers. Help them.

A style guide forms the basis for any integrated content management system.

Asset Control

Keep track of all purchased images — which image came from which stock house. Even when putting together comps, make a note of image origin because you never know which design direction will make the final cut. When presenting concepts to clients, it should be made very clear that the image they are falling in love with could cost them $800 each year for site usage plus additional costs if they want to use it for printing and marketing. Let clients know their options (that other stock images exist), and perhaps they can use a slightly less riveting image that is copyright free for an under-$100 one-time fee. Educate clients early... before opinions lock in. Everyone will save much time and trouble if they understand how usage rights work before the design is approved.

Be sure to get information on all photos and illustrations used. Turn this information over to the client. The Details and Assumptions of your project plan should clearly state that outside costs for photography are not part of the estimate. Also state that obtaining usage rights is the client's responsibility, especially if the client is planning to further use any of the site images (for example, for marketing brochures, mailers, etc.). Today's online stock photography sites (for example, www.gettyimages.com, www.comstock.com, and www.thinkstock.com) have increased functionality to create a streamlined usage acquisition process.

We recommend that you include a core set of components in your Style Guide, as shown in the accompanying chart. How you lay out the Style Guide is entirely up to you. We recommend that it be both visual and informative **[5.10]**. The visual design Style Guide is only the first half of this document. After production is completed, as part of the handoff to maintenance, the HTML production designers will complete the Style Guide with detailed production information.

Standardized treatments for global elements and graphics — rollover states, colors, font choice sizes, headers, background functionality — all need to be established (they will probably be implemented site-wide using style sheets) so that they can be applied across all pages. In addition to defining graphic treatments for global elements, also address any specific design issues that weren't defined and approved in the look and feel. These include items that appear on one page but not another, a random form, a pop-up screen, or an error message. Plus, there might be additional graphics that weren't designed into the final look and feel. And, of course, changes will come in with final content. Without standards for all elements, everyone will generate his or her own way of handling not-yet-standardized issues.

These treatments are not necessarily signed-off on by the client; rather, the client approves the pages that incorporate the established standards. This system of standards is established and approved by the design team to ensure that consistency is maintained throughout this phase, graphic template creation, and after launch during maintenance. Encourage communication among members of your design team so that standardized issues only need to be decided once; create a new standard and then move on. HTML production designers should not have to get too creative.

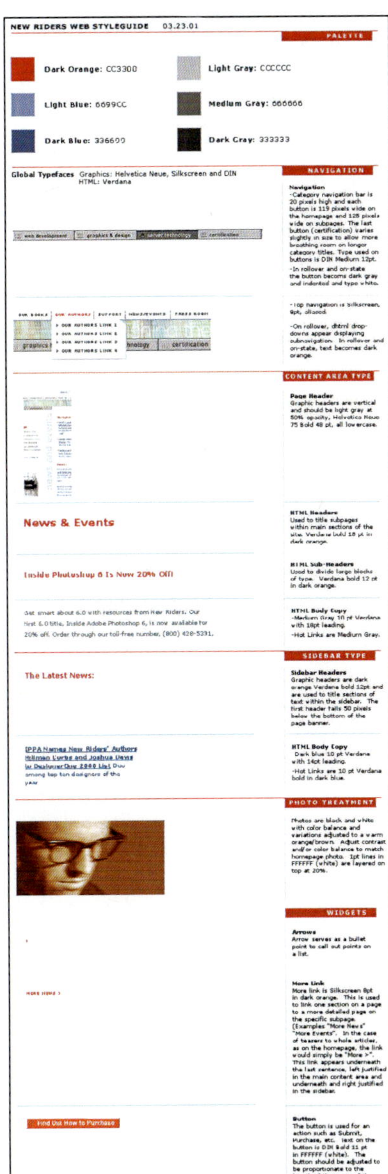

5.10 >

This basic design Style Guide is presented in HTML.

RECOMMENDED STYLE GUIDE COMPONENTS	
SPECIFICATIONS	
Page dimensions	Specify target window size, viewable and maximized. Specify whether liquid pages or fixed width.
Headers	Include navigation and subnavigation callouts such as styles for active vs. inactive states, dimensions, logo and/or tag-line inclusion, banner specifications (if applicable), text sizes and styles for graphic vs. HTML headers, etc.
Colors	Specify hex numbering for the background, main palette, and accents. Clearly indicate which colors get applied to navigation headers, what color for text when background color changes (if it does), what color for buttons, bullets, arrows, stars, and other graphic accents. Be sure to specify all body text/content and links.
HTML text	Describe all text treatments, including color and/or specific HTML font (by name) or size, and include usage for linking.
GRAPHIC TREATMENT	
Graphic type	Identify all graphic type styles. Name the graphical fonts and the HTML fonts. Log point sizes, colors, and any special kerning or leading.
Photo/image treatment	Specify any Photoshop or Fireworks actions (for example, edge or border treatments such as feathering or keylines, or special filters). Also be sure to specify how the photos appear on the HTML page. Are there any standard gutters or spacers? Any other images that always accompany photos?
Embellishments	Describe the treatments for buttons, lines, arrows, and other dingbats. Where and how can they be used? Specify the rules. Otherwise, they will get used in ways the designers never intended.

PHASE 3 CHECK-OFF LIST

Creating

- ☐ Review site goals
- ☐ Develop concepts
- ☐ Present designs
- ☐ Gather feedback

Confirming

- ☐ Confirm navigation and content
- ☐ Test functionality

Handing Off

- ☐ Create graphic templates
- ☐ Create a design Style Guide

PHASE 3 SUMMARY

Visual design is indeed the fun part of the Core Process — watching a design take shape is always exciting. During this phase, the designers create the visual interface: the first thing the world sees when visiting the redesigned site, the first experience the audience has with the client's brand. Thanks to all your preparatory planning from Phase 1: Define and Phase 2: Structure, this "face" of the redesigned site accurately represents the desired tone, the stated goals, and the established structure of the site in a visual format that is ready to be sliced and optimized. As important as the creative product, you have tested functionality in anticipation of Phase 4: Build, and you have confirmed your information design assumptions through testing. On all levels, the designed interface is ready to build and integrate.

But why the rigid process? This is the creative phase; why not simply coach the design team a bit so that they practice Smart Design and then let them do their thing? Here's why: Although visual web design is unquestionably about creativity, it is also about problem solving. It is about effectively communicating information through an appealing and appropriate design that is meaningful to the audience and that also works within technical and budgetary constraints — and doing it all on time.

Staying streamlined is important to the bottom line, and visual design is the spot in the Core Process where both scope and budget can expand out of control. A hundred things can go wrong: Your client may never be happy, the content isn't working, the visual designers create the perfect graphic interface but they go 100 hours over budget, etc. Designing with accessibility and standards in mind from the beginning of the creative process will ensure proper integration at the Build phase. And by sticking with the Core Process and being diligent about tracking and logging hours, the project has a good shot of staying on target.

The next phase is Build and Integrate, the nuts and bolts of the project. If visual design has been done right, the next phase, while hard work, will flow very smoothly.

gotomedia, inc.

Company: gotomedia, inc.
URL: www.gotomedia.com
Design Team: gotomedia in-house
User Experience Director: Kelly Goto

Creative Director: Serena Howeth
Designer: Craig Drake
CSS Production: Rachel Kalman, Jeffrey Chaing
Content Manager: Subha Subramanian

gotomedia, inc., is a strategic consulting firm specializing in user experience and branding. The San Francisco-based firm has worked on successful integration of usability, visual design, and appropriate technologies for web-based applications, embedded devices, and websites.

<PREVIOUS>

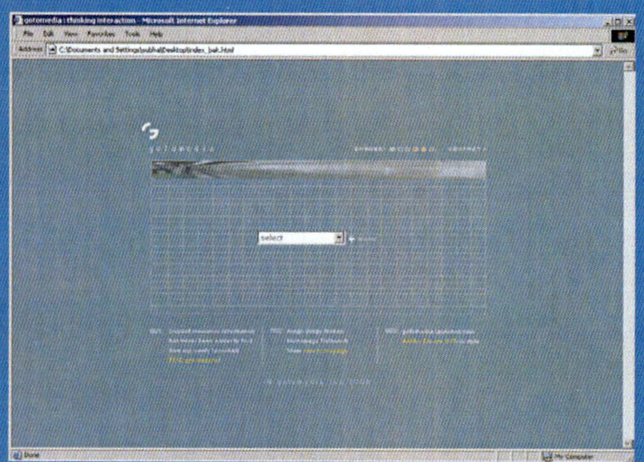

GOTOMEDIA.COM [OLD] was a brochure site with a single point of navigation with no flash or extraneous design. The site, created and launched in 2001, did little to highlight the company's expertise or portfolio.

<CURRENT>

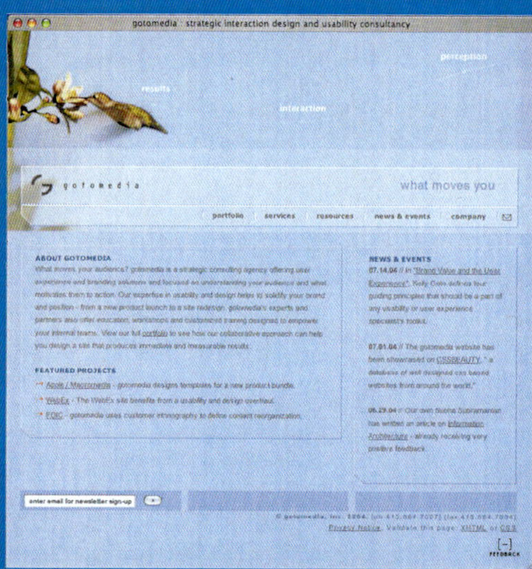

GOTOMEDIA.COM [REDESIGNED] bridges the gap between usability, aesthetics, and functionality. The new site separates content from functionality, using XHTML and CSS for positioning and layout.

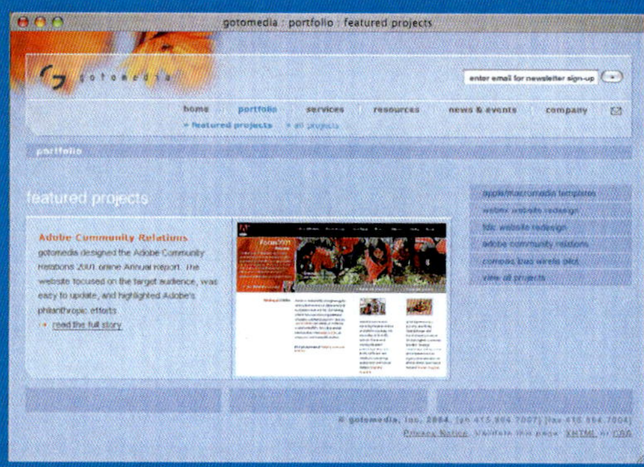

GOTOMEDIA.COM PROJECT PAGE [REDESIGNED] generates random profiled case studies that are also available in detailed format for easy reviewing.

Results: A site that delivers on all three fronts: It's easy to use, aesthetically inspiring, and functionally well designed. Readership of the site increased by more than 40% in the first quarter since launch and continues to grow weekly.

> Readdress your audience capabilities and project goals before building. Use the appropriate technology — not necessarily the latest and greatest.

Phase 4: Build and Integrate 06

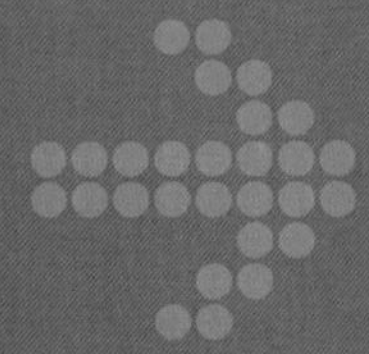

Phase 4: Build and Integrate

With the legwork and planning of the site essentially completed, now is the time to build. Phase 4 is where the actual production happens. You have defined and structured the project and then designed the visual interface. Here is where you put together all the pieces. If this were a house you were constructing instead of a website, consider the end use — summer cabin, single-family home or multiunit apartment building — and match the approach and complexity to the structure you are building.

WHAT THIS CHAPTER COVERS		
PLAN	**BUILD AND INTEGRATE**	**TEST**
> Assessing Project Status > Establishing Guidelines > Setting File Structure	> Slicing and Optimization > Creating HTML Templates and Pages > Implementing Light Scripting > Creating and Populating Pages > Integrating Backend Development (if Applicable)	> Understanding Quality Assurance Testing > Conducting QA Testing > Idenfitying, Prioritizing and Fixing Bugs > Conducting a Final Check

This phase is divided into three sections — Plan, Build and Integrate, and then Test — a production workflow aimed at keeping the project's coding and construction on track. Whether your budget is over $100,000 or under $10,000 or anywhere in between, the steps delineated here work for all web projects — redesigns and initial designs alike. Either way, your goal is simple: practice streamlined coding and build your site in the most appropriate and effective manner.

Choosing the right approach to the technology, tools, and expertise necessary to build your site is a more involved task than it was only a few years ago. Since we are no longer operating in a straight HTML coding environment, our solutions need to consider multiple factors. This chapter is not about how to code, but how to approach site building in a manner that helps you make the best choices up front, thus leading to the most successful implementation in the end.

ASSESSING PROJECT STATUS

Before production actually starts, take a moment to review the project's status. Did the scope increase? Is the project on budget? Has the all-important content arrived? And is your team ready for the production task ahead?

Now that the visual interface is designed and your project's technical parameters are set, reassess your team's coding capabilities. Since the web is driven by HTML, we assume that you or someone on your team has a solid understanding of the HTML process. This can be through pure hand coding (using BBEdit or other text editors) or by using a WYSIWYG editor (such as Adobe GoLive, Macromedia Dreamweaver, or Microsoft FrontPage). But here's the big question: What is the level of that understanding? If you are not qualified to make the assessment, find someone who is.

Coordinating web production takes both ability and experience. Depending on your team's level of expertise, you will need to determine the true level of complexity — or sheer scope — that the site production team can handle. For example, some legacy (inherited and outdated) websites have hundreds if not thousands of pages that need to be updated and redesigned. This behemoth job may require a dozen or more technical resources, many of whom do not need to be experts in HTML but may require some training, a hands-on supervisor, and a clear set of instructions such as a comprehensive Style Guide. If you are creating a 20- to 40-page brochure site with light JavaScript, you can probably get away with using a WYSIWYG editor. However, if the site is more complex (intricate tables, CSS and/or XML, additional scripting and/or DHTML implementation), you will need to have the knowledge to troubleshoot problems along the way. This usually means utilizing people with a fluid understanding of HTML, CSS, DHTML, and JavaScript, and who can understand the code well enough to tweak HTML and troubleshoot during the production process.

While moving into a Content Management System (CMS) or to Java Server Pages (JSP) is a more complex process than we go into in this book, all of these project types have one thing in common: the need to build HTML templates and to integrate the components into the final site. Whatever your need or situation, determining your team's abilities and the skill level necessary for the project at hand is a challenge.

Additionally, before any coding truly begins, a final just-before-production review of audience needs (platform, browsers, screen size, connection speed), technology (plug-ins, scripting, backend needs), and redesign goals (page download size, accessibility goals, search engine optimization) can only help. You will have to address myriad questions about servers, directory structure, and any technical specifics that may have been left until this phase. The Client Spec Sheet, presented in this chapter, will help.

Your goal? No misinterpretation of user capabilities or project goals. No duplication of efforts.

Conversion of Legacy Sites

Do you have hundreds, if not thousands, of pages to convert into the new site standards? Bummer. It's hardly a consolation, but you are far from alone. Unfortunately, there is no quick fix to update and streamline your code or the layout of the pages. You will need to carefully audit your site to see how consistent the current markup is and then determine a strategy of search and replace. Break the site into sections and hit it piece by piece. Accept that this might be part of a multiyear process, depending on the extent of your redesign.

< PLAN
> Assessing Project Status
> Establishing Guidelines
> Setting File Structure

To CSS or not to CSS?

The movement to separate content from presentation isn't abstract, it's happening. Now, with the addition of Cascading Style Sheets, a coder can build a page's look and feel, color, and style separately from the actual content (text) being presented. In most cases, CSS coding enables what we call a "graceful degradation" of look and feel. If the audience is using an older browser or platform, the page will still have the same general appearance, but will perhaps lose some of the finer details. CSS is a big buzzword, and it might be the right move for your site, but it might not be necessary. As with any technology, make sure it fits your needs and goals.

ESTABLISHING GUIDELINES

Establishing clear guidelines for HTML production during the initiation of a web redesign project helps to answer questions and avoid costly backtracking. The Client Spec Sheet can help set parameters for audience capabilities and technical standards for the site. This is a worksheet or a checklist. Either way, it is long and detailed and technical. When questioned about technical parameters, the client will usually say, "I don't know. You're the expert. You tell me." Or the client may request CSS and XML simply because they are catch phrases embedded in his thinking. There might be no valid reason for the use of these technologies, or either might work. Pros will have to be weighed against cons to determine the best solution. You will usually need to make this call, though some discussion is likely necessary.

For instance, the project manager or lead production designer might have to explain the differences and cross-browser stability issues of using DHTML pull-down menus (using graphics) versus using CSS to set styles for menus and rollovers. Or the client's audience may have browser, platform, or connection-speed limitations. Even though that client may want their site to have Flash or DHTML, it may not make sense if their audience is all still using 4.*x* browsers on dial-up connections. And there may be redesign goals (lighten page load time, make site more accessible to lower-end browser, etc.) that will determine what should and should not be used on the site. Often the answers from the Tech Spec sheet will dictate the appropriate direction to take.

The Client Spec Sheet is available for download from www.web-redesign.com. Due to its length, we could not show it in its entirety in this book, so we show only the first two parts: Target Specifications, and Functionality and Features (see worksheet on next page). All told, it is five parts long, as follows:

Part 1: Target Specifications

Part 2: Functionality and Features

Part 3: Design and Layout

Part 4: File Structure and Directory Preferences

Part 5: Server and Hosting Information

As tedious and daunting as going through the Client Spec Sheet may be, the information needs to be addressed and answered. Because handing this worksheet to a client with the expectation of a meaningful response is akin to daydreaming about the lottery, it is far more realistic to simply schedule a meeting between the techiest client-side person and your team's production lead. (The project manager may or may not be as technically savvy.) This worksheet will help you articulate and identify the technical parameters of your site redesign, including specific questions regarding target audience connectivity capabilities, browser versions, functionality, and actual file structure. Get all the information you can and get it back to the team for analysis before the visual designers start developing concepts and definitely before the production starts building.

Scope Expectations Meet Scope Reality

An estimate of 100 hours can easily turn into 300 hours if the complexity of the site has been underestimated. In Phase 1: Define, you estimated the project's budget based on the projected scope. Did you plan on 50 pages and now there are 120, or are you still on target? Assess. Has your scope grown, either through Scope Creep or as a result of client-requested changes and/or additions? Does the client have unrealistic expectations for accessibility standards or cross-browser perfection? If so, you will need to either increase the budget or downsize the allocation of hours... or take a loss. Regardless, if you haven't yet addressed potential budget changes with your client, do it now — before you start coding. And make sure you have included resources for QA along with the time necessary for fixes.

Do a project-wide time check. You should have been tracking your hours on a weekly basis, so this should be a relatively easy assessment. How much of your allocated time and resources have you used up? Are you on budget? Do you have the time left in your budget to comfortably complete the site? Knowing how many resources and hours are necessary to complete a project's production and QA is regularly one of the gray areas in project estimating. The hard truth? Most things that appear to be simple are not and will take much longer than you estimate. Coding an HTML page or template can take a few hours or a few days — it is one of the factors contributing to Scope Creep that is extremely difficult to gauge until actual production begins.

HTML Expertise

Although this chapter concerns HTML, it is not about how to code, the ins and outs of HTML, coding theory, or advanced scripting implementation. We focus on the redesign workflow process and how it relates to the actual site production — keeping your project moving smoothly, staying on schedule and on budget. For guides to hands-on coding, seek alternative resources such as *HTML & Web Artistry 2: More Than Code* (New Riders, 2002) by Susan Harris and Natalie Zee or *Creative HTML Design.2* (New Riders, 2001) by Lynda Weinman. Online resources include Web Monkey (www.webmonkey.com). For CSS, the definitive guide is *Eric Meyer on CSS: Mastering the Language of Web Design* by Eric Meyer (New Riders, 2002). Also highly recommended are *Designing with Web Standards* by Jeffrey Zeldman (New Riders, 2003), *Web Design in a Nutshell* by Jennifer Niederst (O'Reilly and Associates, 2001) and *HTML for the World Wide Web with XHTML and CSS; Visual Quick Start Guide, Fifth Edition* by Elizabeth Castro (Peachpit Press, 2002.)

CHAD KASSIRER ON KNOWING YOUR CLIENT BEFORE YOU CODE

Clear communication with the client is the key to a successful web project. Before beginning the production process, it is important to have agreed on and signed off on two things: a composite of the target audience and the client's expectations concerning the site production details. To assist with this process, I rely on a checklist, such as the Client Spec Sheet. Ideally, this document is administered shortly after the project has been kicked off. This way, there is one central document that can serve as a guideline for everyone contributing to the building process. Not only does this assist in all phases of the process from information architecture to design to production, it also establishes some necessary parameters for the site's requirements and identifies possible limitations early on.

It is every web designer's, programmer's, and production engineer's goal to create a website that looks and works the same for every user. However, with the numerous possible combinations of platforms, browsers, connection speeds, and monitor resolutions, this is nearly impossible to accomplish. To decide the best way to design and build the website, you need to identify the target audience. Once this is established, you can tailor the site to best suit this audience's needs before being concerned about other users. This is not to say that no one other than your target audience is important, but the client's priorities need to be established. These priorities will impact decisions made during the production process. A more realistic goal is to make the site as close to perfect as possible for the target audience while still being functional for everyone else.

By initiating a conversation at the start of the project, a dialog is created between production and the client. During this conversation, the client's expectations and preferences can be discussed before deciding the direction the client wishes to take and documenting this on the Client Spec Sheet. The production lead, as the integrator of design and engineering, uses this document as a reference for making decisions during the design and production phases. When used properly, the Client Spec Sheet is extremely useful and saves time and money by eliminating ambiguities, which cause unnecessary delays and frustration.

I recommend using the Client Spec Sheet early in the process. It documents and clarifies to everyone what the initial goals of the project are, even if changes are made during the process. In case the requirements or expectations of the client change, the Client Spec Sheet also serves as a contract to refer to when additional costs are required or disputed. By using the Client Spec Sheet as a reference to help guide your decisions throughout the project, you can build a site with the client in mind.

Chad Kassirer has been managing website production since 1996. As founder of What? Design (www.whatdesign.com) *and as the former director of production for web development shops Red Eye Digital Media and Idea Integration/San Francisco, Chad has played a key role in the production process for several award-winning websites. Chad also teaches HTML and JavaScript workshops through the University of Hawaii's Outreach College.*

TARGET SPECIFICATIONS (PART 1)

Establishing clear audience specifications enables production to have a targeted goal. It is often difficult, if not impossible, to maintain consistency of experience from one browser or platform to the next. It is important for the HTML production team to understand not only the target and user but also who can be left behind.

	Existing Site Specs (Check One Below)	Priority/Target (Check One Below)	Others to Support (Specify One or More)
Resolution	☐ 378×544 (web tv) ☐ 640×480 ☐ 800×600 ☐ 1024×768 ☐ Other (explain)	☐ 378×544 (web tv) ☐ 640×480 ☐ 800×600 ☐ 1024×768 ☐ Other (explain)	☐ 378×544 (web tv) ☐ 640×480 ☐ 800×600 ☐ 1024×768 ☐ Other (explain)
Browsers	☐ Netscape/Mozilla ☐ Internet Explorer ☐ AOL ☐ Opera ☐ Safari ☐ Other (explain)	☐ Netscape/Mozilla ☐ Internet Explorer ☐ AOL ☐ Opera ☐ Safari ☐ Other (explain)	☐ Netscape/Mozilla ☐ Internet Explorer ☐ AOL ☐ Opera ☐ Safari ☐ Other (explain)
Browser Versions	Browser versions are always changing. For the latest breakdown, refer to upsdell.com/BrowserNews/find.htm and then identify existing specs, target, and others to support. Other sources for up-to-the-minute information follow below.		
Platforms	☐ Macintosh ☐ Windows ☐ Other (explain)	☐ Macintosh ☐ Windows ☐ Other (explain)	☐ Macintosh ☐ Windows ☐ Other (explain)
Connection Speed	☐ DSL/cable ☐ T1/T3 ☐ Dial-up 56.6K and lower ☐ Other (explain)	☐ DSL/cable ☐ T1/T3 ☐ Dial-up 56.6K and lower ☐ Other (explain)	☐ DSL/cable ☐ T1/T3 ☐ Dial-up 56.6K and lower ☐ Other (explain)
Page Download Size (typical page)	☐ 30K and under ☐ 30 to 80K (typical page) ☐ 80K (graphic heavy, animation) ☐ 100K+ (not recommended unless a high-bandwidth site)	☐ 30K and under ☐ 30 to 80K (typical page) ☐ 80K (graphic heavy, animation) ☐ 100K+ (not recommended unless a high-bandwidth site)	☐ 30K and under ☐ 30 to 80K (typical page) ☐ 80K (graphic heavy, animation) ☐ 100K+ (not recommended unless a high-bandwidth site)

For the latest info:
Resolution: www.dreamink.com/design5.shtml
Browsers: www.upsdell.com/BrowserNews
Connection speeds: www.websiteoptimization.com/bw/0402

<<< This worksheet is available in full (all five parts) for download at www.web-redesign.com >>>

FUNCTIONALITY AND FEATURES (PART 2)

The addition of specific technologies that allow greater functionality can greatly enhance your site. These same features can exclude a percentage of your audience, however, and can cause production scope to increase, usually due to unforeseen technical errors and troubleshooting. Please identify which features you already have on your site and how they are currently being used. Please also indicate which features you are looking to add and how you foresee them being used.

	Preferences/Status (Current and New Site)		Issues	Comments and Usage Details (How It Is or Will Be Used)
Flash	☐ Used on current site ☐ Yes (use on new site)	☐ Will not be using ☐ Not sure (list comments)	Requires a plug-in. May cause accessibility/download issues; may require an alternative version of the site/animation to be built. Requires additional code to deal with user accessibility and search engine optimization issues.	
Cascading Style Sheets (CSS)	☐ Used on current site ☐ Yes (use on new site)	☐ Will not be using ☐ Not sure (list comments)	Does not require a plug-in. Allows for global updating of fonts, colors, styles, and positioning. Supported by most 4.x browsers and above although 4.x browser support is limited.	
Dynamic HTML (DHTML)	☐ Used on current site ☐ Yes (use on new site)	☐ Will not be using ☐ Not sure (list comments)	Does not require a plug-in. Used to create special features such as dynamic menus. Supported by most 4.x browsers and above. May require additional testing, programming, and QA.	
JavaScript	☐ Used on current site ☐ Yes (use on new site)	☐ Will not be using ☐ Not sure (list comments)	Does not require a plug-in. Supported by most 4.x browsers and above. Can add noticeable download time.	
Pop-Up Windows	☐ Used on current site ☐ Yes (use on new site)	☐ Will not be using ☐ Not sure (list comments)	May require use of JavaScript; supported by most 4.x browsers and above. Inconsistent size and placement depending on platform and browser. Newer browsers — as well as third-party applications — now include user settings to disable this functionality.	
Forms	☐ Used on current site ☐ Yes (use on new site)	☐ Will not be using ☐ Not sure (list comments)	Requires additional programming and integration. Specific and detailed information about the server and its installed applications is necessary to determine complexity.	
Frames/ Framesets	☐ Used on current site ☐ Yes (use on new site)	☐ Will not be using ☐ Not sure (list comments)	Causes difficulty printing and navigating and may incur extra programming and QA costs, especially with multiframe setup. Causes difficulty for search engines. Not supported by many older browsers.	

FUNCTIONALITY AND FEATURES (PART 2)			
	Preferences/Status (Current and New Site)	**Issues**	**Comments and Usage Details (How It Is or Will Be Used)**
Inline Frame/ iFrame	☐ Used on current site ☐ Will not be using ☐ Yes (use on new site) ☐ Not sure (list comments)	Not supported by 4.x browsers except IE. Search Engine spiders will index the content contained with the iFrame as a separate page (requiring additional code to redirect Search Engine links to the appropriate page). Each browser displays the iFrame (not the content) differently.	
Video/Audio	☐ Used on current site ☐ Will not be using ☐ Yes (use on new site) ☐ Not sure (list comments)	Requires plug-ins. May involve download and processing time. If using any type of media, please list as much detail as possible, including type of media, format, and desired output.	
Output Media ☐ Screen ☐ Print ☐ Aural ☐ Handheld ☐ TV ☐ Projection ☐ Braille/ embossed	☐ Used on current site ☐ Will not be using ☐ Yes (use on new site) ☐ Not sure (list comments)	Used to display page content for specific media types. Is part of CSS and may need additional testing and QA.	

<<< This worksheet is available in full (all five parts) for download at www.web-redesign.com >>>

Readdressing Audience Capabilities

Refocus on your target audience. You are producing the site based on their capabilities, and you cannot translate the visual interface into HTML unless you know your parameters: target operating systems, browsers, monitors, and connection speeds. Use the results from the Client Spec Sheet as a guide.

Checking Content Status

Content should be in — all of it. But chances are it won't be. Back in Phase 1: Define, you were clear: Content must be in before production can commence in earnest. Alert your client that the time has come, that a content freeze is imminent (meaning no more changes to content). For larger sites with a longer template-to-final-integration process, or for a planned phase-in launch of site sections, the content may arrive in staggered delivery. Maintain tight deadlines for content whether in planned batches or if expected all at once.

Announce to the client early in the process, as early as with the initial proposal that accompanies the budget, that if/when content is late, production will be held up and cost overruns will commence. Billing for overruns is never painless, but it will be far more viable if you warn the client of consequences ahead of time.

SCOPE: ARE YOU ON TARGET?	
Sitemap	How big is the site? How many pages/templates? Is it what you planned for?
Visual Complexity	Is the slicing a nightmare or fairly straightforward? Is it set up for a tableless structure using CSS, is it dependent on nested tables, or will you be employing a hybrid approach, some CSS and some table-based?
Light Scripting Needs	Rollovers, pull-down menus, form validations, pop-up windows, rotating and/or random images, time and/or date stamps, browser detection/sniffers, etc. What did you plan for when you initially budgeted/scheduled? What are you now slated to include? Do the two match up?
Backend Engineering	Are the engineers on budget/schedule? Have the requirements been adequately defined, and do they still match the scope/cost expectations?

Accessibility

Imagine your only web access is through a browser that does not support images. Pick any site — if the navigational aids and buttons don't have descriptive ALT text, you won't be able to differentiate between graphics.

The push to support full-access websites is not new. This set of standards, led by the World Wide Web Consortium (www.w3c.org), aims to connect all people to the web regardless of ability, including the handicap of older browsers or outdated technology. Web accessibility and compliance with Section 508 of the federal Rehabilitation Act — which requires that federal agencies' electronic and information technology be accessible to people with disabilities, including employees and members of the public — is essential for all government entities and a best practice for educational sites as well. Understanding accessibility needs before you start coding — especially if your site is legally bound to comply with accessibility standards — will avert the need for damage control later (for example, coding ALT text into 100 pages instead of having done it once at the outset on the HTML template).

Here are two free tools that can help you test your site for accessibility after it's up: Bobby and Macromedia's Section 508 Accessibility Suite.

Bobby (www.cast.org/bobby) is an online tool that rates your web page immediately. Enter a URL, and Bobby identifies the areas that are not accessible and will let you know if your images have proper ALT tags. It's fast and impressive; the results may surprise you ([6.1] and [6.2]). As a bonus, a full-featured commercial version of Bobby can be downloaded (for a fee) and run locally. Like UsableNet's Dreamweaver plug-in [6.3], the full version of Bobby can check entire folders or sites at once and generate compliance reports. Please note, however, that Bobby doesn't authenticate a site's compliancy — it merely gives an overview and a sense of where your site is at the time of analysis.

Dreamweaver MX and MX 2004 make it easy for designers and developers to understand and comply with web accessibility standards with features that include a reference guide, templates, code snippets, and a built-in accessibility validation tools. MX 2004 also includes features designed to handle the creation of accessible forms and data tables. Users of Dreamweaver 4 and Dreamweaver UltraDev 4 can also find free accessibility-checking extensions on the Dreamweaver Exchange.

For a great read on accessibility, see Joe Clark's book *Building Accessible Websites* (Pearson, 2002).

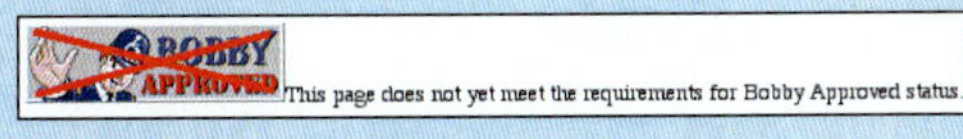

< 6.1 >

A "Bobby Approved" icon appears when a site meets all requirements for accessibility standards. When a site does not meet the standards, Bobby clearly does not approve and lists the site's errors as well as suggestions for improvement.

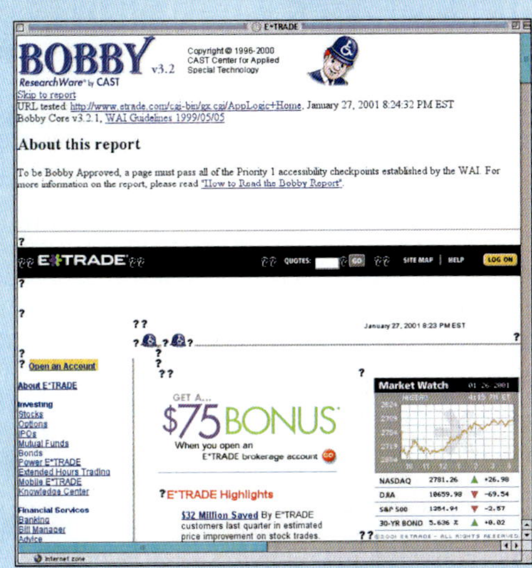

< 6.2 >

This screenshot shows the results of running a URL through Bobby. The question marks show areas that either are non-compliant to ADA standards for accessibility or could be improved upon.

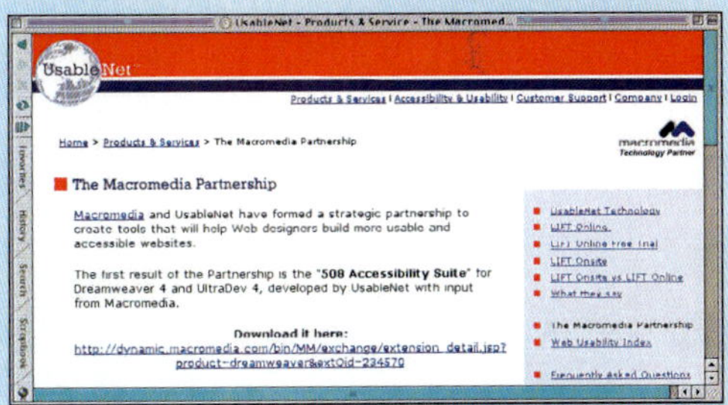

< 6.3 >

UsableNet.com and Macromedia team up to help check for accessibility.

Checking Design Status

Have the graphic templates for the site's main pages been finalized, approved, and turned over to production yet? If not, light a fire under your visual designers; they are holding up production. Set up a delivery schedule so that graphic files can be handed off in a phased process: Do the home page and a representative subpage first and then let production figure out the HTML templates before the remaining pages are delivered.

How many template pages need to be created? Use this simple test: If the page is unique, it needs a template. This includes the home page, of course, and generally all the top-level pages, plus one or more tertiary-level pages. Basically, as many pages as are necessary to create a comprehensive visual guide for the site as a whole, making sure to clearly establish the page structure, CSS, global elements, color and font treatments, and anything else that will need to be carried through the entire site in a consistent manner.

During Phase 3: Design, the visual design team met with production to ensure that the designer's vision could be feasibly carried out through Flash, DHTML, JavaScript, and/or straight HTML. By the first delivery of graphic templates from the visual designers to production, certain issues such as projected K-size download and potential optimization hiccups should be resolved.

Slippage and Consequences

Content will be late; this is predictable. Anticipate it. But what do you do when that magic date has passed, the content officially becomes late, and your production is compromised? After a few gentle reminders via phone and/or email, send a firm yet diplomatic email restating due dates, details, and the costs associated for each day the content is further delayed. What follows is an excerpt of a letter that addressed slippage as it was happening and spelled out the consequences:

> "... for clarification, we have determined some associated costs for the addition of the animated product demo and also for additional production work if our content delivery deadlines slip further.
>
> "We realize you have tight budget constraints and do not wish to incur extra charges unless absolutely necessary. As explained earlier, we have allocated resources for a particular timeframe in order to produce and complete your project, and this time window is quickly evaporating... "

Financial consequences were clearly outlined: For each day until the final content was delivered in full, a rate was applied for "holding" resources. The effect was dramatic. The first part of the content was delivered by the end of the week, and the rest of the project ran smoothly through launch. Should you find yourself seeing deadlines slip by, consider incorporating this slippage and consequences terminology into your workflow.

Confirming the Backend Integration Plan

Is your redesign a static site or a dynamic site? If static, and you are not involved with a backend engineering team, this section does not apply to you. If the site is dynamic, however, plan on having a meeting before production actually starts, a front-end and backend status update. Restate all technical specifications to all team members, review the technical requirements, confirm the integration plan, and clarify responsibilities. For more on backend integration, see Chapter 9: Working with Complex Functionality.

In reality, for internal teams and in-house engineering efforts, such organization is often unrealistic. But instead of haphazard emails, undocumented conversation, or communication akin to messages sent on paper airplanes (sticky notes, anyone?), establish a workable, realistic communication system for tracking on-the-fly changes. (Solid version control here is a must.) Document all that you can, prepare a schedule with deadlines and deliverables, and maintain some sense of sanity amidst what could easily become a three-ring circus.

SETTING FILE STRUCTURE

Often confused with site architecture (Phase 2: Develop Site Structure) by newbies and clients with just enough knowledge to make them dangerous, file structure is, in fact, simple — but very important — housekeeping. Starting out organized will help you stay organized, so make it a priority. (This is especially true for projects with multiple team members.) Although there is no best way to organize a site's file structure, different strategies support different goals (**[6.4]** and **[6.5]**).

For static sites, the file structure of pages will be mirrored in the URL in the browser's address window. For sites employing Content Management Systems however, most content gets dumped into a database, and the URL may be less reflective of hierarchy. Instead of www.site.com/ news/jan/2004/ article2.html, it may appear as www. site.com/news/ article=?2004_01_id02.html. Thus, the overall file structure becomes less important for the user insofar as being able to see where in the site they are. In these cases, it is doubly important for client and team to be in agreement as to how to organize directories so that links and file references (like images) do not have to be recoded at the time of integration.

The Client Spec Sheet asks about redesign specifics regarding existing HTML page-naming conventions and the existing file structure. Does the client want to leave things as they are, and if so,

Three File Structure Questions

Ask a few questions before you start to build. It will ensure a clean and focused directory.

1. How is the folder structure currently set up, and is there a client-desired reason for this method?
2. Does the folder structure follow the content structure in organization of the content?
3. Will the site employ a global images folder at the root level, or be separated into individual folders?

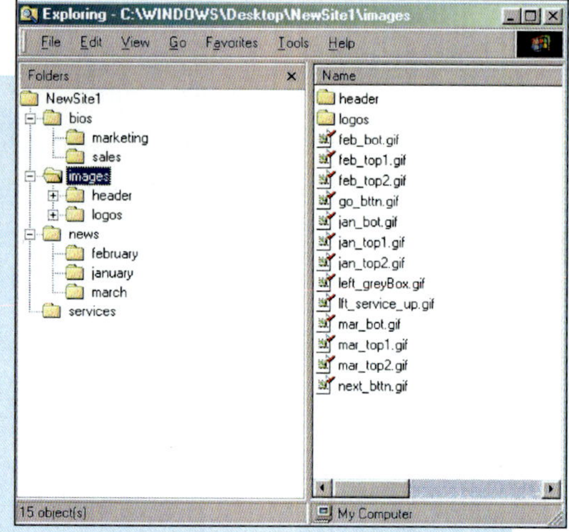

< 6.4

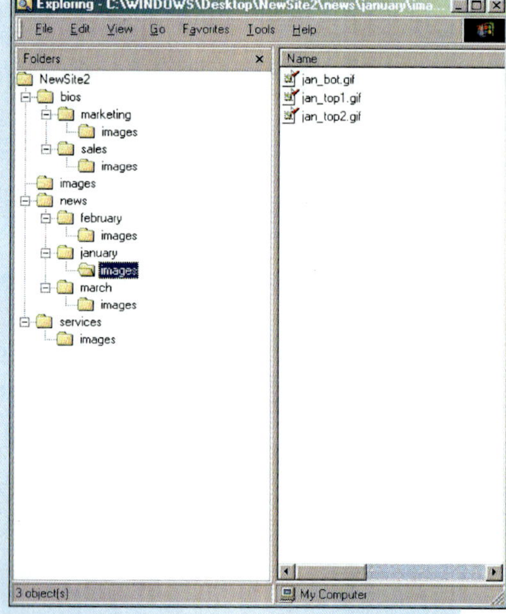

< 6.5

Two structures, different strategies. [6.4] has images listed at the root level, and [6.5] lists images within the current month folder. When to use which strategy totally depends on preference.

why? Whichever method is eventually decided on, it should be aligned with redesign and maintenance goals (such as how the site plans to add and archive postlaunch content).

Redesigning offers an opportunity to start over clean. Chances are, the HTML structure of the old site is a mess: files duplicated, images scattered among folders, old versions of files still up on the server.... Establish a logical, maintainable file structure for the redesign site. The goal? To start out as clean, organized, and scalable as possible.

File Structure and Scalability

How much growth (increased traffic, added content, new products) is anticipated in the 12 months following launch? Are you planning to add additional sections? How do you see them growing? By date? By topic?

When determining the file structure, know that it depends largely on how the client envisions the redesigned site growing and evolving. The plan you adopt for your file structure must be aligned with the anticipated maintenance, including logical archival of outdated content. Create subdirectories that will make sense to the maintenance team after launch and include file directory instructions as they pertain to archived or added pages in the Style Guide. Disorganization and clutter is a regular postlaunch occurrence in situations in which maintenance has been handed over to a new team. An organized file structure that anticipates growth and regular updating can help counter the almost-inevitable degradation of site organization. For setting the file structure, a few pieces of information that are essentially based on client preference should be known. For instance, will the redesign repurpose existing files and the existing file structure, or will it start from scratch? How often will updates be made? Daily? Quarterly? The Client Spec Sheet asks for this information.

The big question here is this: Does the client care? Possibly, but not likely. Does the client even understand? Maybe, but probably not. But whether dictated by the client or established by your team, the file structure should respond to and fit with the answers of the preceding questions. The goal? Be scalable. Stay organized.

SLICING AND OPTIMIZATION

After reviewing your information (the Plan part of this phase) and making sure your redesign project is on track, you are ready to start HTML production in earnest and begin to Build and Integrate. At this point in production, the graphic templates **[6.6]** are processed (sliced and optimized) into HTML elements (graphics) so that they can be put back together (spliced and coded).

Prior to production, during the design phase, before any visual design directions are finalized and approved, they must be reviewed by the production team to ensure that the files are, in fact, sliceable and optimizable under target-audience download requirements. Take this last opportunity to see if your page design can be streamlined to avoid endless nested tables; ideally, the pages are cleanly designed for streamlined HTML and CSS coding. Sometimes

BUILD AND INTEGRATE

> Slicing and Optimization

> Creating HTML Templates and Pages

> Implementing Light Scripting

> Creating and Populating Pages

> Integrating Backend Development

QUICK REFERENCE: STATIC VS. DYNAMIC	
Static Site: Front-End Only	Pages are prebuilt in their entirety and are viewed when referenced by a browser, usually using the .html or .htm extension.
Dynamic Site: Front-End and Backend Teams	Pages are created "on the fly," usually by pulling content-specific information from various places such as from a database. The site usually contains standard HTML pages as well. Additional code (ASP, JAVA, PERL) can be added to the HTML pages to allow for dynamic content population.

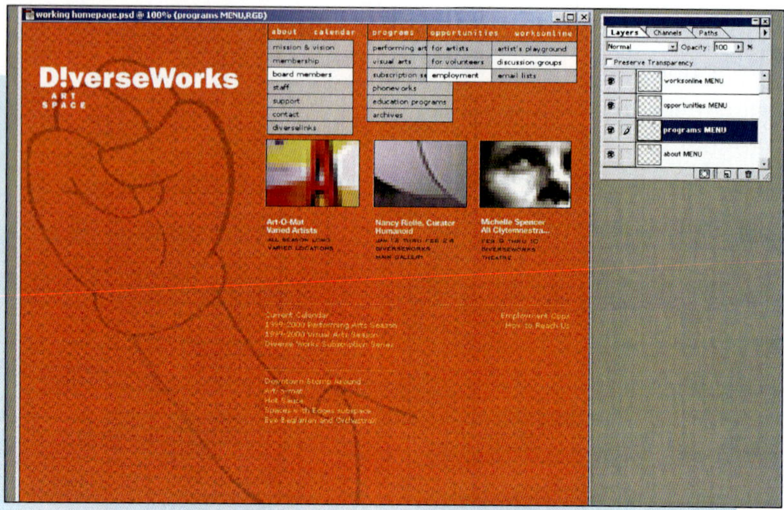

< 6.6

The graphic template for www.diverseworks.org is delivered to production from design as a layered Photoshop or Fireworks file. This file contains all the elements of the page, including all rollover states, each in its own layers. Shown here are the pull-down menu bar graphics shown in their "on" state.

slight design modification can drastically reduce the amount of time coding. Visual designers need to work closely with the HTML production team to determine the best way to slice the graphic templates so that the HTML tables or positioning using CSS can be constructed.

After the Photoshop/Fireworks files are handed off in a state that is producible, production does the actual slicing **[6.7]** and optimization **[6.8]** of the pieces. Note that sometimes, when budget and resources dictate, one designer may fulfill both visual design and production roles.

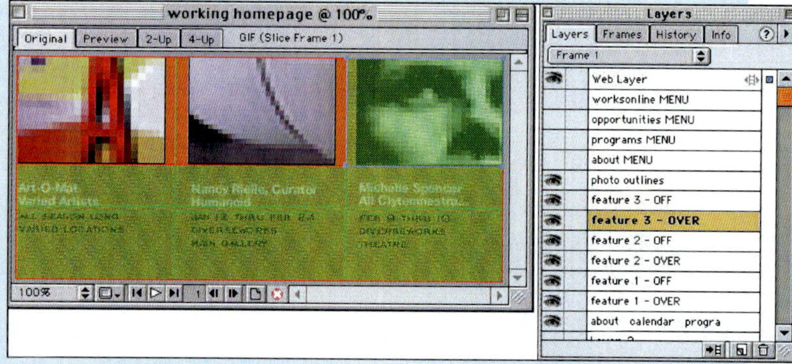

< 6.7 >

Graphic templates are divided into sections and sliced in either Fireworks or Photoshop. Clearly identified layers indicate on/off/over states or DHTML/JavaScript callouts.

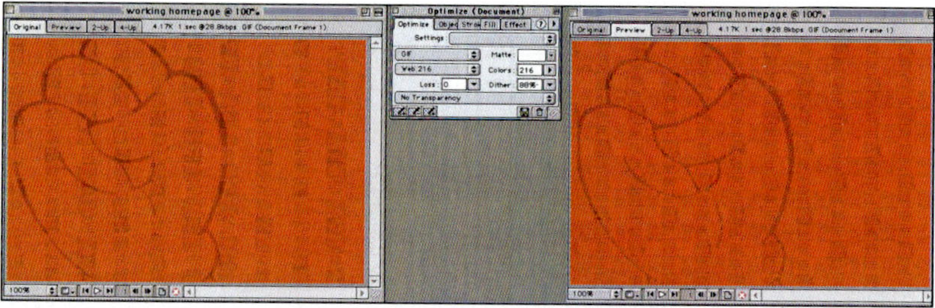

< 6.8 >

Before and after shots of a background image being optimized in Fireworks. The file size is reduced to 16K by reducing colors in GIF format.

CREATING HTML TEMPLATES AND PAGES

The first HTML template sets the standard for globals such as navigation, CSS, HTML font formatting, tag treatments), etc. Take the optimized graphics that were sliced from the graphic template, add any other elements that need to be included (including any light scripting that should be incorporated; light scripting is discussed next in this chapter), and build in HTML.

Test this file on various browsers and platforms. If you are not working with CSS, make sure the HTML tables don't break **[6.9]**. If you are working with a CSS layout, you may not need to worry about table breaking, but you will need to address graceful degradation: Does the layout hold in older browsers or across any targeted wireless devices? Keep in mind that this file will be your base. If it is faulty and you don't fix it here, its errors will propagate in every page saved from it. Note that this testing is not considered QA per se; it is simply standard procedure for the production designer to check for errors.

Save from this initial template to create a page — the first of many. This new page (no longer a template) becomes a designated page within the site and is ready to be populated with content, whether static or dynamic. These pages now can be linked and tested.

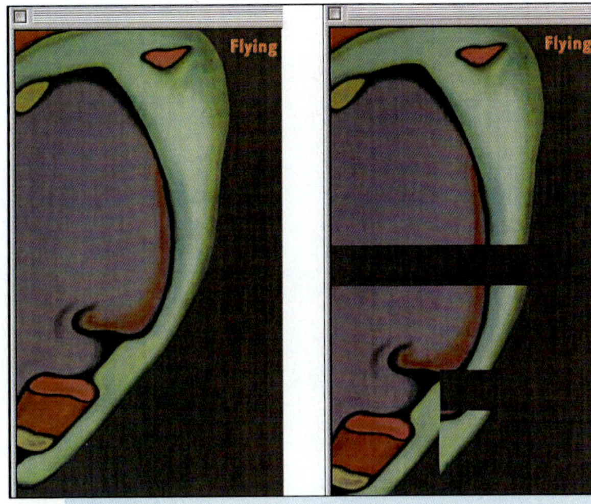

6.9 >

Large graphic elements often get sliced into pieces for easier download. Beware of tables breaking. Shown here: www.flyingsparkfurniture.com with a workable table (on the left) and during pre-QA troubleshooting.

A Few Definitions for the Uninitiated

Cascading Style Sheet (CSS) *n.* Also referred to simply as "style sheets," CSS separates the presentation of an HTML document from the actual content (text) on the page. Styles such as text size, color, and format are defined and applied across multiple pages on a website and are updated globally using that particular style. CSS allows more flexibility for designers and developers by giving them more control over formatting and positioning of text and page elements. In addition, it streamlines page downloading and is easier to update.

Content Management System (CMS) *n.* A tool used to create, modify, organize, and store information pertaining to the content (text and imagery) of a website. A CMS provides nonprogrammers with the capability to create, edit, or delete content on a website without requiring knowledge of HTML.

graphic template *n.* A layered, digital file (usually Photoshop or Fireworks) containing unrendered, editable text, built by a visual designer, that clearly indicates all information necessary for producing the design in HTML. Once a graphic template is sliced, optimized, and coded, it becomes an HTML template or page.

HTML template (also called **HTML shell**) *n.* An HTML page containing no page-specific content, built by the production designer by splicing together all the elements that were sliced and optimized from the graphic template. Visually matches the graphic template. (Utilized by production to create further files using the Save As command.)

optimize *v.* 1. To compress an image or code into as small a file size as possible to minimize download time. Usually saved in GIF or JPG format. 2. To webify, to make web ready.

slice *v.* To separate a graphic (or a portion of agraphic) into two or more images (usually either GIF or JPG). *n.* A sectioned-off area of the Photoshop or Fireworks file designated to be a single image (usually either GIF or JPG).

splice *v.* To reassemble GIF and/or JPG images in a seamless manner using HTML so that the file, when viewed on a browser, looks like the original graphic template.

unique page *n.* A web page that is structurally different than any other page contained within the site.

XHTML *n.* Stands for eXtensible Hypertext Markup Language. Basically, this is an XML-ized version of HTML. Some noticeable differences are the strict formatting conventions including case-sensitivity (all tags must be lowercase) and mandatory closing of all tags (e.g., <br> in HTML is written as <br/>, a self-closing element in XHTML).

XML *n.* Short for eXtensible Markup Language. A commonly used (W3C) standard to mark up HTML documents to allow for easy translation to web pages and other nonweb platforms (such as PDA, kiosks, etc.). Both HTML and XML use customized "tags" that allow flexibility in organizing and presenting information on the web and other nonweb devices.

As you build the HTML templates on which your individual pages will be based, the production designers will need to adhere to visual standards established during the Design phase and written into the Style Guide (see the end of Phase 3: Design). In anticipation of the QA testing you will need to conduct later in this phase, keep checking your work against all browsers and on both the Macs you are probably working on and the PCs most of your audience will use.

Including Includes

Is one of the reasons your site is being redesigned that it became cumbersome to upkeep? Sometimes a simple maintenance need like updating a copyright footer turns into such a mammoth job (as it would be on a site with hundreds of pages) that the updating task often goes undone. When building, you sometimes find yourself repeating things: bits of code, headers and footers, and so on across the entire site or at least on a majority of pages. Using the common example previously mentioned of a copyright footer, how do you change the year on every page? You can do one of the following:

1. Hand open each page (time consuming) and edit each. Reupload each page.
2. Do a global search-and-replace using an HTML editor. (This still requires at least spot-checking pages to ensure nothing was missed due to any code variations.) Reupload each page.
3. Use an include. Edit just one file. Reupload the single page.

An include (noun, not verb) is a chunk of text coded and stored separately but applied globally so that it only needs to be edited once. A JavaScript include is a repeating functionality. Rather than plugging the repeating code into every page, simply reference an external file that is saved on the server separately from the HTML page. No complicated nested frames are necessary. Includes require the SRC attribute (indicating where the file is kept on the server), which is not so different from an IMG tag (image indicator). It is even almost dynamic in this way, except that includes don't require a backend database. And as a bonus, you can have multiple includes on a page. However, using includes does add weight to a page and can slow loading, so use them only when necessary. Assess your priorities: Does ease of updating outweigh the quarter-second of loading? Probably yes, but it's worth the evaluation. Regardless, including an include streamlines future production and is a great feature for redesign projects for which upkeep was identified as a challenge on the old site.

Version Control

Make sure it is very clear to anyone with access to the active HTML files when a file is being worked on. This is, obviously, meant to prevent two or more team members from working on a file at the same time. Such miscommunication usually results in wasted time, overwritten files, and lost work. If you have two or more people working on the HTML, having an established method of version control in place facilitates efficiency. In its last several upgrades, Dreamweaver has included a handy feature that allows people to check in and check out files. Third-party programs such as SourceSafe, Perforce, and WebDAV might be appropriate for your workflow as well.

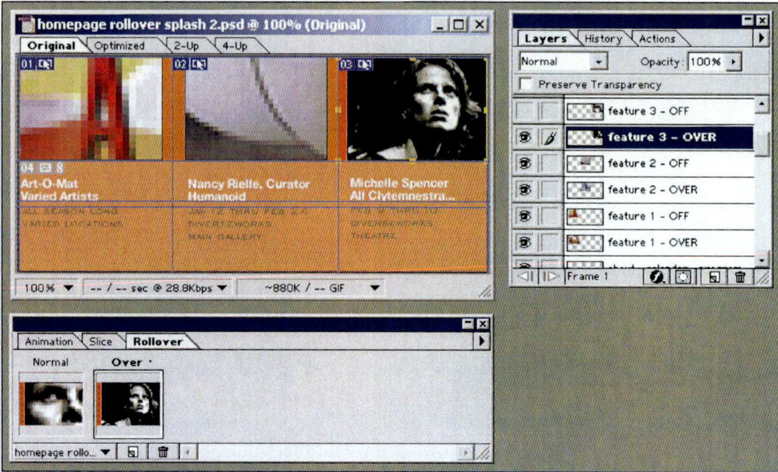

< **6.10**

On the home page of www.diverseworks.org, the rollover is a dithered close-up shot of artwork that rolls over to become sharp. ON and OFF states for the rollover are specified in the layers palette of the graphic template.

IMPLEMENTING LIGHT SCRIPTING

Rollovers, form validation, pull-down menus, pop-up windows — all are the result of light scripting. By "light," we mean essentially do-it-yourself or basic JavaScript that requires very little understanding of complex programming. Light scripting should not be confused with anything like JAVA, ASP, or PHP. Rather, it is standard functionality that appears in site after site, such as rollovers **[6.10]**. CSS can also be used to create rollovers; however, it is not widely browser supported (yet). Light JavaScript is code that is included as part of many of the previously mentioned software tool libraries, including Fireworks, Dreamweaver, and ImageReady, and it can also be "lifted," or shared, and slightly modified to fit to your site's needs.

As software improves, it should come as no surprise that implementing light scripting and special features (such as media requiring plug-ins) gets easier. If you used Fireworks to slice out and optimize your graphics templates, you were able to attach simple behaviors such as rollovers and image swapping as you optimized and exported. If you exported an HTML file of the graphics template, much of your light scripting is already done. However, modifying these scripts to serve a purpose for anything other than what they have specifically been designed for can be a difficult task given that the code is often written in a complex and hard-to-read manner.

Resources abound for code sharing. "Lift" JavaScript from any of these sites: javascript.internet.com, builder.com.com, developer.netscape.com, http://hotwired.lycos.com/webmonkey/programming/javascript/.

It is usually easier — and far cleaner — to code from scratch than to attempt to change the prefabricated, often-proprietary stuff.

Include all light scripting at this point in your workflow. Add browser sniffers and redirects. Drop in QuickTime or Flash files. Test all added functionality against specified browsers and against your audience's capabilities. Test, test, test. Look for errors. Yes, there is still QA coming up, but don't wait until then to catch bugs.

CREATING AND POPULATING PAGES

Your templates are done. Now it is time to use these files to create all the pages. As an external design studio, this may or may not be your responsibility. Oftentimes, you will hand off the HTML shells to the client, and they will create and link all the pages. If so, skip ahead to the section on QA and get ready to beta test. If not, it's up to you to punch out multiple pages based on your shells and build an alpha site, complete with working navigation and globals but with no page-specific content. Refer to your sitemap religiously when doing this; it will prove enormously helpful. When you are done you'll be ready to drop in content, suitable for client review.

Smaller Is Better

Yes, you are responsible for maintaining the K-size for the file. This includes more than just the K-size of the graphics involved; take note of HTML-page K-size (source code) and any outside programming. You have a target audience (and they might still be on modems), and now you have a "finished" piece. Too big? Go back and reoptimize. See if you can shave off a few bytes here and there. Make some decisions. Adjust.

Hand Coding vs. WYSIWYG (What You See Is What You Get)

They say hand coding is a lost art... or is it? Many projects require the knowledge and flexibility that comes with an advanced level of HTML expertise. For many of these projects, the HTML production designers create code one tag at a time — called "hand coding" — using programs such as BBEdit. Hand coding almost always results in "cleaner" code than WYSIWYG editors generate. HTML purists tend to be adamant about the crispness of their code, and even though WYSIWYG editors all can be edited in source code view, many coders avoid them because they tend to add extra and sometimes cumbersome and hard-to-revise proprietary code.

With recent versions, WYSIWYG editors have enabled individuals who are not HTML savvy (designers and nontechnical team members) to create HTML pages with drag-and-drop ease. Adobe GoLive and Macromedia Dreamweaver, the two industry-standard WYSIWYG editors, are each making huge strides to offer more than just an easy-to-use interface. One of the biggest advantages of WYSIWYG editors is saving time. Hand coding can be a tedious and lengthy process.

Even though WYSIWYGs have their downsides — most notably the extra source code — these applications are excellent for getting started in web design and are definitely appropriate for a large percentage of projects. But learn the HTML, too. You will be better able to tackle any development challenge.

JEFFREY ZELDMAN ON WEB STANDARDS

Write once, publish everywhere. That was the goal.

To achieve it, The Web Standards Project (www.webstandards.org) called on browser makers to support a core group of standards. These standards have several names (CSS, XHTML, XML, etc.), but they all support a very basic idea: the separation of presentation from underlying structure and semantics.

What does this mean? It means your design lives in one place (for instance, in a Cascading Style Sheet [CSS]), and your content lives elsewhere (for instance, in HTML or XHTML documents or in a database of XML-formatted text entries).

Why would web designers want this? Why would we want to separate our design from our data? For one thing, if the template for an entire site (or a section of a site) lives in a single CSS document, redesigns are a piece of cake. Need to change your background image, color scheme, margin widths, text size, fonts, leading, and so on? Edit one CSS document, and an entire site (or section of that site) instantly changes to reflect the new design. Try doing that with traditional "HTML-as-design-tool" markup. You can't. Even with sophisticated HTML editors, you're looking at hours or days of monkeywork, not to mention additional hours of browser-specific testing and debugging.

For another thing, if you can separate your design from your data, then people using nontraditional browsers will no longer be barred from your site. Whether they're on web-enabled cell phones, Palm Pilots, nongraphical browsers like Lynx, or special browsers to accommodate a physical disability, they will now enjoy full access to the site's content. With the separation of presentation from structure, you don't have to create alternate versions of entire sites to support these folks (an expensive and time-consuming process in its own right); you simply add a rule or two to your style sheet.

With full support for web standards that facilitate the true separation of style from content, our jobs will get easier, mindless and repetitive tasks will be greatly lessened, and larger audiences will be able to access our sites with fewer problems. Instead of wasting our time and our clients' money on alternate versions and cumbersome hacks and work-arounds, we can spend it on richer content, enhanced design, and additional functionality.

Here's an example. I creative-direct A List Apart (alistapart.com), an online magazine "for people who make websites." Our 1998 layout, like all 1998 layouts, relied on HTML tables to control the presentation. As user needs changed, I modified the site subtly from one issue to the next. But these changes were not retroactive. With no separation of design from data and no transparent content management tools in place, improvements to the latest issue did not appear in older issues unless I manually reformatted the entire magazine each week. With hundreds of articles online, that was never going to happen.

In February 2001, we converted A List Apart to CSS layout and, in so doing, made it possible to change the look and feel of all articles at the same time, simply by editing a single style sheet. Converting to CSS layout also empowered us to provide alternate font sizes for those who needed them, even though our content was not delivered dynamically (http://www.alistapart.com/articles/alternate/). Such techniques are available to all designers regardless of budget and time limitations.

Today, in its third incarnation, ALA not only enjoys a new CSS layout (with that technology's speed and transparency benefits), but the magazine is also finally powered by custom content management tools created by my partner, Brian Alvey.

Jeffrey Zeldman (zeldman.com)*, author of the best-selling* Designing with Web Standards *(New Riders, 2003) and* Taking Your Talent to the Web *(New Riders, 2001), is the publisher and creative director of A List Apart* (alistapart.com)*; co-founder of The Web Standards Project* (webstandards.org)*, a grassroots coalition that helped end the Browser Wars by persuading Microsoft and Netscape to support W3C and ECMA standards in their browsers; and founder of Happy Cog, a web design, consulting, and publishing agency. He lectures everywhere and has written for numerous publications.*

Following HTML template creation, the individual pages are created and linked to create a shell of a site. This is a great time to pour in content, and the perfect time for a content delivery check. Chances are much of the content has been written but is either in draft format or still being approved. At this point, populating the site's shell with content is a great reality check and a chance to get the framework and file structure complete and in working order.

Anticipate this moment. Before the deadline comes, email the person who is responsible for content delivery and let that person know that the content-submission deadline is imminent. Make it clear that as of a certain date, content will be frozen, meaning no longer changeable. Final. If you do not do this, content will continue to trickle in. Content that comes in after the freeze constitutes Scope Creep, and you can charge for it (see the "Slippage and Consequences" sidebar earlier in this chapter). Be aware that content will still come in even after you officially freeze it. Build a cushion into your freeze date if you can.

Once you begin to populate your pages, obviously make sure the content goes into the correct places. Someone, probably the project manager, has been in charge of receiving content from the client. With this person as development-side content coordinator, use the Content Delivery Plan as a checklist, rely on the

Content Buckets

Dynamic sites often have designated areas, or "content buckets," where dynamically generated content (for example, "Today's Top News" or a database-built shopping list) gets placed. There is usually some HTML placeholder code built into your page that will get filled by dynamic content. Content buckets need separate consideration because they are points of integration between back-end and front-end.

If your site is not dynamically driven but you have an area where content regularly changes, make certain you specify clearly in your HTML Style Guide how to properly update that area.

naming conventions of the web-ready files that were delivered, or develop another method of ensuring proper content placement. Whatever the plan, communicate the content-tracking plan to all production designers involved in populating the pages. Make certain nothing gets missed or placed in the wrong spot.

As you place the content, be on the lookout for content that is larger, smaller, or structurally different from what was agreed to. Such changes can "break the design" or negatively impact usability. If the content is significantly different from what was agreed to, some already-created elements and/or pages may have to be reworked, and this may constitute Scope Creep. Additionally, content that was not anticipated most likely has no established layout or HTML text style standard. Ask the visual designers to define the standard right away.

Invisible Content

Populating your pages involves all content, including the frequently forgotten, production-specific "invisible content" — ALT, META, and TITLE tags. Some invisible content, like ALT tags on graphic globals such as navigational elements, should be added at the HTML template creation stage so that it only needs to be done once. Others, like TITLEs, should be included when pages are built from those templates. Invisible content is regularly left until the very end or is flat out forgotten. Keep it in your workflow.

Endeavor to have the invisible content ready to go before the coding process begins. If you didn't address TITLE tagging in the content outlining phase (a great opportunity to establish the standard), work with the client on invisible content during their "off time" while they are waiting on the visual design. Regardless, as long as a naming convention or style is established, the production designers can move forward.

INTEGRATING BACKEND DEVELOPMENT

Communication between the backend development team and the front-end design and production teams has always been important, but at this point in the web development process, it becomes absolutely crucial. Suffering a lack of consistent communication is an exceptionally easy trap for any project to fall into, especially because some backend engineering can take months while the front-end is usually measured in weeks.

The logical place in the workflow for backend and front-end to integrate is during or right after all of the HTML pages are complete. At the beginning of the production phase, however, gather all front-end production and backend engineers and work out a plan for integration and communication. What is the best way to create the HTML templates so that they can be handed off to the backend team for dynamic content population and programming? How much programming should be done in the HTML stage? How much experience with programming do the HTML production designers have? Which team will be responsible for inserting the actual backend code into the HTML pages? What is the timeline for integration? Who will be doing what to the templates from each team? A typical meeting will require the project managers or leads from both teams to meet. Key members from the development team should also be present, including the information designer and the art director. The Technical Specifications document and the Client Spec Sheet should be pulled out and reviewed by everyone.

UNDERSTANDING QUALITY ASSURANCE TESTING

You've built your site; now make sure it works. Quality assurance (QA) is one of the most often skipped steps (besides usability testing) in the development process. Not surprisingly, we highly recommend against skimping on QA. Broadway productions wouldn't go live without a full dress rehearsal complete with sound and lighting in place; you shouldn't launch a site without a comprehensive run-through either.

We recommend shooting for a QA budget of approximately 10% of your total time and resources. You need this time to track and fix mistakes such as spelling errors, orphaned and rogue links, misplaced content, application errors due to integration, etc. **[6.11]**. But the even bigger job is bug tracking and fixing: broken tables, functional errors, browser crashes, everything that is not up to specifications. You need the time to fix those bugs and then to crosscheck once again before the site goes live. And, if you have access to the client server, you will want to QA immediately postlaunch as well.

However, in many projects, there is seldom time left in the budget for QA testing. More often than not, the testing and acceptance of production are slammed right up against launch. All too often, production deadlines have been pushed (usually due to

< **TEST**

- > Understanding Quality Assurance Testing
- > Conducting QA Testing
- > Identifying, Prioritizing and Fixing Bugs
- > Conducting a Final Check

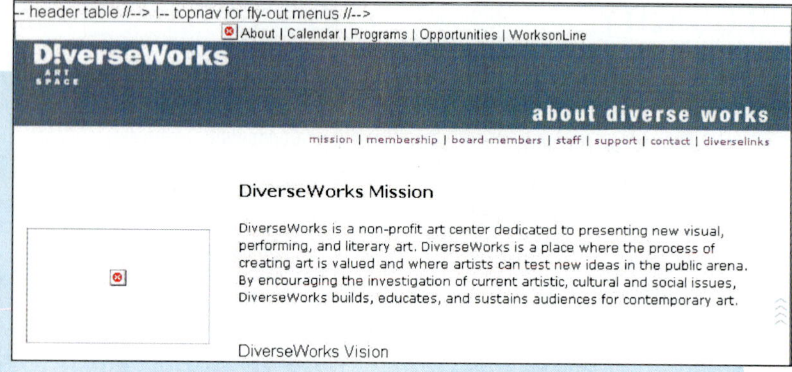

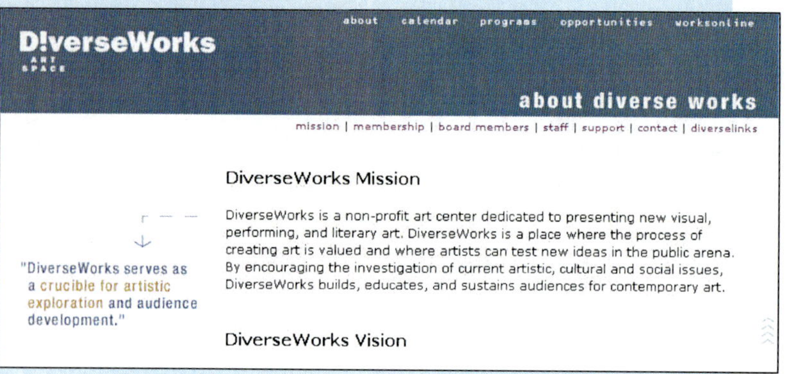

< **6.11**

A typical, simple bug: The image isn't loading (top). A quick directory check and reupload of the image solved the problem (bottom). An example of a bigger bug would be a DHTML pull-down menu that crashes certain browsers. (This is harder to get screenshots of.)

late-arriving content and technical snafus), and the time allotment for QA is compromised. The extent to which you will actually be able to conduct QA will depend largely on three things: 1) how close you are to your launch date — usually a result of how well you were able to adhere to your schedule, 2) acceptance criteria, or how perfect the site needs to be prior to launch, and 3) how flexible, if at all, the launch date is.

This critical testing process can take place informally with just a few team members, or it can be a larger undertaking, done either in-house or by hiring an outside company or team. The real-world tendency is to approach this process haphazardly, but be forewarned: Without a cohesive QA plan, you are taking a big chance. And chance is never a good step to stand on, not when there is a budget at risk. Have a plan.

CONDUCTING QA TESTING

You have known since the beginning of your redesign project that you would need to QA your site and that you would need a plan for it. Chances are, however, the extent of your QA plan is a budgetary/scheduling line that looks something like this: QA = 12 hours. Or five hours. Or 20+ hours. That budgetary line depends on the scope of your project, client expectations, and the expertise of your team.

Reassess your QA plan. Keep in mind that complicated frame sets, intricate HTML templates, scripting, and links all need to be QA tested. There are essentially three levels of QA: light/informal, semiformal, and formal. Make the decision as to the level of QA your project requires.

A core plan for running QA shows resources, time allotted, the extent of expectations, who is involved, criteria for acceptance, and what the development team and the client are each responsible for prior to site launch. Running QA should involve at least two complete run-throughs: first to generate a comprehensive bug list and second to go back over that bug list, make certain that the cited bugs have been fixed, and double check that in the fixing, you have not created additional issues. For informal QA, this basic plan should suffice. For semiformal and formal plans, expand accordingly.

Every test plan or testing situation will contain different criteria for acceptance. Each site will need to check functionality against requirements from simple pop-up windows and submission of forms to complex login procedures and e-commerce ordering systems. And this will be needed across browsers, platforms, and operating systems. If your audience is still largely on dial-up (at press time over 50% of internet users were), make sure dial-up is included. Be up to date with this data; resources abound (www.upsdell.com/BrowserNews, www.dreamink.com/design5.shtml, and www.websiteoptimization.com/bw/0402 are three good places to start). As the web continues to evolve from basic HTML to a functional, application-driven environment, more and more attention needs to be allocated to ensuring integration success.

The QA Lead

In Phase 1: Define, we outlined various roles and responsibilities, one of which was that of the QA lead. Depending on the size of the project or the extent of your development team, you may not have the luxury of having a dedicated individual assigned to overseeing and managing quality assurance. If this is the case, chances are the project manager will have to fill this role. For project managers new to this role, we recommend a crash course in QA — some expertise in the testing and launch of any product is far more valuable than "winging it." For an excellent overview of QA principles and philosophy, go to www.philosophe.com.

If you are managing this task, make sure to keep client expectations in line. Educate your client as to the value of comprehensive QA and to the extent and the cost that QA can take. Make sure the client understands that "comprehensive" calls for more than one day and more than just a few thousand dollars.

QA & Servers

Prior to a site going live, the production team should test on both the staging/development server and then again when the site is moved over to the actual server environment where eventually it will be live. When the site is moved over, the testing environment needs to be exactly the same as the live environment. This means that the folders, file structure, and server-side scripts must be correctly in place; otherwise, many of the scripts and CGI elements may not work properly.

Test Beds

The bank of computers (set up in the testing area) that reflects the target browsers, platforms, and connection speeds of the audience is often called a "test bed." It is difficult to list every combination of browser and platform; at least use the main ones. Even testing a smaller, representative group will result in catching many errors on the site. Test beds are common for semiformal and formal QA. Often for informal testing, the various browsers and platforms are not in the same location.

Quality assurance testing can employ several procedures, most of which typically are used both in software development and for testing websites and web applications. In all testing situations, the extent of testing varies widely depending on technical complexity and the detail of the test plan.

BASIC/STANDARD TESTING PROCEDURES	
Smoke Testing	Testing without a formal test plan, smoke testing is also called "ad hoc" or "guerilla testing." Often, due to time and resources, this is the only type of testing conducted prior to launch.
Alpha Testing	Also referred to as "internal testing," alpha testing is the initial testing of a site after the production and functionality are in place but prior to public display.
User Acceptance	Usually performed through a number of specific tests, user acceptance is dependent on scope, budget, and expertise. User acceptance verifies customer requirements (platform, browser, operating system, connection speed, etc.).
Content Check	The content check confirms content placement (not just copy — check also for image utilization and positioning), spelling, and syntax.
Beta Testing	A final check to confirm that all is functioning as intended prior to the actual launch of a site, beta testing is generally performed on the client staging site or in a subdirectory on the live server.
ADVANCED/FORMAL TESTING PROCEDURES	
Load Testing	Also called "stress testing," load testing utilizes software programs that simulate multiple users hitting the site simultaneously to determine a server's breaking point. (Costs vary widely; research is necessary to determine needs.)
Functional Testing	Also known as "black box" testing, functional testing confirms actual functionality against the specification document. Specific setup involves the person testing the functionality having knowledge of the intended outcome but not the programming details.
Unit Tests	A test of individual components on a web page to make sure they function as specified, unit tests are verifications conducted before the code is submitted for integration of intended versus actual functionality and response.
Regression Testing	Also known by the simple name "retesting," regression testing confirms that all tracked bugs have been fixed, that the old code is still working as intended, and that no new problems were created due to said fixes. Note: The level of regression testing and confirmation varies widely.
Security Testing	A check that confirms that database and transactional information is secure from unauthorized users or hackers; a security test usually involves inside understanding of the server setup.

Informal testing is very basic and is doable by the development team. Formal usually entails hiring an outside, trained team. Semiformal lies, logically, between the two. Most sites with a development budget under $30,000 can usually get away with informal testing. Sites with complex functionality and an application layer normally include formal or at least semiformal testing in their workflow.

Light/Informal QA

For informal QA processes, the QA lead or the project manager coordinates and tracks all planned tests and assigns team members to sections of the site, individual browsers, browser versions, and platforms. The assigned team member then goes through the site and compiles and lists all bugs for the HTML production team to fix. An easy way of doing this involves printing out pages with errors and clearly indicating each error on the printout. Note that these printouts are only complete and helpful if the browser and platform is noted on the printout that notes the bug. Without knowing the browser and platform, it is difficult to re-create the error and therefore fix it.

The project manager also tracks the "bug list," which, in informal testing, is really no more than a

Test Usability During QA

QA testing and usability testing are similar in approach and scope but different in expertise and goal. At times, however, the two overlap, especially when technical errors and complications (checked for during QA) affect a user's ability to move through a site (checked for through usability testing). In fact, usability testing can sometimes be considered a type of QA.

While you are QA testing your site for errors, technical glitches, and cross-browser compatibility, we strongly suggest you also conduct one-on-one usability testing (also called "verification testing" at this stage). Why? Because you can. Watch your testers as they go through the site. You already have them there, so get more from the test if you can. Always take any opportunity to ensure that your site works from the visitor's point of view. Naming and labeling must be clear. Navigation must be intuitive and easy to follow. Your site might be clean and free from bugs, but if it isn't easy to use, the chances are it won't get used and will fail.

Conversely, the redesign might be easy to use (congratulations!), but if you have broken links and spelling errors, visitors won't get very far. Moreover, they will have a poor impression of the site and the company. Make a bug-free and user-friendly site your prelaunch goal. We recommend both QA and usability testing prior to launch. For more on usability testing, see Chapter 8: Testing for Usability.

The Problem with Frames

If your site contains frames, expect QA to take at least twice as long. Nested frames? Even longer. As a rule, the more frames you have, the more QA is needed. Moreover, frames thwart search engines (see Phase 5: Launch). Frames, while appropriate for some situations (for example, portfolios, maintaining several levels of navigation, etc.), are so problematic that most often they are simply not worth it. We recommend no frames unless there is a strong need from a functional standpoint, and only then if you have a tech-savvy production whiz who can hammer out the kinks and troubleshoot along the way. Sometimes frames do enable an elegant solution to tiers of navigation, however they tend to make more problems than solve.

That said, iFrames (inline frames) are a good option to replace clunky frames (using JavaScript and CSS for positioning), however at press time they were only supported on IE 4.0+, Netscape 6.0+, Mozilla and Opera. Stay up to date on this at www.dyn-web.com/dhtml/iframes.

Include the Client

For informal testing, clients should also participate in the QA process in the same fashion as the team members: checking the site and submitting a sheaf of printouts with errors clearly indicated as well as browser and platform types noted. Other alternatives including emails with screenshots and even better, using a bug tracking system such as Bugzilla (www.bugzilla.org). Bug tracking programs need not be cumbersome. In addition to helping with estimating time to complete, track progress on current bug status, and to confirm and regress the fixes, if the program is on the web, then it is easy for everyone to view. For any level of testing, the client should proof the content. Only the client will be able to truly know if content is in the wrong place or is incorrect. The client should be treated as (and should hopefully act as) a partner and not a finger pointer.

stack of printouts with bugs noted. A big red checkmark through the noted bug indicates that it has been addressed, and an accompanying initial indicating "Fixed" or "Deferred" with a date helps track the fixes.

Usually, for small- to medium-size sites (under $30,000 budgets) with very little technical complexity, this informal process is perfectly adequate. Informal testing is also referred to as "ad hoc" or "guerrilla testing" in that it has no formal test plan or approach. Testers are just "banging" on the site, looking for bugs to slay.

Semiformal QA

If your project requires more than "guerrilla testing," yet your budget will not accommodate formal testing with an outside company, the perfect middle ground is semiformal testing. Stepping up from informal to semiformal testing involves more time, expertise, and planning — and if possible, the addition of a trained QA lead and a test bed setup. A semiformal test plan should contain a one- to two-page overview that highlights the scope, timing, and goals of the QA testing process.

A Core QA Plan

- Summary of overall goals for QA including methodology, schedule, and resource allocation.
- List of specific browsers, platforms, and operating systems being tested.
- List of desired connection speeds being tested.
- List of any specific paths or functions that need to be tested.
- A plan for bug tracking (using a web-based program or Excel spreadsheet or printouts).
- A plan for confirming that fixes have been made prior to launch.
- Any stated assumptions (known risks) to protect the team if all fixes cannot be caught prior to launch. These should be listed in the Details and Assumptions section (in Phase 1: Define) of the Project Plan or contract and be signed off on prior to the final site being delivered or launched.
- A plan for fixing bugs that cannot be resolved prior to launch. Who is to handle them, how will any additional costs be identified, etc.

Formal QA

Planning for formal QA testing requires experience, time, budget, and most of all, attention to detail — minute detail. The biggest differences between semi-formal and formal QA are the level of test planning, the cost, the generation of documentation, and the degree of expertise.

Formal QA uses a comprehensive bug-tracking system and a fully trained QA staff (yes, staff) to test requirements and pages against specified browsers and platforms. It includes test plans, tools, use cases, a test bed, and reports. To illustrate the extensiveness of the formal testing process, consider this example of a typical formal QA plan: Identify at least 10 different paths through a site and test each path on three platforms (MAC, WIN, UNIX), with each platform hosting all major browsers (Safari, Netscape, Opera, etc.), with each browser having at least the most recent and second-most-recent versions needing to be tested. Overwhelming? Yes. Impossible? No. Impossible in an informal setting? Yes. Recommended for large sites with a significant backend engineering and extensive functionality? Absolutely.

Bug Reporting

Reporting a bug is easy. Reporting bugs in a way that is meaningful, reproducible, detailed, and solution-oriented is a challenge. Here's the old, serviceable, good-for-informal-testing way: Print the page out, note the browser/platform, circle the error, fix the bug, and then check the error as fixed (or deferred if the bug can't be fixed yet). Here's another (and maybe better) way: Use some kind of tracking device — even an Excel spreadsheet will suffice — although you can only have one person working with the file at a time. Whatever your tracking method, make certain to note the following information:

- Browser type/platform type.
- Operating system.
- URL of page.
- One-line description of problem.
- Detailed description of problem.
- Severity of problem.
- Can the error be reproduced? (If so, list steps taken to reproduce it.)
- Priority level.

<TIPS>

Bug-Tracking Tools

Although you cannot substitute automated software systems for actual QA testing with humans, there are many available tools that can aid in the process. For complete HTML validation testing, links, spelling, load time, and more, try www.netmechanic.com. Fees range from $35 to $200 for testing up to 400 HTML pages.

Other online tools? They are plentiful. Try www.scrubtheweb.com to help check your META information. www.w3.org/People/Raggett/tidy will help you clean up your HTML. For an excellent bug-tracking tool, visit www.alumni.caltech.edu/~dank/gnats.html. Want to learn more about bugs? Go to http://www.bugzilla.org. Mozilla itself is handy for QA as well. Many web editing tools also include HTML, link, spelling, load time, checks/validators (including BBEdit, Homesite, Dreamweaver). There are tons of tools online. A quick search will give you a lot to work with.

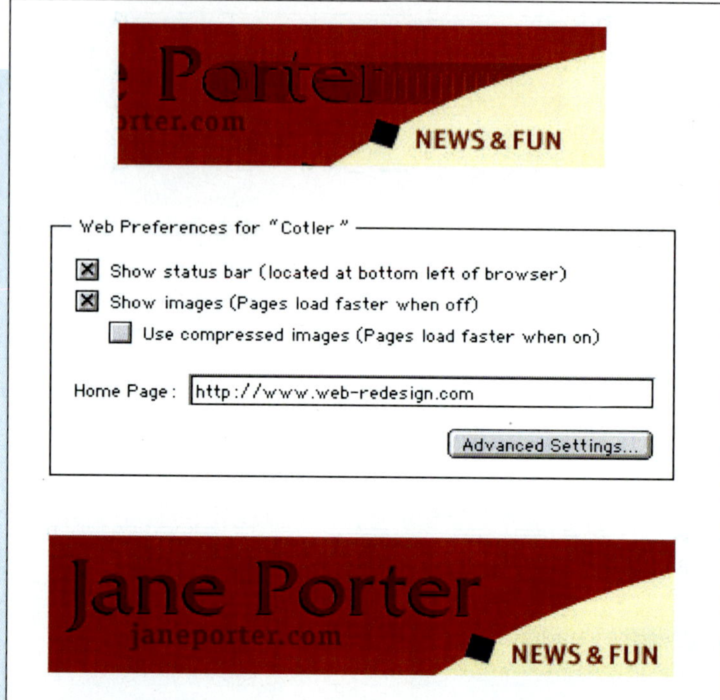

< 6.12

An image glitch (top) shows up on older AOL browsers during the QA process, but randomly — only on some laptops. End-user preferences settings were to blame: Unchecking "Use compressed images" and then dumping the browser cache remedied the glitch and displayed the image correctly (bottom). This random example illustrates a much larger point: End-user-caused bugs are largely out of QA control.

IDENTIFYING, PRIORITIZING AND FIXING BUGS

Decide what needs to be fixed immediately. These are the showstoppers — the glaring errors. Continue your list and prioritize the remainder of the fixes with headings such as showstoppers, high priority, medium priority, and low priority. Understand that some bugs may be unfixable because they are end-user dependent. If you can't re-create the bug, mark it as such. They might be due to nonstandard end-user browser settings **[6.12]**. Depending on the time left before launch and the level of perfection that is necessary at launch, plan for prelaunch fixes and postlaunch fixes alike. Postlaunch fixes should happen in an iterative fashion.

After addressing bugs, test your fixes. Try to re-create the error. Some fixes may require several tries.

QA BUDGET COMPARISONS BY OVERALL PROJECT BUDGET RANGE AND TECHNICAL LEVEL		
Light/Informal QA	**Semiformal QA**	**Formal QA**
For projects with budgets under \$30,000, estimate the QA budget at 1% to 3% of project cost. **Technical level: light.**	For projects with budgets ranging between \$30,000 and \$70,000, estimate the QA budget at 5% of project cost. **Technical level: moderate.**	For projects with budgets over \$70,000, estimate the QA budget at 10% to 20% of project cost. **Technical level: moderate to complex.**

NOTE: For projects at or under the \$10,000 budget mark, a mere \$100 worth of time and resources will not work. You do need to go through the entire site.

CONDUCTING A FINAL CHECK

Conduct a final check with all teams involved. Make sure all systems are go. Here are the key five items to confirm:

- **Design check.** Designers have a keen eye for detail; they might catch misalignments and incorrect graphics that even a good QA team might miss. HTML text might be placed incorrectly; a photo treatment may have been misapplied. Have the art director or designer give the site a thorough look on both Mac and PC to ensure quality control.
- **HTML check.** Confirm that all tables, cells, and graphics are lining up properly. Your team may not have had enough time for ample tweaking. After QA is in full gear and fixes are being implemented, let the HTML team check once more that the site is visually working on both MAC and PCs. Sometimes QA fixes alter or wreck code.
- **Functionality/engineering check (if applicable).** Confirm that all functionality is working in accordance with the technical specifications. Make sure that database integration is complete and that all transactions can be accomplished on the live server.
- **Content check.** Confirm that the headlines are reading as headlines, that body copy reads like body copy… you get the picture. Make sure that the content formatting was appropriately applied by the production team and that everything is lining up as expected. Involve the client on this and get an approval before launch.
- **Client approval.** Making sure the client sees and approves the entire site prior to launch might seem like an obvious check-off item. Surprisingly, it is often the case that, although the redesigned site has been signed off on by the marketing department the entire time, the CEO or advertisers who need to approve the site before it goes live may never have seen the final site. Sometimes it is appropriate to wait until the last possible moment to get the approval from the highest level; sometimes this delay causes chaos.

Showstoppers

There are bugs and then there are big bugs (sort of the difference between a harmless little earwig and a thumb-size Palo Verde beetle). Big bugs are showstoppers — errors that simply cannot go live. These errors have to get fixed before launch (for example, the home page loads incorrectly, a pull-down menu crashes IE, the framesets are mistargeted, etc.). As you track bugs, prioritize. What are showstoppers? What can get fixed in an iterative approach in the first week of launch? Sometimes the launch date is set in stone, and you do not have the time to fix all bugs. Prioritize and slay the showstoppers first. The rest can wait a few days.

PHASE 4 CHECK-OFF LIST

Plan

- ☐ Compose the Client Spec Sheet
- ☐ Assess project status

Build and Integrate

- ☐ Set file structure
- ☐ Receive graphic templates from the visual designers
- ☐ Slice and optimize graphics
- ☐ Create HTML templates
- ☐ Implement light scripting
- ☐ Build individual pages
- ☐ Populate individual pages
- ☐ Include invisible content
- ☐ Freeze production
- ☐ Integrate complex functionality and/or backend engineering

Test

- ☐ Create QA plan
- ☐ Conduct QA testing
- ☐ Prioritize and fix bugs
- ☐ Conduct final check

PHASE 4 SUMMARY

Production — the actual building of a site — is no longer as relatively straightforward a process as when tables and straight HTML were the norm. With so many options available for building pages, more time should be devoted up front to identifying goals, the scalable nature of the site, as well as maintenance and content needs. With the movement toward separating design and content, using style sheets to establish consistency, and moving away from traditional table structures to create a simplified page layout, designers and coders are needing to educate themselves not only on how to build and integrate in this manner but *why* they are doing so. With a larger understanding of the big picture, we begin to shift into this new way of thinking.

Why involve the production team throughout the entire process? Quite simply, without advance checking, testing, and confirming, the building phase can be risky. You may as well get off a ski lift and ride down any random run without checking its skill level. Think of the possible crises: finding out as you build the HTML templates that your pull-down menus block the contracted advertising space, or trying to slice and optimize a layout that simply does not translate to HTML. Either of these scenarios would involve chalking up as a loss the numerous hours spent coding. The team would have to backtrack, and if the launch date is firm, you might not have enough time.

Not to worry, however. The Core Process sets you up to pull off production with minimal hitches. Sure, you encountered bugs — every site has them. Be thrilled that production is done! Well, almost. Yes, your site is built. It is logically organized and will be easy to maintain thanks to well-thought-through HTML. You've slain all the bugs you can (and those still extant are on your list). Your site is user friendly. It looks as close to what your visual designers intended as the limitations of code will allow. Congratulations. You are ready to take care of launch and what follows.

Melanie Craft

Client: Melanie Craft
URL: www.melaniecraft.com
Design Team: Waxcreative Design
Creative Director/Art Director/ Information Designer: Emily Cotler

Designer: Caitlin Lang
Production: Renée White
Copywriting: Melanie Craft

Melanie Craft is a successful novelist currently focusing on the romantic comedy genre. Like many authors and creative professionals, she is her own small-but-thriving business with needs to connect with readers, industry professionals, and press.

<PREVIOUS>

MELANIECRAFT.COM [OLD] was cute, but that was not the image Ms. Craft was looking for. While the site served as an online brochure, adequately presenting good content, it did not project the level of professionalism desired. As a result, the content wasn't taken seriously.

<CURRENT>

MELANIECRAFT.COM [REDESIGNED] presents a clean and professional look that directs visitors to the main event: the current book.

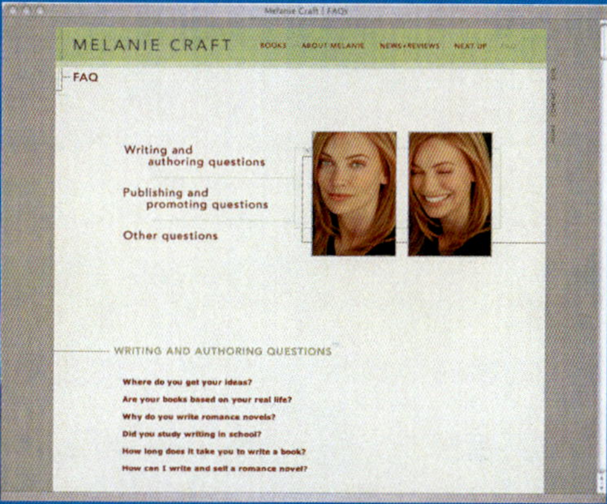

MELANIECRAFT.COM [REDESIGNED] is open and sparse, while presenting accessible information in the novelist's own words, offering a feeling of conversation that is important for any fan-based website. The FAQ page proved to be a valuable and easy-to-use resource, with several members of the press quoting directly from it.

Results: Better industry positioning. Also, increased fan mail applauded the ease-of-use and attractiveness of the site.

> Launching your site is a major milestone. But it is only a step; a website is an evolving production.

Phase 5: Launch and Beyond 07

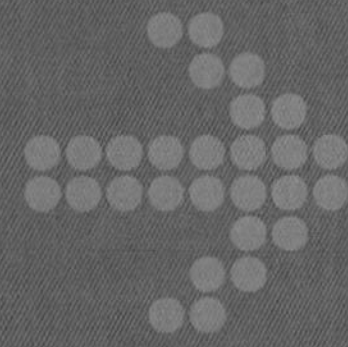

Phase 5: Launch and Beyond

In today's web development world, this moment — launch — should not be an end; it is a transition into an entirely different workflow: maintenance and evaluation. Who will maintain the site, and what are their qualifications and capabilities? Who will be responsible for the creation of postlaunch content? And don't forget about evaluation — you still need to determine the measurable success of your site. Did the site meet the original goals of the Communication Brief? Are visitors finding it usable? Are visitors finding it at all?

WHAT THIS CHAPTER COVERS

DELIVERY	LAUNCH	MAINTENANCE
> Handing Off	> Going Live	> Maintaining the Site
> Completing the Production Style Guide	> Prepping an Announcement Plan	> Assessing Maintenance Team Capability
> Creating the Handoff Packet	> Optimizing for Search Engines	> Internal vs. External Maintenance Teams
> Tracking Documentation	> Launching the Site	> Developing a Maintenance Plan
> Conducting a Postlaunch Meeting		> Confirming Site Security
> Scheduling Maintenance Training		> Planning Iterative Initiatives
		> Measuring Success

Here, in the fifth and final phase of the Core Process, the distinction between internal and external teams becomes even sharper — and therefore, so does the difference in the usage of the word "client." In the beginning of this book, we explained how we broadly use the term "client." If a company contracts a web development or design firm to produce its site, the "client" is the company that does the contracting. We also use "client" to denote the decision-makers in a company in which the web/design department is in-house. In either case, the client is whoever signs off on budgets, schedules, and designs. Interpret the word "client" as it best suits your particular situation.

The workflow involved in this phase covers what you need to know as you smoothly transition your redesign project out of the hands of the web development team and into the care of the maintenance team. Even if these teams are made up of the same people, their roles are very different.

Specifically, this chapter is about launching your site and what you need to think about before, during, and after your site goes live, including planning

what should get done next on the site to keep it tuned. Phase 5 includes loose ends that need tying up, some suggestions on how to announce your site and register with search engines, and also some tips on how to assess and measure the site's success and usability. Whether your project is small or large, refer to this chapter to help make sure important things don't slip through the cracks during the final hours.

HANDING OFF

As any designer or developer will tell you, it is difficult to actually "freeze" development. It always feels like more refinement is possible. Establish a point in time when the design, production, and development of the redesign project has reached a full cycle — if for nothing else than to send the final invoice. Understand that there may never be a perfect moment to do this; errors and issues will continue to crop up. The client and development team should mutually decide in advance what defines the point of transition between a site-in-development and a site-in-maintenance. Clearly defining responsibilities and transition points, as well as handing off a packet of materials, helps make the gray area between development and maintenance much more black and white. Refer back to the original contract, which should clearly outline the deliverables. If these have changed during the process, there should be (hopefully) an email trail and a signed additional charge (AC) form or change order request. The ease with which you can manage the client's expectations at this phase is a direct result of effective communication throughout the process.

Most projects have one team responsible for the building and launch of a site and another team set to take care of the site's ongoing maintenance. Even for internal teams, the individuals who created the site are often not the ones maintaining it. But regardless of who is transitioning the project to whom (or when — sometimes the project is handed over after pages are built and populated and sometimes before, with only the templates handed off), now is the time when several items need to be wrapped up so that the maintenance team can do its job.

COMPLETING THE PRODUCTION STYLE GUIDE

After the site is launched, the integration team has a moment to breathe and recoup. Now, before too much time passes, have them add production information to the Style Guide that was started by the visual designers in Phase 3: Design.

Production complexity will vary from site to site. Following web standards helps the QA process by alleviating some of the variables from browser to browser and also the use of external style sheets helps by forcing consistency during the coding process. Heavily nested tables, complex frame sets, and includes — not to mention content management

< **DELIVERY**

- > Handing Off
- > Completing the Production Style Guide
- > Creating the Handoff Packet
- > Tracking Documentation
- > Conducting a Postlaunch Meeting
- > Scheduling Maintenance Training

Who Broke It?

In any web development project with multiple teams, there are bound to be some back and forth issues and unresolved errors. Who should fix an error that is found post-QA? In order to address this issue (which happens in every project), either factor in a stated amount of hours and a timeframe that the outsourced firm is available (for example, one month with an estimate of 12 hours) for requests for fixes and changes to the delivered pages/code, or clearly determine the "point of no return" when the integration/maintenance team is responsible for all bugs and fixes to the site after the stated point is passed.

RECOMMENDED PRODUCTION STYLE GUIDE COMPONENTS	
DEFINITION OF GRAPHIC ELEMENTS	
Sample code for all graphic elements	For all visual design elements (page dimensions, headers, colors, type, photo treatments, embellishments — reviewed in Phase 3's Style Guide), include a sample of the accompanying HTML code (for style sheet standards, navigation and sidebar elements, and for image insertion, etc.).
NAMING CONVENTIONS	
For TITLE tags	Specify how the names of each page appear in the browser bar. Will there always be the company name? How will subsections be shown?
For images	Are you using any prefixes and/or suffixes to identify images (e.g., hd_contact.gif or nav_services.gif)? Are you using underscores and/or mixed case (e.g., nav_contact_on.gif or navContactOn.gif)? Where are images kept (e.g., images used in multiple sections are kept in /images/global/, whereas section-specific images are kept in /images/section/; or they could be divided by type such as /images/header/ and /images/nav/)?
For Cascading Style Sheets	What are the CSS names for each font set? The font may be Arial Regular 8-point gray, but if you are using CSS, you create a style and name it. List those names and the treatments for naming the styles.
For files/folders	Are you using prefixes and/or suffixes to identify files? The same considerations as for images (above) also apply here.
FORMATTING OF CODE	
Tab	When to tab? When to break lines?
Comment tags	When and how to use? Include sample code.
Case sensitivity	Uppercase versus lowercase (for example, tags are UPPERCASE; attributes are lowercase).
Absolute vs. relative links	Define when to use which and where (if applicable).
Includes	Define when, where, and how to use (if applicable).
JavaScript	Define code conventions for ease of manipulations (how to create additional rollovers, how to change link references, etc.). Graphic and code examples of these elements may need to be included.
Definition of templates (if used)	Describe how the template is broken down into parts and how to properly populate it. This section should include code and graphical elements examples.

RECOMMENDED PRODUCTION STYLE GUIDE COMPONENTS	
STRUCTURE/ORGANIZATION	
Site structure	Identify where everything is being physically kept in the directory. Identify where new files (as a result of maintenance) will be kept.
PAGE LAYOUT	
Page layout	Add code illustrating the basic outline of the page layout, including **<body>** tag info and margin attributes. Layout might also include CSS tags of used for positioning.
Type/fonts	Add code illustrating the CSS being used; for example, a.red:link { font-family: verdana, arial, helvetica,sans-serif; font-size: 10px; color: #CC3300; } .body { font-family: verdana, arial, helvetica, sans-serif; font-size: 10px; color: #666666; }.
Sizes/colors	Add code illustrating the fonts being used with their sizes and colors; for example, <font face= "verdana" size=2 color="#c9c9c9">.
Navigation	Include sample code illustrating the navigation if explanation is necessary. If JavaScript functions pertaining to navigational elements warrant, describe with a brief walk-through of code.
Menus	Show sample code illustrating the menus (if applicable). Include explanation of any JavaScript functions pertaining to menu elements with a brief walk-through of code.
Forms	Walk-through of code for form elements (if applicable). What information is being passed, where is it being sent, how is it processed, where is it stored, how can information be reviewed, etc.
Additional elements	Banner ads, placements, and sizes. Integration with third-party vendors. User tracking: How is the info collected, where is it stored, etc. Additional JavaScript, PERL, ASP components that need explanation.

Company Style Guide

Maintaining consistent brand standards is critical for companies, whether established or newly formed. Create a password-protected area on the site to serve the entire company, particularly marketing and sales teams, vendors and internal staff. Keep this intranet updated as necessary with accurate brand standards, downloadable logos in EPS format, styles for company collateral, and any other elements that might be inadvertently misused.

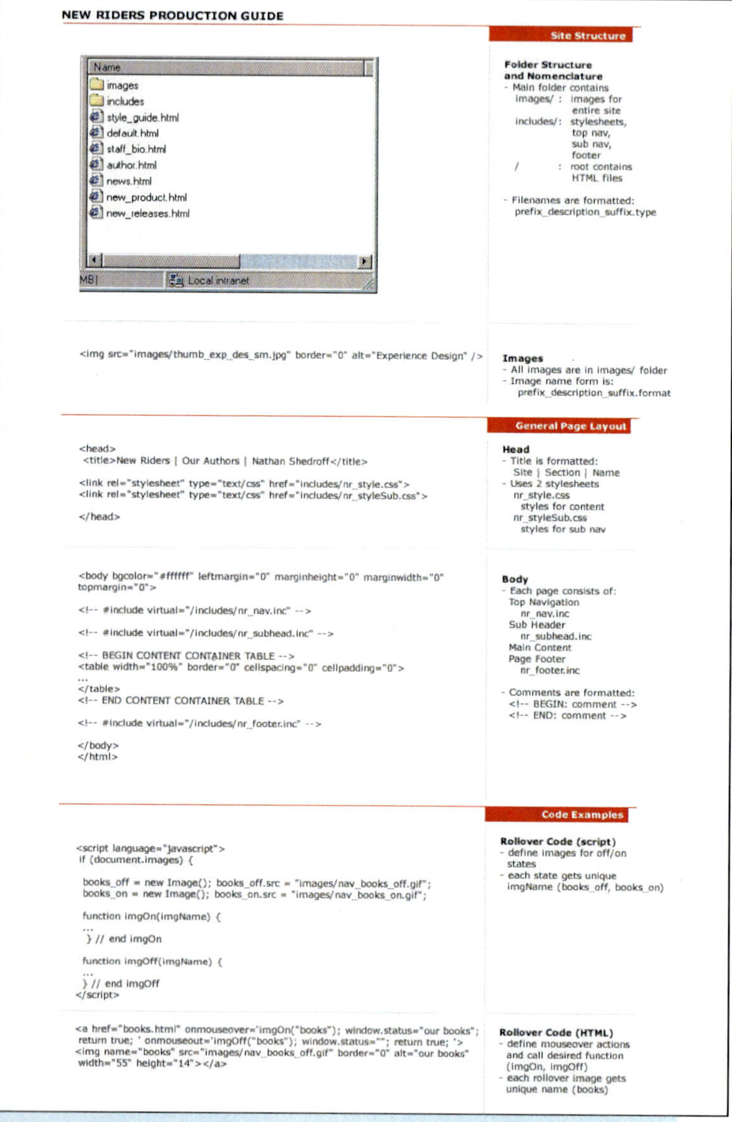

NEW RIDERS PRODUCTION GUIDE

Site Structure

```
Name
images
includes
style_guide.html
default.html
staff_bio.html
author.html
news.html
new_product.html
new_releases.html
```

Folder Structure and Nomenclature
- Main folder contains
  images/ : images for entire site
  includes/: stylesheets, top nav, sub nav, footer
  / : root contains HTML files
- Filenames are formatted:
  prefix_description_suffix.type

```
<img src="images/thumb_exp_des_sm.jpg" border="0" alt="Experience Design" />
```

Images
- All images are in images/ folder
- Image name form is:
  prefix_description_suffix.format

General Page Layout

```
<head>
 <title>New Riders | Our Authors | Nathan Shedroff</title>

<link rel="stylesheet" type="text/css" href="includes/nr_style.css">
<link rel="stylesheet" type="text/css" href="includes/nr_styleSub.css">

</head>
```

Head
- Title is formatted:
  Site | Section | Name
- Uses 2 stylesheets
  nr_style.css
    styles for content
  nr_styleSub.css
    styles for sub nav

```
<body bgcolor="#ffffff" leftmargin="0" marginheight="0" marginwidth="0"
topmargin="0">

<!-- #include virtual="/includes/nr_nav.inc" -->

<!-- #include virtual="/includes/nr_subhead.inc" -->

<!-- BEGIN CONTENT CONTAINER TABLE -->
<table width="100%" border="0" cellspacing="0" cellpadding="0">
...
</table>
<!-- END CONTENT CONTAINER TABLE -->

<!-- #include virtual="/includes/nr_footer.inc" -->

</body>
</html>
```

Body
- Each page consists of:
  Top Navigation
    nr_nav.inc
  Sub Header
    nr_subhead.inc
  Main Content
  Page Footer
    nr_footer.inc
- Comments are formatted:
  <!-- BEGIN: comment -->
  <!-- END: comment -->

Code Examples

```
<script language="javascript">
 if (document.images) {

  books_off = new Image(); books_off.src = "images/nav_books_off.gif";
  books_on = new Image(); books_on.src = "images/nav_books_on.gif";

  function imgOn(imgName) {
  ...
   } // end imgOn

  function imgOff(imgName) {
  ...
  } // end imgOff
</script>
```

Rollover Code (script)
- define images for off/on states
- each state gets unique imgName (books_off, books_on)

```
<a href="books.html" onmouseover='imgOn("books"); window.status="our books";
 return true; ' onmouseout='imgOff("books"); window.status=""; return true; '>
<img name="books" src="images/nav_books_off.gif" border="0" alt="our books"
 width="55" height="14"></a>
```

Rollover Code (HTML)
- define mouseover actions and call desired function (imgOn, imgOff)
- each rollover image gets unique name (books)

< **7.1**

A portion of the Production Style Guide for newriders.com.

systems and other backend functionality — all add to potential confusion as a second team takes over.

Make the Style Guide comprehensive because it will be used as a reference guide for the maintenance team when adding or modifying HTML pages or graphics. Build it in HTML format so that it is accessible as a "microsite" to all integration and maintenance teams via a simple link on a company intranet or extranet. While this might seem obvious, it is amazing how often this information is not shared, especially when a team transitions or new hires are put onto the project down the road. Include any and all information necessary to update and maintain the site. Be clear and concise and be available should the maintenance team have questions.

The production portion of the Style Guide should include code information for HTML tags, attributes, and definitions of graphic elements. Please refer to the comprehensive set of components to include in your Style Guide. The level of detail is project dependent. The layout of the Production Style Guide should compliment the layout of the Design Style Guide. We recommend that it be both visual and informative [7.1]. Portions of your project may be very straightforward and not need code called out. Conversely, your project may require additional items to support the inevitable changes that are inherent to maintenance.

CREATING THE HANDOFF PACKET

Consider the handoff packet to be like a baton in a relay race — you are passing on what is needed to keep running. The handoff packet is the collection of all the assets, materials, and documentation of the project. It contains all source files, images, templates, and specs necessary for another team or individual to understand the site after the initial launch.

Gather all files relevant to the site's production. Communicate clearly between team members when determining which files — both design and HTML — are worth archiving. You probably have many intermediary files, perhaps called layout_01, layout_02, layout_06, final, final_2, final-final, etc. Clean up files you want to keep and name and archive everything clearly.

Materials will vary from project to project, but a complete packet should be burned to CD-ROM and should contain at least the following:

- **All Photoshop/Fireworks files (in layers, text *not* rendered)**
- **Fonts (or information on where to purchase fonts)**
- **All photos/illustrations (including copyright information — don't forget about usage rights!)**
- **HTML pages and templates**
- **Style Guide (design and production) in HTML**
- **The root folder of the site and other relevant files**

This handoff packet should be approved by the project manager, lead production designer, and art director. Once the packet is handed off, the transition has happened. At this point, the site is the maintenance team's responsibility.

Timeframe for Transitional Tutoring

Establish — and get it in writing — a predetermined timeframe for back-and-forth questions and technical consulting following handoff. A few weeks of emails flying back and forth should be expected. A few questions within a few months after that are also acceptable. But three to six months down the road, if the maintenance team still needs regular assistance from the original web development team, then that constitutes billable services. Long in advance of the handoff, set up a firm understanding that postlaunch technical assistance and maintenance needs will be billable as of x number of days after handoff. Whether it's 30 days or 45, 60, or 90, the point is to preset the duration. State this in writing and have the client sign off on it.

Plan for Usability Testing

Conducting usability tests on the live site is the first chance to see how real users interact with the site. One of the best comparison methods for obtaining measurable results is to conduct usability testing on the existing/outgoing site — and then compare results to the newly launched redesigned site. If any areas are still hard to use, incorporate appropriate modifications into the maintenance plan and retest for usability after a subsequent update of the site. For more on Usability Testing, see chapter 8.

TRACKING DOCUMENTATION

Although you don't need to print out every last email, gather the relevant ones for internal archival — especially anything that demonstrates client approval. Make certain to account for anything that discusses scope change (AC forms with signatures, memos, project plans, contracts, etc.). In the possible case of a dispute over the invoice, these documents go a long way toward clearing up miscommunication. Furthermore, when it comes time to bid on the next redesign project, you can refer to actual costs versus guesswork.

Sort through all documents, both hard copies and electronic, and cull. Archive everything relevant by whatever method your company uses to handle archival: a binder, folders, CD-ROM. As always, the more organized you are throughout a project, the less work will be required to wrap it up.

CONDUCTING A POSTLAUNCH MEETING

The postlaunch meeting, often somewhat somberly called the "postmortem" meeting, is an excellent chance to reflect on the project as a whole and revisit lessons learned. Ideally, all team members (client and development teams alike) should have a brief rest before the meeting occurs. This allows everyone to get out of the moment and stay at a high level of conversation during the meeting.

What Archived Documentation Should Include

- Budget approvals: initial budget and weekly budget reports (signed and dated whenever possible)
- Additional charge forms (ACs) — signed!
- Emails (especially those with any approved changes or requests from the client)
- The original proposal (in PDF and editable format)
- The project scope or project plan
- Submitted documents: reports or studies generated during the project, including the Creative Brief, competitive analysis (if conducted), usability testing reports, etc.
- Printouts, records, or sketches of information from the design and visual design phases (original Visio, OmniGraffle, or FreeHand files if possible)
- A copy of the Style Guide in HTML or editable format

Every project is a learning experience. Some projects go well; others are challenging. Begin the post-launch meeting with a broad overview of the project from start to finish and then isolate areas where there were innovative breakthroughs, issues, communication gaps, and/or places to improve on methodology. Maintain a positive approach and avoid blame or finger pointing. Don't turn the meeting into a gripe session (you may still need to work with these people); rather, identify the spots in production where the flow was impeded. What caused slowdowns? What ran smoothly, and how can that successful workflow be duplicated in the future? Think positively. This meeting is a perfect opportunity to reflect upon the upcoming next phase of the site, or to kick around thoughts on a new project.

SCHEDULING MAINTENANCE TRAINING

With most sites in maintenance, the unfortunate tendency is for the layout, graphic treatment, and information design to slowly break down and lose cohesion. With the original designers no longer choosing photos, laying out pages, and signing off on new content placement, the maintenance team begins to impart its own sense of design and organization, especially when incorporating new content. Although the maintenance team may have a background in design and layout, and even if its members are creative individuals with design ideas of their own, the integrity of the site depends on maintaining the look and feel that has been established. It is heartbreaking to watch the redesigned site slowly fall apart, often through no fault of the maintenance team. Usually, it is because they have not been adequately prepared for the task.

Because no one knows a site as well as those who built it, training and direction will almost always have to accompany the handoff materials. When planning maintenance training, set up a predetermined number of hours for the task; otherwise, it may turn into a never-ending process. Be timely with handoff materials; maintenance starts right away. Communicate clearly by explaining the Style Guide, the graphic and HTML standards, and the technical goals of the site. Consider it preventative medicine for your redesigned site.

STEPHAN SPENCER ON INFORMATION AS POWER

Most companies don't even realize that their competitors are ranking higher in the search engines, getting more traffic, converting more visitors into buyers, and enjoying better returns on their website investment. They simply don't know how well their website is performing. And they are missing out on valuable e-business opportunities.

What do you need to know? For starters: how well your site is performing. And how it stacks up against competitors.

How Effective Is Your Site?

Measuring the effectiveness of your site's design, content, and functionality is a business imperative. The following metrics will give you information critical for maximizing your ROI:

- **Abandonment.** What percentage of visitors gets no further than your home page? What percentage abandons shopping carts? What is the ratio of abandoned carts to completed purchases per day? How many items are in an abandoned cart? In a purchased cart? What items do people abandon?
- **Conversion.** What percentage of visitors becomes customers or, at least, takes some action? What is the cost per conversion?
- **Retention.** How many customers make repeat purchases? Retained customers are cheaper than new ones.
- **Lifetime value (LTV).** What's the value of a given customer relationship over his lifetime? Improve a customer's LTV by upselling, cross-selling, increasing buying frequency, and reducing the cost of sales and support.
- **Referral source.** Determine which websites (search engines, industry portals, partners, and affiliates), email campaigns, and online promotions deliver the most sales, inquiries, and customers.
- **Recency, frequency, and monetary value (RFM).** How recently did a given customer visit your site and/or make a purchase? How often does he visit or purchase? How much does he spend? Take good care of customers who rate high in all three areas.

Other web metrics include stickiness, slipperiness, attrition, churn, etc. Two great sources for more on web metrics are Jim Sterne's book, *Web Metrics*, and his "E-Metrics" white paper, available from www.emetrics.org/articles/whitepaper.html.

Competitive Intelligence Online

Answer these key questions to gauge the effectiveness of your online presence versus that of your competition:

How much traffic are your competitors getting? Find out with the Alexa.com site, which provides traffic data, historical graphs showing traffic trends, and even what other sites your competitors' users visit. (You can also track site competitor site changes with Alexa's Wayback Machine [www.archive.org], which shows changes to web pages since 1996.)

How many pages do you and your competitors have in Google and Yahoo!? Find out by searching both search engines for "site:" followed by your domain name (for example, "site: amazon.com"). Note that the www was intentionally omitted, as "site:www.amazon.com" doesn't return as comprehensive of a results set." Even easier, use our free tool at netconcepts.com/urlcheck to check all major search engines.

How "important" is your site to Google and Yahoo!? An important site enjoys better rankings. Find out by installing the following:

- The Google Toolbar is a browser plug-in for Internet Explorer for Windows (http://toolbar.google.com) which among other things, will check any web page's PageRank score, a numerical representation of Google's importance-scoring algorithm.
- The Yahoo! Companion Toolbar, another Internet Explorer plug-in (http://companion.yahoo.com) to check your Web Rank score, Yahoo!'s rough equivalent.

Who links to you? Find out by searching Google for "link:" followed by your web address (for example, "link:www.amazon.com") and then searching Yahoo! for "linkdomain:" followed by your web address. Easier yet, use our free link-popularity-checking tool at netconcepts.com/linkcheck.

How are your PR campaigns, advertising, email marketing, and search engine optimization affecting your market share? Consider signing up with a service like Hitwise for day-by-day monitoring of your online market share.

What's the word on the e-streets? Search for discussions about you and your competitors on the forums at http://groups.google.com. Search news sites for articles mentioning competitors and your own company.

What are your competitors offering? Subscribe to your competitors' email newsletters to stay informed about what offers, contests, sales, products, and features they're launching.

Automated monitoring services can make keeping up with your competitive position easy. GoogleAlert (www.googlealert.com) monitors chosen Google search results and emails you when the results change. ChangeDetect (www.changedetect.com) can "watch" any page on the web and email you when the page is updated.

Collecting and monitoring site data and your site's effectiveness in the context of your competition will allow you to identify weaknesses that need to be fixed and competitive challenges that need to be met.

An online wine shop seized the web metrics opportunity. Metrics guided its redesign efforts and allowed it to laser-focus web marketing initiatives. Breaking its visitors into five distinct audience segments revealed that one segment — less than 10% of its total audience — accounted for over 80% of its revenue. This knowledge allowed the site to target that sector aggressively. New site visitors from that segment received special treatment in the form of discounts and customized content. Metrics also revealed other opportunities: For instance, cross-selling bakery products and white wine was particularly effective.

Remember, the first step toward maximum return on your website investment is building a clear understanding of your website's effectiveness.

Stephan Spencer (www.stephanspencer.com) is founder and president of Netconcepts (www.netconcepts.com), a full-service web agency specializing in search engine optimization, e-commerce, website auditing, and email marketing. Clients include Gorton's, Cabela's, Verizon, REI, InfoSpace, Sharper Image, Wella, Sara Lee, and MP3.com. Stephan has authored articles for Catalog Age, MarketingProfs, Unlimited, Building Online Business, NZ Marketing, and others. He co-authored Catalog Age's research report "State of Search Engine Marketing 1.0." He is also a frequent speaker at conferences around the globe.

LAUNCH

> Going Live

> Prepping an Announcement Plan

> Optimizing for Search Engines

> Launching the Site

GOING LIVE

With the site poised to move to the live server, all testing should be complete, and production must be frozen. Because there are probably still bugs to be slain, have a solid plan in place for postlaunch fixes. But with the QA process essentially finished, the site is ready for public viewing. Congratulations! Just as moving to a new location provides the impetus to send moving announcements, a new site launch offers the opportunity to announce a new, redesigned site at the same, familiar URL.

Plan your announcement strategy long in advance of the launch date. Know how you intend to advertise and promote the site once it goes live and know who will be involved. Is the external web development team involved? Is the internal team handling it all? Has an advertising firm been brought into the mix? What about timing? Often there is an immovable "drop-dead" date for launch. This can depend on a variety of outside factors, any of which might announce the redesigned site. These might include an upcoming tradeshow or company presentation, the release of an annual report, or anything else associated with a firm date. If outside factors are fueling the launch schedule, make sure to know in advance who is in charge (for example, the marketing department or an outside advertising agency — establish this when identifying all client contacts in Phase 1: Define). That person can be contacted should schedules slip or content radically change.

Soft Launch

Imagine a schedule that has breathing room. Imagine the luxury to launch on the live server and test there without the timing constraints of outside factors such as an expensive advertising campaign or the release of an annual report. A soft launch is a non-pressured posting of the site to the live server, giving time to test on a live audience, conduct usability tests and watch for technical errors. Sometimes a soft launch also means the site is not yet complete, as in "We are soft launching on October 1 with 85% of content in place. We plan to fill in the remaining content by December 1 and advertise the redesign then." Some larger companies running on multiple servers have pushed a site live without announcement on a few "test" servers and watched to see if audience usage of the site dropped or changed dramatically, addressing audience feedback prior to making a public announcement.

A hard launch is simply a situation with a hard deadline — a "drop-dead" date that is usually accompanied by outside timing restraints. If possible, always plan for a soft launch. If the client can't accommodate, make the risks abundantly clear: If there are bugs associated with the live server (this includes firewall issues), they may not be found before going live.

SITE ANNOUNCEMENT PLAN TIPS			
Before Launch	**During Launch**	**After Launch**	**Off Site (Should Be Planned Far in Advance)**
• A month or so prior to launch, announce the impending launch of the new website on your existing site [7.2]. • A few weeks prior to launch, preview the redesigned site from your home page [7.3].	• If customers will notice that your site is down while you are uploading and checking live, put up a temporary page announcing that the redesigned site is launching "right now" [7.4]. • Some companies launch sections in phases and announce certain times when the site will be down for maintenance while the sections are being updated.	• Send an announcement inviting customers to see the "new and improved site." • Have an area on the new site explaining what changed, why it changed, and how the improvements will help the customer experience. • Take screenshots for promotional use.	• Determine how you can promote your site using links on other sites with a similar audience profile. Set up agreements early so that after launch, and after an advertising delay, links can run. • Determine what offline printed materials can announce the re-launch: monthly newsletters, brochures, a new mailer, etc. Have the plan in place so that after launch, and after an advertising delay, printed materials can run. • Confirm traditional offline marketing methods. Depending on advertising budget and the marketing effort supported by the client, this campaign could be local, regional, or national in print and media. Get everything in place so that after launch, and after an advertising delay, advertising can run.

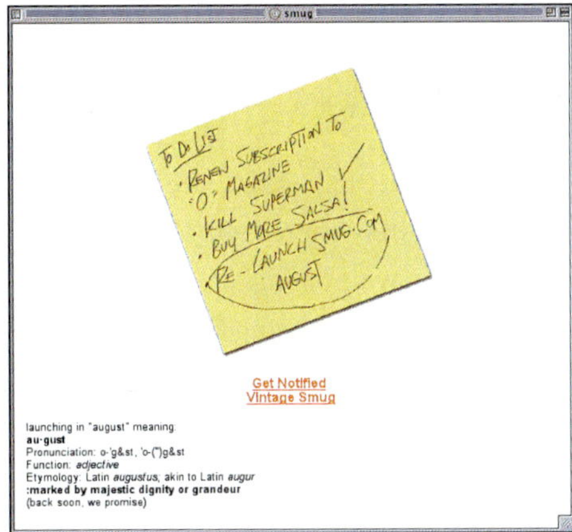

< 7.2 >

Smug.com ran this humorous splash-page announcement for months prior to the scheduled launch of its redesign. The options smug.com offered were entry into the existing site or an email link that offered notification of when the redesign would be launched. The danger of this setup is the very real possibility that the temporary home page stays live for far longer than intended.

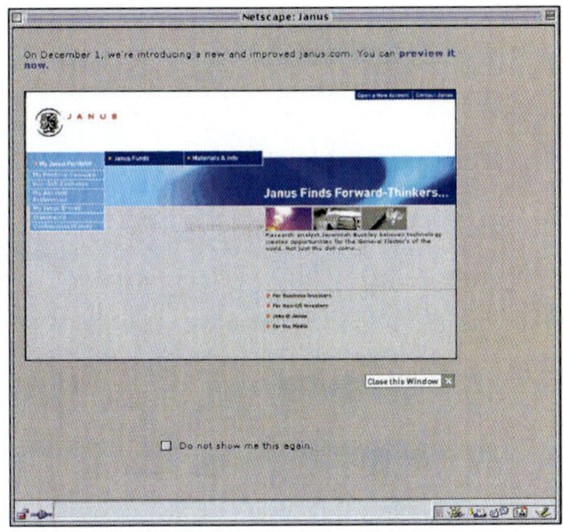

< 7.3 >

Allow users to become familiar with the changes. (Remember that people generally dislike change, even if it is for the better.) Before launching their redesign in late 2000, Janus Funds (www.janus.com) had a pop-up window offering the option of previewing the new site or closing the window.

< 7.4 >

Author Julia Quinn (www.juliaquinn.com) pushed a soft launch that allowed for QA of some potentially fussy code on the live server before going truly live to users. This page, announcing that the redesign was uploading right then, sat on the URL for the two-day duration of testing, and included a product-ordering link.

Advertising Delay

Don't book paid advertising until at least two weeks after the projected live date. Things can and will go wrong. The QA process may have revealed more errors than were expected. Your team might be unable to fix everything by the specified date. If you can, allow for a few weeks of postlaunch testing to ensure that the site is working on the live server (soft launch) — then begin your outside marketing campaign. Think of how frustrating it would be to pay for advertising that leads new users to a broken site. You have one chance to make a good impression. Make it count.

Your Current Audience and Its Comfort Zone

Part of easing your current audience into accepting your redesign is to let these people know about it in advance. Create a page to introduce the redesign and clearly identify the new features and navigation. Link it directly from the home page. Make your current audience part of your newly launched redesign. Consider the following list as a guide:

- **Redesigned.** Tell your audience that you've redesigned your site. Let people know that this will only help you do a better job for them.
- **New features.** List your new content features. Did you add new media? Add more FAQ items? If you are launching your redesign in iterative sublaunches, list what is coming soon.
- **New navigation.** Tell your audience what you've done. Here is an example: "We've restructured our site and provided more page-to-page links to make it easier than ever to get around and to get the information you look for regularly. We've broken up long pages that required lots of scrolling and added "bread crumbs" at the tops of pages so that you always know what part of the site you are in."
- **Feedback.** Make it easy to get feedback. Try the following text: "Like the redesigned site? Have any suggestions? Find any broken links or glitches? Email us. We'd love to hear from you."

PREPPING AN ANNOUNCEMENT PLAN

Depending on your audience, the redesigned site can be announced both online and offline. Use existing methods already in place with current materials (advertising, business cards, printed collateral, brochures) and explore new options as well. Regardless of whether you are working toward a soft launch or a drop-dead launch date, make sure marketing and promotional cues are in place, but don't let marketing drive your launch to the detriment of the integrity of the site (if you can help it). See the Site Announcement Plan Tips chart for several suggestions as to how to announce the redesigned site.

OPTIMIZING FOR SEARCH ENGINES

Search engines are like your site's life support. If your site is not adequately represented in the search engines, you might as well be cut off from your air supply. Put another way, not being in the search engines is like having an unlisted phone number. The market leader among search engines — Google — has been deemed by internet luminaries as the "operating system of the internet." Google is the shortest path between points A and B, even when A and B are both part of your same website. So it follows that being well represented in the search engines — particularly Google, Yahoo!, and MSN — is a business imperative.

You may be tempted to submit your site to an array of search engines in one fell swoop using a submission service or software, something akin to the "$99 will submit your site to ALL THE TOP SEARCH ENGINES!" spam that continues to intrude upon our email inboxes. These services will most likely do more harm than good. They will submit your URL to "link farms" and various unsavory online neighborhoods. In the court of the search engines, you're "guilty by association," and the punishment is being penalized in the search results or even being banned.

You may be considering simply submitting your site to the major search engines by hand, one at a time. Again, we don't advise it. First of all, it shouldn't be necessary. Spiders for Google, Yahoo!, MSN, Teoma, and so forth will find your new site on their own just by the fact that other sites link to you.

So instead of submitting, focus your energy on getting some inbound links from sites that are already included in the search engines. Even just one inbound link can be enough to get your site spidered and included, particularly if the page that links to you is considered reasonably "important" in the eyes of the major search engine. How can you know what a search engine considers to be important? In the case of Google and Yahoo!, it's simple: Both companies offer a free, downloadable toolbar that displays the importance score, from 0 to 10, measured in PageRank by Google and WebRank by Yahoo!

If, after a month or two of waiting, your site is still not included, *then* perhaps consider a manual submission. Because search engines do not like automated submissions, you won't get much benefit from tools like WebPosition Gold.) Only submit your home page URL and only submit it once. Monthly submissions are no longer necessary.

And just because the search engine spiders do find you, it doesn't mean their spiders will do a thorough job of exploring your site. Search engines actually tend to skip over pages with overly complex URLs (such as too many variables in the query string, session IDs, etc.). This is usually the case with database-driven websites. Even the nontechnical layman can identify such search engine–unfriendly URLs: Just look at the URL for ampersands, equal signs, the word "cgi-bin," or long strings of characters that look like they could be unique identifiers (for tagging users or sessions). Search spiders also have problems exploring sites with frames or with navigation that relies on JavaScript, Java, or Flash. You can check to see how much of your site has been included in all the major engines by using the handy tool from SEO specialists Netconcepts at www.netconcepts.com/urlcheck.

Search Engines and the Dreaded 404 Page

Error pages, a pesky web reality, are usually caused by outdated links from emails, indexed pages that have changed, or typos. A search engine remembers outdated pages until it visits and your server returns a 404 code. Your IT department needs to turn on the error trapping function. See Barbara "WebMama" Coll's site for more information on turning error pages into selling opportunities. www.webmama.com/error404-advice.htm.

BARBARA COLL ON DESIGNING FOR OPTIMAL PLACEMENT IN SEARCH ENGINE RESULTS

Consider search engines one of your most important audiences. If this audience cannot access and understand the contents of your website, it will severely reduce the number of visitors who can find you using search engines.

There are four elements to designing for optimal placement of your website in search engine results: the right architecture, the right technology, the right source code, and the right keywords. Getting these right means being sure your team includes "empowered" people from marketing, graphic design, and IT, so get buy-in and committed hours from all key stakeholders. Don't count on outside vendors (including off-site hosts) for design or programming being up-to-speed in SEO.

Getting the Architecture, Technology, and Source Code Right

Think about optimization early in the redesign process. Each of the following architecture and technology concerns has a direct effect on SEO:

Architecture Decisions Relevant to SEO

- File/directory structure and naming
- Navigation schemes
- Password protected areas
- Error trapping

Technology and Source Code Decisions Relevant to SEO

- Tracking systems
- Entry pages
- Intro or splash pages
- Wizzy technology
- Frames

Keep in mind that users — both humans and search engines — often don't start at your home page. Because of this, your site needs detailed navigation information, and you should design each major page as able to stand alone (like your home page).

Pay attention to "Error 404" trapping; your users should never see the default Error 404 page. To prevent this, your site should "trap" error pages and replace them with a smarter custom page; tailored to take advantage of the visitor's (thwarted) desire to find something on your site by giving your customers a branded, easy-to-navigate page. The text should be polite and non-technical.

Include a detailed sitemap in your redesign and link to it from your home page. This entry page is full of text links — the favorite food of search bots and spiders. If you have a sitemap filled with detailed text links (use your keywords in the links!), the bots and spiders will follow them and the pages, improving your ranking.

Your design team won't like it, but do not use splash movies or content-free intro pages — search engine spiders and bots require text. Movies and other technologies have their place, but on the home page, they act as barriers to indexing and frustrate visitors.

You have to be sure that you don't look like a spammer to the search engines. (See *Search Engine Spam* by Shari Thurow, December 8, 2003; www.clickz.com/experts/search/results/print.php/3116421.)

Finally, make sure that referring URLs are turned on and being collected and analyzed, if you use server-side includes set them up so that the tags are different for each page. Also, use separate files for JavaScript and Cascading Style Sheet (CSS) files, and handle redirects at the DNS level.

Getting the Words Right (and in All the Right Places)

Getting the words right means including words that your users will search on to find your pages. Don't just ask yourself — ask your customers, your team, maybe even your mail carrier, what terms they would type into a search engine to find your product, services, or information about your industry.

What's the biggest challenge? Getting past "marketing speak." Remember that folks searching for your site will be searching in plain language; they certainly won't know the latest buzzwords!

Because each page of your site is different, you will need to use different keywords on different pages so that users can click straight to what they are looking for. Do not use your competitors' brands (unless in comparison charts, etc.) and do not use terms for anything that does not appear on the relevant page. The formula for search results includes how often a word appears (in text) on a page, so this is particularly crucial.

The bottom line? Remember the search engines as you build or redesign your website!

SITE ARCHITECTURE NAVIGATION SCHEMES

Navigation Scheme	How Do Search Engines Like It?
Flash	Not at all — although they are working on it.
Image maps	Not at all, cannot read images, however can read ALT tags.
Search or Fill in the Box	No way.
JavaScript	Some do, some do not.
Drop-down menus	Sort of, it depends on how they are coded.
Text links	Love it! The best!

DIRECTORY AND FILE NAMING

Do's	Don'ts
Use key *phrases* — a big win!	Use underlines.
Separate words by (up to two) hyphens	Rely on dynamic additions to the URL.
Use words relevant to the user.	Use long URLs.
Use subdomains to drive traffic deeper into your site.	Include session IDs.
Put keyword-laden content pages near the root level.	Have more than two parameters per URL.
Use no more than three directory levels for any page.	

Barbara "WebMama" Coll has been involved with product and program marketing in Silicon Valley for 17 years, combining her engineering education with business/market know-how. She founded WebMama.com Inc. in 1996 to provide online businesses with low-cost lead-generation programs and now specializes in search engine marketing. Barbara is a sought-after presenter for industry conferences. She is president of the newly formed Search Engine Marketing Professional Organization (www.sempo.org).

Preserving Bookmarks and Search Engine Links

As you retire the current site, consider that a significant percentage of your existing audience — an audience that you want to keep — may have bookmarked heavily frequented pages from your old site. Due to information design changes, specifically with file/directory structure and naming conventions, many of your site's URLs may now be obsolete. Don't lose traffic due to this potential hiccup. Use redirects.

Some search engines offer paid inclusion services, whereby you periodically submit an XML feed to that search engine, and they re-spider the pages listed in the feed on a frequent basis. Yahoo! offers such a service; Google does not and openly rejects the notion of ever offering such a service. It may be worth considering if you cannot fix what is making your site search engine unfriendly, even with the help of an SEO consultant. Be forewarned, paid inclusion could get very expensive.

Directories, unlike search engines, *require* that you submit to them to get included. Definitely submit to the handful of important directories like Open Directory, JoeAnt, and GoGuides. Also hunt out niche directories and topically relevant guides for your industry or special interest. For each directory submission, craft a good site name and site description that includes relevant keywords, each tailored to the directory's unique length, format, and editorial requirements.

For the latest information on the ever-changing and often-complicated world of search engines, make frequent visits to www.searchenginewatch.com.

Four Surefire Ways to Hide from Search Engines

1. **Poor choices for TITLE tags.** Avoid fancy or irrelevant TITLE tags. Some designers like to lay out titles like this: "a c m e h o m e" so that it looks nicely designed in the browser. While this may be prettier than "ACME HOME" and simpler/sleeker than "ACME ROAD RUNNER EXTERMINATION COMPANY," a search for the word "acme" won't match the four one-letter words "a c m e."
2. **Splash pages.** We have already recommended not having a splash page, but if you must, give it a descriptive TITLE tag and META "description" and "keyword" information. Remember, search engines consider your home page to be the most important page of your site. That's because search engines like Google and Yahoo! measure importance in terms of links and most of the links that point to your site point to your home page rather than to internal pages.
3. **Frames.** If you want to hide the contents of your site from search engines, use frames. Enough said.
4. **Complex URLs.** Sites that are database-driven tend to have problematic "stop characters" in the URLs of their web pages – characters such as question marks, ampersands, and equal signs – that in many cases cause the search engine spiders to turn up their noses to the pages. It's even worse if session IDs, user IDs, or other various "flags" are embedded in the URL. You can have a database-driven website and simple URLs that resemble those of static web pages; it's not an either-or proposition.

OPTIMIZING YOUR SITE FOR SEARCH ENGINE

Optimizing your site for search engines is not unlike aiming at a moving target. For the latest information and suggested strategies, check searchenginewatch.com. For an overview, refer to this chart. It is not an exhaustive list, but it is a good starting point.

ITEM	BENEFIT
<TITLE> tag	Leading with good keywords in the title makes your page more relevant to those keywords in a search
Heading tags (<H1>, <H2>, etc.)	Heading tags are considered much more important than the rest of the body copy by the search engines. <H1> gets more weight than <H2>.
<IMG ALT> tags	All navigation and product images should have alt text defined that contain relevant keywords to make your page more relevant to those keywords in a search.
Body copy	Ideally, have at least 200 words on the page and have it be keyword-rich. Keywords near the top of the HTML get more weight than if they are near the bottom.
Text links	Google associates the anchor text in the hyperlink as highly relevant to the page being linked to. So, use good keywords and not "click here," unless you're aiming to be #1 in Google for the words "click here." It's especially important to do a good job of this on your home page.
URL	Dynamic content coming from a database should still have a URL that looks static, rather than one with question marks, ampersands, etc.
Inbound links	Try to garner links from other, relevant sites, as links from other sites increase your position in the search results. The more relevant and more important the site is, the better. Google's measure of importance is called PageRank score.
Keyword choices	Keywords that you are targeting for high search engine rankings should not only be relevant, but also popular with searchers. Check this with a keyword research tool such as inventory.overture.com or wordtracker.com.
<META NAME=description CONTENT="..."> tag	Having a META description won't improve your rankings, but it can influence the snippet displayed in on the search results page. Incorporate relevant keywords into the description and make it a compelling call-to-action.

To Blog or not to Blog

Blogs (web logs) and moblogs (mobile logs) have become one of the most effective ways of driving appropriate traffic to your site. Starting as a medium for sharing of opinions and information (sometimes called "ranting"), blogs have evolved from online journals into one of the most compelling content sources online. Moveable Type (moveabletype.org) is an inexpensive way to get started. Or, for blogging basics, start with www.technorati.com/help/blogging101.html.

Prioritize Fixes

You may not be able to catch every last thing prior to launch. You should have a list of prioritized changes and fixes for postlaunch maintenance. A perfect site is very hard to achieve, even with QA completed and usability testing performed. Issues will always crop up; there has to be some threshold for acceptable losses. First take care of showstoppers — bugs that must be fixed prior to launch — and then launch. Fix the next most important bugs immediately postlaunch and then fix the rest in due course. If you are an external team readying for handoff, determine what is feasible for the maintenance team to handle. Hand off when appropriate.

MAINTENANCE

> Maintaining the Site

> Assessing Maintenance Team Capability

> Internal vs. External Maintenance Teams

> Developing a Maintenance Plan

> Confirming Site Security

> Planning Iterative Initiatives

> Measuring Success

LAUNCHING THE SITE

All testing has been completed on the staging server, fixes have been made, production is frozen, and the announcement plan is in place. All systems are go. Plan to upload to the live server during off-peak hours to allow for downtime to interfere as little as possible with the regular web traffic. Then... launch! Have a "live" moment. Be accessible to your real audience and customer base.

An important part of launch is an immediate QA test on the live server. If you were able to schedule a soft launch, this is a nonpressured event, and testing can be conducted in a relatively leisurely timeframe (a few days, close to the first 24 hours but hopefully no overtime). If you launched on a drop-dead date, some rushing is probably in order to test on the live server. Be prepared to roll back to the old site if any showstopper bugs pop up.

Launch is a big black dot in the very gray area between development and maintenance. Client and development teams need to agree on when the site is truly ready to go live. This may sound simple, but often there is a lot of going back and forth between fixing and refining, and finally having the okay to go live. There is also the potential problem of handing off a site to a client without first being able to test on the client's server. All kinds of issues can pop up at that point. And whose responsibility is the immediate postlaunch testing? The maintenance team's or the development team's? Make sure this is clear. And if you are an external team launching on a client's server on a drop-dead date, make certain you have the access you need.

When it is finally time to go live, go live. Voilà! You are now in maintenance. Have a celebration. Get some sleep. Then get ready to track the results of your labor.

A rollback is the last saved and approved version of a site. Have a rollback of the old site standing by just in case something goes horribly wrong with the launch.

MAINTAINING THE SITE

Maintenance is the fuel that keeps a site alive. Your announcement plan may get visitors to your site, but will they come back? What about regularly? In one study, Forrester Research Inc. interviewed 8,600 web-using households to find out why people return to websites **[7.5]**. High-quality content led the poll, closely followed by ease of use, quick download time, and frequent updating. Consider that only regular updating keeps high-quality content fresh and new. This makes maintenance responsible for both the first and the fourth top reason why a visitor returns to a website.

Maintenance is really just the regular introduction of new content. Why make such a fuss and spend so much time developing guidelines and plans? The alarming fact is that a significant percentage of sites launched grow stale through lack of good, planned upkeep. Winging it rarely works. In fact, many sites slated for redesign stagnated in "No-Plan Land" before the decision to redesign was finally acted on. Keep your redesigned site healthy and growing with iterative relaunches that smoothly introduce improvements and changes that respond to user needs.

Maintenance, however, doesn't just happen. There needs to be a plan for immediate, postlaunch fixes and ongoing, long-term, regular updating. A 6- to 12-month maintenance plan is a good timeline to undertake. Include in the plan ways for dealing with glitches, usability issues, scheduled updates, as well as the next iteration of the site. Don't forget about getting user feedback and usability testing results both immediately after the site is live and a few months later. User feedback is integral to shaping the redesigned site and planning for how to approach your next refresh/redesign.

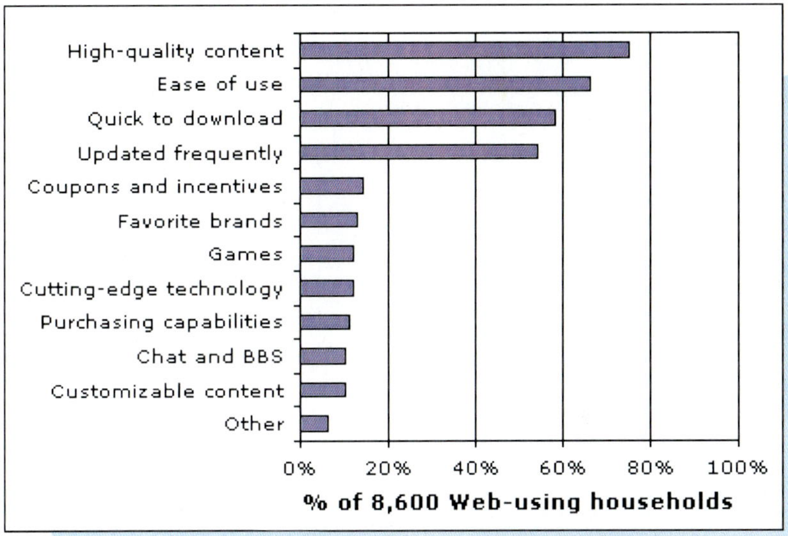

7.5 >

Forrester Research Inc. interviewed 8,600 web-using households to find out why people return to websites. Chart courtesy of system concepts (www.system-concepts.com/articles/forrester.html).

High-quality content
Ease of use
Quick to download
Updated frequently
Coupons and incentives
Favorite brands
Games
Cutting-edge technology
Purchasing capabilities
Chat and BBS
Customizable content
Other
0% 20% 40% 60% 80% 100%
% of 8,600 Web-using households

Contribute

Many clients want to update their own sites. Whether to save resources or because their workflow demands a more hands-on approach, they need the control. However, due to the proclivity of client mayhem over HTML, the mere idea of clients working on the actual files makes many developers fearfully grimace. Finally, a solution has emerged: Contribute from Macromedia (www.macromedia.com). Contribute allows the client to make updates through the Contribute browser without requiring access to the code. Furthermore, developers can lock the client out of selected areas (using Dreamweaver), thus ensuring against inadvertent breakdown of code. Contribute is not for everyone. Sites that haven't been developed with Contribute in mind may require more set up than might be worth it. For some clients, Contribute doesn't allow enough control for their purposes, and they do, in fact, need the HTML files. But the idea is stellar, and the kinks are sure to be worked out.

ASSESSING MAINTENANCE TEAM CAPABILITY

In most situations, the development team hands off to a maintenance team already in place. "Who'll be maintaining the site?" the development team asks. It is not uncommon for the client to answer with pride, "Charlie in marketing knows some HTML. He's been posting our press releases for six months. We think he's doing a bang-up job. We're planning on having him take care of the new site, too."

Here is a simple, straightforward fact: The individuals responsible for updating need to have a high enough level of skill to handle the maintenance of the redesigned site — especially if there is complex functionality involved. The web development team should assess the capabilities of the maintenance team against the complexity of the redesigned site. It presents an obvious problem for someone like "Charlie in marketing" to suddenly maintain a dynamically driven site or a complex CSS-based layout if all he has is an only-slightly-above-basic understanding of FrontPage. Either Charlie needs tens of thousands of dollars worth of training or the client should be advised to hire an expert or two and let Charlie do some of the less technical production work.

We recommend a test. Far in advance of handoff, preferably after the Client Spec Sheet is filled out and analyzed so that the production designers have an idea of the complexity of the redesign, give the maintenance team a proficiency test (and pay them for their time). Resurrect an old project, one on roughly the same level of complexity as the maintenance team will need to deal with, and have them update it. Have them fix code. See how they handle adding information that breaks tables or challenges the CSS layout. Suggest that they add information and archive the old. Can they follow the file structure and cleanly add to it? Can they read the HTML and understand it enough to troubleshoot? What about the backend programming? Do they know Flash or DHTML (if either is applicable)? Do they understand the content management application (if applicable)? Watch them. Do they understand what they are doing, or are they guessing?

If a test isn't feasible, at least review previous sites they have coded. If you aren't qualified to review the code, find someone you trust to take a look. Keep in mind that there is no absolute right or wrong, especially when it comes to the intricacies of CSS. If they are well versed in Dreamweaver or GoLive, this might be adequate for a simple site, but often it is best if you find someone who can hand code or at least problem solve from scratch.

Web maintenance folks quite often possess an admirable level of production knowledge and only need some training on the specifics of the site. In other situations, it becomes clear that additional maintenance personnel will be needed.

INTERNAL VS. EXTERNAL MAINTENANCE TEAMS

For many companies, increasing expectations for daily site updates, dynamic content generation, management of e-commerce systems, and effective customer service have engendered the development of web-savvy and detail-oriented in-house maintenance teams.

Maintenance needs vary. Depending on the depth of postlaunch content and the frequency of updates, the development of a maintenance team can be as simple as hiring one HTML production designer for straightforward content updates. For more complex sites, a full team, complete with a full-time project manager, may be required. If you are working on a

MAINTENANCE TEAM SCENARIOS		
Much of the Time...	**Sometimes...**	**With Increasing Frequency...**
The client company hires an experienced web development firm to create the redesigned site but expects its own internal team to handle all postlaunch maintenance.	Some companies (usually smaller businesses) have the web development firm that designed the site maintain it, or they hire a third-party firm or outside consultant and keep that person/firm on retainer for site maintenance.	Many companies are developing and maintaining in-house and are recruiting experienced talent (art directors, visual designers, information designers, production designers, and engineers) for their internal teams.
Pros: • The experience and resources of the web development firm. • The cost savings of conducting the maintenance in-house.	**Pros:** • Having the same web development team develop, design, and maintain the site is obviously optimal. (It combats the natural degradation of a site over time.) • Hiring expertise for site maintenance can be cheaper than hiring staff if hours per month are low. • Lower overhead.	**Pros:** • The experience and resources of professional expertise for the web development team. • Having the same web development team develop, design, and maintain the site is obviously optimal.
Cons: • The expertise of in-house maintenance teams tends to be on a lower level than the web development team's, resulting in site degradation over time. • Higher overhead for internal maintenance.	**Cons:** • The cost of an outside web development team to maintain the site can be high. • Dealing with an outside firm can be cumbersome.	**Cons:** • Keeping the talent happy in a situation in which they only have one project to work on is difficult. Turnover can be high. • The cost of expertise on a full-time basis can be high.

fairly static site with very simple daily or weekly changes (or even brochure sites with relatively few monthly or quarterly changes), an outside contractor or part-time in-house individual might be a better bet.

There are several things to consider when comparing in-house maintenance to paying an outside development company a retainer (an ongoing payment, usually on a month-to-month or, for more static sites, quarterly basis). It is almost always cheaper to hire internal resources for full-time work. If your maintenance need is only 20 hours per week, however, it doesn't make sense to hire a full-time staffer. There are pros and cons for different scenarios; it must make sense from several standpoints: facilities, management, and financial.

DEVELOPING A MAINTENANCE PLAN

In the first phase of web development (Phase 1: Define), we recommended that your client fill out the Maintenance Survey to help align and define postlaunch goals. You used the information gathered to help structure the redesigned site so that it could grow with the planned maintenance.

Revisit the Maintenance Survey. What were the goals? Daily news updates? Weekly HTML advertising emails? Press releases? Product additions? Housekeeping concerns like copyright updates, archival of articles, etc.? Now that production is complete, update the answers from the survey to include anything the client may have added during the course of development. Now is the time to plan for all these things. Be aware of what is required for maintenance and make sure the resources will cover it. A simple spreadsheet — with time on one axis (in hours/days/weeks/months) and the site sections to be updated on the other — clearly communicates what gets updated and when **[7.6]**.

SAMPLE MAINTENANCE SCHEDULE
for a simple site that updates monthly

	HOME	PRODUCTS	NEWS PAGE	BIO/FAQ	OTHER
March 01	Announce new product	Post new product info	Announce new product		Register with Yahoo
April 01			Post reviews of new product	New FAQ	
May 01			Preview new product		Register with Google
June 01	Announce new product	Post new product info	Announce new product	Update Bio to include new product info	
July 01			Post reviews of new product, Preview new product		Register with HotBot
August 01	Announce new product	Post new product info	Announce new product		
Sept 01			Post reviews of new product	New FAQ	Register with Alta Vista
etc.					

< **7.6**

A simple spreadsheet provides a guide for scheduled maintenance.

When Bad Links Happen to Good Maintenance Teams

Broken links are a web reality. They pop up even after QA testers have crawled all over the site. And, as maintenance pours new content into the site and removes what is outdated, the possibilities for error multiply. Over time, broken links can become a persistent problem.

There are resources on the web that help track bad links, slow pages, and errors. Two of the top ones are Web Site Garage [7.7] and Net Mechanic [7.8]. Both sites help to monitor, maintain, and promote your site. Different tools and services are offered for free, with others at a fairly low fee.

If you are working in Dreamweaver, take advantage of the Check Links Sitewide feature [7.9]. Although this will not catch links going to the wrong place, it will find broken or orphaned links. A double-click will bring up the HTML file and highlight the errant link.

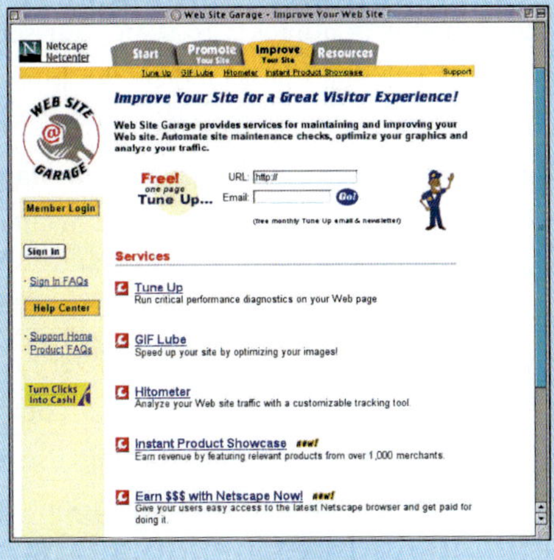

< 7.7 >

websitegarage.netscape.com (no www.).

< 7.8 >

www.netmechanic.com.

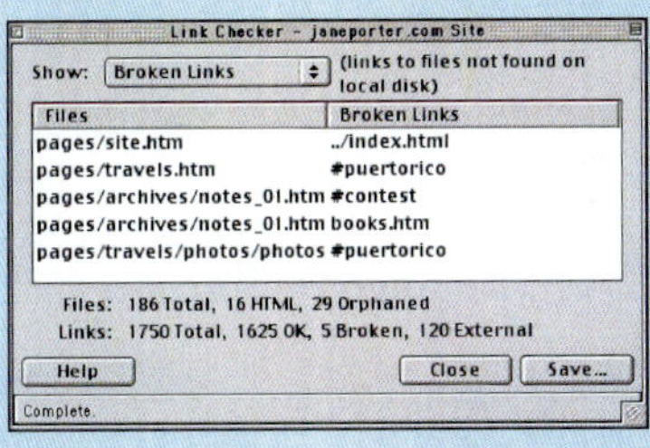

< 7.9 >

Dreamweaver's easy-to-use Check Links Sitewide feature.

CONFIRMING SITE SECURITY

Site security is usually not the responsibility of the external web development team. Typically, the in-house team does not specialize in this particular area; however, the responsibility may fall on them whether they are trained for it or not. Hopefully there is a security-minded member of the staff to protect against intruder attacks and to perform damage control if site security is compromised.

The unfortunate reality is that hackers are abundant and relentless. Hacking these days requires very little high-level knowledge. Most hackers run programs that automatically determine the vulnerabilities of your website and break into the system once a soft spot has been detected. This process happens largely without the direct interaction of the intended intruder. At the click of a button, a hacker can trigger a process that scans thousands of sites and breaks into those that are vulnerable.

Since the intrusion process is so largely automated, you can expect a hacker to scan your server within hours of it being connected to the Internet. System intruders can steal personal information, cause chaos, or use your web server as a staging ground for other web-based attacks. But whatever their reasons, *you* lose credibility and revenue when hackers force you offline **[7.10]**.

What we present here in this section is very rudimentary; it should not be mistaken for a comprehensive how-to on site security. Rather, use this section as an overview of items to think about.

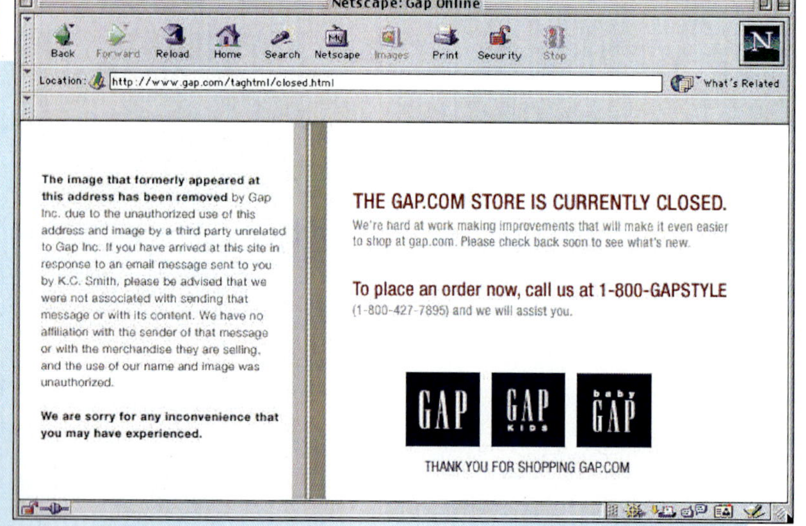

< **7.10**

In December 2000, a hacker broke into The Gap's online store and caused enough damage to force the online store to close while the problems were fixed.

A Few Tips to Consider as You Plan for Your Redesign's Security

- Protect yourself by outsourcing hosting to a larger service provider, one that has firewalls and aggressive monitoring and response systems.
- Avoid easy passwords based on dictionary words. Always use a combination of numbers, letters and characters. Change passwords frequently, especially after any layoffs. Disgruntled employees are always a risk.
- If you do choose to host your own web server, hire a Systems Administrator to monitor and maintain the server and to handle ongoing security issues.
- BACK UP YOUR DATA!!!! Even the most stringent security policy is not fail-safe. Always make sure that you have a recent copy of your business' data.
- Avoid using outdated, insecure methods of transferring data to your web site like FTP (File Transfer Protocol) or Telnet. Use secure programs like SCP (Secure Copy), SFTP (secure file transfer program), or SSH (Secure Shell) that encrypt data before it is sent and prevent hackers from stealing passwords and information.
- Use the most current versions of software and update all older software to the current version. Most hackers exploit vulnerabilities in older software. Make sure that your web server and any web-based technologies you use are up to date. For current information about vulnerabilities, visit the web site of the Computer Emergency Response Team Coordination Center www.cert.org.
- Install a firewall, a configured mechanism that permits or denies access to your internal server.
- Restrict physical access to your equipment. Keep your server in a restricted area away from public access.
- If your site is compromised it is best to rebuild it from the ground up. Hackers usually install back doors to allow a return visit to your site. These back doors are often quite difficult to discover. After your system has been hacked, it is recommended that you reinstall from scratch.
- Pay attention! If you know the warning signs, you have a much better chance of protecting your site from intruders. Monitor your site's traffic and activity, check server logs, and be aware!

Hacker Alert

How will you know if your site has been broken into? The evidence might be glaring: You have no site, or all your text has been suddenly replaced by gibberish. It might be offensive: All your site images have been replaced with pornographic material (true story, actually happened). Most often, however, it is far more subtle and subversive: Unexplained increases in regular traffic patterns, blocked user accounts, or the absence of expected services could indicate infiltration. The more you monitor your site, the better you will be at noticing when something is amiss. Stay aware!

PLANNING ITERATIVE INITIATIVES

With site improvements and refreshes ideally occurring regularly, revisiting planned initiatives should happen right after launch. If these plans were only abstractly addressed during development, waste no time in assessing what still needs to be done. Now is the time to begin planning quarterly releases. Out-of-scope items raised during the development process should be scheduled.

Plan on gathering information from current data, along with site logs, tracking software, and customer feedback. Additionally, post-launch usability testing and stats analysis will yield areas ripe for improvement. These should be tied to discrete business goals and prioritized. Return on investment (ROI) often drives these initiatives. However, it is important to note that not all iterative site improvements will be visible to the visitor (such as implementing CSS or incorporating a CMS).

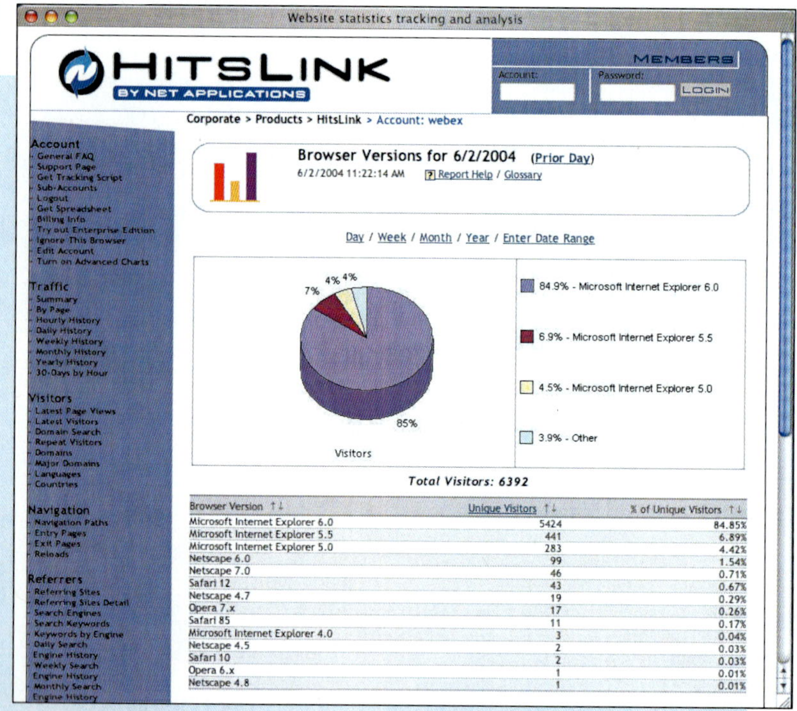

< 7.11

www.hitslink.com offers hard data about how your site is performing.

MEASURING SUCCESS

With the rapidly changing internet economy and the evolving nature of the web, it is more important than ever to track your site's postlaunch success. Return on investment (ROI) is not just a buzzword, it's a driving force. An overall goal of a site redesign should not be just to change it but to improve on specific business objectives. These goals, stated in the Communication Brief, might include increased usage/traffic, increased online sales, fewer customer calls, greater visibility, etc. Understanding these goals both qualitatively and quantitatively is integral to determining the best methods of measuring the success of the redesigned site.

Often a site's success is measured by logins or increasing subscriptions. Sales, especially direct from the website, are another success indicator. But because advertising is also one of the sources of revenue for companies, it continues to be increasingly important to understand site traffic and page hits as well as the demographics of your user base. This understanding helps not only to provide advertisers with specific data so that they can meet their own revenue goals, but also to help companies understand which parts of their sites are getting used the most, which features are working, and — just as important — which aren't. Your own server logs can help measure (if you can decipher them), and online tools such as www.hitslink.com **[7.11]** are also available for a very reasonable fee.

Many companies spend a lot of money and time analyzing server logs that monitor who is coming to their site (and from where), how long they stay at the site, what major paths they take, and where they usually end a session. This is great information if relevant data can truly be gleaned from pages and pages of barely comprehensible user logs. Unfortunately, it is not easy to decipher this raw data and turn it into meaningful summaries. Few companies actually allocate the time and resources to do it. An alternative would be one of the many software packages that specialize in gathering information, tracking results, and coming up with methods to increase usage **[7.13]**.

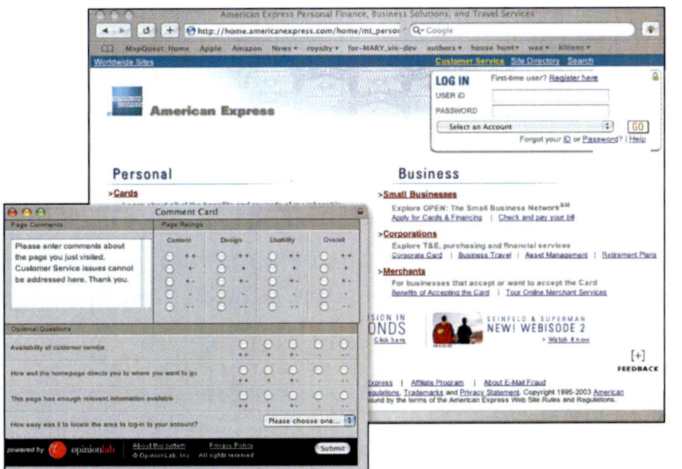

< **7.12** >

OnlineOpinion is used by adobe.com, sprintpcs.com, americanexpress.com, gotomedia.com, and others.

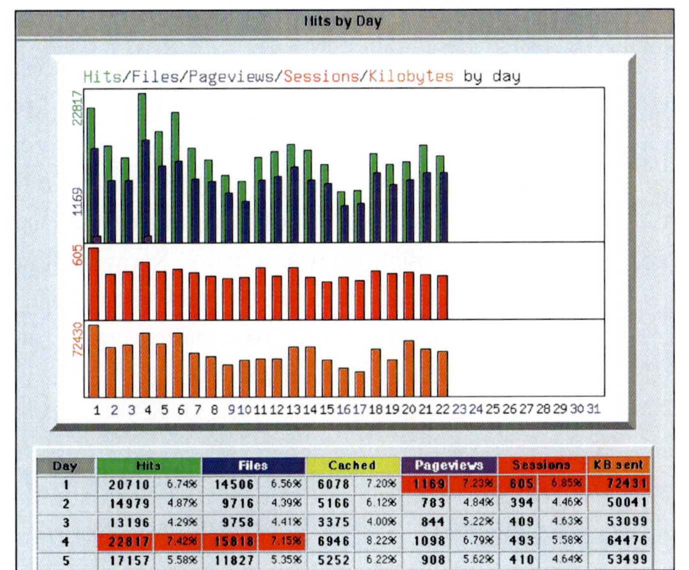

Day	Hits		Files		Cached		Pageviews		Sessions		KB sent
1	20710	6.74%	14506	6.56%	6078	7.20%	1169	7.23%	605	6.85%	72431
2	14979	4.87%	9716	4.39%	5166	6.12%	783	4.84%	394	4.46%	50041
3	13196	4.29%	9758	4.41%	3375	4.00%	844	5.22%	409	4.63%	53099
4	22817	7.42%	15818	7.15%	6946	8.22%	1098	6.79%	493	5.58%	64476
5	17157	5.58%	11827	5.35%	5252	6.22%	908	5.62%	410	4.64%	53499

Gather User Feedback

An excellent way to gauge a site's success upon launch is through user feedback. Gather comments, complaints, and accolades on your site's redesign quickly and easily. Have a prominent link — a feedback button — on each page. Ask users to comment specifically on the redesign's new features. Quantitative data can be tricky to obtain. Some sites have advanced features for gathering customer feedback. OpinionLab's (www.opinionlab.com) product, OnlineOpinion, provides a page-specific rating system that allows sites to capture instant feedback **[7.12]**. A key factor here is that the user does not need to do more than click.

< **7.13**

What are the most popular pages on your site? Can you define user behavior and patterns? This sample graph was generated by a simple server log and shows top pages by visits.

PHASE 5 CHECK-OFF LIST

Delivery

- ☐ Complete the Production Style Guide
- ☐ Create the handoff packet
- ☐ Track and archive documentation
- ☐ Conduct a postlaunch ("postmortem") meeting
- ☐ Schedule maintenance training

Launch

- ☐ Prepare an announcement plan
- ☐ Search engine optimization
- ☐ Launch the site

Maintenance

- ☐ Assess maintenance team capability
- ☐ Develop a maintenance plan
- ☐ Confirm site security
- ☐ Measure the success of the site

PHASE 5 SUMMARY

Congratulations! Your redesigned site has been launched and transitioned from development into maintenance. If you are an external team, maintenance is a weaning time. Hand off and evaluate the success of the project. Did the Core Process work for you? Where did things run smoothly? Where were there hiccups? Assess and adjust the Core Process to fit your own developing workflow and move on to planning the next iteration of the site.

If you are an internal team and are just receiving hand-off of the redesigned site for launch, you have a significant ongoing responsibility ahead of you. Regularly optimizing your site for search engines and continued analyses of measurable results is up to you. Continued development of ongoing initiatives — such as upgrading to a content management system, upgrading to a new e-commerce tool, or adding new sections to the site — will now need to be addressed. Maintaining standards and incorporating new content will be a daily/weekly/monthly job. The redesigned site is like an engine that has been rebuilt using many new parts. Knowing how that machine was built, however, is always insightful.

Then you won't have to redesign again for years... or at least the next few months.

CORE PROCESS SUMMARY

With launch, you've successfully completed the five phases of redesign site development: Define the Project, Develop Site Structure, Design Visual Interface, Build and Integrate, and Launch and Beyond. But don't stop here. The next three chapters, Chapter 8: Testing for Usability, Chapter 9: Working with Complex Functionality, and Chapter 10: Analyzing Your Competition, contain helpful processes to add into your workflow should your project warrant. We highly recommend them.

Website development is an ongoing process. With the Core Process as a set of suggested practices, you are armed with many options for how to construct your own workflow. Here's to it working, and may all your user feedback be good.

Coldwell Banker Walter Williams

Company: Coldwell Banker Walter Williams Realty, Inc.
URL: www.northfloridahomes.com
Design Team: nGen Works (Bruce Cooke, Stockton Eller, Varick Rosete, Travis Schmeisser, and Carl Smith)

Coldwell Banker Walter Williams Realty, Inc., provides residential, commercial, property-management, and other real estate services in the Northeast Florida area. The CBWW site redesign goal was to attract inquiries about residential properties as well as commercial properties.

<PREVIOUS>

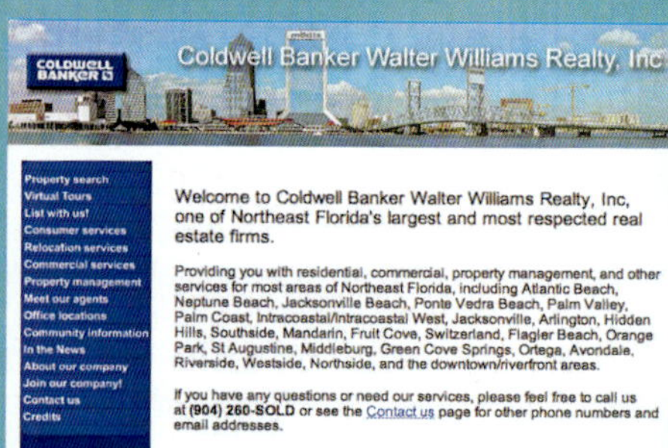

COLDWELL BANKER WALTER WILLIAMS [OLD] was outdated, and the plethora of choices confused users. Informal research indicated that there are only three things people want from a residential real estate website: the ability to buy, sell, or rent a home.

<CURRENT>

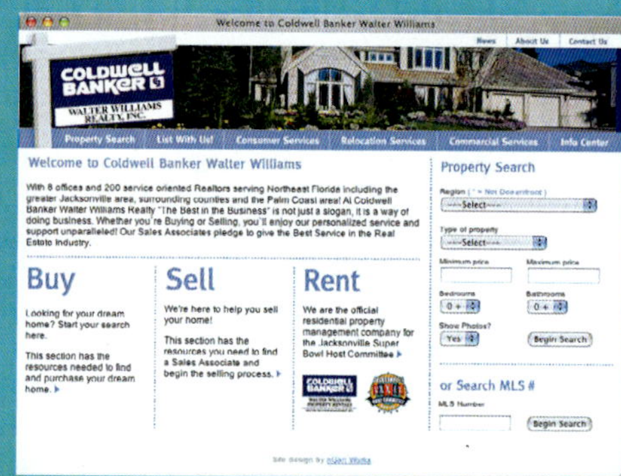

COLDWELL BANKER WALTER WILLIAMS [REDESIGNED] incorporated straightforward, action-oriented navigation that allows site visitors to easily direct themselves to their primary goals. The search feature was also rebuilt as a result of user feedback to make it as simple as the site itself.

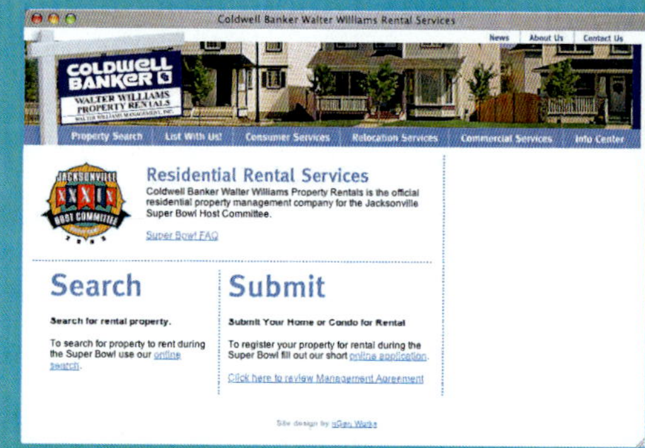

COLDWELL BANKER WALTER WILLIAMS RENTAL [REDESIGNED] carries the navigation system intact to subpages of the site, allowing the target audience continued easy access to desired actions.

Results: Thousands of unique visitors, hundreds of qualified leads, and several complimentary emails from users each week.

> Focus group results are what site visitors think they might do. Usability testing shows what visitors actually do.

Testing for Usability 08

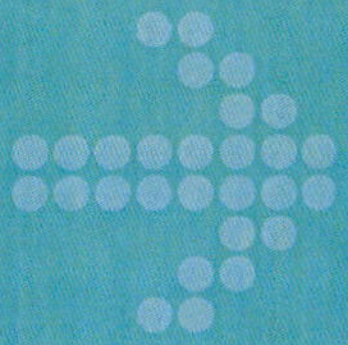

Testing for Usability

Why does a site get redesigned, whether in part or completely? Often it comes from a group of people brainstorming: "We need this on our new site," or "This aspect about our current site doesn't work." Unfortunately, ideas like these are often based on speculation and the unsubstantiated personal opinions and prejudices of the people running the company.

The burning question ought to be, "How easy is our site to use?" And by that we mean more than the ability to get from point A to point B without broken links. How easy is it for your site visitors to get the information they want? And closely related, how easy is it on your site to lead your visitors to do what you want them to do?

WHAT THIS CHAPTER COVERS	
UNDERSTANDING USABILITY	**CONDUCTING USABILITY TESTS**
> Getting Started	> Plan and Prep
> Usability and Redesign	> Find Participants
> When to Test	> Conduct the Session
> Costs of Testing	> Analyze Data and Make Recommendations

Ease of use continues to be a top reason why customers repeatedly return to a site. It usually only takes one bad experience for a site to lose a customer. Guesswork has no place here; besides, you are probably too close to your site to be an impartial judge.

UNDERSTANDING USABILITY

Usability is defined as "ease of use." How easy is it to make something work? Operating a can opener is easy. Operating the space shuttle is complex. Using an upgrade to a familiar software application should be easy, but it often isn't.

As Karen Donoghue points out in her book *Built For Use: Driving Profitability Through the User Experience* (McGraw-Hill, 2002)...

> "Successful user experiences deliver a firm's value proposition — the brand promise — to customers in the most effective and appropriate way. Usability is now linked to revenues — and profits — as never before. If a customer can't engage in the full brand experience because of usability issues, the value proposition is diminished in the customer's mind."

Website usability is the measure of how an individual user actually navigates, finds information, and interacts with your website. Note that we use the word "actually." Usability is not about how you *think* users will navigate, search, or interact.

Many companies think they are already conducting usability tests, but in actuality they are running focus groups or online surveys. These are not usability tests. Some companies even feel they are testing usability by analyzing site statistics to gain a high-level understanding of patterns and behavior. Although all these kinds of feedback can be valuable and will probably provide interesting insight, simply getting feedback does not a usability problem solve, or even identify.

Unlike surveys or focus groups, usability testing is a one-on-one process that incorporates a watch-and-learn approach. One moderator observes one user. Results are immediate and indisputable. If users click the wrong link, they're not wrong ... the interface is. Usability testing displays how users actually use the site.

Usability testing helps to identify website problem areas. It would be nice to be able to test the entire site, but that usually isn't possible. Since you only have test subjects for a set span of time, testing is focused on specific tasks and sections within your site. With the resulting data, the development team and company management can better understand how closely business goals are tied to user experience goals. Usability testing continues to be the most immediate and effective way to determine whether a website is meeting its business objectives. It works toward creating a successful user experience.

We believe strongly in the value of conducting usability tests. Understanding usability testing is important, and this chapter will help orient you. It is designed give a quick overview of the basics so that your team can determine the best solutions for obtaining direct audience feedback. When redesigning a site, conducting usability testing throughout the process may or may not be possible. You may have time and resource constraints. Regardless of real-world reality during development, we still advocate testing. Do it after launch and incorporate feedback into the (scheduled) next release of your site three or four months down the road. As companies move away from full redesigns (site-wide changes in branding, structure, look and feel) and move toward adopting an ongoing improvement practice for their sites, it is important to regularly focus on specific areas that can be improved. Focusing on trouble spots and employing small-sample usability tests (five to eight screened participants, outlined in this chapter's Expert Topic) to gather data and insight from the actual audience is the best way to determine how to improve the areas (specific paths for registration, lead generation forms, purchasing or application design) where site visitors get frustrated and leave.

For a comprehensive and meticulous look into usability, Jakob Nielsen's book *Designing Web*

Usable vs. Useful

Ensuring ease-of-use is important, yes, but don't lose site of the site's usefulness. How relevant is the site's content and information? Would the participant return to the site on their own? Take the time to gather additional information through interviews and post-test surveys. Was the site useful? Was it likeable? How could it serve to be more useful? Be prepared to make adjustments.

Usability (New Riders, 1999) is about as complete a tome as exists, and it remains applicable years after its first publication. Plus, his online articles are top notch (www.useit.com). For a look into the business side of usability testing, read Karen Donoghue's book *Built For Use: Driving Profitability Through the User Experience* (McGraw-Hill, 2002). Steve Krug's book *Don't Make Me Think* (New Riders, 2000) continues to be a bestseller and is as entertaining as it is insightful. In this chapter, we are setting theory aside and are simply explaining how you can fit usability testing into your daily workflow.

Getting Started

It's easy: You need a pen, paper, computer, and browser. You need a plan, participants, and possibly some simple legal forms like a nondisclosure agreement (NDA) or consent to videotape. You can add a video camera and a testing facility, but often you can conduct tests on a more modest scale, even within the user's own environment. The hard part is finding the time. Having a printed version of the main paths through the site is helpful for note-taking. Be prepared to be surprised; usability testing is never predictable.

One-On-One Testing

- Testing duration is one to two days with four to six participants each day but only one participant in a room at a time.
- Individual session length is approximately one hour.
- Tasks performed are predetermined.
- Tasks test specific areas or user paths, not the whole site.
- Tasks to be performed are pretested by a member of the development team to make sure they are feasible.
- The test moderator watches, keeps quiet, and takes notes. One test moderator can test all participants but only one participant at a time.
- Sessions can be videotaped.
- Sessions can be watched by the development team. Formal testing environments often incorporate a one-way mirror to avoid making the test subjects uncomfortable.
- Results show what is working and what is not working.

Usability and Redesign

Test your current, about-to-be-redesigned site. Testing the current site for usability will yield valuable results (see this chapter's Expert Topic with Jakob Nielsen) and will give pointers as to where to begin with site improvements. You are probably already well aware of areas that need improvement, whether through complaints or lack of sales. Draw on existing data for your tests.

Here's a prickly point in testing redesigns: Testing new looks and navigation on your current site's regular users will almost always yield skewed results. As a rule, people dislike change. If a site is changed, many regular users will have something negative to say, even if the redesign is easier to use. Don't test solely on your existing audience.

When to Test

It is difficult to determine when to test within the workflow. The obvious time to test is at the end of the production phase, while you're QA-ing but before launch. However, this is also a difficult time to test, primarily because the focus is on getting the site live, not adding more processes. Also, just before launch, the schedule is already tight, and what if testing forces the team back to the drawing board when there isn't time to do so? But what if the site goes live and is flawed? It is a mistake to leave the site until the last minute without having someone besides the development team or client take a look.

Test early. Conducting usability tests early in the process not only is cheaper in the long run, but also is easier on the schedule (and on the team and on the

Hire Experts Whenever Possible

Usability as an industry long predates the web. Although in recent years many individuals have specialized in web usability, human factors specialists and ergonomic engineers have long studied user needs as they pertain to a wide range of products and situations. The data to draw from in the field is substantial. Consider bringing a pro on board. A web usability expert has experience not only in conducting the testing, but also in analyzing the results and making recommendations.

The Little Site That Could

Once upon a time, way back at the beginning of the dot-com boom, Carl Smith of Husk Jennings Advertising received a call from a large media company inquiring whether Carl and his team could build them a website in two weeks. Carl assured them he could make their deadline. After all, they had a budget of $8,000.

The site was delivered on time. It was a very simple, clean site that had brief text with a single custom icon on each page. Carl and his team did what was reasonable with the given time and budget. They kept it streamlined and within user-download capabilities.

A few days later, the client called and read Carl the riot act. It turned out that a different department of the client's company had hired another (now absorbed/defunct) web agency to build the site as well. It was beautiful. It blinked! It flashed! It actually had sound! The other design firm obviously knew how to build a site. Husk Jennings Advertising obviously did not.

A week went by, and Carl got another call from the client. Suddenly the client loved him. "You're brilliant," the client said. "Your site rated #1 in usability testing. It is easy to use and straightforward. Not at all like that complicated other site."

And the lesson here is?

JAKOB NIELSEN ON THE VALUE OF SMALL-STUDY USABILITY TESTING

The web development situation now is different than it was in the mid-nineties before usability became a real factor in web development. Now many redesign projects are, in fact, driven by usability needs. Many existing websites are poor matches with user needs and much too difficult to use. People are finally starting to realize this. I predict that once enough websites are truly driven by usability, they will become so superior that competing websites will see a significant reduction in traffic and therefore business. The result will be a real impetus to redesign with usability in mind.

Unfortunately, while it seems that most people know they should test for usability, the reality is that they don't. The barrier for many is the false notion that usability testing has to be an elaborate and costly project. If you always wait until you have the budget for the perfect study, you will never get anything done.

If you, as is common, find yourself with no budget or time, you may be tempted to view testing for usability as an expendable step. My standard advice is still to test but on an abbreviated scale. A very small study with just three or four people — really just a day's work and requiring a very small budget — is incredibly valuable. Focus on just one of the top three core things the site does and test that. With small-study testing, there will be a richness that is lost — you will not be able to test the secondary features, nor will you be able to start obsessing about audience segmentation. But the difference between no testing at all and some data... That difference is immense.

Never say, "We can only afford a small study, so it probably is not worth doing." That's one of the biggest mistakes. I regularly emphasize the notion of many small, fast tests. What almost always happens is that the results of those first simple tests are so valuable, so revealing, that you will get the budget for future studies because everybody realizes how very helpful the testing is.

You can conduct these small studies all along the development process. With redesign projects, one of the most overlooked testing opportunities is right at the beginning, with the outgoing site itself. Here are two reasons not to pass up testing the outgoing site:

1. What's Wrong?

There are probably a lot of opinions within the company as to what's wrong with the outgoing site — everybody has their own theory. But without empirical insight from real users, any analysis is based in myth. What if you consider an aspect of the website to be wrong, but in reality it is not a big problem? You would be focusing your resources in the wrong place. There is substantial benefit to actually knowing what is wrong with the outgoing site before redesigning it.

2. What's Good?

The old site is bad, granted, but it probably is not all bad. It likely has some elements that are good and should be preserved. It would be a shame to lose those benefits in the redesign process. Look for what is working in the outgoing site. The old site is, by definition, trying to achieve some of the same goals that the redesign will have. Recommended usability methodology has always been to test several versions of a prototype as it evolves. Testing the old design will give you insight into how users behave with the type of features and content the site offers, as well as the types of products being sold.

Of course, just because people redesign and improve their websites does not mean that they will get a perfect website. First of all, no perfect website exists. Second, there is the real-life factor that, as a development team, they have to get the project done in a specified time-frame. Think of web development as a never-ending process — every two years or so you have to go over this again and redesign. There will always be substantial room for improvement, and usability is always a great place to start analyzing.

Dr. Jakob Nielsen (www.useit.com) *has been called "The world's leading expert on web usability"* (U.S. News & World Report), *"The smartest person on the web"* (ZDNet), *and "Knows more about what makes websites work than anyone else on the planet"* (Chicago Tribune). *His most recent book,* Designing Web Usability: The Practice of Simplicity *has about a quarter million copies in print in 13 languages, and his Alertbox column about web usability — published on the internet since 1995* (www.useit.com/alertbox) *— currently has about 200,000 readers. Dr. Nielsen holds 53 United States patents, mainly on ways to make the internet easier to use.*

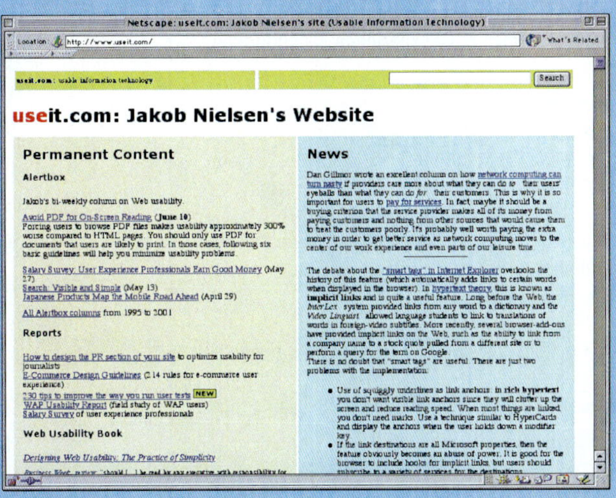

Why You Haven't Tested

Usability testing: We know we should be doing it, but we tend to push it aside in favor of what may seem to be more important issues. It's like New Year's resolutions. (I will work out.... I will eat organic vegetables.... I will drink eight glasses of water a day....) We know we should, but we don't often follow through. More pressing issues always seem to demand our attention because the consequences do not seem immediate.

What a mistake. Don't test and the consequences can be dire, regardless of tight development schedules and budgets. Make testing a priority instead of making excuses.

INFORMAL, SEMIFORMAL, AND FORMAL COST COMPARISONS	
All levels of testing are valuable. Mixing levels of formality at different points of development is also valid: perhaps semiformal testing at the outset on the existing, to-be-redesigned site; informal testing at several stages during development; and then formal testing upon launch. It depends on the budget, the timing, and the client's dedication to make the site user-centric.	
$0	**Informal testing:** Use friends/co-workers as unpaid subjects.
$500–$1000	**Informal to semiformal testing:** Find outside participants through postings and pay them $35 to $75 each.
$2,000+	**Semiformal testing:** An outside company finds and prescreens participants.
$5,000–$20,000+	**Formal, professional testing with experts and a laboratory or formal testing environment:** Use impartial and consistent specialists trained in human factors. They should be trained to plan, set up, conduct, analyze, and report results.

FORMAL VS. INFORMAL TESTING	
In addition to budget and time requirements, the biggest difference between formal and informal testing is expertise. Formal testing requires an expert in human factors engineering and/or cognitive psychology who has experience in the testing-and-analysis process. This person or team should also have experience in conducting and analyzing test results.	
Informal Testing	Informal testing usually takes place in the participant's own work environment or in a casual office setting. Participants are often family or co-workers. A simple test plan and task list is prepared and is observed and noted by an impartial moderator.
Semiformal Testing	Semiformal testing, like formal testing, may or may not take place in a formal facility. Participants are prescreened and selected from a pool of applicants. Moderating is usually handled by a member of the team.
Formal Testing	Formal testing usually takes place in a formal facility with a human factors specialist moderating and running the testing process. Participants are prescreened and selected from a large pool of applicants. There are viewing facilities through a one-way mirror, and intricate video-monitoring practices often are used.

budget). When you test early, you can quickly identify problems and make changes before you build structures on top of fault lines. If you are too far along in the process to change things, the tendency is to simply launch and hope for the best. But note: No business school trains its MBAs to go forward with a flawed business plan and "hope for the best."

We recommend testing at as many critical junctures as possible. A little bit of testing at the wireframe or paper prototype stage requires little time or budget. And yet, it puts your project in a far better position to move forward into visual design than if you didn't test at all. Testing visual design flat screens or an HTML Protosite also brings potential issues to light. And again, start early enough in the process to avoid having to backtrack too far.

Costs of Testing

Informal testing is one-on-one testing with friends and colleagues who closely fit the specific user profiles and who are not directly involved with the project. The cost for this is usually minimal. Semiformal testing raises the bar to the next level; outside participants are recruited and paid. A makeshift testing area is often set up. Formal testing can take many forms, but it is common to have a paid usability consultant who is a human factors specialist, as well as to rent a testing facility. Hence the higher budget.

CONDUCTING USABILITY TESTS: A FOUR-STEP PROCESS

Throughout this book, we focus on core processes. This chapter is no exception. Usability as a topic is extensive. In the interests of discussing simply how to fit usability into your workflow, we have distilled the process of usability testing into an overview that incorporates these four key steps:

Step 1: Plan and Prep

Step 2: Find Participants

Step 3: Conduct the Session

Step 4: Analyze Data and Make Recommendations

Each of these steps can be applied to any of the three levels of formality: a simplified, informal approach; a semiformal, more expanded plan; or a formal, expanded, full-blown production. The main difference between the levels is in the expertise involved.

Step 1: Plan and Prep

Your tests don't need to be complex, but they do need to have specific goals. The point here is to stay focused. Your time while testing is limited — you only have about an hour for each session. You will need a plan.

Test Plans

A test plan should be the overview and guide to your version of the testing process. Your test plan **[8.1]** should contain at least the following:

- Overall goals/objectives
- Methodology (testing procedure, equipment, facility, etc.)
- Target audience profile (whom you will be testing)
- Testing outline (orientation, check-off lists, test questions)
- Specific task list
- Final evaluation (analysis of data)
- Reporting structure (how you plan to submit results and recommendations)

A test plan allows you to align expectations and goals. Make sure you are focused on specific tasks; you will not have time to test everything. Remember that the testing plan is a work in progress and may vary from session to session.

Café Testing

Looking for a low-cost solution to usability testing or customer feedback? Café testing is here. Many cafés offering free wireless have a plethora of remote workers among their clientele who are looking for a short break. Most of the time, a sign offering "$20 for 20 minutes of time" is a good incentive. Be aware however, that this particular user group may not fit your target profile, unless caffeine intake is part of your demographic. For testing tips see www.gotomedia.com/gotoreport/news_0607_wantfreebeer.html

Usability Testing Plan

Overall goal: To provide specific feedback on search, login, and e-commerce features. To determine expected performance on the current site and identify serious problems prior to the next phase of production.

Specific questions that need to be answered:

1. Are the basic search features intuitive for a new user?
2. Are the advanced search features intuitive to use and learnable?
3. Is the purchasing process clear?
4. Are user login and member requirements clear to the user?

User profile: Participants will fit the target market profile of being versed in current internet practices and adaptive technology. The target market is internet users ages 25 to 45 with moderate to high internet experience. To qualify, participants should access the web at least once a week, purchase products online at least twice per month, and be familiar with basic search and e-commerce functions.

Methodology: Usability testing of six to eight individuals will be held at an outside testing facility. Each session will take approximately one hour. The test monitor will greet and orient participants. Participants are asked to fill out a basic questionnaire and background information, and nondisclosures will be signed.

Testing outline:

I. Orientation

II. Background: Testing Site

III. Begin Task List

IV. Fill Out Post-Test Survey

V. Debrief Participant

Summary of results: All participant testing notes will be compiled. Observations and specific findings will be summarized. Other data (time taken for each task, ability to complete each task, post-testing information) will be summarized.

Recommendations report: The report will include the complete testing plan and task list, result summary, and findings/recommendations. All notes and participant comments will be included.

< **8.1**

A sample test plan: Test plans should outline basic requirements, including overall testing goals, the audience profile, the methodology, and the testing outline. Note that this plan is an example — your user profile (for example) will likely differ from this semigeneric example.

Task Lists

Choose straightforward tasks to test potential problem areas. For instance, if you are not sure about your login, plan for a series of testing tasks to cover the whole login process. Your users should be prompted to do something that requires a login so that they discover on their own that they need to log in. How easy and intuitive was it for the user to figure it out?

Create a list of tasks that a general user can (hopefully) finish in about an hour. Have additional tasks prepared in case the tasks take less time than you predicted. Make sure the tasks are neither too simple nor too difficult to accomplish within the set timeframe — either situation defeats the purpose of the session. Pretest the tasks to weed out any problematic ones.

When developing your list of tasks, keep in mind that the usability test session should be casual, informative, and low stress. Let your subjects get comfortable and confident, as they would be in their own environment — usually their home or office. Developing the proper site-specific task list takes both time and practice.

Tasks should obviously relate to the site, but make them as real world as possible. Have one task relate to the next in a comprehensive manner — like a real user experience. Although you don't want to combine tasks that might skew results, neither do you want the user to perform random tasks. Keep the individual in a flow. Here are a few examples:

- If the site you are redesigning is for a national housewares chain, one sample task could be to have subjects order a gift off of a wedding registry. Then have them request a catalog.
- If your redesign is for a bank, have the subjects check their balance or investigate mortgage applications. Next have them sign up to pay bills or make a transfer.
- Is it a site that indexes restaurants? Have your participants save three restaurants to their favorites folder (which they will have to create). This would require a login as well. Next have them locate an Italian bistro that delivers to their neighborhood or a medium-priced restaurant with live jazz. Then have them make a reservation.
- If the project is for a bed-and-breakfast, have them attempt to reserve a room, find directions, and then inquire about large parties or large dogs.

Sample Test Script

The moderator needs to keep the flow of the test moving. Getting chatty with your test subject is an easy trap to fall into, but it wastes valuable time. To aid you in staying on target and to make sure you don't miss anything during the actual test, have a test script on hand [8.2].

Orientation & Greeting

Greet the Participant — Orient to testing and expectations:

"Hello, my name is John, and I'll be working with you in today's session. I would like to give you a brief idea of what you should expect and what we are trying to accomplish.

"Today we are testing the online ordering process and determining how effective and intuitive it is to use. Your experience here today will help us evaluate our website. Remember, you are not being evaluated in any way — we are simply trying to see how users navigate through the site. Do your best, but don't be concerned with the results. While you are working, I'll be watching and taking notes. Feel free to talk aloud as you go through the site. You may ask questions, but I probably won't answer them, because it is important for you to go through the site as if I were not present.

"Afterwards we will have some time to talk about the site and your experience. I will also have a short survey for you to fill out before you leave.

"Do you have any questions?"

(Give the NDA form if applicable, and begin the testing.)

Begin Task List

8.2 >

A sample test script: This is a sample of what you might say, based on a test script developed by Jeffrey Rubin in Handbook of Usability Testing. *Remember: Don't read the script word for word.*

Test Often!

Small-scale testing at several points during development is arguably more beneficial than testing only once. Develop methods of quick, iterative testing to allow for feedback on specific issues throughout the development process. In design meetings, whenever there is a question or discussion regarding navigation, functionality, or user response, cheerfully add it to the list for the next round of testing. Use testing to settle arguments — nothing speaks more loudly than the actual site visitor.

A test script should cover the following: introductions, the test-session schedule, and a brief explanation of methodology. Put the test subject at ease when you explain the testing setup and expectations. When orienting your participant on the day of the test, you need to cover the following important points, so make sure to include them in your test script:

- Introduce yourself and your role as a moderator.
- Explain that your role is as a silent observer. You shouldn't answer any questions directly; you're just here to observe and take notes.
- Give an overview of the testing goals.
- Assure participants that they are not being tested in any way. It's the site that is being tested.
- Encourage participants to "talk aloud" during the testing process.
- Get an NDA signed (if applicable) and ask if there are any questions.

Step 2: Find Participants

Finding potential participants is one of the more challenging aspects of conducting usability testing. For informal and most semiformal testing, you can enlist people you know — they just have to fit the profile. You can recruit the easy targets: your mother, your neighbor, the kid who delivers the Friday staff pizza... but regardless of their convenience, they are only good choices if they match your target audience. Select with care. If your site is B2B auto supply and your mother couldn't identify a carburetor if world peace depended on it, she is not a good test subject.

Drafting co-workers may seem convenient, and although they may be adequate for many informal tests, we suggest recruiting outside your office. Testing with individuals who are not associated with your company or your site will give better results, and gathering an ongoing user base for use in both focus groups and usability tests is valuable for any web development team — whether in-house or not.

That said, co-workers and friends are great candidates for a "dry run" of the usability testing session. Since co-workers or friends are familiar with you, they will feel comfortable providing feedback on your methods and processes. Plus, this kind of preliminary run-though provides the moderator with an opportunity to work out bugs in the script.

Setting up sessions and tracking down ideal candidates can be a formidable time investment. Depending on available methods of advertising in your local area, you can secure ideal candidates in less than a week's time. First, determine your best methods for reaching your target audience. Would they be responsive to the local weekly? Is there an online resource for jobs and postings? Would posting a flyer at a college work? Post an ad in the local job listings (**[8.3]** and **[8.4]**). You will see quick results.

Screen Participants

One of the differences between informal and formal testing procedures is the professional screening of participants. Professional testing facilities and companies are paid up to $1,000 per participant (usually targeting a group of 8 to 12) to locate, screen, and recruit participants for usability-testing purposes. The value of this service lies in the opportunity for a precisely targeted group to be selected according to specific demographics determined by a usability expert. Furthermore, it allows for screening and recruiting to be conducted in other cities (if testing is to be done in several locations), which allows for a wider sampling.

The more closely targeted the participants, the more viable the results. Specific profiles may include CEOs, day traders, or long-distance truckers — none of whom might be readily targeted using traditional posting or advertising methods.

8.3 >

A sample job posting for usability testing subjects where the target audience is wide. Note that you may have to pay a participant more than the going rate if the session is on super-short notice.

Earn $50 for an hour of surfing the web!
Participate in an online usability study.
Contact information@________.com

8.4 >

A sample job posting for usability testing subjects where the target audience is narrower.

Looking for women over 45. Earn $50 for an hour of surfing the web! Participate in an online usability study.
Contact information@________.com

Test Subjects for Intranet Sites

Usability testing on an intranet or a site where your target audience is exclusively internal can be tricky. On the one hand, you absolutely know who your audience is. When it comes to testing for usability, however, you may have a problem finding good participants. Actually, the problem may be that your participants are *too* good. Often, when you contact a department and request that someone be sent over for usability testing, they send you a "star." Departments want to shine, so they send their absolute best: "Rudy is the biology department's resident internet expert" or "Pamela knows computers better than anyone else in the human resources department." Congrats to Rudy and Pamela, but they aren't typical. When you request participants from departments, request "typical" site visitors, not whiz kids. Choose by random selection.

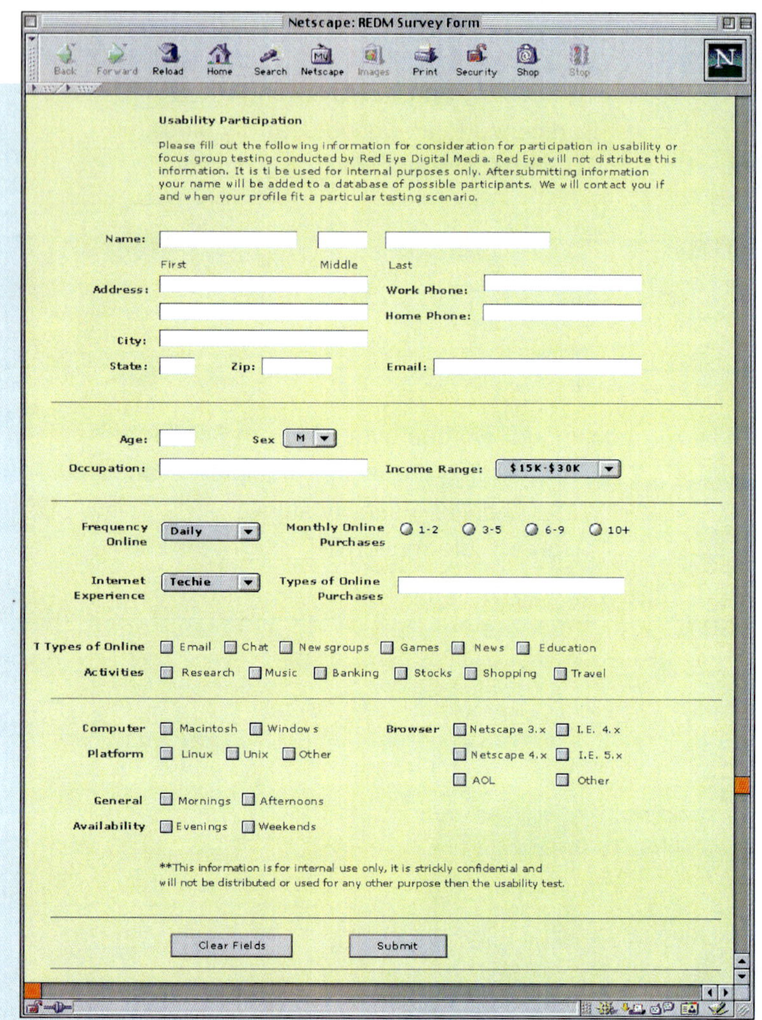

Netscape: REDM Survey Form

Back Forward Reload Home Search Netscape Images Print Security Shop Stop

Usability Participation

Please fill out the following information for consideration for participation in usability or focus group testing conducted by Red Eye Digital Media. Red Eye will not distribute this information. It is ti be used for internal purposes only. Aftersubmitting information your name will be added to a database of possible participants. We will contact you if and when your profile fit a particular testing scenario.

Name: First Middle Last

Address: Work Phone:

Home Phone:

City:

State: Zip: Email:

Age: Sex M

Occupation: Income Range: $15K-$30K

Frequency Online: Daily — Monthly Online Purchases: 1-2, 3-5, 6-9, 10+

Internet Experience: Techie — Types of Online Purchases:

T Types of Online Activities: Email, Chat, Newsgroups, Games, News, Education, Research, Music, Banking, Stocks, Shopping, Travel

Computer Platform: Macintosh, Windows, Linux, Unix, Other

Browser: Netscape 3.x, I.E. 4.x, Netscape 4.x, I.E. 5.x, AOL, Other

General Availability: Mornings, Afternoons, Evenings, Weekends

**This information is for internal use only, it is strickly confidential and will not be distributed or used for any other purpose then the usability test.

Clear Fields Submit

< **8.5**

This online test subject profiling form gives you the information you need to identify potential test subjects as aligning with your target audience. It can also be faxed, but since you are testing online habits and usage, most subjects will have access to the internet.

Profile Test Subjects

Direct potential subjects (from ads, postings, and referrals) to fill out an online or faxed form that asks for basic demographic information as well as internet usage patterns **[8.5]**. On any form you distribute that asks for personal information, note that all information is confidential and that no information will be distributed.

The reasons for wanting this information should be obvious: When you test for usability, you want your test subjects to match your target audience as closely as possible. Otherwise, what's the point? Compile your collected information into a grid or some other easy-to-reference format and sort **[8.6]**. Narrow your results. Schedule a few more than you need in case someone cancels. These extra participants, called floaters, should still get paid.

Send an introductory email to applicants who fit the desired profile. Explain briefly when they should expect to be contacted and what they will be doing, but don't get too specific. Follow up with an email or a phone call closer to the confirmed date **[8.7]**.

ID	Sex	Occupation	Household Income	Web Experience	Time Online	Online Activities	Purchases Per Month
5	F	Partner development	70K–100K	Web savvy	Daily	Email, news, research, stocks, shopping, travel	1 to 2
6	F	Marketing	50K–70K	Web savvy	Daily	Email, chat, news, research, banking, stocks, shopping, travel	3 to 5
8	M	Music therapist	15K–30K	Intermed	Daily	Email, newsgrp, news, research, music, shopping, travel	3 to 5
9	F	Teacher; director catalog content	30K–50K	Web savvy	Daily	Email, chat, newsgrp, news, educ, research, shopping	1 to 2
18	F	Housewife/ mother	70K–100K	Web savvy	Daily	Email, chat, newsgrp, games, news, research, music, stocks, shopping, travel	1 to 2
30	M	Employee operations	30K–50K	Web savvy	Daily	Email, chat, newsgrp, news, educ, research, banking, shopping, travel	3 to 5
46	M	Interior designer	50K–70K	Intermed	Daily	Email, newsgrp, educ, banking, stocks, shopping, travel	3 to 5
75	M	Student	15K–30K	Techie	Daily	Email, newsgrp, news, educ, research, music, banking, shopping, travel	1 to 2
87	F	Office manager	30K–50K	Web savvy	Daily	Email, chat, games, news, research, music, banking, stocks, shopping, travel	6 to 9

< **8.6**

This sample grid of potential test subjects shows the information collected from the online profile form [8.5]. This data has been poured into an Excel file. Out of 400 responses, 40 were selected for client review. Eight were eventually selected as participants.

Initial Contact

Hello,

Thank you in advance for your participation in our usability testing. You have been selected based on your online profile. We will contact you via email to confirm the testing dates and your availability. Currently we are scheduled for the 17th and 18th of this month. Testing will be held at our offices downtown, located at 1200 24th Avenue, Suite 100. That's between East 12th and East 14th on the south side of the street. The entire session should take approximately one hour. You will be paid $50 for your participation at the end of the session.

If you have any questions, please do not hesitate to contact us via email or phone.

Thanks!

< **8.7**

A sample script for contacting participants.

"Two distinct advantages to formal testing: It provides feedback for site development, and it is an educational opportunity for designers and engineers, allowing them to see firsthand the decision-making process of an average site visitor."

— Jupiter 1999, www.jup.com

Step 3: Conduct the Session

Begin each session with a pleasant and patient attitude. Introduce yourself and explain the process — that the participant will be asked to perform a set of predetermined tasks. Take care with your choice of words; don't prejudice your results by telling the test subject the number or length of tasks. Make it clear that you are an observer, not a helper. Have an NDA and any other paperwork prepared in advance. Keep the formalities light and make the participant feel as comfortable as possible. Refer to your test script to keep you on track.

Remain neutral during the testing process. As a facilitator, you will be a silent observer, speaking only when giving a new task and taking notes throughout the process. If the participant asks you a question, respond only if necessary and in a very nonspecific manner. Do not give any hints, verbally or by eye or hand motion. You might be tempted to "rescue" the individual, but this would defeat the purpose of the testing. If the participant becomes frustrated, read the level of frustration and note "Failed task" only when all other options have been taken. Do not consider a failed task to be a testing failure. It's quite the opposite. By uncovering site flaws, you should diminish the number of site visitors who click out of websites in frustration. (That's lost business and perhaps a permanently lost customer.) Videotaping the session is also helpful for later review and to show to other members of the development team.

Make sure to have everything you need before starting. Here is a handy checklist:

- Have an NDA ready for signing.
- Make sure your internet connection works.
- If you are videotaping, have batteries charged for your video camera because cords can be problematic. (Note: We do not recommend videotaping for informal testing.)
- Have a printout of the site handy for easier note-taking (pages associated with the task).
- Have your list of sequenced and predetermined tasks.
- Have the survey form ready for post-testing.
- Have the site bookmarked and ready to use.

Basic Data Collection

Take meticulous notes during the testing process. A blank form to write notes on is always helpful [8.8]. Use the same form for all test subjects. This streamlining will be handy for compiling notes and comparing findings.

Make certain to note all of the following points for each task:

- Could the test subject complete the task?
- Did he need help? Did the task fail?
- How much time did it take?
- What stumbling blocks did he encounter? Describe problems and obstacles.
- Note overall observations. Add commentary. Did the test subject mutter in frustration? Did he say, "Cool!"?

Know When to Quit

If a participant becomes too frustrated or goes too far off track, it is time to have him quit the task. Make it clear that if he does not or cannot perform a task to completion, he has neither ruined the test nor demonstrated incompetence (except perhaps the development team's!). Flustered test subjects will not perform well.

Moderating Do's and Don'ts

DO introduce yourself and your role as a silent observer.

DO explain that participants should think aloud as they feel comfortable. Keep the session relaxed, use humor when appropriate, and stay impartial.

DON'T describe the tasks in advance. Say only that participants will be performing a certain number of tasks in one hour's time.

DO make it clear that they are not being tested and that there are no wrong answers.

DON'T set expectations. Don't say, "This is so easy, you'll have no problem."

DON'T rescue the participants when they struggle.

DO recognize when a participant is getting really frustrated. Know when to "give up" and list a task as failed.

CHAPTER 8

Participant ID#

Date: | Site URL

Time	Task Description	Observations/Comments/Notes

< **8.8**

Use this sample observation form to help take notes during a typical session. The form is available for download at www.web-redesign.com.

You don't need to write down absolutely every click or hesitation, but make certain to be thorough when you report problem areas. Follow closely enough to track a task's flow. You will base your conclusions on the data you collect.

After the Session

Keep an eye on the clock. A few things need to happen before the test subject is finished and can leave. First give the participant a brief post-test survey, then conduct a quick debriefing interview, and finally pay the test subject for his time.

Prepare the post-test survey in advance **[8.9]**. It should contain questions about the person's overall impressions and experiences with the site. Offer the participant the opportunity to rate each question/component on a scale of 1 to 10. The survey should take no longer than five minutes to complete.

Debrief the participant. If you have allocated time, let him say whatever is on his mind and then ask him questions. Begin with overall, high-level issues and move on to specifics — the areas you marked in your notes. Have the payment ready for the participant once the session is complete. Don't forget to thank him. Be sure to keep the door open

> Participants may have suggestions for how to improve the user experience. Make a note of any suggestions, but don't get involved in a dialogue. As a moderator, you should not be interacting with participants.

for further correspondence and further testing — maybe on the same project, maybe on a different project down the road.

After the participant leaves, if you have time before the next test subject comes in, prepare a short summary of the session and the results. Outline specific problem areas and surprising results. Include personal observations if appropriate. Some test sessions schedule subject after subject, and there isn't time in between to summarize. Take good notes; you won't be able to remember many specifics after three or four test subjects.

Step 4: Analyze Data and Make Recommendations

Here is where experience will show. Understanding how and why a user fails at a task or seeing where problem spots exist — this is easy. Determining how to fix the problem takes expertise. Even if you aren't an expert, however, you can still make educated recommendations for improvement.

Gather data as you go — this is obvious. Compile and summarize this data while the test is still fresh in your mind and don't forget to transfer handwritten notes to a digital file. Summarize all data in one format (a grid works well for this) showing the results of each test, problem areas, comments, and user feedback from the post-test survey.

When calling out problem areas, note why there was difficulty. If you can determine it, indicate the source of the problem — even use a screenshot. This

Post Session Survey

Please fill out the following questions based on how you are feeling overall about the site:

Name: (First Name, Last Initial) ____________________
Date: ________________

1. Able to complete tasks as requested
Frustrating 1 2 3 4 5 Easy

2. Able to navigate through the site
Confusing 1 2 3 4 5 Very Clear

3. Overall look and feel of site
Not pleasing 1 2 3 4 5 Pleasing

4. Relevance of site images to content
Not relevant 1 2 3 4 5 Relevant

5. Relevance of site content (text)
Not relevant 1 2 3 4 5 Relevant

6. Overall ease of use
Confusing 1 2 3 4 5 Very Clear

7. Overall page layout and organization
Confusing 1 2 3 4 5 Very Clear

8. Was the site inviting to use?
Not inviting 1 2 3 4 5 Inviting

9. Were the naming and labeling of links clear?
Confusing 1 2 3 4 5 Very clear

10. Would you recommend this site to a friend?
Never 1 2 3 4 5 Absolutely

Please list any additional comments about the site and your experience:

____

____

____

____

8.9 >

Have the participant complete a survey like this one after the testing is finished. Post-test feedback and comments are an excellent basis for understanding user preferences. This form is available for download at www.web-redesign.com.

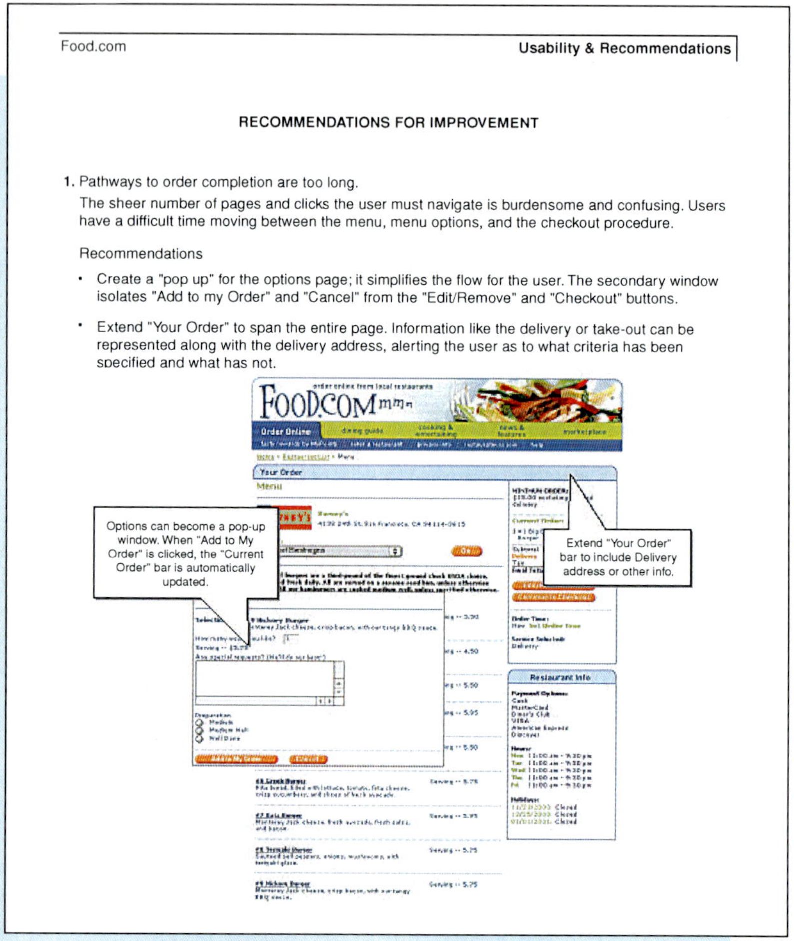

Food.com Usability & Recommendations

RECOMMENDATIONS FOR IMPROVEMENT

1. Pathways to order completion are too long.

The sheer number of pages and clicks the user must navigate is burdensome and confusing. Users have a difficult time moving between the menu, menu options, and the checkout procedure.

Recommendations

- Create a "pop up" for the options page; it simplifies the flow for the user. The secondary window isolates "Add to my Order" and "Cancel" from the "Edit/Remove" and "Checkout" buttons.
- Extend "Your Order" to span the entire page. Information like the delivery or take-out can be represented along with the delivery address, alerting the user as to what criteria has been specified and what has not.

Options can become a pop-up window. When "Add to My Order" is clicked, the "Current Order" bar is automatically updated.

Extend "Your Order" bar to include Delivery address or other info.

< 8.10

For the final report, recommendations are shown here using screenshots and caption callouts to emphasize specific points. Not all reports need to be this detailed.

will help immeasurably when thinking up ways to improve these areas. Identify user interaction with specific factors such as navigation, text, graphics, etc., as well as global issues such as consistent logo placement and branding or inconsistent naming and labeling. If there was a particular problem in the course of carrying out a task, note the issue in detail. Rank all these problems in order of frequency and then prioritize. Concentrate on high-level functionality first: issues with global navigation, text links vs. graphic links, page layout, etc. Then focus on specific areas and recommendations for improved user experience.

After all sessions are complete, compile your findings into a final report. Translate the collected data into recommendations; much of the information may validate thoughts you already have regarding your site. Divide recommendations into short-term and long-term goals. Determine an implementation plan for putting your findings into action and adjust your site to better fit the way it will actually get used.

The Final Report

Putting all of your findings into a final report provides a concise reference for your client and your team [8.10]. Unless you selected prejudiced or inappropriate test subjects, usability testing results are incontrovertible. Report these findings; any recommendations based on them will have to be taken seriously. An improved site is almost guaranteed as the result.

A final report should contain the following:

- **Executive summary.** A brief synopsis of major findings, recommendations, and suggestions of areas on which to focus. Overview what is working and what is not working on the site.
- **Methodology.** A description of the nature of the research, how it was set up, user profiles, data collection methods, etc.
- **Results.** A clear, comprehensive display of all test results, survey feedback, etc.
- **Findings and recommendations.** A presentation of general and specific information, short- and long-term changes recommended, and the type of changes suggested (for instance, graphic only, text or backend programming, etc.). Include information about the given task, the reason for the problem, and the recommended solution.
- **Appendices.** Raw data, notes, samples of test materials, background data (no names) for participants, etc.

CHAPTER SUMMARY

Although usability testing will neither create nor perfect a website, it will yield a more usable, more successful site. It can identify disaster... and help you avert it. Feedback is valuable. Observation is critical. Once you remove yourself, switching roles from developer to observer, and watch a typical site visitor navigate through the site — attempting to click on graphics, finding his way back to the home page, executing fairly simple tasks — you quickly realize that a little observation goes a long way toward knowing what makes for a positive user experience.

Have tangible goals. It is impossible to test all aspects of a site's design, architecture, and navigation. Break down your site's needs. With specific goals in mind, it is easier to tailor your tasks to a particularly questionable area. Sometimes when upper management finally agrees to a budget for usability testing, they expect to be able to test the entire site in one fell swoop. Test often, and may all your user feedback be good.

Educate Yourself

For some projects, hiring an outside consultant might be overkill. In these instances, do some reading. Besides Jakob Nielsen's *Designing Web Usability*, there is also *Don't Make Me Think* by Steve Krug (New Riders, 2000 — this one is funny!) and *Handbook of Usability Testing* by Jeffrey Rubin (John Wiley & Sons, 1994). Although you will not become an expert overnight, you will undoubtedly benefit from some research before you embark on your own informal usability testing.

Usability Testing...

... settles disputes with data instead of guesses.

... provides real feedback from actual users.

... is low cost for valuable results.

... shows that what is obvious to the developer might not be obvious to the user.

... minimizes risk prior to public launch.

WebEx

Company: WebEx Communications
URL: www.webex.com
Design Team: gotomedia, inc.
User Experience Director: Kelly Goto
Creative Director/Information Designer: Serena Howeth

Design/Production: Rachel Kalman
Usability Associate: Subha Subramanian
WebEx In-House:
Director of Web Marketing: Sindy Braun
Visual Design: Johnny Au
Content Management: Paul Fehrnstrom
Web Developer: Mark Mahle

WebEx delivers a range of web application services, including services for web conferencing, web-based support, remote training, and online events. Its suite of award-winning application services drives results for sales, marketing, support, training, and other professionals.

<PREVIOUS>

<DURING>

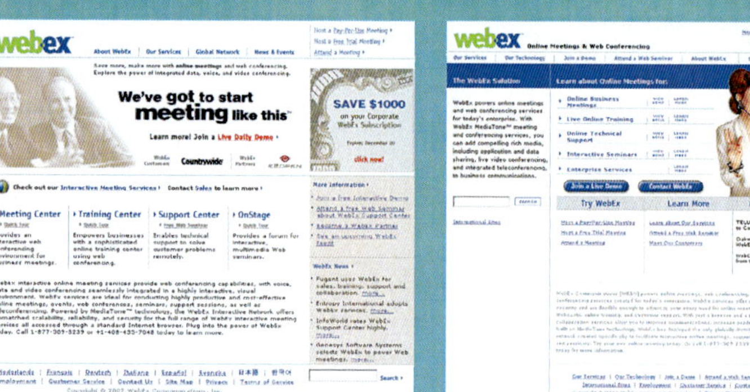

WEBEX HOME PAGE [OLDEST] offered a flood of text-heavy information, clutter, and nonbranded design. Usability testing showed paths were undirected and the purpose of the site was unclear (2002).

WEBEX HOMEPAGE [OLDER] was launched in just a few weeks with the same home-page content but with revised information architecture, labeling, and imagery. Strategic HTML text positioning also increased search rankings enormously (2002).

WEBEX [OLD] reflected a contemporary yet corporate look and feel, matching its new branding initiatives. Further enhancements to the primary path flows led to increased lead generation and traffic to primary actions within the site (2003).

<CURRENT>

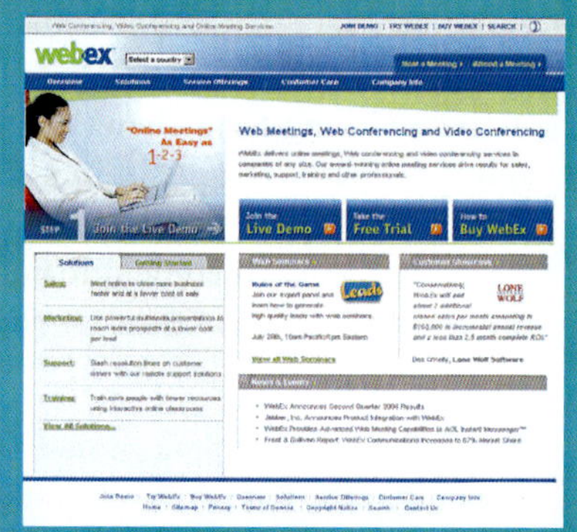

WEBEX [NEW] reaches a sophisticated, enterprise audience without sacrificing the existing WebEx identity (fun and friendly). The site's content (completely revised) and page design were published dynamically using an integrated CMS system (2004).

Results: Usability testing and click-through analysis show that primary paths are clear and easy to follow, search rankings remain high, and the site reflects the professionalism intended.

> Assumptions lead to miscommunication and confusion. Complexity demands clear documentation — leaving nothing for the engineers or site users to question.

Working with Complex Functionality 09

Working with Complex Functionality

Today's sites offer more than simple browsing. Purchases, on-demand content, and personalization have never been easier or more accessible online. Mega sites such as Amazon.com, E*TRADE, and Expedia.com have led the way, creating an expectation of evolving, thinking sites that respond to specific needs. And as web functionality becomes easier to use and offers more options for site visitors, the desire and demand for complexity widens. Shopping carts, newsletter sign-ups, online polls, Content Management Systems — these functional pieces are weaving their way into site design and development as a result of expectation and necessity.

In the Core Process, we discuss Discovery as a key component at the beginnig of Phase 1: Define, during which the design team works closely with the client to thoroughly understand and clarify both the goals and the scope of the project. When your project requires complex functionality, it is during Discovery that you must gather requirements, delving into deeper and more specific detail to understand how the functional components should work.

WHAT THIS CHAPTER COVERS

ASSESS	CREATE	IMPLEMENT
> Gathering Requirements	> Drafting a Functional Specification	> Managing Two Workflows
> Documenting Requirements	> Getting Sign-Off	> Integrating Your Efforts
> Prioritizing, Rating, & Analyzing		> Preparing to Launch

In this book, "functionality," as it pertains to web development, refers specifically to the methods and means by which a site visitor makes requests of a website and the manner in which the website is constructed to respond. In today's internet industry, "functionality" usually demands a more sophisticated layer of technology that hides behind the graphical user interface (GUI). It's where processes invisible to the end-user (functions beyond simple browsing) can operate. Some common examples of these types of functionality include:

- Promotion or advertising [9.1]
- Online polls [9.2]
- Registrations and logins [9.3]
- Search [9.4]
- E-commerce [9.5]
- Dynamic content (customized by the user, on-the-fly) [9.6]

9.1 >

Using JavaScript to change the ad with each reload (and over time), CNN.com can display a wide variety of ads.

< **9.2**

Hello! Magazine (*www.hellomagazine.com*), *a popular celebrity gossip magazine, offers irreverent polls that have absolutely nothing directly to do with revenue generation or the dissemination of information, but they do provide visitors with immediate gratification (instantly tabulated results).*

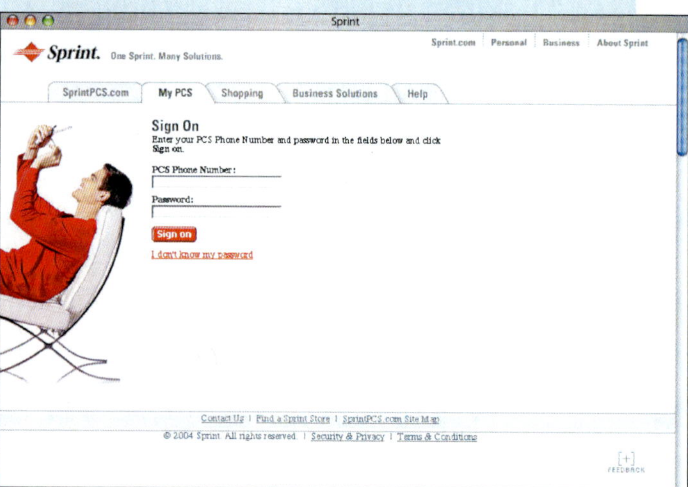

< **9.3**

Sprint PCS (www.sprintpcs.com) offers customers an area to check up on many aspects of their account: how many minutes are left in their billing cycle, the amount due, and a lot more. But to get into that secure area, you have to pass through this login screen: login, password, and option to retrieve a forgotten password.

Here's where it gets complex. Considerably more involved than simple browsing, these kinds of sites require detailed documentation before and during development to ensure that designers and developers alike understand *how* this complex functionality should work. The Core Process we've outlined in the previous chapters is a baseline for all sites undergoing visual and/or architectural modifications, but as the web continues to evolve and these types of value-added functions become mainstream, many smaller companies with limited budgets and resources need to grow and adjust accordingly. Amazon.com, eBay, CNN.com and the like no longer corner the market on providing site visitors with tremendous quantities of personalized content as well as a lot to do. Complexity is becoming the expected norm, and the need to integrate a backend workflow into the Core Process is being impressed on a greater audience than ever before. And yes, there is a workflow for it. It means, from the very start, incorporating an additional, parallel, and integrated approach into the way your site is defined and documented.

This chapter is divided into three sections. The first shows how to gather and assess the complex requirements and requests associated with the proposed functionality. The second section describes how to create a functional specification (referred to in this chapter as a *Functional Spec)* that documents the requirements and communicates this extremely detailed information to the entire team: project managers, visual and information designers, and engineers and technical information architects (sometimes referred to as an interaction architect). The Functional Spec will be the team's guideline for the implementation of some serious code. Complex really does mean complex; it is frightfully easy here to make simplistic assumptions and leave out important details.

The third section of this chapter presents an overview on how to integrate and implement back-end development into the Core Process. What we outline here are some general steps necessary to communicate properly and effectively with your engineering team and your client, and what the minimal amount of work is that you will need to do. The operative words here are *general* and *minimal*; this is an overview.

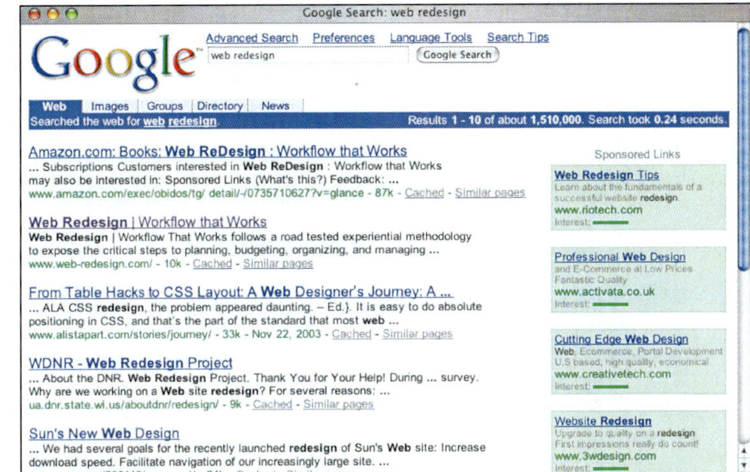

9.4 > *Search by site or across the internet. Talk about a dynamic database! "Google" has become a verb in today's lexicon.*

9.5 > *This is an example of a straightforward e-commerce order screen. Notice all the options on this one screen beyond the identification of purchaser (which has already been retrieved from a database) and the product selection: a spot to change quantity, a notice of the promotional shipping method, an option to see like items, and a choice to proceed to checkout or to continue shopping.*

< 9.6

My.yahoo.com allows the site visitor to customize their own page with user-specified content. With dozens of different information tools like news feeds, calendar, email, stock quotes, horoscope, and weather, my.yahoo.com can be organized in a fashion that is meaningful to each individual visitor.

Engineering runs a parallel workflow to the front-end development, and although timelines may vary considerably, the two must intersect at some point [9.7–9.8] But while it may not be our goal to go into details regarding the project management of the engineering efforts (there are already plenty of resources available for this task) or any of the actual engineering itself (again, other resources abound), we do hope that when you've finished this chapter you have a strong sense of how the project manager can:

- Gather and document the requirements for the complex functional aspects of your project
- Translate these requirements into a Functional Spec that illustrates how the functionality should work in a language that both teams can understand and follow
- Make sure the client understands the process
- Manage the implementation of this Functional Spec throughout the entire design process

And though it is not our intention to do so, this chapter, more than any other, will separate the newbies and non-tech types from those deeply entrenched in the web development field. However, this chapter does hold information for everyone. It is what makes the difference between assumptions (a terrible thing) and written, established, and understood specifications.

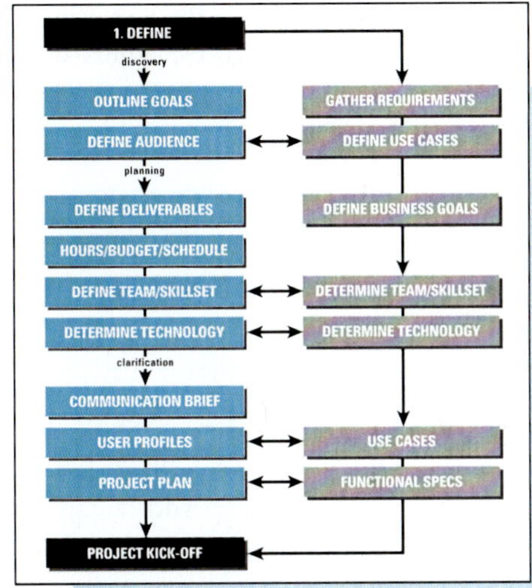

9.7 > This chart, showing the traditional Core Process on the left and the parallel backend workflow on the right, clearly identifies the points where the two meet during Phase 1: Define.

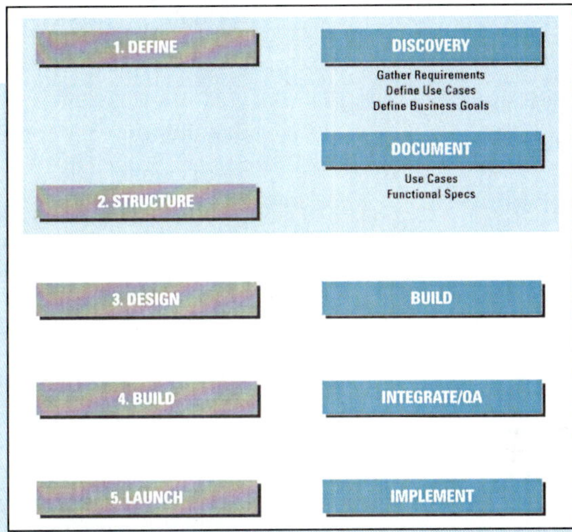

9.8 > This chart, showing the traditional Core Process on the left and the parallel backend workflow on the right, clearly identifies the points where the two meet during the entire Core Process.

A Viable, Though Risky, Option

In recent years, another method of developing software has emerged from programmers who eschew the documentation process we present here, who regularly advocate and follow an *Agile Manifesto*, a.k.a. *Fly By The Seat Of Your Pants* or *Extreme Programming* (www.agilemanifesto.org/). This means creating only minimal documentation or even just a basic request. For example: The request involves reference to an existing site feature/function and being asked to "build something like that." The programmer(s) then goes into a rapid cycle of prototyping over days or weeks. Instead of spending that time documenting and building detailed use cases, the team jumps right into programming and actually makes something that then gets tested against users and is modified over and over inside a small window of time. This rapid and iterative approach requires a well-established relationship between programmer, client, and project manager, and *extensive* experience in complex functionality on all sides — including the clear understanding of the costs involved. This process is a refreshing change for small, focused, in-house or independent engineering teams.

But programmer beware: This approach does not generate the paper trail that supports your methodology in the instance of a dispute between you and your client come invoice time. Please note that although this approach can save time and money if everything goes smoothly, it can also be very costly. Pushing forward with a knowingly haphazard approach may create more problems down the road.

ASSESS

> Gathering Requirements

> Documenting Requirements

> Prioritizing, Rating, & Analyzing

GATHERING & DOCUMENTING REQUIREMENTS

It's far too easy for anyone — team and client alike — to wave a hand at a proposed design sketch and say blithely, "And that's where the content will be dropped in dynamically," or "Login should go here," and in the next breath return to the "real" business of creating a sitemap. But what happens later on in the process when someone asks, "But how does it *really* work?"

There are many gray areas in web design and development, and more often than not, we approach complex problems with a cavalier assumption that the answers are obvious. But avoiding complexity breeds the project manager's mortal enemy: assumptions. Designers will assume that the particulars of a piece of complex functionality will be clear to the engineers; engineers will assume that all the choices they've made while coding will work with the interface being developed. The result? Interfaces designed by engineers (who are generally not visual or information designers) or interfaces requiring functionality that the code cannot provide. There's no way around it: Designing functionality for a website can be hard work, meticulous, and even tedious. And it can get very expensive, especially if your teams don't communicate as well as they should.

A Simple Request

Clients may ask for something that they consider to be a straightforward request: "We would like to add a username and password area to the site. How much will it cost?" It's a common item for most e-commerce and community sites, but it's far easier requested than done. There are answers needed. Where and how is the data stored and accessed? Is the process handled in real-time by the system, or is it manually operated? What if customers forget their passwords? Can they automatically retrieve the information through the website, or do they need to wait for a return email or until a service technician contacts them? While these requests may appear to be simple, the nuances (such as allowing immediate retrieval of a forgotten password) are what make the difference between a $10,000 request and a $100,000 request. Taking each request seriously means going through the discovery and requirements definition process to accurately estimate budget, resources, and timing. Beware of gray areas: a simple request is not always a straightforward one.

Determining When Requirements Are Necessary

For every action a user takes on a website beyond the basic click-and-link (and sometimes even then), there are several reactions that the system needs to perform to satisfy the user's request. Identifying these reactions and all their variables is the goal of gathering and specifying requirements. This process is especially necessary when the site's functionality is too complex to show in a simple sitemap or wireframe. Gathering and specifying requirements goes significantly deeper, breaking down a task or action that a site visitor can take past the simple log-in screen into detailed specifics that may be invisible to the end user.

An easy example would be a customer log-in. While assigning a user name and password may seem like a simple process, questions quickly arise that need more details in order to properly estimate time, resources, and budget to complete. Examples of some potential questions might include:

- **Should the visitor be able to automatically generate their own user name and password?**
- **Will the user name and password be generated in real-time?**
- **If the visitor forgets their password will they be able to retrieve automatically or will it be a delayed process?**

Generally, any such complex functionality requires more detailed documentation than just "User name and password will be generated in real-time," which is why we delve deeper. You need to determine what processes, as the end user goes through the log-in process, must take place invisibly.

First identify all the necessary steps, paying careful attention to divide each step into specific tasks. For instance, for the preceding list, the client may have only identified "site visitor logs in" as a requirement.

Understanding Requirements

To understand the manner in which the website will be *required* to respond to user requests, one must first align the company's business needs to these requirements. And unless the client is incredibly tech savvy (not the usual case), translating overall business needs into individual elements will also help the client better understand how these functional pieces fit into the overall success of the company.

Think of requirements as project components, each its own little subproject with a mini-workflow of its own. Each requirement — once known, agreed upon, and documented — gets mapped to specifications that explain in detail how the website's functionality should work in respect to this requirement. The specification can then be used by front-end designers and engineers to design and construct their respective aspects of the website.

Practice Makes Perfect

Over time documenting requirements does get easier, though at times your requirements may seem too detailed or too broad. This is a common frustration and source of anxiety, but as you get more experienced with detailing requirements, and your team gets used to reading them, you'll quickly find a happy medium that everyone is comfortable with. No one is perfect, but experience gets you close.

Assign a Requirements Coordinator

Project requirements can come from many places within a company. Assign a single person to coordinate gathering requirements. Typically this falls to the project manager, but it could also be the responsibility of a marketing person, a designer, a business analyst, or an account manager. Regardless, it should be the primary responsibility of one and only one person. This is not only efficient; it also avoids duplication of effort. Having a background in engineering or systems integration is helpful, although it is not necessary to have hands-on programming experience. It is critical, however, for this person to have a solid understanding of the business goals, user goals, and capabilities of the system.

Gathering Requirements

Gathering requirements can often be difficult, frustrating, and problematic. It involves working with clients and helping them take their hazy, often incomplete understanding of their needs and solidifying them into concrete elements based on priority and what functionality is required vs. desired.

When interviewing the client during Discovery, the project manager must dig for as many details as possible. And we mean dig — don't rely on information provided. Strive to interview as many client representatives as possible, including the site maintenance team lead. Interview customers and users; these are the people who have needs that the redesigned site should be meant to address.

Avoid discussion as to how you will implement the actual requirements. People will always get ahead of themselves if you let them. Stay focused on what the website should allow users to do, not specifically how it will be designed to allow them to do it. That comes later. Client comments such as "I should be able to select my optional shipping addresses from a drop-down menu," or "I like how Amazon.com can show me my past orders on one page," are examples of requests driven less by business needs, but more from familiarity and preference. Stay focused on why the request is being made. Without truly understanding the business needs, you will have no real understanding of how to meet them through the site.

Documenting Requirements

With the requirements gathered, the Requirements Coordinator (assign someone; see accompanying tip) will need to translate your requirements into brief and easy-to-digest-by-everyone text. Keep the definition of each requirement to one sentence; anything more is too long and probably means that the requirement should be broken down into at least two separate pieces.

Once documented, requirements should be assembled in some manner that is easy to keep track of and reference. We suggest that you also cross-reference each requirement to the business need it represents and to the "proprietor" of the requirement [9.9] — the person who is advocating the particular requirement (usually the person who'll be fired if it doesn't get done right). That person is good to have in the loop, even if he isn't actually authorized to sign off on anything.

There are several software suites out there to assist with more sophisticated requirements organization. (Rational Requisite Pro from IBM is a particularly robust application for this.) But you can also achieve quality organization by numbering the requirements in a simple but well-organized spreadsheet. No specific numbering convention is necessary. There is no hard-and-fast rule for organizing. Select a system that suits you and facilitates easy sorting. Numbering is important, but the numbering system is not.

REQUIREMENTS FOR E-COMMERCE MODULE		
#	Title	Description
1.1	Personalize Content	The website shall allow all customers to access personalized shopping lists.
2.1	Browse Inventory	The website shall allow all visitors to browse available products.
3.1	Save Addresses	The website shall allow all customers to save mailing addresses.
3.2	Save Credit Card Information	The website shall allow all customers to save their credit card information.
4.1	Review Past Purchases	The website shall allow all customers to review past purchases.
4.2	Track Delivery	The website shall allow all customers to track the delivery status of orders.
4.3	Cancel Orders in Process	The website shall allow all customers to cancel placed orders within a specified window post submission.
5.1	Personalize Discounts	The website shall offer visitors special discounts based on previous activity or purchases.
5.2	Promote Specials	The website shall promote current special deals.
5.3	Feature Content	The website shall feature content in designated areas based on previous activity or purchases.
6.1	Contact Customer Service	The website shall allow visitors to contact customer service agents via the website.

REQUIREMENTS FOR E-COMMERCE MODULE				
#	Owner	Need	Title	Description
1.1	Mktg	Drive repeat customers conversion	Personalize Content	The website shall allow all customers to access personalized shopping lists.
2.1	Sales	Increase customer awareness of new product lines	Browse Inventory	The website shall allow all visitors to easily browse available products.

< 9.9

"The website shall allow..." Yes, this gets repetitive, but it ensures consistency of meaning. We recommend using this wording. It's short and to the point with each requirement written as a single sentence that is descriptive enough to clearly communicate its intent and differentiate it from other requirements.

Set Realistic Target Dates

Trying to assign a target date before scope is set is a very real project development problem. Don't be surprised by "real-world" pressures to get *something* up by a release date that is determined before the actual scope of the project is set. Do remember that workflow is designed in the other order — prioritize ahead of risk rating — for a reason: It provides a vital check to ensure that you're not putting something out there just because it is possible, but rather because it will meet correct and crucial business needs. Ideally, scope determines schedule, but the opposite happens all the time, thrusting risk rating ahead of business priorities, or at least forcing the combining of these tasks.

PRIORITIZING, RATING, AND ANALYZING

The next step: Prioritize the listed requirements according to business needs. This has to come from the client. After priorities are set, rate the requirements according to perceived risks of failing at implementation. This doesn't really involve the client (unless the engineering team is internal to the client). Finally, analyze — meaning that you find the right mixture of priority and risk and then put those in scope for the project. This requires that both the project manager (or requirements coordinator if you have one) and the client work together.

Prioritizing Business Needs

Priorities should be determined according to business need. Do not stifle a requirement because it seems to be too costly, too time consuming, or too complex. Instead, concentrate on how necessary the requirement is for the business needs of the client, divorced from any consideration of implementation. It is seductive to combine prioritization with ease of implementation and make decisions accordingly, but avoid that temptation.

Additionally, prioritizing based on business need means that when the time comes to cut some of the requirements from the scope of the project — and that time will certainly come — you have a solid basis on which to exclude them. We suggest a simple numeric scale such as:

1 = Critical. Must have.

2 = High.

3 = Moderate.

4 = Low.

5 = Optional.

6 = Postpone for next release.

This is a crucial stage in which the client can see how their business needs can be prioritized *before* focusing on what is or is not possible with regard to site development. This is a bit of an abstraction, and in reality these two things often get conflated, resulting in real business needs being discounted out of hand because of perceived risk. Example: "We really need to implement the Content Management System (CMS), but we don't have time."

Rating Requirements

Once the requirements are prioritized, each must pass through a risk assessment. What is the chance of failure? What is the probability of implementing on time or on budget when the following are all taken into account: **complexity**, **cost restrictions**, **personnel availability**, and **external factors**. You should determine this risk in conjunction with the workflows of both your engineering and design teams. Leaving either out will render your assessment a mere guess.

At this early stage, risk assessment analyses will necessarily be preliminary, but you should be able to get a rough idea of the resources necessary based on industry standards and past experience. We recommend using a rating method similar to that used for priorities:

1 = Minimal risk.

2 = Low risk.

3 = Moderate risk.

4 = High risk.

5 = Unrealistic.

6 = Unknown

Analyzing Requirements

Once you've determined priorities and assessed the risks, schedule a meeting with your client for the all-important analysis review. Be prepared with a spreadsheet or matrix containing all the necessary information **[9.10]**. This provides an easy visual showing which requirements (think of them as project components) have the highest business need and the lowest risk. Items with a lower score are "better" in that they meet the best of both worlds, but they're not necessarily better for the project, so don't hastily select for implementation based on score alone. Often requirements must be implemented when they have a high priority *and* a high risk. This is the reality of business and is a decision for the client to make. But it is always helpful to know what you are getting yourself into.

REQUIREMENTS FOR E-COMMERCE MODULE				
#	**Title**	**Priority**	**Risk**	**Score (Priority + Risk)**
1.1	Personalize Content	3	3	6
2.1	Browse Inventory	1	3	4
3.1	Save Addresses	2	2	4
3.2	Save Credit Card Information	2	2	4
4.1	Review Past Purchases	4	2	6
4.2	Track Delivery	5	4	9
4.3	Cancel Orders in Process	5	4	9
5.1	Personalize Discounts	2	1	3
5.2	Promote Specials	2	1	3
5.3	Feature Content	4	4	8
6.1	Contact Customer Service	2	2	4

< 9.10 >

Sample analysis. This chart shows priority, risk and final scoring — an analysis which will allow a business to make decisions about pieces of complex functionality on their site.

Make It a Team Effort

The Functional Spec document is usually created by the Requirements Coordinator/Project Manager (or sometimes a business analyst) in conjunction with the information designers, graphic designers, and engineers. While the project manager may lead this process, the insights and talents of all team members are crucial to fully explore the best way a site visitor can utilize the website to complete a task, making sure nothing is left out. Designers will see things that an engineer will miss and vice versa. If possible, include the client as well — they can validate that all variables are being considered. In short, include all stakeholders.

CREATE

> Drafting a Functional Specification

> Getting Sign-Off

Getting the client to make decisions at this seemingly abstract point in the workflow will be a challenge. The tendency is for clients to provide frustratingly partial answers such as, "We know that these three requirements are critical, but I will have to get back to you on the others." And if there are multiple decision-makers, each with agendas and conflicting schedules, you'll contend with the possibility of not getting a cohesive, coherent answer. The requirements coordinator will probably have to crack a whip and force the issue. You cannot move forward until an approved list is in hand.

DRAFTING A FUNCTIONAL SPECIFICATION

With your gathered and documented requirements, you can create a specification document that acts as a blueprint from which both your design and engineering teams can work. Referred to as a "requirements specification," it often gets shortened to a "spec." We call it a Functional Spec. Think of it as a compendium of your project scope requirements, elaborated upon by adding step-by-step detail showing how the functionality will actually work.

At this point in your redesign-with-complex-functionality project, you've completed all the steps that comprise the first phase of the Core Process. The next step usually takes place at the same time you are creating your sitemap in Phase 2: Structure. If it helps to consider construction of the Functional Spec to be part of flow chart development, you wouldn't be off base. The sitemap provides a high-level view of overall site flow and organization, while the Functional Spec drills down into greater detail on those areas of the sitemap that represent complex functionality. The two documents complement each other. Creating and combining these two documents can be a powerful tool in planning and presenting the developing vision of the redesigned site.

Creating a Functional Spec is a meticulous process and is often more time-consuming than was budgeted for. It can be difficult and often tedious, although problem-solving, analytical types thrive on this sort of thing. Depending on overall site complexity, some projects can burn up to 25% of the total schedule and budget on this without being either unrealistic or wasteful. Despite project size, however, determining clear requirements for complex functionality up front goes a long way toward avoiding problems later on in the process.

What to Include in the Functional Specification

In the Functional Spec, each of the requirements is described in step-by-step überdetail, explaining in terms of functionality what each actually means when implemented. Though there are a variety of formats for creating your Functional Spec, we recommend Use Cases **[9.11]**. As the name implies, Use Cases **specify** (describe) each **case** (task) for which a visitor **uses** (interacts with) a website. Simple enough. And since these are developed from a user experience perspective, Use Cases are easy for both designers and engineers to understand. Use Cases are gaining in popularity, and many fine books explain them in more detail than the general overview we present here. We recommend *Use Cases: Requirements in Context* by Daryll Kulak and Eamonn Guiney (Addison-Wesley, 2003) or *Writing Effective Use Cases* by Alistair Cockburn (Addison-Wesley, 2000).

For each requirement or task, you should include the following:

- **A description of the required functionality — keep it short.**
- **A description of when this functionality will be used and under what conditions.**
- **An overview of how a site visitor would use that functionality, usually including a step-by-step breakdown of the expected steps by the user and how the website responds.**
- **Any alternative paths a user could take that would deviate from the expected steps but still achieve the same result.**
- **A description of what happens when the user makes an error or takes a path that results in the task not being able to be completed.**
- **A list of any requirements that are related to the one you're currently discussing and upon which this requirement might be dependent.**
- **Any assumptions about the user or the website that must be true in order for the functionality to work as you detailed in your step-by-step breakdown.**

You should also note the business rules — basically any standard operating procedures specifically dealing with the company and the website — that are inherent to your Use Cases. Some people put these rules in each Use Case, and others create a single list for all business rules within the specification. If business rules tend to apply to all Use Cases, then a single repository should be fine. If each Use Case tends to have particular rules, include them individually in the Use Case itself.

Usage Scenarios

Supplement your Use Cases with the inclusion of scenarios in your specification. A scenario depicts a real-world example to flesh out how the step-by-step might actually look when sample users are inserted. This is an optional step, but it's recommended if you have the resources — even if you only create scenarios for particularly important and/or highly complicated requirements. Note that scenarios are already part of Phase 2: Structure **[4.19]**, except that what we recommend here includes complex functionality and is necessarily more detailed.

Field	Description	Example
Use Case Name	Descriptive Title of the Use Case (What Is Being Accomplished by the User)	User Purchase of Product from Saved Items
Use Case Specifier	The author/updater of the Use Case	John Smith, Project Manager
Version History	A list of the dates on which versions of this use case were created.	Version 003 – 03/03/04 Version 002 – 02/15/04 Version 001 – 01/12/04
Summary	A description of what this Use Case describes. Keep it brief. A few sentences should be enough since the purpose of the summary is to allow a reader of the Use Case to quickly scan for the content of the Use Case.	This Use Case describes the process by which a user returns to the website and purchases items he/she has previously saved for later purchase in the MyItems listing under the Member area (MyStuff).
Trigger	Describe the situation that makes this Use Case necessary or what the user is trying to accomplish.	The user desires to purchase an item from his/her previously selected list of saved items.
Outline of Events	In a step-by-step fashion, outline each of the steps the user takes and each way in which the system (website) reacts as the user completes the task. To best illustrate the interactivity that the Use Case is meant to describe, we suggest that your outline should be 1. User acts 2. System responds 3. User acts 4. System responds 5. User acts 6. etc. until the user has completed the task.	1. The Use Case begins when the user returns to the website and logs in to the system. 2. The system responds by delivering the user to his/her personalized page (termed the MyStuff area). 3. The user selects the previously saved items feature (MyItems). 4. The system responds by delivering the user's previously saved items. 5. The user selects the item(s) that he/she wishes to now purchase. 6. The system pulls the item(s) into an active shopping cart with the current price(s). 7. The user proceeds with the checkout process. 8. The system removes the previously saved item(s) from the MyItems list.

9.11 >

This Functional Spec sample uses the Use Case format. All descriptions, jargon, organization, and the general thought process is courtesy of Sean Dolan (see this chapter's Expert Topic) and is based on his extensive experience.

Field	Description	Example
Alternative Paths	Describe any alternative paths the user might take to accomplish the same task or alternative decisions the user might make within the task. This should primarily describe uncommon or unusual steps the user might take. If the path the user takes is common or usual, you should create a separate Use Case to describe it.	In step 6, if the price has changed since the time when an item was originally saved to the MyItems list, a message will convey this information to the user, and the user will be given the option to continue with the purchase process or cancel the process.
Exception Paths	Describe what happens if there is an error or if the system cannot respond to the user's actions. For example, if the user enters information into a form that is incorrect. Describe how the system would respond to such a situation.	In step 3, if an item is no longer in available inventory, the system will notify the user that the previously saved item is no longer for sale and will give the user the choice of canceling the process or viewing a list of similar items.
Extension Points	List any other Use Cases that are related to this Use Case.	Once the user has added an item to the cart for purchase, the course of events will be identical to those outlined in Use Case 2.2: User Purchase of Products in Shopping Cart.
Assumptions	Describe any assumptions about the user or the system that must be true (or are assumed to be true) for the user to successfully complete the Use Case. These may be assumptions about the user or about the system.	1. The user already has a valid login/password for the website. 2. The system is accessible to the user. 3. The user is logged in to the website. 4. The system has access to current pricing information. 5. The system has access to stored user profile information.
Preconditions	Describe any conditions that must be true for the Use Case to be initiated.	The user has previously saved items to the MyItems list.
Post conditions	Describe the result of the successful completion of the Use Case.	The user completes purchase of previously saved item.
Business Rule	List any business rules that are involved in the successful completion of the Use Case.	1. All products previously saved will have their prices updated as prices change, regardless of the price applicable when the user originally saved the item. 2. If the product qualifies for free shipping, this will be applied to the item when it is added to the active shopping cart.

The Visual Design Factor

After you get your initial Functional Spec done and distributed, and you turn to concentrate on designing the site's visual look and feel, the GUI will and should come into play. It will possibly even spark new issues or questions that might not have surfaced otherwise. Some design elements such as buttons and menus do affect the actual coding process. In order to keep communication flowing as the project moves forward, it may be beneficial to include visual mock-ups in subsequent versions of the Spec.

How Detailed Should the Specification Be?

The targeted level of detail for the Functional Spec is difficult to pinpoint. The more experienced your team is individually and with each other, the easier this level is to discern. Regardless, each requirement should be specified in as much detail as necessary to communicate all the pertinent information, yet it should be brief and concise enough to be digestible without overwhelming the team members who will actually need to use the document. This is a balancing act: needs against resources.

It is important initially to keep all references to interface design *out* of your Functional Spec. It is easy to unconsciously employ interface assumptions such as "using a drop-down menu" or "pushes a button." But you are not yet at the wireframe stage in the Core Process, and therefore you should not be trying to visualize what the actual interface is going to look like. Endeavor to keep your specifications as "interface neutral" as possible at the outset; don't breed assumptions into your documents. If you write "using a drop-down menu" in your Spec, the engineer working on the project will assume a decision has been made. And then, when the designer instead suggests a DHTML menu or buttons, there will be confusion and frustration. Use these examples as a guide:

- **Instead of "user pushes a button" choose "user submits information."**
- **Instead of "using a drop-down menu" choose "user selects from list."**
- **Instead of "user selects tab" choose "user selects category."**

In all versions of the Spec, keep it simple and modular so that it's easy to search and sort. Avoid ambiguity as well as excessive repetition. If you find that a particular requirement specification is becoming overly long and complex, break it into multiple requirements. It is always better to have four brief documents that can be quickly understood than a single document that is a wall of words. The former will be cherished and support a streamlined process; the latter will be loathed and lend itself to inefficiency.

GETTING SIGN-OFF

Review the completed Functional Spec with your team. Once both the designers and engineers (as well as any IT folks) are clear on it and all necessary revisions have been made, review it with the client. They will want to be walked through it, so a face-to-face is encouraged. The key here is to be very, very clear about the implications of changes made after they sign off on this document. Explanation and mutual understanding of the Functional Spec is critical to avoid the "that's not really what I meant" syndrome down the road. Plus, if the client is not completely sold and is adopting a "we'll see how it goes" attitude, you can be sure there will be costly changes. Cover yourself by getting a client signature and then distribute the Functional Spec to your engineering team so they can begin to build all the code.

That is the next step: the coding necessary to make all the requirements happen. This step happens parallel to Phase 3: Design. The two workflows may not meet at all during this step, but they will come together when it is time to integrate and implement.

Be aware that revisions to the Spec are likely to occur. As with any highly detailed documentation, indicate specifically what has changed and make sure to implement a clear revision history so there is never any question as to which version is current. Be scrupulous in distribution of subsequent versions; one team member missing a version can cause a lot of problems. In addition, keeping everyone up to date offers the opportunity for any team member at any time to apply his expertise to its development. Each team member — from designer to production lead to engineer to IT — will be looking at the Spec from a different perspective, and they will be able to spot potential areas of concern before it reaches them and/or become a critical issue.

SEAN DOLAN ON FOSTERING PRODUCTIVE COLLABORATION BETWEEN DESIGNERS AND ENGINEERS

As a project team grows, the chance for miscommunication grows exponentially. This is particularly vexing once you've entered the actual construction phase. Designers are designing. Engineers are engineering. Production is producing. There is a tendency for each to view the others as separate entities. Designers often view programming as simply supporting their beautiful interfaces. Likewise, engineers may view the interface as nothing more than the façade of the "real" work they are doing to make the whole site run. An effective project manager strives to prevent such predictable tensions by fostering the feeling that all parties are collaboratively creating the entire user experience and that one aspect cannot succeed without the other. An interface that lacks robust engineering will falter and fail to meet user expectations, and code that lacks a clear interface will simply not be used. Here's a truth: Designers and engineers are talented professionals, each providing innovative and creative solutions to problems. In this sense, they are more similar than not. Building on this sentiment keeps these teams in constant collaboration rather than in isolation.

Design and engineering usually happen on independent, parallel paths, but eventually the products of both efforts must merge. It's a daunting task. Making sure that this happens smoothly is one of the most difficult yet crucial tasks a project manager will face. To accomplish this, you should keep in mind some common issues and their solutions.

- **Avoid rabbit holes.** It's common for specialists such as designers and engineers to get their marching orders and proceed to create elegant solutions in seclusion. This is the rabbit-hole mentality, where everyone is off on their own paths, digging ever deeper with the hope that eventually their path will intersect with everyone else's. As you might suspect, the chances of success are limited. (More often than not, you'll face delays in schedule, mismatched efforts, and results that don't meet the overall goals of the project.) Meet to brainstorm and share information between the two teams regularly. As much as you might face resistance, it's crucial to keep the team together by keeping them all on the same page.
- **Avoid the mad scientist mentality.** Some designers and developers show little interest in the "why" of a project. They just want to come up with solutions individually. Working in relative isolation, their solutions may begin to diverge from the goals of the project, and while innovative or even brilliant, they won't meet the business goals of the project or conform to the technical standards. Review the business logic of the project with everyone on a regular basis. Reinforce the "why" of the project so that when your designers and engineers are working on the "how," they have a broader context and understanding of how their efforts will integrate with each other.

- **Force process.** Schedule your project so that discrete components are designed and engineered on roughly the same schedule. Not only can you do dry-run testing of integration throughout, you keep both teams on the same schedule. The design and development process can take weeks or months, and during this period, team members may work at different speeds. Some work steadily. Others procrastinate and then produce work in a flurry as the deadline approaches. Some others fall so far behind that you find yourself with little to show for months of effort. That's a catastrophe. By having the project scheduled in discrete and simultaneous components, you can take a very large project and break it down into manageable chunks. Reinforce a team mentality, ensure regular workflow, and you'll chart progress and milestones more effectively.
- **Protosite it.** Aside from being a valuable presentation tool for the client so that they can understand what the site will eventually look like, a Protosite also forces your designers and engineers to work collaboratively throughout the process to uncover issues that individually they might not have noticed. Protosites (also called prototypes) come in varying levels of functionality and completion, but by integrating even provisional design/code, you'll see how well the efforts are matching up during the process. Even better, if you do usability testing on the Protosite, both engineers and designers can see how well their in-progress efforts are working and can change things as necessary.

Every designer has a little engineer in her, and every engineer has some sense of user interface. Though the roles may be distinctly different, create an atmosphere in which each team feels empowered to provide insights into how the other might create a more effective product. Encourage your engineers to explain to your designers on a high level how the back-end will function. Oftentimes, a designer can see how certain steps within the programming might be streamlined. Similarly, an engineer can suggest functionality in which the interface might be optimized to take advantage of the coding. Build on the seasoned talent of both worlds while maintaining clear role definition, and you'll foster a tremendous sense of collegiality and innovation for your product.

Sean Dolan is Senior Producer / Project Manager for gotomedia, inc., in San Francisco where he has guided the development of projects for clients such as the FDIC and WebEx. Prior to gotomedia, Sean was Director of Program Management for Idea Integration/ San Francisco and Executive Producer at Food.com. He was also Senior Managing Producer at AOL / Digital City in Boston.

IMPLEMENT
> Integrating Your Efforts
> Preparing to Launch

IMPLEMENTING THE FUNCTIONAL SPECIFICATION

With the sitemap and Functional Spec signed off on and established as the collective springboard from which all team members will work, the engineers can use it to build the code, and the designers can use it to create the GUI that the code will work within. Now, with both of those major tasks completed, the two workflows come back together and implementation begins. At this point, the project manager has a challenge ahead of her. Validating requirements/specifications — making sure that the actual work done and the requirements do, in fact, match — is a constant task throughout the rest of the design process, starting with the wireframes. And if a Protosite is created (either in HTML only or including a rough version of the functionality), this should be validated against the requirements/specification as well. The project manager will need to monitor progress, manage damage control, and resolve all sorts of problems. Scope creep will need to be identified, combated, and controlled.

Inevitably, the design and development efforts will uncover issues that cannot be solved or that were unanticipated. Hopefully these will be small and easily resolved, but if not, the Functional Spec should be updated (or the project scope would need to be altered). Changing the Spec or scope after development has begun is not optimal (obviously!), but if it happens, make sure everyone involved — client and team alike — clearly understands exactly what is changing and how.

Integrating Your Efforts

Production time. Phase 4 of the Core Process is already one big building exercise; here is where you add to it. As your HTML and engineering efforts are nearing completion and the two teams necessarily come together, you reach the point where you can see how creating the Functional Spec — and regularly validating progress against it — really pays off. Seamless integration of interface and engineering is one of the most difficult aspects of the entire redesign process. And though the teams have been in regular contact with each other (hopefully), they have been working somewhat independently from each other for weeks or, more probably, months. Integration can be a tense time. It is not uncommon for a project to move smoothly until this stage and then encounter significant delays. Whether due to plain bad luck (the code is compatible with the staging environment but not with the live environment) or due to misconceptions and contradictory assumptions about how the site should really work, delays cost money. Rotten luck we can't speak to (though we definitely commiserate), but if your Functional Spec has been done well and you've communicated effectively throughout the design and development process, the obstacles should be minimal and manageable.

In anticipation of the actual point of integration, there has probably been a dummy placeholder built into the HTML that the front-end team works around, knowing it will be switched out at some moment before launch (and hopefully before QA). This switch is — at the risk of melodrama — a magical moment. It is one of those cool moments when people call co-workers over to their workstation and say, "Hey, look at this." Of course, often it doesn't work. It's a hard fact that very few projects don't encounter some hitch at the point of integration.

Ideally, the process of gathering, documenting, analyzing, and specifying requirements will help you avoid most integration issues (or at least manage them more effectively) by forcing team members to investigate and plan at the beginning of a project rather than in the middle or, even worse, at the end. While not every problem can be anticipated, we can say with certainty that this process will greatly reduce the nasty and expensive surprises that usually arise during integration.

Preparing to Launch

Finally, once integration and delivery have taken place, your Functional Spec can be a powerful tool to assist in showing the client how you met with the contractual obligations of the project. Using the Spec, you can show how you logically took the business needs, mapped them to requirements, and implemented them as interface elements and features on the site. This point-by-point process removes some of the vagueness that often plagues the wrap of design projects. And if the client ever complains or wonders aloud whether you're actually done — Did you do everything they wanted you to do? — you have it there in plain English (or Serbo-Croatian, if you happen to live along the Aegean coast). Additionally, any requirements that were set aside for the current project and deferred for later implementation can be seen as business development opportunities.

Using the Functional Spec to Conduct QA

For companies with a budget for QA and a qualified (and hopefully experienced) person to run the testing process, the Functional Spec can be quite helpful. Using the document as reference, the QA team can develop test cases — specific paths or tasks designed to QA the site in the most comprehensive manner possible, even before the feature highlighted in the test case is created. With the obvious benefit of reducing the amount of time necessary for QA, test cases get the QA team involved earlier in the process. While this method might successfully uncover many common errors, it is nevertheless impossible to test everything. But for a complex site, developing a test plan with test cases is always recommended.

CHAPTER SUMMARY

The Core Process, as enhanced by the integration of backend workflow, will work for huge projects as well as the small e-commerce site with a few products in its database. The key is simply scale. But for any site that needs to employ a complex functionality (and not every site will need to), taking a detailed, step-by-step approach and documenting requirements up front lays a sturdy foundation to build upon.

But perhaps the best postlaunch consequence of the meticulous process presented in this chapter is that the client will actually have a document that details how their website works both for maintenance and for when the team begins work on the next iteration of the site. Redesigning is a constant process, and any tool that effectively shares knowledge about the site will give you and the client an immediate head start when planning for the future.

Banana Republic

Company: Banana Republic
URL: www.bananarepublic.com
Design Team: Banana Republic in-house

Creative Director: An-Ching Chang
Copy Director: Sarah Seipel
Associate Art Director: Jaime Gabriel

Banana Republic aims to offer a premier shopping experience online and off. Launched originally in October 1999, the site has grown to match the cybershoppers' expectations. Timely merchandise updates make it easy to browse and shop online.

<PREVIOUS>

BANANA REPUBLIC [OLD] used a simplistic element of squares to create a navigational system used throughout the site. The high-concept navigation was nonscalable and difficult to learn and use

<CURRENT>

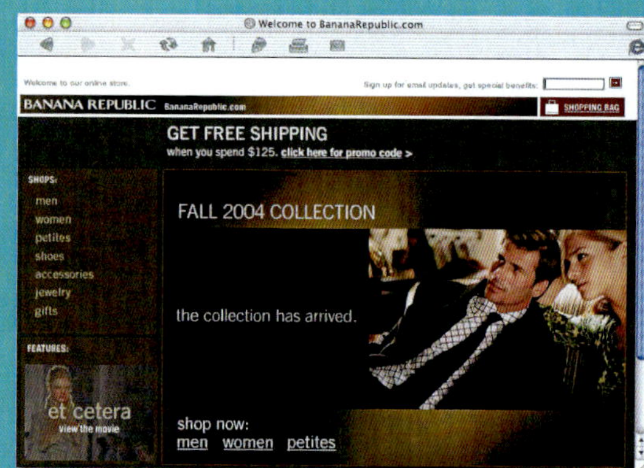

BANANA REPUBLIC [REDESIGNED] completely expanded the navigation to highlight all of its business categories, including new initiatives.

BANANA REPUBLIC SHOES [REDESIGNED] maintains navigational and visual integrity throughout the site.

Results: By shifting its priority from form to function, the redesigned website invites its customers to become more engaged with the site. By paying close attention to brand during the process, none of Banana Republic's modern, classic sensibility was sacrificed.

> To become better partners with our clients, we must understand the client's industry online, against its competition. What are the goals of the company, product, and market as they relate to the web?

Analyzing Your Competition 10

Analyzing Your Competition

A competitive analysis should be part of the web redesign process no matter the level of approach — and the levels can get very lofty. With large, fiercely competitive industries such as commercial airlines or personal computer hardware, there might be both the need and the budget for a formal industry analysis. In these situations, plan on spending up to six figures for an outside marketing or research company to deliver an exhaustive document the size of Tolstoy's *War And Peace*. For projects without mammoth budgets, we recommend conducting an informal features analysis.

WHAT THIS CHAPTER COVERS	
DEFINE AND PREP	**CONDUCT AND ANALYZE**
> Determining Analysis Plan	> Performing Evaluations
> Becoming an Expert in the Client's Industry	> Conducting Usability Testing
> Defining the Competitive Set	> Creating a Final Report
> Creating a Features List	

What's the difference between comparing industries and features? Expertise, budget, and approach. A full-blown formal industry analysis is generally conducted by marketing- and strategy-focused teams with solid research methodologies driven by experience. It focuses largely on markets and business positioning in a broad competitive landscape. A features analysis, whether formal or informal, focuses on comparing the actual customer experience — primarily online but sometimes offline as well. It provides a snapshot view of the competition's services and features from a customer standpoint.

The results generated from this analysis will be used by both the web development team and the client. The team gains the invaluable experience of being able to simulate the user experience within the client's industry. The client — whether external or internal — receives data that helps them see what their online competition is offering in the way of content, features, and services. Through conducting a features analysis, the team and the client each gain a better understanding of what is working and — just as important — what is not working for users.

When your site was first built, you (or your predecessor) probably surfed extensively to see who was doing what in your field. You leveraged some ideas from competitors and rejected others. Now that the site is being redesigned, it is time to take another, updated look. The industry has likely changed — even if it's only been a year since the site was originally built. Significant industry change may even be the primary reason why the site is being redesigned. Include the existing site in your analysis. Looking at the existing site alongside its competition enables you not only to compare features and audience expectations, but also to look at how the existing site measures up (or doesn't measure up) against the competition. This will help to establish redesign goals.

Throughout this book, we advocate hiring experts whenever possible. Conducting competitive analyses is no exception. Expertly gathered information is always incredibly worthwhile and usually hits on points that non-research types may not even consider. But conducting an informal features analysis is valuable for a different reason — it enables the team designing and developing the redesigned site to engage in the information-gathering process. Part of the value of conducting an informal competitive analysis is that it helps the team begin to think like your audience within the your industry, and that type of thinking is priceless.

FORMAL INDUSTRY ANALYSIS VS. INFORMAL FEATURES ANALYSIS

Understand that the informal analysis we recommend in this chapter involves online features and customer experience, not marketing or branding or product analyses of the company's current or future business position. These other analyses may have already been developed by the company and may provide an understanding of where the company has been and where it is going — especially as it relates to redesign goals. Gather as much information from the client as you can during this Discovery process.

FORMAL VS. INFORMAL COMPARISON

	Formal Industry Analysis	Informal Features Analysis
Team	An independent research team with expertise and background in marketing, communications, research, and/or strategy.	Members of the web development team who will be re-creating the user experience online.
Approach	Formal analysis of industry, market segmentation, trends and forecasts, and customer needs.	Informal analysis of competitive sites focusing on features and user experience.
Results	Quantitative data–driven, market- and research-centered focus.	Feature-driven, qualitative information; show what is working and what is not working.
Report	A huge book of information.	5 to 20 pages, short and sweet.
Budget	$20,000 and up.	Lunch to $20,000.
Goals	Provide comprehensive, detailed, strategy-based recommendations on changing marketplaces, evolving business models, and customer habits and segmentation.	Gain firsthand view of customer experience. Provide relevant documentation and industry information to the client.

Obscure Industries

Unless the company's field is so technically obscure that you cannot understand even the basic terminology (for example, genetically engineered livestock food supplements, FAA-mandated commercial jet engine maintenance, or Shih-tzu breeding), you should be able to use and review several sites right away and form solid opinions. (Note: If you are redesigning a jet engine maintenance company's website, you should plan on a crash course in aeronautical terminology, hire yourself a jet engine expert, or better yet, have the client give you a detailed tour of their plant.)

The ultimate goal of a features analysis is quite direct in that it answers this question: What are competitors (and other "best practice" sites) doing to provide services and content that is positive and meaningful to users? For the purposes of this book, we focus primarily on online competition, though the brick-and-mortar world should not be ignored. Sometimes most, if not all, of your competition is offline and just a phone call away. But to analyze the entire industry is outside the scope of what we suggest. The job of the web development team as it embarks on a features analysis is to look at the goals of the company, product, and market as they relate to the web.

Becoming an Expert in the Client's Industry

The process of becoming an industry expert begins much the same way as you might begin online research for personal reasons — with a search at Yahoo! or Google or the like and then visits to several competitor sites. Perhaps one of the site's products is fingerless fleece gloves. By plugging those three keywords, "fingerless fleece gloves," into a search engine, you will get a dozen or more online catalog sites specializing in sporting wear or outdoor clothing. All these sites are in the same industry and therefore make up a competitive set. Perhaps some of them are even on the list of perceived competitors the

Gaining a Customer Perspective

A small design group embarked on a complete redesign and rebranding of an online food delivery website. "Make it a better experience" was the goal. "Increase customer usage." It was a straightforward challenge: Take a site and identify what needed to be changed and how the experience could be improved.

The team started by looking at other sites within the industry. Online food delivery, online grocery delivery, online dining guides, offline food delivery, cooking sites, etc. What worked with these sites? What didn't work? The only way to find out was to become actual users. The team compared site features. They went through checkout ordering processes. They registered and became members. They searched for restaurants and ordered food — a lot of food. They called customer service to complain when food was delivered late or the orders were incorrect. They felt the pains of a user when a particular menu couldn't be found or a restaurant was closed. They quickly saw what was successful and why.

In the end, they became experts by doing. Not just observing or researching but being real users. What did they learn? The design needed to be simple and straightforward. The ordering process needed to be as easy as picking up the phone — even easier. They knew the site needed to do more, think faster, and perform better than the main competition: the offline, phone-in delivery services.

The upshot? The redesigned site wasn't just usable; it got used.

client provided (from the Client Survey in Phase 1: Define). By looking through many of these sites, you — a typical user for that industry — become better versed not only on the specific product but also on the industry itself.

A big theme throughout this book is to THINK LIKE YOUR CUSTOMERS. The competitive analysis is no exception. Approach this task with the mindset of a typical site visitor and "shop" through the client's industry much the way you "shopped" for fingerless fleece gloves. Compare competitors. Use the competitors' sites to complete transactions and find information. It takes time, but by being a typical customer on site after site within the competitive set, you quickly become an expert customer in your company's industry. Be reasonable, of course. If your client's company sells cars, you certainly don't need to purchase several of the newest models. But take it as far as possible without committing serious dollars.

Analyzing the competition from an audience perspective enables you to remove yourself from your web developer's get-it-done, make-it-work point of view. Making decisions based on things that matter to your audience — ease of use, likes and dislikes, and other fickle attributes that site visitors with little patience or aptitude might apply to their actual online experiences — helps immeasurably in understanding the your industry online.

CONDUCTING AN ANALYSIS

Conducting a features analysis is a basic, easy-to-follow process that can be expanded or scaled back depending on time, resources, and budget. Whether 20 hours or 200 hours, the process contains the same four steps: define the process, create a features list, conduct analysis and usability testing, and lastly, create a report. Use the accompanying chart as a guide. Modify as your time, resources, and industry dictate.

In-House Expertise

If you are part of an in-house web development department, chances are you are already exceedingly familiar with your industry. Most likely, you have spent considerable time browsing through competitor sites... but how long ago? If your research is more than a year old, your industry's online landscape has probably changed. Perhaps you have new competition. Perhaps your competition is no longer in existence.

Perhaps you are too close. Internal teams are often biased and would benefit by having an outside team's vantage point. Regardless of circumstance, being at the brink of redesign is a critical juncture at which the competition should be looked at closely ... and as objectively as possible.

Staying Current

Maintenance teams should regularly check in on the competition. Industries fluctuate and markets are volatile. Always know who you are vying with for online customers and visit those sites frequently. Is the competition introducing new features or functionality? Do any across-the-industry customer needs make themselves apparent? Fill them on your own site. Only by continual analysis can you know where you are within the pack.

STEP 1: DEFINING THE PROCESS	
Build a Plan for Analysis	Outline basic goals, process, and deliverables. Establish team, timeframe, methodology, allocated hours, and deliverables.
Define the Competitive Set	Using existing information, search engines, and research, identify a range of companies that fall into the competitive set.
Categorize Your Competitive Set	Break the defined competitive set into categories within the overall industry. Note that each site should fall into only one category.
STEP 2: CREATING A FEATURES LIST	
Create a Features List	After the initial evaluation, create a list of features that apply to most or all sites within the competitive set. Include relevant offline features. Break these features down into individual categories.
STEP 3: CONDUCTING ANALYSIS AND TESTING	
Perform Individual Evaluations	Each person working on the analysis should conduct an individual study of each site, answering basic questions about overall experience, perceived company objectives, and types of services provided. They should also add to the features list as they get deeper into the site.
Conduct Informal Usability Testing	Determine key tasks that can be conducted on most or all sites. Perform informal usability testing (see Chapter 8: Testing for Usability) and record observations and effectiveness from site to site.
STEP 4: CREATING A FINAL REPORT	
Create a Features Grid	Using the features list, create a comprehensive grid showing all sites and the categories and listing features that exist within each.
Make Overall Evaluations	Create a final report (in short, executive summary format). Outline the main findings and indicate how they apply to the company's direction and business goals. Follow with screenshots, evaluations, and summaries about each site in the competitive set. Include a features grid that lists main features within each site. Overall evaluations rank each site for overall use, usability, and likeability.

Step 1: Defining the Process

Clearly identify what information you intend to generate. Specifically, who will be using the final results? Is this primarily to benefit the design team? To generate ideas for content? To better understand the industry? Have clear goals. Whether it is a budgeted deliverable for the client, an exercise for the team as part of the Discovery process, or both, define what you hope to gain from this analysis.

Building a Plan for Analysis

Create a plan for analysis that details overall objectives, methodology, deliverables, schedule, and budget **[10.1]**. Competitive analyses differ widely in size and scope, depending on the details sought. Analyses should be conducted by at least two people because this allows for different perspectives. Depending on time and resources, this process can take a week (for small to mid-size budgets of 20 to 70 hours) or up to a month (for budgets of larger scale). If you can charge for this work, do so. Many firms conduct exactly this type of analysis and charge a meaningful fee for it. If you can't invoice for the competitive analysis on its own budgetary line, build the cost of an abbreviated analysis as part of the Discovery process.

Defining the Competitive Set

The goal here is to identify several things: Who are the key industry players? The heavy hitters? The smaller firms with new innovations? The up-and-comers? Who are the ones to beat? Who are your client's direct competitors — the sites the target audience might visit in lieu of your client's?

First, choose broadly. Gather information the way an actual customer might: using search engines, marketing influences (what billboards have you seen lately?), and other resources like the phone book or referrals. Collect as much information as possible. The client already provided the team with a list of its perceived main competition (from the Client Survey). Now is the time to really look at those sites. Look beyond the client's list as well; the client might have a biased or narrow view of the industry or might have forgotten some key players, especially in the offline arena. This last bit might require extra sleuthing and research on your part.

Competitive Analysis: Overview

Overall Goals and Objectives

Provide a comprehensive industry analysis and comparison of competitive sites. Evaluate features, technology, content, usability, and overall effectiveness. Compile a list of features in a matrix format to establish detailed site offerings and simple comparison methods. Generate a report of what works and what doesn't work within each site, individual site analysis and comments, and final recommendations for possible implementation into the redesigned site.

Methodology

The analysis will be conducted and compiled by team members including the Creative Director, Marketing Analyst, and Information Designer. Individuals participating in this analysis are classified as potential users and will be conducting several task-oriented tests for each of the sites with a user-based orientation instead of a developer's point of view. This analysis, though informal, will allow a range of observations, input, and overall use of each site.

The analysis will be conducted in three phases:

1. Individual analysis (heuristic)
2. Informal usability testing (task-oriented)
3. Features comparison

Deliverables

The report will contain a detailed overview of each site, including screenshots, specific features and differentiating factors, and ratings, which will include usability, ease of use, and overall rating. Also included will be a comprehensive features grid, which shows a breakdown of the competitive sites into specific industry categories, and specific features divided into graphic, technical, content, and site-specific categories. The final report will also contain overall recommendations for the possible implementation of specific features that were highly rated and should be considered in the site's redesign.

(Note: The information compiled in this report is not statistically significant. It is based on general use and informal opinions and should be taken for recommendations only.)

10.1 >

This is an example of an analysis plan that outlines overall goals and objectives, basic methodology, and deliverables. In a more detailed version, include specifics about team and project scope (with schedule and hours allocated) and details about both the user and general tasks associated with the company's site and industry.

Hours and Budgeting

At the barest minimum, allocate at least one hour to analyze each site in the competitive set, including testing, tallying features, and making recommendations.

It's simple math: A 12-site competitive set equals a solid day and a half of work, at minimum. Obviously, more time per site will yield better results; if you have the resources, several hours per site is advantageous. If you don't have the resources or budget, limit the number of sites you are analyzing or limit the time you spend analyzing each site.

Are there any sites that match your client's to a T? Select the primary ones. Also choose several others that are only partial overlaps. Here's an example: The redesign project is an online travel agency. Look at direct competitors' sites — other travel agency sites — as well as at portals like Expedia.com or Travelocity.com, and don't forget airlines like southwest.com or united.com. Also consider more specialized travel sites, like one or two of the many and widely varied adventure travel sites such as Away.com, and don't ignore brochure sites like Lonely Planet or Let's Go. Keep in mind that there are also offline competitors such as 1-800 numbers, 24-hour customer service lines, and (gasp!) actual travel agencies with storefronts or phone-in customer-service representatives.

The client's site? The existing, getting-redesigned site? Make sure to include it in the competitive set. The redesign goals will become more focused if you can clearly see what needs attention alongside competitors' sites.

Now narrow your competition. Limiting the analysis to 12 sites or fewer can be a difficult task. There are bound to be dozens, even a hundred, depending on the industry. Choose roughly 20 for starters. Sorting them will pare that number down. You should have as many sites as necessary to give you a broad yet focused perspective on your industry. Have at least five but no more than a dozen. Presented here is an example of a competitive set within the travel industry (**[10.2]** to **[10.7]**).

< 10.2 >
Expedia.com: www.expedia.com (Category: portal).

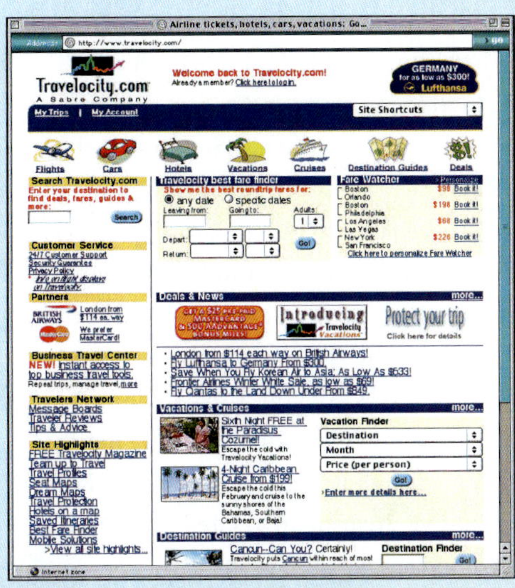

< 10.3 >
Travelocity.com: www.travelocity.com (Category: portal).

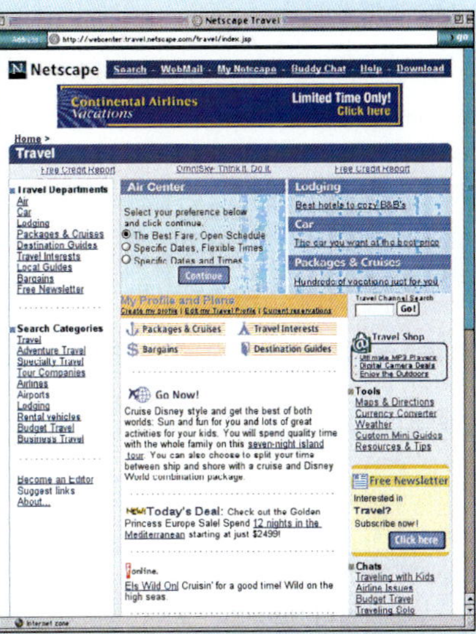

< 10.4 >
Netscape Travel Center: http://webcenter.travel.netscape.com (Category: search engine portal).

< 10.5 >
Away.com: www.away.com (Category: adventure travel).

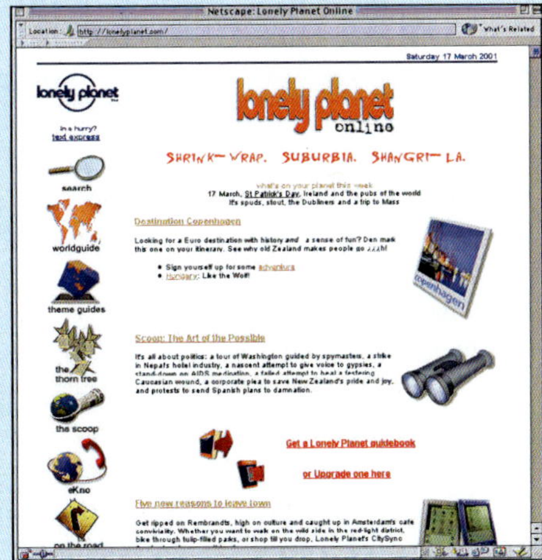

< 10.6 >
Lonely Planet: www.lonelyplanet.com (Category: brochure site).

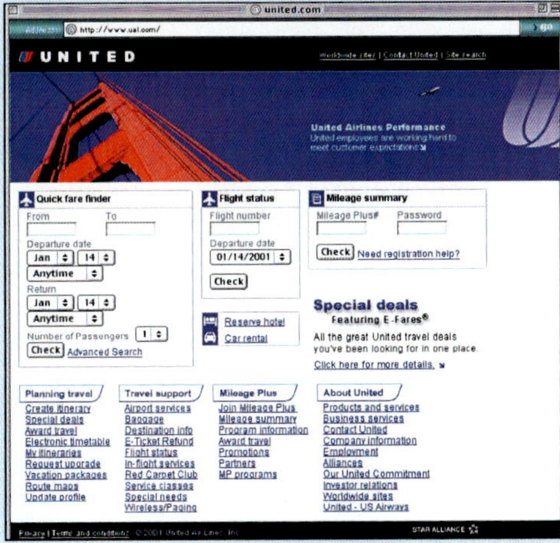

< 10.7 >
United Airlines: www.united.com (Category: airlines).

Partial Analysis

A competitive analysis can focus on a specific feature or functional item of the site. It does not have to be industry specific. For example, when creating an online ordering process for a particular services package, you might want to conduct an analysis of various ways in which people select and order similar services. First you will want to look at industry competitors. Then you may want to branch out and research a similar process in different consumer industries. The point is that you need not analyze your entire site against the competition. Test a portion; keep it simple and specific. Check what works and what doesn't by actually going through the process using heuristic evaluation techniques (usability testing with just one person — yourself!).

Categorizing Your Competitive Set

You have your list; now quickly evaluate each site (a five-minute evaluation, nothing intensive) for category placement within the industry. Start with the existing site: Where does it fit into its industry's big picture? These are broad categories; don't get too specific. Looking back at the travel industry example, categories might be eco-tours, adventure travel, travel portals, airlines, etc. All are definitely travel sites, but each specializes. If you are working on something as specific as Shih-tzu breeding, make sure you look at sites that focus on other small breeds. Be imaginative. Investigate related categories such as purebred dog shows or veterinary obstetrics.

The idea here is to sort and categorize. Although you may have a category with several sites in it, each site should be in only one category. This limiting factor will help clarify true market segmentation and will undoubtedly simplify the total process. Determine industry relevance. Make final cuts.

Step 2: Creating a Features List

A features list is a concise inventory of what each of the selected sites has to offer (**[10.8]** and **[10.9]**). Content, graphics, media, functionality, things to do, things to see, actions to take... List them all. Take all elements into consideration. Identify the download speeds and graphic weight of the different competitive sites. Include features such as search, registration, and message boards. Determine the best

Scarcity of Choices?

What if there aren't even five sites for your comparison? You may have been the first in your industry to go online, or perhaps you found a niche with essentially no competition. Much of the reason you are conducting the informal features analysis is to get deep into the company and to discover what it is like to be a customer in this particular industry. Get creative. If you are unable to find more than three to five sites to compare within your industry, or if most of the competition is offline or traditionally functioning (brick-and-mortar types), try to find areas of similarity with other sites and companies. Look for similar information, similar choices, similar e-commerce functionality. Begin to test functions against your site. If need be, assess the offline competition in greater depth. How? Explore, purchase, and contact offline competition through traditional means. Locally, this might mean driving to a facility or store. Nationally, it might entail contacting the company by phone and requesting a catalog or other information.

Graphic & Content Comparison	Competition A Brochure-site	Competition B Interactive	Competition C Dynamic
Company Name			
Company URL	samplea.com	sampleb.com	samplec.com
Site Classification	brochure	destimation	portal
Frames based	x		
Use of animation	x		
Splash screen	x		
Scrolling on homepage		x	x
Scrolling content on sub-pages		x	x
Graphic buttons	x		
Text/HTML links		x	x
Ad on homepage			x
URL on homepage	x	x	x
Printable homepage	x	x	x
Global navigation on subpages	x	x	x
Sitemap/Site Index		x	x
Dynamic content (changes daily)			x
Rollover navigation	x	x	
Email or feedback ability	x		
Pull-down menus		x	
Download less than 50k		x	x
Total # of features per site	9	10	10
Rank Effectiveness:	*	**	****

< 10.8 >

Here is a generic example of graphic and content features that might appear on competitive sites. Note that this example focuses on graphics and functionality...

Feature Comparison	Competition A Brochure-site	Competition B Interactive	Competition C Dynamic
Company Name			
Company URL	samplea.com	sampleb.com	samplec.com
Site Classification	brochure	destination	portal
Search Function		x	x
Contests/Games	x	x	x
Email	x	x	x
E-Commerce	x		x
Ad Banners		x	x
Chat			x
Press Releases	x	x	x
Company Information	x	x	x
Video/Music Clips		x	x
Web Links	x	x	x
Contact Information	x	x	x
Client List	x	x	x
Feedback	x	x	x
Message Boards			x
Flash Animation		x	x
Other	x	x	x
Total # of features per site	10	13	16
Rank Effectiveness:	*	**	****

< 10.9 >

...And this example is content oriented. Your features list should be likewise grouped.

Categorizing

Make categorizing easier by using self-stick notes. Spread out on a conference table or use a big, white, dry-erase board. Draw a grid and create initial categories. Print out the company logos and URLs and tape the information to the notes. Place the companies in the appropriate categories on the grid. Rename categories if you need to split them (the dry-erase board is handy for that) or move sites to other categories if it becomes appropriate (self-stick-note mobility makes this a snap). Remember, each site should fall under only one category. Some, like portals, will logically qualify for more than one category, so select the category that best fits.

navigation methods. Customize your features list to best fit the industry. Keep it feasible and within budget; an exhaustive list is not necessary. You can get a comprehensive view of the online competition without listing every last feature on every last site.

While evaluating a site, rank the importance of each feature. Determine how it applies to the overall site goals. Decide as a customer if you like it or hate it, or could take it or leave it. Be as diligent and as detailed as possible in the time allowed. In the final competitive analysis report, you will compile these features lists and create a grand master grid for an ultimate comparison experience.

Step 3: Conducting Analysis and Testing

With the competitive set defined and the features list created, you are ready for the actual "doing" part. Gathering data from each site in the competitive set is the most laborious part of the entire analysis. This is the step, depending on the depth and complexity of research conducted, that can quickly blow a budget.

We present two approaches here: individual evaluation and informal usability testing. Each will work on its own, or you may determine that your budget will only allow for one approach (individual evaluation). Again, determine what your goals are for the analysis and testing and be realistic with time and resources.

Brainstorming for Features

When generating a features list, begin by logging every feature (graphics, content, functionality, etc.), then narrow down to specific categories, and finally hone in on features that repeat across several sites. In the end, the features listed and compared should cover as many sites as possible but need not go across the board. The final number of features compared will depend on resources and the detail desired, but a target of 20 to 30 after narrowing down is a good goal. Here are some things to look for as you begin your features list:

- **Media.** Audio clips, video clips, etc.
- **Graphics.** Splash screen, Flash animation, GIF animation, frames, ads, etc.
- **Content.** Press releases, a description of products/services, a company description, bios, a client list, whether the content is static or dynamic, etc.
- **Functionality.** Search, login, community boards, online chats, registration, online purchasing, security, etc.
- **GUI:** High design? Lame design? Professional looking or do-it-yourself?

Performing Individual Evaluations

After all sites in the competitive set are appropriately checked against the features list, each evaluator should give his or her opinion on each site from a customer perspective. Prepare a simple document [10.10] to fill out for each site in the competitive set. Take a look at each site in detail. You did so while checking for features; do more now if time and budget allow. The more you investigate the competitive set, the better versed in the industry you will be.

Conducting Informal Usability Testing

Informal usability testing takes the evaluation a step further. If you have the resources, we highly recommend testing a feature or two across the competitive set for ease of use. Identify some basic tasks that can be performed within the set of competitive sites. If there is more than one audience for your redesign project, choose tasks aimed at each audience.

Consider again the travel industry. How hard it is to find and book a trip for two to Tokyo? To check on flight arrival times? Try to find a motel in Madagascar, a rental car in Reykjavik, or hiking trails in Helsinki. If you are doing an analysis on the lighting industry, order some light bulbs. How easy or difficult it is to find the size, type, and brightness you want? Now wait a few days until your order actually arrives. Return a few items. How easy is that? Call customer service for assistance. Complain. Be an actual customer.

Competitive Analysis Site: ______

Date:
Tester name:

1. What is your initial response to this site?

______

2. After a brief examination (less than five minutes), please describe your impression of this company's purpose.

______

3. List the services that this site provides.

______

4. Using a rating of 1–5, 1 being poor, 5 being excellent, rate the following aspects of the site:

Ease of use:	1	2	3	4	5
Look & feel:	1	2	3	4	5
Navigation:	1	2	3	4	5
Overall:	1	2	3	4	5

5. Additional comments:

______

10.10 >

This individual evaluation worksheet outlines some of the basic things you should think about when taking a look at each website during the individual analysis.

Travel.com Competitive Analysis | Expedia.com

Classification: Portal Site

Expedia.com meets users' needs. It is a travel portal that enables a user to search easily for flights and make online reservations, book hotels and plan an effective vacation. Personalization on the site enables quick and easy flight booking and a one-button flight reference area. Clear labeling and copy enables a user to feel comfortable navigating the site.

excerpt from the food.com website

Effectiveness Rating

Overall Experience: ✪ ✪ ✪ ✪ 1/2

Functionality/Ease of Use: ✪ ✪ ✪

Look & Feel: ✪ ✪ ✪ 1/2

✪ = worst ✪ ✪ ✪ ✪ ✪= best

< **10.11**

This final report sample page shows one of the sites being analyzed, along with several subscreens. This page will have an overview and will take the ratings (from the bottom of the final grid) to give an overall ratings score.

Depending on the objectives of your redesign project, these tasks might be very simple or highly complex. For the most part, this type of testing will be more in-depth than what one site visitor can accomplish in one hour. You will want to analyze tasks from start to finish, and in some cases, that will require actual purchases. Invest a little time and money. The results are worth it.

Step 4: Creating a Final Report

Putting your findings and information together in official report format is the final step of competitive analyses, regardless of formality. The final report will be most effective if it is put into an "executive summary," easy-to-read (easy-to-skim) format. In one or two pages, convey your top findings and recommendations. Get straight to the point. What were the most surprising results? What made the customer experience a positive one? What was infuriating? The rest of the report should explain methodology and process and should include screenshots and overview pages of the sites reviewed, along with the comparison grids you so painstakingly produced (and checked and double-checked) **[10.11]**.

Obviously, the formality of the final report depends on whom it is for: the web development team or the client. Most often it is for both. Primarily, the entire competitive analysis is for the team to wrap its collective head around the project. However, this exercise can be extremely valuable as a deliverable to the client as well — especially if the client is starting to evaluate its services and features for a redesign. This report can show what other industry leaders or competitors are offering, which is important in evaluating what content should appear on the new site.

Creating a Features Grid

Before completing the report, we highly recommend taking the time to compile the gathered information into a visual grid. Take the features list for each site analyzed and merge them, putting features down the side and sites across the top. Put the existing site first. Add your usability-tested tasks into your features grid. Chunk the features together into comprehensive categories such as "Search" and "Personalization." List subcategories if further definition is necessary **[10.12]**. This grid will probably be several pages long, but the more detailed and specific the features list, the more comprehensive the report.

The Final Report Should Contain at Least the Following:

- An executive summary (a one- to two-page overview)
- A description of the methodology/process/approach
- Screenshots and an overview of each site (two to three screenshots, final ratings from the grid, a brief overview of collected experiences)
- Findings and recommendations (can be included in the executive summary or expanded as necessary)
- A features grid (created next)
- Overall ratings (included in the features grid)
- Notes and raw data

Site Name	Travelocity .com	Expedia.com	travelnow	Yahoo/ Travel	Netscape/ Travel	Lufthansa	Icelandic Air	Southwest	Alaska	United	Away.com	LonelyPlanet
CLASSIFICATION	Portal Sites					Airline Sites					Adventure Travel	
GENERAL FEATURES												
Search for Flights									•	•		
Make Online Reservations												
Search for Hotels	•	•	•	•	•		•				•	•
Make Online Hotel Reservations	•	•	•	•		•	•				•	•
Search for Rental Cars	•	•					•				•	•
Search for Vacation Packages	•	•					•				•	
Customer Service 1-800#	•	•				•	•				•	•
Customer Service Online Chat												•
BOOK FLIGHT FEATURES												
Search for Flights			•									•
By City			•									•
By Date	•	•					•					
By Price	•	•	•	•	•	•	•	•	•	•		
Sort Flights		•				•	•	•			•	•
By Airlines	•	•									•	•
By Lowest Fare											•	•
By Non-stop											•	

< 10.12 >

This is a sample features grid for the travel industry showing the 12 selected sites in three categories: portals, airline sites, and adventure travel. The features (listed on the left) are then compared across the board for a direct side-by-side comparison.

Note: *This is a sample used for display purposes only and should not be considered actual data.*

Making Overall Evaluations

At the end of the analysis, prepare two evaluations. First give an overall rating for each site in the competitive set. Select at least three main areas to evaluate and use a standard rating system of one to five stars (**[10.13]** and **[10.14]**). Get feedback from all involved — one team member may have had a horrible experience with a site, and another may have had major success. The main areas for rating might include the following:

- **Overall experience.** What was the general experience when using the site? Favorable? Frustrating? Did you feel the company was responsive to your needs as a customer? Were you able to complete tasks successfully? Would you want to return to the site?
- **Functionality.** From a functionality standpoint, was it easy to complete actual tasks, or did you hit dead ends? Was registration and ordering problematic or smooth?
- **Look and feel.** Was the site visually appealing? How did it make you feel about the company or the brand? Did it appear professional, targeted, and clean? Did it seem dated, overloaded, or badly executed?

Another form of evaluation is a more comprehensive, written piece summarizing the experiences, pros and cons, and overall impression of the site from a collection of customer responses. This summary should be accompanied by screenshots, be brief and to the point, and outline the most relevant findings.

10.13 >

Ratings for overall experience, functionality, and look and feel are shown here. Also included is the K size for the home page download for comparison purposes.

Ratings								
Overall Experience	✪ ½	✪ ✪	✪ ✪ ½	✪ ½	✪ ✪ ½	✪	✪ ✪	✪ ✪ ✪ ✪ ✪
Functionality	✪ ½	✪ ✪ ✪	✪ ✪ ½	✪ ✪	✪ ✪ ✪	✪	✪ ✪	✪ ✪ ✪ ✪ ✪
Look & Feel	✪ ✪ ½	✪ ✪	✪ ✪	✪	✪ ½	½	✪ ✪	✪ ✪ ✪ ✪ ✪
Homepage Download (graphics only)	54K	10K	30K	120K	8K	24K	18K	110K 2nd page

* = Recommended feature
(•) = Hidden feature

10.14 >

For individual site overview pages, relist the ratings information next to screenshots of each site [10.11].

Effectiveness Rating
Overall Experience: ✪ ✪
Functionality/Ease of Use: ✪ ✪ ✪
Look & Feel: ✪ ✪
✪ = worst ✪ ✪ ✪ ✪ ✪= best

CHAPTER SUMMARY

Out of a need to become better partners with our clients, conducting analyses like the informal features analysis described in this chapter is a valuable part of the Discovery process. Although the final report is often surprising and sometimes enlightening, understand that the process itself is as important as the results for one big reason: It enables both the client and the development team to see the client's industry from a customer's perspective. Yes, you are evaluating the industry's current online and offline competitive landscape and are making pertinent comparisons. And yes, those results go a long way toward understanding how the client's company fits into its competitive set. But as a web development team, the ultimate point of this analysis is to achieve a better understanding of the client company's site that's slated for a redesign, the overall industry, and the customer experience for which you are ardently aiming.

Index

Numbers

404 code, 193

A

About.com Website, 118
AC (Additional Charge) form, 74
access
  expert redesign tips, 15
  full access Websites, 153
Additional Charge (AC) form, 74
advertising, 192
  complex functionality, 235
Agile Manifesto, Website, 239
alpha testing, 170
analysis
  competitive, 36, 260–261
    creating features list, 268–270
    defining process, 264–268
    final report, 272–275
    formal industry versus *informal features, 261–263*
    testing, 270–272
  complex functionality requirements, 244–246
  customer surveys, 46–47
  surveys, 21
  usability testing data, 229–231
announcements
  planning, 35, 191
  preparations, 192
Appen, Allyson, Baby Center, 8
approvals, 24
archived documentation, 186
Art Director, 78
asset control, 137
assignments, project teams, 24, 78–79
Au, Johnny, WebEx Communications, 232
audiences. *See also* users
  Core Process discovery, 22
  creating visual interface, 124–125
  expert redesign tips, 14
  feedback, 130
  understanding, 49–57
audit methodology, 93

B

Baby Center Website, 8
backend
  engineering, 32
    building, 166–167
    plan, 155
  programming needs
    Core Process discovery, 22
    sitemapping, 102
Backend Engineer, 78
Banana Republic Website, 258
Bearing Point Website, 86
beta testing, 170
billable services, post launch, 185
blogs, 197
Bobby Website, 153
bookmarks, redirects, 196
branding, Shedroff, Nathan, 58–59
Braun, Sindy, WebEx Communications, 232
buckets, content, 165
budgets
  competition analysis, 266
  project planning, 23, 67–74
  QA (quality assurance) testing, 174
bugs
  fixing, 33
  integration testing, 174
  prioritizing, 198
  showstoppers, 175
  tracking tools, 173
Bugzilla Website, 173
building, integration, 31–32
  backend development, 166–167
  HTML templates, 159–161
  light scripting, 161–162
  populating pages, 163–166
  slicing and optimization, 157–158
Building Accessible Websites, 153
Built for Use: Driving Profitability Through the User Experience, 212
Burgess, Mark, Port of Seattle Website, 16
buttons, naming, 27
Byrd, Jikta, Bearing Point, 86

C

café testing, 219
Cascading Style Sheets (CSS), 146, 160
  Meyer, Eric, 126
Castro, Elizabeth, *HTML for the World Wide Web with XHTML and CSS: VQS*, 147
Catalyst Design Group, NYC, About.com, 118
Chaing, Jeffrey, gotomedia, inc., 142
Chang, An-Ching, Banana Republic Website, 258
check lists
  discovery, 61
  visual design, 131
chunking, 94
clarification of goals, project definition, 22–23, 62–65
Clark, Joe, *Building Accessible Websites*, 153
clients
  communications, Kassirer, Chad, 148
  controls, 130
  documentation signatures, 69
  informal testing, 172
  spec sheets, 146–155
CMS (Content Management System), 160
Coldwell Banker Walter Williams Realty, Inc. Website, 210
Coll, Barbara
  optimal search engine p lacement, 194–195
  WebMama Website, 193
colors, 139
  setting gamma, 124
Colter, Emily
  Melanie Craft Website, 178
  Waxcreative Design, ix
Communication Brief, 22–23
  preparation, 62–64
competitive analysis, 36, 260–261
  creating features list, 268–270
  defining process, 264–268
  final report, 272–275
  formal industry *versus* informal features, 261–263
  testing, 270–272
competitive sets, 265–268
complex functionality, 233–239
  Functional Specification, 246
    drafting, 246–250
    implementation, 254–255
    sign-off, 251
  requirements
    analyzing, 244–246
    documenting, 242–243
    gathering, 240–242
concepts, creating visual interface, 123–124
content, 90
  auditing, 91
  buckets, 165
  checks, 170
  creating delivery plan, 95–98
  delay, 26
  expert redesign tips, 15
  features lists, 270
  invisible, 32, 166
  outlining, 94–95
  status, 152
Content Management System (CMS), 160
Content Manager, 79
content-view, site structure, 25–26, 90–97
Cooke, Bruce, Coldwell Banker Walter Williams Realty, Inc. Website, 210
Copywriter, 79
Core Process, 11, 20
  complex functionality, 233–239
  define project
    clarification of goals, 22–23, 62–65
    discovery, 21–22, 43–61
    planning, 23–24, 65–83
  flow chart, 18–19
  integration
    building, 31–32, 157–167
    planning, 30–31, 145–157
    testing, 32–33, 167–175
  launch, 34–35, 190–198
    delivery, 33–34, 180–189
    maintenance, 35–36, 198–207
  site structure development. *See also* sites, structure
    content-view, 25–26, 90–97
    page-view, 106–111
    site-view, 98–105
    user-view, 27
  visual interface. *See also* visual interface
    creating, 28, 121–131
    hand off, 29, 134–139
    testing, 29, 132
costs, usability testing, 218
Craft, Melanie, Website, 178
Creative HTML Design.2, 147
CSS (Cascading Style Sheets), 146, 160
  Meyer, Eric, 126
Currens, Amy, Bearing Point, 86
customer surveys
  analyzing, 46–47
  customizing, 42–45
customized processes, expert redesign tips, 15
cycles, redesign, 11

D

data, usability testing
  analyzing, 229–231
  gathering, 226–229
delivery
  content planning, 95–98
  launch, 33–34, 180
    documentation tracking, 186
    handoff packets, 185
    post launch meeting, 186–187
    production style guide, 181–184
    scheduled maintenance training, 187
Design Style Guides, 29, 137–139
Designing Web Usability, 213
designs, status, 154
detailed schedules, 76–77
discovery
  check list, 61
  gathering information, 60
    audience understanding, 49–57
    client surveys, 42–47
    maintenance surveys, 47–48
  project definition, 21–22
documentation
  signatures, 69
  tracking, 34
    launch delivery, 186
Dolan, Sean
  productive collaboration, 252–253
Don't Make Me Think, 214
Donoghue, Karen, *Built for Use: Driving Profitability Through the User Experience*, 212
Dorff, Todd, Bearing Point, 86
Dowker, Sandra, Bearing Point, 86
Drake, Craig, gotomedia, inc., 142
due dates, 95
Duncan, Leigh, redesign issues and strategies, 13
dynamic content, complex functionality, 235
dynamic sites *versus* static sites, 157

E

e-commerce
  complex functionality, 235
  module requirements, 243, 245
Eller, Stockton, Coldwell Banker Walter Williams Realty, Inc. Website, 210
embellishments, 139
Eric Meyer on CSS: Mastering the Language of Web Design, 147
error pages, 193
estimating projects, 69–70, 72

F

features
  competitive analysis
    grid, 273–274
    list, 268–270
  worksheet, 150–151
feedback
  creating visual interface, 127–131
  users, success measurement, 207
Fehrnstrom, Paul, WebEx Communications, 232
file structure, 30, 155–157
fixed bids, 69
Flash, 125
flow charts, Core Process, 18–19
focus groups, testing, 82
formal industry analysis *versus* informal features analysis, 261–263
formal testing *versus* informal testing, 218
forms, AC (Additional Charge), 74
frames, QA (quality assurance) testing, 171
Functional Specification
  drafting, 246–250
  implementation, 254–255
  sign-off, 251
functionality
  complex, 233–239
    Functional Specification, 246–255
    requirements, 240–243
  features lists, 270
  testing, 132, 170
  worksheet, 150–151

G

Gabriel, Jaime, Banana Republic Website, 258
gamma, setting, 124
gathering information, client surveys, 42–47
Go to Media Website, 95
goals
- clarification, project definition, 22–23, 62
- creating visual interface, 122
- expert redesign tips, 14
- technical, 56–57
- unifying, 43

Gomoll, Kate, user profiling, 52–53
Goto, Kelly
- gotomedia, inc., 142, ix
- WebEx Communications, 232

gotomedia, inc.
- WebEx Communications, 232
- Website, 142

graphics
- features lists, 270
- templates, 29, 134–136, 160
  - *integration, 157–158*
  - *slicing, 31*
- type, 139

GUI, features lists, 270
guidelines, 30
- client spec sheets, 146–155

H

hackers, 205
hand coding *versus* WYSIWYG, 163
Handbook of Usability Testing, 231
Handel, Kate, Baby Center, 8
handoff packets, 34
- Design Style Guides, 137–139
- launch delivery, 185

Harris, Susan, *HTML & Web Artistry 2: More Than Code,* 147
headers, 139
Heid, Jim, workflow, 11
Hit box Website, 56
Hits Link Website, 56
Hivner, Brady, Bearing Point, 86
Howeth, Serena
- gotomedia, inc., 142
- WebEx Communications, 232

HTML
- creating templates and pages, 31
- naming, 104–105
- protosite development, 27, 113–114
- shells, 160
- templates, 159–161, 160
  - *scripting, 161–162*
- text, 139
- WYSIWYG *versus* hand coding, 163

HTML & Web Artistry 2: More Than Code, 147
HTML for the World Wide Web with XHTML and CSS: VQS, 147

I

IA toolkits, Wodtke, Christina, 92–93
Iacona, Nick, Bearing Point, 86
images, treatment, 139
includes, 161
industries, analyzing competition, 260–263
industry analysis, 59
- Core Process discovery, 22

informal features analysis *versus* formal industry analysis, 261–263
informal testing *versus* formal testing, 218
information
- client surveys, 42–47
- Core Process discovery, 21
- industry analysis, 59
- maintenance surveys, 47–48

Information Designer, 79
integration
- planning
  - *client spec sheets, 146–155*
  - *file structure, 155–157*
  - *project status, 145*
- testing, 32–33
  - *bugs, 174*
  - *final checks, 175*
  - *QA (quality assurance), 167–173*

invisible content, 32, 166
invoices, 69
iterative approaches, 12, 206

J-K

Janus Capital Group, 38

Kalman, Rachel
- gotomedia, inc., 142
- WebEx Communications, 232

Kassirer, Chad, x
- client communications, 148

kickoff meetings, 24
Krug, Steve, *Don't Make Me Think,* 214

L

labeling, page-view, 27
Lang, Caitlin, Melanie Craft Website, 178
launch, 198
- announcement preparation, 191–192
- Core Process, 34–35
- delivery, 180
  - *documentation tracking, 186*
  - *handoff packets, 185*
  - *post launch meeting, 186–187*
  - *production style guide, 181–184*
  - *scheduled maintenance training, 187*
- going live, 190
- maintenance, 35–36, 198–199
  - *assessing team capabilities, 200*
  - *developing plan, 202–203*
  - *internal* versus *external teams, 201–202*
  - *planned iterative initiatives, 206*
  - *site security, 204–205*
  - *success measurement, 206–207*
- optimizing for search engines, 192–197

light scripting, 31
load testing, 170
logins, complex functionality, 235
Long, Tara, About.com, 118
Luong, Sayuri, About.com, 118

M

Mac *versus* PC, 124
Macromedia Website, 125
Mahle, Mark, WebEx Communications, 232
maintenance
- expert redesign tips, 14
- launch, 35–36, 198–199
  - *assessing team capabilities, 200*
  - *developing plan, 202–203*
  - *internal* versus *external teams, 201–202*
  - *planned iterative initiatives, 206*
  - *site security, 204–205*
  - *success measurement, 206–207*
- scheduled training, 187
- surveys, 47–48
- training, 34

management, projects, 75
marketing, Core Process discovery, 21
markups, 68
measurable goals, expert redesign tips, 14
media, features lists, 270
methodology steps, 75
Meyer, Eric
- CSS, 126
- *Eric Meyer on CSS: Mastering the Language of Web Design,* 147

Meyerhoffer, Mary Kate, Baby Center, 8
Microsoft Project, 75
Milar, Shannon, Baby Center, 8
milestones, 95
Miller, Dave, Port of Seattle Website, 16
mobile logs (moblogs), 197
monitors, screen sizes, 127

N

naming
- buttons and labels, 27
- conventions, 26, 103–105
- HTML, 104–105

navigation, page-view, 27
nested frames, QA (quality assurance) testing, 171
Net Mechanic Website, 173
New Riders Website, 128–129
nGen Works, Coldwell Banker Walter Williams Realty, Inc. Website, 210
Niederst, Jennifer, *Web Design in a Nutshell,* 147
Nielsen, Jakob
- *Designing Web Usability,* 213
- small-study usability, 216–217

O

- Omnigroup Website, 104
- one-on-one testing, 214
- online polls, complex functionality, 235
- online surveys, user testing, 81
- optimization, 160
  - building integration, 157–158
  - graphics templates, 31
  - search engines, 192–197
- organizations
  - chunking, 94
  - current site, 26, 100
  - naming, 105
- overview schedules, 76

P

- page-view, site structure, 26–27, 106–111
- pages
  - dimensions, 139
  - HTML, 31
  - populating, 31–32, 163–166
- partial analysis, competition, 268
- participants, usability testing, 222–225
- PC *versus* Mac, 124
- Philosophe Website, 169
- Phinney, Leslie, Port of Seattle Website, 16
- Phinney/Bischoff Design House, Port of Seattle Website, 16
- photos, treatment, 139
- planning, 30–31
  - announcements, 191
  - budgets, 67–74, 83
  - integration, 30–31
    - *client spec sheets, 146–155*
    - *file structure, 155–157*
    - *project status, 145*
  - projects, 23
    - *assigning team, 78–79*
    - *definition, 23–24, 65–67*
  - redesign, 11
  - schedules, 75–77
  - staging areas, 80
  - usability testing, 219–220
  - user testing, 81–82
  - workflow, 11–12
- *PMBOK Guide*, 67
- PMI (Project Management Instituted), 67
- polls, complex functionality, 235
- populating pages, 31–32, 163–166
- Port of Seattle Website, 16
- post launch meetings, 34, 186–187
- processes, expert redesign tips, 15
- Production Designer, 79
- Production Lead, 79
- production style guides, launch delivery, 181–184
- profiling
  - test participants, 224–225
  - users, 52–53
- Programmer, 78
- programming needs, Core Process discovery, 22
- Project Management Instituted (PMI), 67
- Project Managers, 78
- projects
  - definition, 40–41
    - *audience understanding, 49–50*
    - *clarification of goals, 22–23, 62–65*
    - *discovery, 21–22, 42–48.* See also *discovery*
    - *industry analysis, 59*
    - *planning, 23–24, 65–83.* See also *planning*
  - estimating, 69–70, 72
  - management, 75
  - status, 30
  - team assignments, 24, 78–79
- promotions, complex functionality, 235
- protosite development, HTML, 27, 113–114

Q

- QA (quality assurance)
  - budgets, 174
  - Functional Specification, 255
  - Lead, 79, 169
  - testing, 32
    - *basics, 167–168*
    - *conducting, 168–173*
- quality assurance (QA)
  - budgets, 174
  - Functional Specification, 255
  - Lead, 79, 169
  - testing, 32
    - *basics, 167–168*
    - *conducting, 168–173*

R

- rebranding, redesign cycle, 11
- redesign
  - cycles, 11
  - expert tips, 14–15
  - need for book, 10–11
  - *versus* refreshing, 46
  - workflow, 11–12
- redirects, bookmarks, 196
- refreshing sites *versus* redesign, 46
- registrations, complex functionality, 235
- regression testing, 170
- Reiter, Alissa Cohen, Baby Center, 8
- reports
  - bugs, 173
  - competition analysis, 272–275
  - usability testing data, 230–231
- repositioning, redesign cycle, 11
- Rosete, Varick, Coldwell Banker Walter Williams Realty, Inc. Website, 210
- Rubin, Jeffrey, *Handbook of Usability Testing*, 231

S

- Saam, Eric, About.com, 118
- scalability, file structure, 156–157
- scenarios, users, 115
- schedules
  - creating, 24
  - planning, 75–77
- Schmeisser, Travis, Coldwell Banker Walter Williams Realty, Inc. Website, 210
- Scope Creep, 22, 68–69
- scopes
  - client expectations, 147
  - status checks, 152
- screen sizes, 127
- scripting
  - HTML templates, 161–162
  - light, 31
- Scrub the Web Website, 173
- Search Engine Watch Website, 197
- search engines
  - expert redesign tips, 15
  - optimization for, 192–197
  - optimizing site for, 35
- searches, complex functionality, 235
- security, sites, 204–205
- security testing, 170
- Seipel, Sarah, Banana Republic Website, 258
- Sen, Mike, Bearing Point, 86
- servers, QA (quality assurance) testing, 169
- Shedroff, Nathan, branding, 58–59
- shells, HTML, 160
- signatures, documentation, 69
- site-view, site structure, 26, 98–105
- sitemapping, 98–100, 103
  - site-view, 26
- sites
  - current site organization, 26, 100
  - launch, 35
  - maintenance, expert redesign tips, 14
  - naming conventions, 103–105
  - security, 204–205
  - statistics, 56
  - structure
    - *content-view, 25–26, 90–97*
    - *determination, 101–103*
    - *page-view, 26–27, 106–111*
    - *site-view, 26, 98–105*
    - *user-view, 27, 112–115*
- Skolnick, Jared, About.com, 118
- slicing, 160
  - building integration, 157–158
  - graphics templates, 31
- small-study usability, Nielsen, Jakob, 216–217
- Smart Design, 29
  - creating visual interface, 121
- Smith, Carl, Coldwell Banker Walter Williams Realty, Inc. Website, 210
- smoke testing, 170
- soft launch, 190
- software, sitemapping, 104
- Spencer, Stephan, site effectiveness, 188–189
- splicing, 160
- staging areas, 24, 80
- standards, Web
  - expert redesign tips, 15
  - Zeldman, Jeffrey, 164–165
- static sites *versus* dynamic sites, 157
- Stross, Jon, Baby Center, 8
- structures
  - files, 30
  - sites
    - *content-view, 25–26, 90–97*
    - *determination, 101–103*
    - *page-view, 26–27, 106–111*
    - *site-view, 26, 98–105*
    - *user-view, 27, 112–115*

Style Guides
launch delivery, 181–184
production-specific guidelines, 34
Subramanian, Subha
gotomedia, inc., 142
WebEx Communications, 232
success measurements, 206–207
SurveyMonkey.com Website, 81
surveys
Core Process discovery, 21
customer
analyzing, 46–47
customizing, 42–45
maintenance, 47–48

T

target specifications, 149
task lists, usability testing, 220–221
teams
assignments, 24, 78–79
maintenance
assessing capabilities, 200
internal versus *external, 201–202*
Tech-Check worksheet, 56–57
technical goals, 56–57
audience understanding, 51
expert redesign tips, 14
Template Monster Website, 127
templates
graphic, 29, 134–136, 160
integration, 157–158
slicing, 31
HTML, 31, 160
scripting, 161–162
Website design, 127
testing
beds, 169
competition analysis, 270–272
expert redesign tips, 15
integration, 32–33
bugs, 174
final checks, 175
QA (quality assurance), 167–173
planning, 24
usability, 31, 171
basics, 212–218
competition analysis, 271–272
conducting, 219–231
expert redesign tips, 15
planning, 24, 82
users, 81–82
visual interface, 29
text, HTML, 139
time tracking, 71–73
project planning, 23
Timeslice Website, 73
tracking
bugs, 173
documentation, 34
launch delivery, 186
time, 23, 71–73
training
launch delivery, 187
maintenance, 34
Tuttle, Jonathan, Baby Center, 8

U

unifying goals, 43
unique pages, 160
unit tests, 170
Usability Lead, 79
usability testing, 31, 171
basics, 212–214
costs, 218
redesign, 215
when to test, 215–218
competition analysis, 271–272
conducting
analyzing data, 229–231
participants, 222–225
planning and preparation, 219–222
session, 226–229
expert redesign tips, 15
planning, 24, 82
UsableNet.com Websites, 153
user-view, site structure, 27, 112–115
users. ***See also*** **audiences**
acceptance testing, 170
defining key paths, 27, 112–113
feedback, success measurement, 207
profiling, 52–53
scenarios, 115
testing, 81–82

V

Visual Designer, 78
visual interface
creating, 28
audience, 124–125
defining Smart Design, 121
developing concepts, 123–124
presentation and feedback, 127–131
reviewing goals, 122
design check list, 131
hand off, 29
Design Style Guides, 137–139
graphic templates, 134–136
testing, 29, 132

W

Waxcreative Design
Colter, Emily, ix
Melanie Craft Website, 178
Web
copy ready, 95
logs (blogs), 197
standards
expert redesign tips, 15
Zeldman, Jeffrey, 164–165
***Web Design in a Nutshell*, 147**
Web Trends Website, 56
Web-Redesign Website, 23
WebEx Communications Website, 232
WebMama Website, 193
Websites
About.com, 118
Agile Manifesto, 239
Baby Center, 8
Banana Republic, 258
Bearing Point, 86
Bobby, 153
Bugzilla, 173
Coldwell Banker Walter Williams Realty, Inc., 210
Craft, Melanie, 178
current site organization, 26, 100
Go to Media, 95
gotomedia, inc., 142
Hit box, 56
Hits Link, 56
Janus Capital Group, 38
launch, 35
Macromedia, 125
maintenance, expert redesign tips, 14
naming conventions, 103–105
Net Mechanic, 173
New Riders, 128–129
Omnigroup, 104
Philosophe, 169
Port of Seattle Website, 16
Scrub the Web, 173
Search Engine Watch, 197
security, 204–205
statistics, 56
structure
content-view, 25–26, 90–97
determination, 101–103
page-view, 26–27, 106–111
site-view, 26, 98–105
user-view, 27, 112–115
SurveyMonkey.com, 81
Template Monster, 127
Timeslice, 73
UsableNet.com, 153
Web Trends, 56
Web-Redesign, 7, 23
WebEx Communications, 232
WebMama, 193
What? Design, 148
Zoomerang, 81
Weinman, Lynda
Creative HTML Design.2, 147
designers as problem solvers, 133
Weinrich, Lars, About.com, 118
What? Design Website, 148
White, Renée, Melanie Craft Website, 178
wireframing, page-view, 27, 106–110
Wodtke, Christina, IA toolkits, 92–93
workflow, 11–12
WYSIWYG, *versus* hand coding, 163

X-Y-Z

XHTML, 160
XML, 160

Zee, Natalie, *HTML & Web Artistry 2: More Than Code*, 147
Zeldman, Jeffrey, xiii
Designing with Web Standards, 147
Web standards, 164–165
Zoomerang Website, 81

COLOPHON

We wrote the first edition of this book using Microsoft Word (which we cursed regularly) on several machines, including Kelly's generic Dell PC Pentium, super-fast, organizational behemoth and Emily's Apple Macintosh G4 (Graphite), as well as three Apple Macintosh Powerbooks — two G3s that crisscrossed the Bay Bridge and the country often enough to warrant better carrying cases for each, and one antique 520C that met an untimely (and still unsolved) death in a hotel room in Seattle.

The second edition also relied heavily on MS Word (with no abatement of frustration), as well as better, faster machines — Quicksilver replaced Graphite, and the PC was completely abandoned. One G3 laptop was replaced with a G4 iBook in the eleventh hour of production, and the other G3 was upgraded to two successive G4 PowerBooks, the first of which met an untimely (and easily and embarrassingly explained) death in a parking lot at SFO.

This book was laid out using QuarkXPress. Illustrations were completed using Adobe Illustrator, Macromedia FreeHand, and Adobe Photoshop — several versions of each employed. Also used: Macromedia Dreamweaver, Macromedia Fireworks, several browsers (most predominately Safari, then Internet Explorer, and to some extent Netscape), Omnigraffle, and Inspiration. Fonts: Sabon (body copy), InfoText, and Univers Condensed (headers and captions).

Mascot support was provided unconditionally by Malcolm The Wonder Kitty (in memoriam).

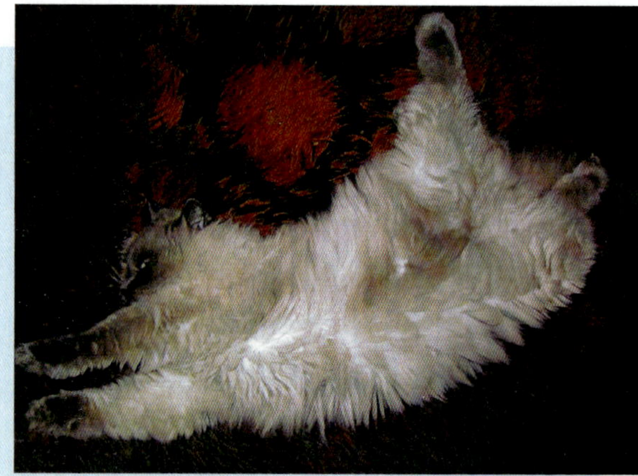

Malcolm The Wonder Kitty.